Y0-CPC-026

SOCIETY
of
ACTUARIES

Transactions

The work of science is to substitute facts for appearances and demonstrations for impressions. —RUSKIN

1988-89-90 REPORTS
OF MORTALITY, MORBIDITY
AND OTHER EXPERIENCE

MANUFACTURED FOR THE SOCIETY BY IPC PUBLISHING SERVICES,
ST. JOSEPH, MICHIGAN

PRINTED IN THE UNITED STATES OF AMERICA

ISBN 0-938959-21-2

The *Transactions* are published by the Society of Actuaries, successor to the Actuarial Society of America and the American Institute of Actuaries, in lieu of *Transactions* and the *Record*, respectively, heretofore published by the two former organizations.

CONTENTS OF 1988-89-90 REPORTS OF MORTALITY, MORBIDITY AND OTHER EXPERIENCE

*This report replaces the one that appears in the *1985-86-87 Reports of Mortality, Morbidity and Other Experience*; that report contains incorrect bar graphs and should not be used.

SOCIETY OF ACTUARIES

JOHN E. O'CONNOR, JR., *Executive Director*
JUDY F. ANDERSON, F.S.A., *Education Actuary*
BERNARD A. BARTELS, *Registrar*
RICHARD BILISOLY, F.S.A., *Education Actuary*
RACHEL L. BRODY, *Assistant to the Executive Director*
BARBARA M. CHOYKE, *Director of Continuing Education*
LINDEN N. COLE, F.S.A., *Education Actuary*
LINDA M. DELGADILLO, C.A.E., *Director of Communications*
MARK G. DOHERTY, C.A.E., *Director of Research*
LAWRENCE C. HENZE, J.D., *Director of Development*
MARTA L. HOLMBERG, PH.D., *Education Executive*
WILLIAM KEPRAIOS, C.P.A., *Director of Finance*
WARREN R. LUCKNER, F.S.A., *Research Actuary*
JOHN A. (JACK) LUFF, F.S.A., F.C.I.A., *Experience Studies Actuary*
RICHARD MATTISON, F.S.A., *Education Actuary*
JAMES WEISS, *Director of Information Services*

475 N. MARTINGALE ROAD, SCHAUMBURG, ILLINOIS 60173

MORTALITY AND MORBIDITY EXPERIENCE COMMITTEES

INDIVIDUAL LIFE INSURANCE

INDIVIDUAL LIFE INSURANCE EXPERIENCE COMMITTEE:

JOHN W. PADDON, *Chairperson*
KENT DOUGLAS SLUYTER, *Secretary*
RICHARD D. ASHTON
JOHN E. BAILEY
DARRELL W. BEERNINK
JAMES D. BROCK
BARRY EDENBAUM
ALFRED B. HARPER
YVES LANEUVILLE
MELVIN C. MCFALL
GARY N. SARGENT
LETA WORLEY UNGAR
JEYARAJ VADIVELOO
ROBERT W. VOSE
HARRY A. WOODMAN

AVIATION AND HAZARDOUS SPORTS EXPERIENCE COMMITTEE:

STEPHEN N. PATZMAN, *Chairperson*
GUY VINCENT BARKER
MICHAEL V. ECKMAN
V. DANIEL LACROIX
ROBERT J. LALONDE
ORRIN S. TOVSON

HIV RESEARCH COMMITTEE:

THOMAS W. REESE, *Chairperson*
ARTHUR L. BALDWIN, III
RICHARD L. BERGSTROM
DANIEL F. CASE
MICHAEL J. COWELL
JOHN B. DINIUS
WALTER H. HOSKINS
DONALD B. MAIER
RICHARD W. MATHES
THOMAS KEVIN MEEHAN
JOHN W. PADDON
PAUL J. SULEK
HARRY A. WOODMAN
MICHAEL L. ZURCHER

MEDICAL IMPAIRMENT EXPERIENCE COMMITTEE:

HARRY A. WOODMAN, F.S.A., *Chairperson*
DONALD C. CHAMBERS, M.D.
JAMES L. COMPERE, F.S.A.
DONALD L. GAUER, F.S.A.
DENIS W. LORING, F.S.A.
BRIAN MCCRACKEN, M.D.
THEODORE E. PLUCINSKI, M.D.

ASSOCIATION OF LIFE INSURANCE MEDICAL DIRECTORS OF AMERICA AND SOCIETY OF ACTUARIES JOINT LIAISON COMMITTEE:

HARRY A. WOODMAN, F.S.A., *Chairperson*
SAM GUTTERMAN, F.S.A.
WARREN KLEINSASSER, M.D.
JAMES W. PILGRIM, F.S.A.
JOHN SWANSON, M.D.
DAVID WESLEY, M.D.

OTHER EXPERIENCE

INDIVIDUAL HEALTH INSURANCE EXPERIENCE COMMITTEE:

SAM GUTTERMAN, *Chairperson*
DAVID S. BEER, *Vice-Chairperson*
GERALD AGRIMSON
RICHARD J. ESTELL
SHIRAZALI JETHA
GARY L. KIONTKE
JOHN M. LENSER
GREGORY M. MILLS
LEONARD M. PRESSEY
FRANK G. REYNOLDS
JEROME F. SEAMAN
ROBERT SHAPLAND
DOUGLAS W. TAYLOR
ROBERT P. VROLYK
CHARLES M. WALDRON

GROUP LIFE AND HEALTH INSURANCE EXPERIENCE COMMITTEE:

TED L. DUNN, *Chairperson*
BARRY T. ALLEN
JEFFREY P. BASH
DOROTHEA D. CARDAMONE
DAVID WILLIAM COOK
THOMAS G. COULTER
PETER J. DA SILVA
AIDA S. DAVID
JAMES GUTTERMAN
WILLIAM J. HAUSER
SANFORD B. HERMAN
ALAN HOFFMAN
FRANCIS E. KEENAN
STEPHEN M. MAHER
CRAIG S. NIEHAUS
SUSAN E. PIERCE
GEORGE E. POLLINO
RALPH B. REESE
G. NICHOLAS SMITH
DOUGLAS E. WEED
MICHAEL WELSH

RETIREMENT PLANS EXPERIENCE COMMITTEE:

EDWIN C. HUSTEAD, *Chairperson*
MARK S. HANRAHAN
RICHARD JOSS
ROBERT T. MCCRORY
WALTER J. MCLAUGHLIN
KENNETH L. PITZER
BARTHUS PRIEN
MICHAEL VIRGA
ALICE H. WADE

ANNUITY VALUATION TABLE COMMITTEE:

LINDSAY J. MALKIEWICH, *Chairperson*
DAVID BENJAMIN BERG
NEIL J. BRODERICK
JOEL L. COLEMAN
JOHN B. GOULD
EDWIN C. HUSTEAD

ANNUITY EXPERIENCE COMMITTEE:

PHILIP J. BIELUCH, *Chairperson*
DAVID BENJAMIN BERG
CATHARINE NEALE BISULCA, F.C.A.S.
WILLIAM R. CLAYPOOL
DENNIS M. CORBETT
ALAN DUBIN
JEAN GREGOIRE
ROGER F. HARBIN
ANTHONY L. HOLLOBON
JAMES ROBERT HOPSON
DONALD E. KELLER
SUSAN LIN
LINDSAY J. MALKIEWICH
STEVEN D. POWELL
ZENAIDA M. SAMANIEGO
FREDERIC SELTZER
STEVEN A. SMITH

CREDIT INSURANCE EXPERIENCE COMMITTEE:

JAY M. JAFFE, *Chairperson*
RICHARD L. BERGSTROM
J. RAMSAY BOYD
GARY FAGG
WILLIAM R. HORBATT
E. PERRY KUPFERMAN
KEITH E. NELSON
HARRY PLOSS
CHARLES M. UNDERWOOD, II
MICHAEL G. WARREN

LONG-TERM-CARE EXPERIENCE COMMITTEE:

SAM GUTTERMAN, *Chairperson*
FAYE ALBERT
HAROLD L. BARNEY
JAY P. BOEKHOFF
GARY L. CORLISS
TED L. DUNN
RICHARD J. ESTELL
KAREN LYNN GERVASONI
STEPHEN C. GOSS
ROBERT A. HALL
DAVID M. KLEVER
MICHELLE L. KUNZMAN
BARTLEY L. MUNSON
MARK C. ROWLEY
ROBERT SHAPLAND
CARL D. SMITH
MORRIS SNOW
JOHN C. WILKIN
JEROME WINKELSTEIN
ROBERT YEE

TRANSACTIONS

1988-89-90 REPORTS OF MORTALITY, MORBIDITY AND OTHER EXPERIENCE

INTRODUCTION

Included in the *1988-1989-1990 Reports* are the following reports of the Society of Actuaries' experience committees:

- 1986–87 Individual Life Mortality Experience
- 1985–86 Aviation Experience
- 1987–88 Group Annuity Experience
- 1985 National Nursing Home Survey Utilization Data.

In addition, the following reports of experience studies of interest to actuaries, prepared by other organizations, are also included:

- Mortality under Canadian Standard Ordinary Insurance Issues Studied between the 1987 and 1988 Anniversaries (Committee on Life Insurance Expected Experience of the Canadian Institute of Actuaries)
- Individual Annuitant Mortality Study, Policy Years 1980–1988 (Subcommittee on Annuity Mortality of the Committee on Expected Experience of the Canadian Institute of Actuaries)
- Improvement in Annuitant Mortality—Canada (Subcommittee on Annuity Mortality of the Committee on Expected Experience of the Canadian Institute of Actuaries)
- Long-Term Ordinary Lapse Survey in the United States and in Canada between 1987 and 1988 Anniversaries (Life Insurance Marketing and Research Association, Inc.)

We thank these organizations for permitting us to reproduce these studies in this volume.

Discussions of these reports are encouraged and may be submitted to the office of the Society of Actuaries prior to September 30, 1992. They will be published in the next *Reports* volume.

These experience reports include an aggregation of historical experience from several insurance companies or other sources. As a result, the experience included in these reports should not be assumed to apply prospectively or to a specific company, because of differences in marketing and underwriting of business written, mix or type of products sold, and trends between the experience period and the period for which expected experience will be effective.

Certain portions of the historical experience included in these reports may not be fully credible for a variety of reasons. Every attempt has been made to provide appropriate measures, such as amounts of exposures or claims, from which an actuary can determine the degree to which the reported measures can be relied upon statistically.

In addition, trends in experience between those reported here and in previously published reports should be viewed with caution; for example, they might have resulted from changes in mix of companies that have contributed or mix of business over time.

SAM GUTTERMAN, *Chairperson*
Society of Actuaries' Committee on Experience

REPORT OF THE INDIVIDUAL LIFE INSURANCE EXPERIENCE COMMITTEE

MORTALITY UNDER STANDARD INDIVIDUALLY UNDERWRITTEN LIFE INSURANCE BETWEEN 1986 AND 1987 ANNIVERSARIES

ABSTRACT

This study is the latest in continuing annual reports on intercompany mortality experience under standard individually underwritten life insurance. Because of changes in the number of companies contributing from year to year, direct comparisons with previous studies are affected.

The mortality ratios in this report are based on the 1975–80 Basic Tables. The primary results for this study are as follows:

- The overall mortality ratio for experience between 1986 and 1987 anniversaries, during policy years 1–15, is 86.3 percent, down about 2 percent from the prior year and continuing the ongoing trend. Virtually all this mortality improvement is in medical experience.
- The mortality ratios for experience between 1982 and 1987 anniversaries, during policy years 1–15, show that there has been greater improvement from the 1975–80 period for males (89.3 percent) than for females (95.0 percent) and that the greatest combined improvement has occurred at issue ages 25–39.
- For 1980–86 issues observed between 1982 and 1987 anniversaries, the mortality ratio for smokers is 152.1 percent and that for nonsmokers is 70.3 percent. Subdivisions of these data into medical, paramedical and nonmedical and into male and female produced little difference in these overall ratios.
- For experience between 1986 and 1987 anniversaries, during policy years 16 and later, the overall mortality ratio is 90.8 percent, about a 1 percent increase from the prior year. The comparable mortality ratios using expected deaths based on the 1980 CSO Tables and the 1979–81 U.S. Population Tables are 68.4 percent and 68.0 percent, respectively.

INTRODUCTION

This report covers the intercompany (U.S.) mortality experience by amount of life insurance under standard individually underwritten issues between 1986 and 1987 anniversaries. The report also combines experience between 1982 and 1987 anniversaries to provide a larger volume of data so that more adequate comparisons of results, particularly for males-females and smokers-nonsmokers, can be made.

INDEX OF PRIMARY TABLES

Table	Exposure Period	Policy Years*	Medical, Paramedical, or Nonmedical	Male or Female	Smoker/ Nonsmoker	Mortality Ratios by
1	1986–87	1–15	Combined	Combined	Combined	Issue age
2	1986–87	1–15	Combined	Combined	Combined	Policy year
3	1986–87	1–15	Separately	Combined	Combined	Issue age
4	1986–87	1–15	Separately	Combined	Combined	Policy year
5	1986–87	1–15	Separately	Combined	Combined	Issue age and policy year
6	1986–87	1–15	Separately	Combined	Combined	Issue age and policy year
7	1982–87	1–15	Combined	Separately	Combined	Issue age
8	1982–87	1–15	Combined	Separately	Combined	Policy year
9	1982–87	1–15	Separately	Separately	Combined	Issue age
10	1982–87	1–15	Separately	Separately	Combined	Policy year
11	1982–87	1–15	Medical	Separately	Combined	Issue age and policy year
12	1982–87	1–15	Paramedical	Separately	Combined	Issue age and policy year
13	1982–87	1–15	Nonmedical	Separately	Combined	Issue age and policy year
14	1982–87	1–15	Combined	Separately	Combined	Issue age and policy year
15	1982–87	1–15	Separately	Separately	Combined	Issue age and policy year
16	1986–87	1–7	Separately	Combined	Separately	Issue age
17	1986–87	1–7	Separately	Combined	Separately	Policy year
18	1982–87	1–7	Separately	Combined	Separately	Issue age
19	1982–87	1–7	Separately	Combined	Separately	Policy year
20	1982–87	1–7	Combined	Separately	Separately	Issue age
21	1982–87	1–7	Combined	Separately	Separately	Policy year
22	1986–87	16 and over	Combined	Combined	Combined	Attained age
23	1982–87	16 and over	Combined	Combined	Combined	Attained age
24	1982–87	16 and over	Separately	Combined	Combined	Attained age
25	1982–87	16 and over	Combined	Separately	Combined	Attained age

Appendix A — Names of the contributing companies and percentage of total 1986–87 exposures contributed by each company

*Select (1–15); smoker-nonsmoker (1–7); ultimate (16 and over).

The report is divided into four primary sections:

I. Select Experience (first 15 policy years) between 1986 and 1987 anniversaries for issues of 1972–1986 (Tables 1–6).

II. Select Experience (first 15 policy years) between 1982 and 1987 anniversaries for issues of 1972–1986 (Tables 7–15).

III. Smoker-Nonsmoker Experience (first seven policy years) between 1986–1987 anniversaries and between 1982 and 1987 anniversaries for issues of 1980–1986 (Tables 16–21).

IV. Ultimate Experience (policy years 16 and over) between 1986 and 1987 anniversaries and between 1982 and 1987 anniversaries (Tables 22–25).

Each section subdivides experience by insurance issued subject to a medical examination (medical), insurance issued subject to a paramedical examination (paramedical), and insurance issued without a paramedical or medical examination (nonmedical).

Most of the tables in this report show actual amounts of death claims (to the nearest $1,000) and mortality ratios of actual-to-expected death claims based on the 1975–80 Male and Female Basic Tables. (Tables 1, 2 and 22 also show mortality ratios based on the 1965–70 Basic Tables.) In addition, Tables 1, 2, 7, 8, 16–21, and 22 show amounts exposed to risk (to the nearest $1,000,000). All data in Sections I, II and III were submitted separately for males and females.

The 1986–87 select and ultimate experience is derived from the contributions of 19 companies. The 1982–87 select and ultimate experience is derived from the contributions of 23 companies, 18 of which contributed data for the entire 1982–87 period. The 1986–87 smoker-nonsmoker experience is derived from the contributions of 13 companies, and the 1982–87 smoker-nonsmoker data is derived from the contributions of 15 companies. Appendix A gives the names and proportionate contributions of companies that contributed 1986–87 experience. Appendixes B, C, and D, which are not published here but can be obtained from the Society Research Department, contain detailed medical, paramedical and nonmedical experience, respectively, by ages at issue for each year of issue, for males and females separately.

The following summary tables show some interesting trends. Table A shows the change in proportions of policies issued by type of underwriting and reflects the decreasing use of medical examinations and the increasing use of nonmedicals. Table B shows mortality ratios by exposure years since the introduction of the 1965–70 Basic Tables. The decreases are a continuation of the trend that has continued almost without exception since these annual studies were started.

TABLE A

EXPOSURES FOR POLICY YEAR 1
AS PERCENTAGE OF TOTAL EXPOSURES

Year of Issue	Medical	Paramedical	Nonmedical
1977	34.7%	28.9%	36.4%
1978	35.1	28.5	36.4
1979	35.1	30.5	34.4
1980	38.2	32.5	29.3
1981	33.1	30.6	36.3
1982	29.2	25.1	45.7
1983	24.7	23.5	51.8
1984	22.5	25.3	52.2
1985	20.7	27.1	52.1
1986	15.7	27.4	56.9

TABLE B

AGGREGATE MORTALITY RATIOS BASED ON 1965–70 SELECT BASIC TABLES
(NUMBERS IN PARENTHESIS ARE MORTALITY RATIOS
BASED ON THE 1975–80 BASIC TABLES)

Exposure Year	Policy Years 1–15				Policy Years 16 and Over
	Medical	Paramedical	Nonmedical	Combined	
1973–74	88.0%	84.1%	99.1%	89.9%	93.4%
1974–75	85.1	85.5	94.9	87.8	87.1
1975–76	80.9	81.4	88.5	82.3	85.0
1976–77	75.5	78.0	87.9	77.9	82.0
1977–78	75.0	80.5	85.9	77.4	80.5
1978–79	68.7	74.5	84.9	72.1	77.0
1979–80	69.8	80.3	82.9	73.3	77.1
1980–81	69.5	70.1	79.8	71.0	75.2
1981–82	67.8	73.2	79.2	70.7	72.8
1982–83	68.0	69.9	74.2	69.6	73.2
1983–84	68.6 (93.6)	68.8 (92.2)	70.8 (89.6)	69.1 (92.4)	71.2 (91.8)
1984–85	66.2 (90.5)	69.9 (94.3)	72.4 (92.5)	68.5 (91.9)	71.0 (91.1)
1985–86	61.2 (83.7)	67.9 (91.8)	72.0 (92.4)	65.5 (88.0)	70.0 (89.8)
1986–87	58.6 (80.1)	66.5 (90.3)	71.6 (92.2)	64.3 (86.4)	70.8 (90.5)

Table C shows the proportions of medical, paramedical and nonmedical exposures in policy years 1 and policy years 1–15 by issue age groups. This indicates that the use of nonmedicals predominates at issue ages under 30 and that medicals account for about half of the exposures (which are based on amounts of insurance) at issue ages 50 and over.

TABLE C

EXPOSURES AS PERCENTAGE OF TOTAL EXPOSURES FOR 1986–1987 EXPERIENCE

	Policy Year 1			Policy Years 1–15		
Ages at Issue	Medical	Paramedical	Nonmedical	Medical	Paramedical	Nonmedical
0–9	2.0%	0.9%	97.1%	4.3%	1.0%	94.6%
10–19	2.1	2.6	95.4	4.5	2.9	92.6
20–29	2.5	7.8	89.7	7.2	10.7	82.1
30–39	11.6	29.0	59.4	19.6	30.3	50.2
40–49	28.2	49.0	22.8	37.1	43.5	19.4
50 and over ..	49.5	42.3	8.2	55.4	37.4	7.2
All Ages	15.7	27.3	57.0	22.0	26.0	52.0

It would be desirable for the comparisons of medical, paramedical and nonmedical experience to be based on strictly comparable policies, but such comparisons are not possible. Medically underwritten business generally includes larger amounts of insurance issued to persons at higher socioeconomic levels than nonmedical and paramedical business. However, medical business also includes policies issued to individuals within nonmedical or paramedical amount limits who were not acceptable on these bases because of medical histories. Similarly, paramedical policies include persons not acceptable on a nonmedical basis. In addition, there are considerable variations in amount limits and proportions of medical, nonmedical, and paramedical policies among contributing companies. In this comparison and throughout this report, the difference in the mix of companies from that in previous studies may account for some of the differences in mortality ratios.

Note also that some of the more recent nonmedical issues are likely based on applications with limited medical history questions (that is, simplified underwriting). In addition, nonmedical issues over age 50 often arise from business issued under pension trust and salary allotment plans. So-called policyholder's nonmedical, issued on the basis of a previous medical examination within 6 or 12 months, is also included in nonmedical issues for some companies.

I. 1986–87 SELECT EXPERIENCE (MALES AND FEMALES COMBINED)

The experience between 1986 and 1987 anniversaries during the first 15 policy years presented in Tables 1–6 includes exposures of $672 billion and actual deaths of $980 million. The corresponding amounts in the 1985–86 experience were $691 billion and $1,005 million, respectively. As previously mentioned, there were differences in the mix of companies; 18 companies contributed data for both 1985–86 and 1986–87, whereas 2 companies contributed data for only 1985–86 and 1 company contributed data for only 1986–87.

The experience for the first 15 policy years compared by issue age group is shown in Table 1 and that by policy year is shown in Table 2. Separate data for medical, paramedical and nonmedical are shown by issue age group in Table 3 and by policy year in Table 4. Separate data for males and females (Section II, Tables 7–15) and for smokers and nonsmokers (Section III, Tables 16–21) are shown later in this report.

TABLE 1

1986–87 EXPERIENCE BY ISSUE AGE
MALE AND FEMALE LIVES COMBINED; MEDICAL, PARAMEDICAL, NONMEDICAL COMBINED
ISSUES OF 1972–86 STUDIED BETWEEN 1986 AND 1987 ANNIVERSARIES
EXPECTED DEATHS BASED ON 1965–70 AND 1975–80 BASIC TABLES
(EXPOSURES IN $1,000,000 UNITS; ACTUAL DEATHS IN $1,000 UNITS)

Ages at Issue	Exposure	Actual Deaths	Expected Deaths	Mortality Ratio 1975–80 Basic Tables	Mortality Ratio 1965–70 Basic Tables
0–9	$ 33,440	$ 8,298	$ 12,530	66.2%	33.1%
10–14	10,609	5,850	6,645	88.0	87.7
15–19	21,097	17,772	17,797	99.9	99.2
20–24	53,902	36,037	35,722	100.9	86.7
25–29	105,065	63,594	73,855	86.1	72.9
30–34	131,105	93,507	118,589	78.9	60.9
35–39	119,017	126,335	153,563	82.3	63.6
40–44	80,668	128,106	157,830	81.2	59.5
45–49	50,074	128,534	156,205	82.3	61.5
50–54	32,114	124,826	136,775	91.3	61.2
55–59	20,413	111,352	126,805	87.8	65.5
60–64	9,874	79,967	81,555	98.1	66.2
65–69	3,267	37,953	42,950	88.4	66.8
70 and over	913	17,655	14,553	121.3	88.9
Total	$671,558	$979,786	$1,135,374	86.3%	64.2%

TABLE 2

1986–87 EXPERIENCE BY POLICY YEAR
MALE AND FEMALE LIVES COMBINED; MEDICAL, PARAMEDICAL, NONMEDICAL COMBINED
ISSUES OF 1972–86 STUDIED BETWEEN 1986 AND 1987 ANNIVERSARIES
EXPECTED DEATHS BASED ON 1965–70 AND 1975–80 BASIC TABLES
(EXPOSURES IN $1,000,000 UNITS; ACTUAL DEATHS IN $1,000 UNITS)

Policy Year	Exposure	Actual Deaths	Expected Deaths	Mortality Ratio 1975–80 Basic Tables	Mortality Ratio 1965–70 Basic Tables
1	$150,207	$ 91,977	$ 128,575	71.5%	51.4%
2	110,892	116,649	125,720	92.8	67.0
3	89,326	117,061	131,865	88.8	64.7
4	85,796	124,907	146,489	85.3	62.8
5	55,629	86,542	103,843	83.3	64.1
6	37,274	65,382	75,245	86.9	65.6
7	27,019	55,410	59,892	92.5	69.1
8	21,749	49,032	51,699	94.8	70.8
9	18,134	42,484	46,246	91.9	68.9
10	17,142	41,776	47,241	88.4	66.6
11	14,455	37,225	46,110	80.7	62.0
12	12,450	42,142	43,358	97.2	74.8
13	11,563	35,878	43,279	82.9	63.5
14	10,431	37,034	42,914	86.3	66.1
15	9,490	36,286	42,897	84.6	64.6
Total	$671,558	$979,786	$1,135,374	86.3%	64.2%

TABLE 3

MEDICAL, PARAMEDICAL, NONMEDICAL 1986–87 EXPERIENCE BY ISSUE AGE
MALE AND FEMALE LIVES COMBINED
ISSUES OF 1972–86 STUDIED BETWEEN 1986 AND 1987 ANNIVERSARIES
EXPECTED DEATHS BASED ON 1975–80 BASIC TABLES
(ACTUAL DEATHS IN $1,000 UNITS)

Ages at Issue	Medical		Paramedical		Nonmedical		Combined	
	Actual Deaths	Mortality Ratio	Actual Deaths	Mortality Ratio	Actual Deaths	Mortality Ratio	Actual Deaths	Mortality Ratio
0–9	$ 300	54.0%	$ 50	41.3%	$ 7,848	66.9%	$ 8,298	66.2%
10–14	262	56.3	55	31.6	5,534	93.2	5,850	88.0
15–19	824	108.8	740	121.5	15,956	98.9	17,772	99.9
20–24	2,294	107.7	2,023	84.9	31,124	102.7	36,037	100.9
25–29	8,523	107.7	6,181	61.2	46,298	86.9	63,594	86.1
30–34	16,588	69.7	24,752	83.7	49,784	81.8	93,507	78.9
35–39	34,952	73.9	42,818	80.3	43,092	90.9	126,335	82.3
40–44	47,401	72.9	48,465	81.3	27,037	98.6	128,106	81.2
45–49	52,513	68.6	54,384	95.1	16,420	99.2	128,534	82.3
50–54	64,089	80.2	44,826	100.5	10,941	142.8	124,826	91.3
55–59	59,663	76.9	41,079	106.6	7,770	119.8	111,352	87.8
60–64	53,917	95.2	21,787	112.9	2,017	65.8	79,967	98.1
65–69	26,933	83.5	9,168	111.1	868	66.4	37,953	88.4
70 and over	13,111	116.7	3,367	136.9	911	161.7	17,655	121.3
Total	$381,370	79.1%	$299,694	91.9%	$265,600	92.0%	$979,786	86.3%

TABLE 4

MEDICAL, PARAMEDICAL, NONMEDICAL 1986–87 EXPERIENCE BY POLICY YEAR
MALE AND FEMALE LIVES COMBINED
ISSUES OF 1972–86 STUDIED BETWEEN 1986 AND 1987 ANNIVERSARIES
EXPECTED DEATHS BASED ON 1975–80 BASIC TABLES
(ACTUAL DEATHS IN $1,000 UNITS)

Policy Year	Medical		Paramedical		Nonmedical		Combined	
	Actual Deaths	Mortality Ratio	Actual Deaths	Mortality Ratio	Actual Deaths	Mortality Ratio	Actual Deaths	Mortality Ratio
1	$ 17,187	54.4%	$ 31,233	78.7%	$ 37,253	76.0%	$ 91,977	71.5%
2	28,429	83.4	39,756	98.3	38,726	97.7	116,649	92.8
3	35,831	91.6	34,914	82.9	36,079	90.3	117,061	88.8
4	38,919	76.2	42,744	90.0	41,752	92.7	124,907	85.3
5	28,277	70.8	31,396	91.1	26,376	91.5	86,542	83.3
6	24,395	75.7	23,959	90.9	15,384	95.4	65,382	86.9
7	25,224	86.6	20,956	99.7	8,614	92.6	55,410	92.5
8	21,530	82.2	18,266	110.4	8,979	104.9	49,032	94.8
9	20,370	83.7	13,478	99.2	8,297	103.2	42,484	91.9
10	21,745	82.0	12,749	97.9	7,254	97.6	41,776	88.4
11	19,552	70.3	10,262	95.0	7,253	101.7	37,225	80.7
12	25,604	93.9	9,156	106.3	7,250	103.8	42,142	97.2
13	22,057	75.7	5,704	91.2	7,013	95.7	35,878	82.9
14	25,713	83.8	3,384	84.1	7,758	102.0	37,034	86.3
15	26,537	80.7	1,738	94.8	7,613	98.4	36,286	84.6
Total	$381,370	79.1%	$299,694	91.9%	$265,600	92.0%	$979,786	86.3%

The mortality ratio for medical, paramedical and nonmedical combined based on the 1975–80 Basic Tables is 86.3 percent. The mortality ratios for the subdivided experience are 79.1 percent for medical, 91.9 percent for paramedical and 92.0 percent for nonmedical. These aggregate ratios do not present an accurate comparison of these three sets of data because of the different age distributions.

By Issue Age (Tables 1 and 3)

The pattern of mortality ratios by issue age shows virtually no improvement in mortality from the 1975–80 experience (that is, the experience underlying the 1975–80 Basic Tables) at issue ages 15–24 and 60–64 (a 21 percent deterioration at issue ages 70 and over), with the most substantial improvement at issue ages 30–49.

The bulk of the exposures are nonmedical through issue age 29, and the nonmedical experience is generally more favorable than medical and paramedical at these ages—presumably because much of the medical and paramedical issues were within nonmedical amount limits but required examinations because of medical history. The data for issue ages 30–39 include a substantial proportion of medical, paramedical and nonmedical, and not unexpectedly the mortality ratios are lowest for medical, almost as low as for paramedical, but higher for nonmedical, particularly at issue ages 35–39.

At issue ages 40–59, the bulk of the experience is medical and paramedical. The medical experience has relatively low mortality ratios, and the mortality ratios for paramedical increase with age. The amount of nonmedical data decreases with age and the mortality ratios increase with age.

At issue ages 60 and over, the medical experience continues to show relatively low mortality ratios (except at issue ages 70 and over), and the paramedical mortality experience produces high mortality ratios. The nonmedical data are very limited.

By Policy Year (Tables 2 and 4)

The mortality ratios by policy year for medical, paramedical and nonmedical separately are generally lowest in the first six policy years and highest in policy years 7–12. This pattern is particularly pronounced for paramedical and nonmedical and may reflect lapsation antiselection due to replacement of policies issued just prior to the introduction of interest-sensitive products in the early 1980s. Note that the paramedical experience is less mature (that is, there were relatively few paramedical issues before the mid–1970s) and therefore the amount of exposure is relatively small at the longer durations.

By Issue Age and Policy Year (Tables 5 and 6)

The 1986–87 experience is subdivided, separately for medical, paramedical and nonmedical, in Table 5 into six issue age groups, each further subdivided into four policy-year groups. These subdivisions provide an opportunity to examine the separate medical, paramedical and nonmedical data in more detail than that provided by issue age for all policy years combined (Table 3) and by policy year for all issue ages combined (Table 4).

Table 6 shows the ratios of mortality ratios: paramedical to medical, nonmedical to paramedical, and nonmedical to medical. Each of these ratios would be expected to exceed 100 percent because in each case the ratio is that of the less exacting underwriting requirement to the more exacting. This is generally true for the age groups for which the comparisons are not distorted by small amounts of data (for example, medical experience at ages under 30 and nonmedical experience at ages 60 and over).

TABLE 5

MEDICAL, PARAMEDICAL, NONMEDICAL 1986–87 EXPERIENCE BY ISSUE AGE AND POLICY YEAR
MALE AND FEMALE LIVES COMBINED
ISSUES OF 1972–86 STUDIED BETWEEN 1986 AND 1987 ANNIVERSARIES
EXPECTED DEATHS BASED ON 1975–80 BASIC TABLES
(ACTUAL DEATHS IN $1,000 UNITS)

Ages at Issue	Policy Years 1–2		Policy Years 3–5		Policy Years 6–10		Policy Years 11–15		Policy Years 1–15	
	Actual Deaths	Mortality Ratio	Actual Deaths	Mortality Ratio	Actual Deaths	Mortality Ratio	Actual Deaths	Mortality Ratio	Actual Deaths	Mortality Ratio
Medical										
0–19	$ 50	24.6%	$ 270	103.4%	$ 321	47.1%	$ 744	118.0%	$ 1,385	78.0%
20–29	173	17.7	2,970	192.7	2,648	93.9	5,026	106.8	10,818	107.7
30–39	3,681	44.8	12,068	68.7	17,919	85.5	17,872	73.4	51,540	72.5
40–49	9,030	48.5	25,032	65.9	26,661	72.9	39,191	81.1	99,914	70.6
50–59	15,437	74.1	33,513	85.1	35,351	74.3	39,452	79.6	123,752	78.6
60 and over	17,245	102.4	29,174	87.4	30,363	102.1	17,177	85.1	93,960	93.8
All Ages	$ 45,616	69.4%	$103,027	79.2%	$113,264	81.8%	$119,462	80.8%	$381,370	79.1%
Paramedical										
0–19	$ 81	54.4%	$ 44	29.4%	$ 557	124.8%	$ 163	102.2%	$ 845	93.4%
20–29	1,387	50.6	1,170	44.1	3,776	77.1	1,871	85.5	8,204	65.8
30–39	17,712	93.6	18,711	68.7	24,007	85.8	7,140	81.7	67,570	81.5
40–49	25,949	86.5	35,613	77.5	29,266	99.2	12,020	105.8	102,848	88.0
50–59	17,780	87.0	36,257	108.9	24,383	112.6	7,485	96.5	85,906	103.3
60 and over	8,079	102.3	17,258	116.7	7,419	123.3	1,566	118.7	34,322	114.4
All Ages	$ 70,989	88.6%	$109,054	87.9%	$ 89,409	98.8%	$ 30,243	95.9%	$299,694	91.9%

TABLE 5—*Continued*

Ages at Issue	Policy Years 1–2		Policy Years 3–5		Policy Years 6–10		Policy Years 11–15		Policy Years 1–15	
	Actual Deaths	Mortality Ratio	Actual Deaths	Mortality Ratio	Actual Deaths	Mortality Ratio	Actual Deaths	Mortality Ratio	Actual Deaths	Mortality Ratio
Nonmedical										
0–19	$ 5,893	67.3%	$ 7,979	92.8%	$ 8,022	88.3%	$ 7,444	100.9%	$ 29,338	86.8%
20–29	21,401	78.4	24,210	94.7	17,637	106.0	14,174	100.7	77,422	92.6
30–39	27,978	82.0	39,458	83.3	14,477	91.9	10,963	99.4	92,876	85.8
40–49	12,519	95.9	21,410	97.1	6,052	108.6	3,476	105.5	43,457	98.8
50–59	6,970	173.3	9,074	120.5	1,892	107.9	776	91.9	18,711	132.3
60 and over	1,217	87.5	2,076	75.9	448	68.1	55	35.8	3,796	76.9
All Ages	$ 75,979	85.7%	$104,207	91.5%	$ 48,528	98.1%	$ 36,886	100.3%	$265,600	92.0%
Combined										
0–19	$ 6,276	66.3%	$ 8,393	92.1%	$ 8,900	87.1%	$ 8,351	102.2%	$ 31,920	86.3%
20–29	25,110	75.9	29,209	95.1	24,167	98.2	21,145	99.8	99,631	90.9
30–39	52,436	79.8	73,023	76.4	58,033	88.3	36,350	80.7	219,843	80.8
40–49	52,090	77.2	85,556	77.3	62,999	87.3	55,995	87.7	256,640	81.7
50–59	44,210	88.3	82,339	98.4	61,755	86.8	47,875	81.6	236,179	89.6
60 and over	28,503	100.1	49,990	95.3	38,230	105.0	18,851	87.0	135,574	97.5
All Ages	$208,626	82.0%	$328,510	86.0%	$254,084	90.6%	$188,566	86.3%	$979,786	86.3%

TABLE 6

SUMMARY OF MEDICAL, PARAMEDICAL, NONMEDICAL 1986–87 MORTALITY RATIOS
MALE AND FEMALE LIVES COMBINED
ISSUES OF 1972–86 STUDIED BETWEEN 1986 AND 1987 ANNIVERSARIES
EXPECTED DEATHS BASED ON 1975–80 BASIC TABLES

Ages at Issue	Policy Years 1–2			Policy Years 3–5			Policy Years 6–10			Policy Years 11–15			Policy Years 1–15		
	Mortality Ratios														
	Med	Para	Non	Med	Para	Non	Med	Para	Non	Med	Para	Non	Med	Para	Non
0–19	24.6%	54.4%	67.3%	103.4%	29.4%	92.8%	47.1%	124.8%	88.3%	118.0%	102.2%	100.9%	78.0%	93.4%	86.8%
20–29	17.7	50.6	78.4	192.7	44.1	94.7	93.9	77.1	106.0	106.8	85.5	100.7	107.7	65.8	92.6
30–39	44.8	93.6	82.0	68.7	68.7	83.3	85.5	85.8	91.9	73.4	81.7	99.4	72.5	81.5	85.8
40–49	48.5	86.5	95.9	65.9	77.5	97.1	72.9	99.2	108.6	81.1	105.8	105.5	70.6	88.0	98.8
50–59	74.1	87.0	173.3	85.1	108.9	120.5	74.3	112.6	107.9	79.6	96.5	91.9	78.6	103.3	132.3
60 and over	102.4	102.3	87.5	87.4	116.7	75.9	102.1	123.3	68.1	85.1	118.7	35.8	93.8	114.4	76.9
All Ages	69.4%	88.6%	85.7%	79.2%	87.9%	91.5%	81.8%	98.8%	98.1%	80.8%	95.9%	100.3%	79.1%	91.9%	92.0%
	Ratio of Mortality Ratios														
	Para to Med	Non to Para	Non to Med	Para to Med	Non to Para	Non to Med	Para to Med	Non to Para	Non to Med	Para to Med	Non to Para	Non to Med	Para to Med	Non to Para	Non to Med
0–19	2.21	1.24	2.74	0.28	3.16	0.90	2.65	0.71	1.88	0.87	0.99	0.85	1.20	0.93	1.11
20–29	2.86	1.55	4.43	0.23	2.14	0.49	0.82	1.37	1.13	0.80	1.18	0.94	0.61	1.41	0.86
30–39	2.09	0.88	1.83	1.00	1.21	1.21	1.00	1.07	1.07	1.11	1.22	1.35	1.12	1.05	1.18
40–49	1.78	1.11	1.98	1.18	1.25	1.47	1.36	1.10	1.49	1.30	1.00	1.30	1.25	1.12	1.40
50–59	1.17	1.99	2.34	1.28	1.11	1.42	1.52	0.96	1.45	1.21	0.95	1.15	1.31	1.28	1.68
60 and over	1.00	0.85	0.85	1.34	0.65	0.87	1.21	0.55	0.67	1.39	0.30	0.42	1.22	0.67	0.82
All Ages	1.28	0.97	1.23	1.11	1.04	1.16	1.21	0.99	1.20	1.19	1.05	1.24	1.16	1.00	1.16

Key: Med = medical
Para = paramedical
Non = nonmedical.

II. 1982–87 SELECT EXPERIENCE (MALES AND FEMALES SEPARATELY)

The experience between 1982 and 1987 anniversaries during the first 15 policy years is presented in Tables 7–15 in the same format as that presented for the 1986–87 experience in Tables 1–6 except that data for males and females are presented separately.

The mortality ratio for 1982–87 medical, paramedical and nonmedical experience combined (Table 7) is 90.1 percent (compared to 86.3 percent for the 1986–87 experience). The mortality ratio for males is 89.3 percent and that for females is 95.0 percent. These mortality ratios are based on expected deaths derived from the separate male and female 1975–80 Basic Tables as are all mortality ratios in this report.

By Issue Age (Tables 7 and 9)

The mortality ratios by issue age (Tables 7 and 9) show a pattern for both males and females that is somewhat similar to the 1986–87 experience (Tables 1 and 3): relatively high ratios at issue ages 15–24 and relatively low ratios at ages 25–39. However, the mortality ratios for females are much more than 100 percent at issue ages 55 and over, which is a rather unexpected result. These patterns are consistent throughout the experience when subdivided into medical, paramedical and nonmedical.

By Policy Year (Tables 8 and 10)

The mortality ratios by policy year (Tables 8 and 10) are highest in policy years 3–10 as compared to policy years 7–9 in the 1986–87 experience (Tables 2 and 4), again reflecting possible lapsation antiselection produced by the heavy replacement activities in recent years. The same pattern is less apparent for females than for males, although the relatively favorable mortality in policy years 1–2 is also apparent for females. This pattern applies primarily to the medical experience. The highest paramedical mortality is for policy years 5–12, and the highest nonmedical mortality is for policy years 6 and over.

TABLE 7

MALE AND FEMALE 1982–87 EXPERIENCE BY ISSUE AGE
MEDICAL, PARAMEDICAL, NONMEDICAL COMBINED
ISSUES OF 1972–86 STUDIED BETWEEN 1982 AND 1987 ANNIVERSARIES
EXPECTED DEATHS BASED ON 1975–80 BASIC TABLES
(EXPOSURES IN $1,000,000 UNITS; ACTUAL DEATHS IN $1,000 UNITS)

Ages at Issue	Male			Female			Combined		
	Exposure	Actual Deaths	Mortality Ratio	Exposure	Actual Deaths	Mortality Ratio	Exposure	Actual Deaths	Mortality Ratio
0–9	$ 88,692	$ 30,713	76.9%	$ 70,633	$ 13,854	68.0%	$ 159,325	$ 44,567	73.9%
10–14	30,754	22,810	89.3	21,156	7,040	89.5	51,910	29,850	89.4
15–19	75,698	78,011	93.1	41,751	17,094	95.5	117,449	95,105	93.5
20–24	211,219	168,174	98.6	94,747	34,343	88.3	305,967	202,517	96.7
25–29	392,543	276,532	86.9	145,745	54,076	79.3	538,289	330,607	85.6
30–34	491,727	404,986	83.4	151,849	74,009	75.4	643,579	478,995	82.0
35–39	452,839	539,556	86.2	113,629	83,755	81.0	566,472	623,311	85.5
40–44	314,379	578,548	88.2	67,028	89,325	89.5	381,410	667,873	88.4
45–49	201,483	616,273	90.9	41,039	87,522	97.4	242,527	703,796	91.6
50–54	131,374	565,350	95.2	27,051	80,834	102.4	158,427	646,184	96.1
55–59	77,586	457,913	88.5	17,334	80,115	122.9	94,922	538,028	92.3
60–64	33,174	276,084	93.1	9,201	57,789	122.6	42,376	333,874	97.2
65–69	9,822	121,748	81.3	3,750	33,659	134.9	13,573	155,407	88.9
70 and over	2,193	46,727	109.7	1,231	21,212	168.3	3,424	67,939	123.0
Total	$2,513,484	$4,183,426	89.3%	$806,143	$734,628	95.0%	$3,319,651	$4,918,053	90.1%

TABLE 8

MALE AND FEMALE 1982–87 EXPERIENCE BY POLICY YEAR
MEDICAL, PARAMEDICAL, NONMEDICAL COMBINED
ISSUES OF 1972–86 STUDIED BETWEEN 1982 AND 1987 ANNIVERSARIES
EXPECTED DEATHS BASED ON 1975–80 BASIC TABLES
(EXPOSURES IN $1,000,000 UNITS; ACTUAL DEATHS IN $1,000 UNITS)

Policy Year	Male			Female			Combined		
	Exposure	Actual Deaths	Mortality Ratio	Exposure	Actual Deaths	Mortality Ratio	Exposure	Actual Deaths	Mortality Ratio
1	$ 561,550	$ 449,916	81.5%	$198,788	$ 81,237	77.9%	$ 760,359	$ 531,153	80.9%
2	447,151	508,706	89.4	149,881	92,676	93.9	597,036	601,382	90.1
3	338,754	496,583	91.0	111,254	90,092	100.6	450,008	586,675	92.4
4	251,192	428,365	92.9	81,978	75,700	97.1	333,169	504,065	93.5
5	178,270	334,461	93.1	57,475	61,558	99.0	235,745	396,019	94.0
6	135,762	266,904	91.4	42,989	49,580	96.2	178,751	316,484	92.1
7	109,304	236,495	92.7	33,850	42,484	95.1	143,153	278,978	93.0
8	91,234	217,514	94.8	27,757	36,292	90.5	118,991	253,806	94.1
9	78,802	193,410	90.2	23,217	38,616	106.3	102,019	232,026	92.6
10	70,365	187,376	89.8	19,793	34,918	103.2	90,158	222,293	91.7
11	61,072	176,636	87.5	16,277	30,506	97.5	77,349	207,143	88.8
12	54,503	173,947	87.7	13,566	25,518	90.2	68,069	199,465	88.0
13	49,377	168,351	85.1	11,439	26,083	100.2	60,816	194,434	86.9
14	44,994	172,108	86.5	9,637	25,090	100.5	54,631	197,198	88.0
15	41,153	172,654	86.1	8,244	24,279	102.8	49,397	196,933	87.9
Total	$2,513,484	$4,183,426	89.3%	$806,143	$734,628	95.0%	$3,319,651	$4,918,053	90.1%

TABLE 9

MALE AND FEMALE 1982–87 EXPERIENCE BY ISSUE AGE
MEDICAL, PARAMEDICAL AND NONMEDICAL SEPARATELY
ISSUES OF 1972–86 STUDIED BETWEEN 1982 AND 1987 ANNIVERSARIES
EXPECTED DEATHS BASED ON 1975–80 BASIC TABLES
(ACTUAL DEATHS IN $1,000 UNITS)

Ages at Issue	Medical		Paramedical		Nonmedical		All Issues	
	Actual Deaths	Mortality Ratio	Actual Deaths	Mortality Ratio	Actual Deaths	Mortality Ratio	Actual Deaths	Mortality Ratio
				Male				
0–9	$ 1,579	62.4%	$ 385	98.1%	$ 28,699	77.7%	$ 30,713	76.9%
10–14	2,039	80.8	427	60.4	20,344	91.4	22,810	89.3
15–19	4,611	91.7	2,819	87.7	70,329	93.4	78,011	93.1
20–24	16,681	99.5	13,915	96.6	137,062	98.9	168,174	98.6
25–29	53,727	91.8	44,202	80.0	176,126	87.1	276,532	86.9
30–34	130,716	82.1	109,493	79.1	162,794	88.1	404,986	83.4
35–39	246,026	85.9	160,845	77.4	127,977	100.9	539,556	86.2
40–44	319,817	83.9	180,124	89.1	73,511	108.4	578,548	88.2
45–49	381,387	87.1	188,982	98.0	41,415	97.6	616,273	90.9
50–54	383,117	90.0	151,494	104.9	26,439	134.8	565,350	95.2
55–59	316,699	83.1	120,598	103.4	18,286	113.2	457,913	88.5
60–64	214,429	90.3	54,742	112.3	4,868	60.5	276,084	93.1
65–69	99,328	78.7	19,221	99.6	2,603	77.4	121,748	81.3
70 and over	38,972	106.6	6,188	129.9	1,414	131.9	46,727	109.7
Total	$2,209,129	86.4%	$1,053,434	91.7%	$ 891,867	94.3%	$4,183,426	89.3%

TABLE 9—*Continued*

Ages at Issue	Medical		Paramedical		Nonmedical		All Issues	
	Actual Deaths	Mortality Ratio	Actual Deaths	Mortality Ratio	Actual Deaths	Mortality Ratio	Actual Deaths	Mortality Ratio
				Female				
0–9	$ 402	42.9%	$ 30	17.3%	$ 13,372	69.6%	$ 13,854	68.0%
10–14	730	129.4	45	23.8	6,264	88.3	7,040	89.5
15–19	300	45.4	485	103.3	16,310	97.5	17,094	95.5
20–24	1,855	132.0	1,670	108.1	30,740	86.0	34,343	88.3
25–29	4,633	102.5	5,925	96.7	43,402	76.1	54,076	79.3
30–34	12,349	94.6	13,183	68.6	48,076	73.8	74,009	75.4
35–39	19,434	83.8	24,031	78.7	39,525	81.0	83,755	81.0
40–44	33,562	100.1	27,789	80.0	27,867	91.0	89,325	89.5
45–49	41,251	97.0	32,243	95.1	13,302	105.4	87,522	97.4
50–54	41,761	94.3	30,512	106.8	7,891	144.2	80,834	102.4
55–59	45,391	116.2	27,689	129.1	6,525	153.4	80,115	122.9
60–64	40,193	122.0	16,087	127.2	1,309	104.0	57,789	122.6
65–69	25,184	131.1	7,572	143.7	516	156.0	33,659	134.9
70 and over	16,449	162.5	3,874	179.7	776	297.9	21,212	168.3
Total	$ 283,494	106.6%	$ 191,136	97.1%	$ 255,872	84.0%	$ 734,628	95.0%

TABLE 9—*Continued*

Ages at Issue	Medical		Paramedical		Nonmedical		All Issues	
	Actual Deaths	Mortality Ratio	Actual Deaths	Mortality Ratio	Actual Deaths	Mortality Ratio	Actual Deaths	Mortality Ratio
				Combined				
0–9	$ 1,981	57.1%	$ 415	73.3%	$ 42,070	74.9%	$ 44,567	73.9%
10–14	2,769	89.7	472	52.7	26,608	90.7	29,850	89.4
15–19	4,911	86.3	3,304	89.7	86,639	94.1	95,105	93.5
20–24	18,536	102.0	15,584	97.7	167,802	96.2	202,517	96.7
25–29	58,360	92.5	50,128	81.7	219,528	84.7	330,607	85.6
30–34	143,066	83.1	122,676	77.8	210,870	84.4	478,995	82.0
35–39	265,461	85.7	184,876	77.6	167,502	95.4	623,311	85.5
40–44	353,379	85.2	207,913	87.8	101,378	103.0	667,873	88.4
45–49	422,637	88.0	221,225	97.6	54,716	99.4	703,796	91.6
50–54	424,878	90.4	182,006	105.2	34,330	136.9	646,184	96.1
55–59	362,090	86.2	148,287	107.4	24,811	121.5	538,028	92.3
60–64	254,622	94.2	70,829	115.4	6,176	66.4	333,874	97.2
65–69	124,512	85.6	26,793	109.1	3,119	84.5	155,407	88.9
70 and over	55,421	118.7	10,062	145.5	2,190	164.4	67,939	123.0
Total	$2,492,623	88.3%	$1,244,570	92.5%	$1,147,739	91.8%	$4,918,053	90.1%

TABLE 10

MALE AND FEMALE 1982–87 EXPERIENCE BY POLICY YEAR
MEDICAL, PARAMEDICAL AND NONMEDICAL SEPARATELY
ISSUES OF 1972–86 STUDIED BETWEEN 1982 AND 1987 ANNIVERSARIES
EXPECTED DEATHS BASED ON 1975–80 BASIC TABLES
(ACTUAL DEATHS IN $1,000 UNITS)

Policy Year	Medical		Paramedical		Nonmedical		All Issues	
	Actual Deaths	Mortality Ratio	Actual Deaths	Mortality Ratio	Actual Deaths	Mortality Ratio	Actual Deaths	Mortality Ratio
Male								
1	$ 153,086	76.9%	$ 138,166	83.1%	$ 153,126	84.8%	$ 449,916	81.5%
2	194,353	83.5	166,220	94.5	139,807	92.8	508,706	89.4
3	217,685	91.8	151,504	87.8	118,690	93.7	496,583	91.0
4	202,795	94.3	132,145	89.7	92,009	95.9	428,365	92.9
5	166,183	91.5	107,824	95.0	59,960	94.4	334,461	93.1
6	135,928	86.4	83,521	93.6	45,925	102.2	266,904	91.4
7	131,433	89.7	69,364	96.1	35,081	97.2	236,495	92.7
8	125,506	91.0	58,664	100.3	33,087	101.0	217,514	94.8
9	117,610	86.6	45,048	95.3	30,448	98.5	193,410	90.2
10	121,854	87.3	36,269	94.2	29,225	96.2	187,376	89.8
11	117,548	81.9	27,458	97.9	31,472	104.7	176,636	87.5
12	124,217	83.6	18,823	97.9	30,886	102.4	173,947	87.7
13	126,019	81.4	10,527	88.3	30,700	100.9	168,351	85.1
14	136,007	84.2	5,771	94.4	30,204	97.9	172,108	86.5
15	138,904	83.6	2,130	89.1	31,248	99.1	172,654	86.1
Total	$2,209,129	86.4%	$1,053,434	91.7%	$ 891,867	94.3%	$4,183,426	89.3%

TABLE 10—*Continued*

Policy Year	Medical		Paramedical		Nonmedical		All Issues	
	Actual Deaths	Mortality Ratio	Actual Deaths	Mortality Ratio	Actual Deaths	Mortality Ratio	Actual Deaths	Mortality Ratio
				Female				
1	$ 16,084	86.3%	$ 21,634	83.3%	$ 42,755	73.7%	$ 81,237	77.9%
2	28,721	132.6	24,588	89.3	37,954	79.8	92,676	93.9
3	28,028	125.2	27,165	103.7	33,365	84.5	90,092	100.6
4	22,877	104.3	24,398	101.4	28,350	89.7	75,700	97.1
5	21,360	108.8	20,867	102.5	19,331	87.5	61,558	99.0
6	16,715	92.3	18,695	107.5	14,056	87.9	49,580	96.2
7	16,663	97.3	15,049	103.9	10,772	82.9	42,484	95.1
8	15,221	92.7	11,030	92.4	10,042	85.6	36,292	90.5
9	18,878	118.5	9,423	98.2	10,278	95.3	38,616	106.3
10	18,939	118.5	6,983	91.8	8,995	87.9	34,918	103.2
11	16,712	104.3	5,107	96.2	8,688	87.3	30,506	97.5
12	14,131	90.7	3,011	89.4	8,264	88.8	25,518	90.2
13	15,966	103.7	1,843	99.1	8,274	94.6	26,083	100.2
14	16,519	105.0	977	107.4	7,542	90.9	25,090	100.5
15	16,680	107.7	366	115.6	7,206	92.6	24,279	102.8
Total	$ 283,494	106.6%	$ 191,136	97.1%	$ 255,872	84.0%	$ 734,628	95.0%

TABLE 10—*Continued*

Policy Year	Medical		Paramedical		Nonmedical		All Issues	
	Actual Deaths	Mortality Ratio	Actual Deaths	Mortality Ratio	Actual Deaths	Mortality Ratio	Actual Deaths	Mortality Ratio
				Combined				
1	$ 169,169	77.7%	$ 159,799	83.2%	$ 195,881	82.1%	$ 531,153	80.9%
2	223,074	87.7	190,808	93.8	177,761	89.7	601,382	90.1
3	245,714	94.6	178,669	89.9	152,055	91.5	586,675	92.4
4	225,672	95.2	156,543	91.4	120,359	94.4	504,065	93.5
5	187,543	93.1	128,691	96.2	79,291	92.6	396,019	94.0
6	152,643	87.0	102,216	95.9	59,981	98.4	316,484	92.1
7	148,096	90.5	84,413	97.4	45,853	93.4	278,978	93.0
8	140,727	91.2	69,694	99.0	43,128	97.0	253,806	94.1
9	136,489	89.9	54,472	95.8	40,727	97.6	232,026	92.6
10	140,793	90.5	43,252	93.8	38,221	94.1	222,293	91.7
11	134,260	84.2	32,565	97.6	40,160	100.3	207,143	88.8
12	138,348	84.3	21,835	96.6	39,150	99.2	199,465	88.0
13	141,985	83.4	12,369	89.7	38,974	99.5	194,434	86.9
14	152,526	86.1	6,748	96.1	37,746	96.4	197,198	88.0
15	155,585	85.7	2,496	92.2	38,454	97.8	196,933	87.9
Total	$2,492,623	88.3%	$1,244,570	92.5%	$1,147,739	91.8%	$4,918,053	90.1%

Comparison of Medical, Paramedical and Nonmedical Experience

In the 1982–87 experience, the mortality ratios (using expected deaths based on the 1975–80 Basic Tables) of medical, paramedical and nonmedical separately, subdivided by males and females as compared to the combined mortality ratios in the 1986–87 experience, are summarized as follows:

	1982–87			1986–87
	Males	Females	Combined	Combined
Medical	86.4%	106.6%	88.3%	79.1%
Paramedical	91.7	97.1	92.5	91.9
Nonmedical	94.3	84.0	91.8	92.0
All	89.3%	95.0%	90.1%	86.3%

These mortality ratios suggest the following observations:

1. The more favorable medical mortality ratio for the 1986–87 experience (79.1 percent) relative to the 1982–87 experience (88.3 percent) may be due to the increasingly greater proportion of medicals on large policies for which underwriting investigations are more extensive.
2. The more favorable 1982–87 nonmedical ratio for females (84.0 percent) relative to paramedical (97.1 percent) and medical (106.6 percent) suggests that examinations, because they largely identify cardiovascular risk profile characteristics (that is, build, blood pressure, pulse), may be of relatively less value in underwriting females at the older ages, where most of the relatively unfavorable paramedical and medical experience occurs.
3. The higher 1982–87 mortality ratio for females (95.0 percent) relative to males (89.3 percent) indicates less improvement for females since the 1975–80 observation period for the 1975–80 Basic Tables.

By Issue Age and Policy Year (Tables 11–15)

Tables 11–14 subdivide the 1982–87 experience into the same six issue-age groups and the same four policy-year groups as in Table 5. This provides an opportunity to examine the experience by issue age-policy year cells.

TABLE 11

MALE AND FEMALE MEDICAL 1982–87 EXPERIENCE BY ISSUE AGE AND POLICY YEAR
ISSUES OF 1972–86 STUDIED BETWEEN 1982 AND 1987 ANNIVERSARIES
EXPECTED DEATHS BASED ON 1975–80 BASIC TABLES
(ACTUAL DEATHS IN $1,000 UNITS)

Ages at Issue	Policy Years 1–2		Policy Years 3–5		Policy Years 6–10		Policy Years 11–15		Policy Years 1–15	
	Actual Deaths	Mortality Ratio	Actual Deaths	Mortality Ratio	Actual Deaths	Mortality Ratio	Actual Deaths	Mortality Ratio	Actual Deaths	Mortality Ratio
Male										
0–19	$ 1,102	97.5%	$ 1,320	68.2%	$ 2,706	76.6%	$ 3,101	88.9%	$ 8,229	81.6%
20–29	8,182	83.1	12,831	100.6	22,373	100.5	27,022	88.7	70,408	93.5
30–39	59,023	81.8	100,572	96.2	101,284	81.6	115,864	79.9	376,743	84.5
40–49	99,165	73.5	171,900	87.9	191,388	90.9	238,751	85.8	701,204	85.6
50–59	109,836	81.4	190,747	99.0	208,010	86.5	191,223	80.1	699,816	86.7
60 and over	70,131	89.1	109,294	86.3	106,570	91.6	66,734	85.0	352,729	88.1
All Ages	$347,438	80.5%	$586,664	92.5%	$632,331	88.2%	$642,695	83.0%	$2,209,129	86.4%
Female										
0–19	$ 32	9.1%	$ 512	97.7%	$ 547	75.2%	$ 342	61.1%	$ 1,433	66.2%
20–29	1,089	120.9	1,589	119.3	2,436	128.8	1,374	76.3	6,488	109.5
30–39	4,140	73.1	10,207	116.0	9,326	78.1	8,110	82.4	31,784	87.7
40–49	12,047	118.0	16,853	103.5	19,121	83.1	26,792	100.8	74,813	98.4
50–59	15,348	140.6	17,935	95.7	27,403	97.8	26,466	103.1	87,152	104.6
60 and over	12,150	99.1	25,169	137.7	27,583	153.3	16,924	122.9	81,826	131.3
All Ages	$ 44,805	111.2%	$ 72,265	113.0%	$ 86,416	103.4%	$ 80,008	102.3%	$ 283,494	106.6%
Combined										
0–19	$ 1,134	76.5%	$ 1,832	74.5%	$ 3,253	76.4%	$ 3,442	85.1%	$ 9,661	78.9%
20–29	9,270	86.3	14,420	102.4	24,809	102.7	28,397	88.0	76,896	94.7
30–39	63,162	81.1	110,779	97.7	110,610	81.3	123,974	80.1	408,526	84.8
40–49	111,212	76.7	188,753	89.1	210,509	90.2	265,542	87.1	776,016	86.7
50–59	125,183	85.9	208,682	98.7	235,414	87.7	217,689	82.3	786,968	88.4
60 and over	82,281	90.4	134,463	92.8	134,152	99.9	83,658	90.7	434,555	94.0
All Ages	$392,243	83.1%	$658,928	94.4%	$718,748	89.8%	$722,703	84.8%	$2,492,623	88.3%

TABLE 12

Male and Female Paramedical 1982–87 Experience by Issue Age and Policy Year
Issues of 1972–86 Studied Between 1982 and 1987 Anniversaries
Expected Deaths Based on 1975–80 Basic Tables
(Actual Deaths in $1,000 Units)

Ages at Issue	Policy Years 1–2		Policy Years 3–5		Policy Years 6–10		Policy Years 11–15		Policy Years 1–15	
	Actual Deaths	Mortality Ratio	Actual Deaths	Mortality Ratio	Actual Deaths	Mortality Ratio	Actual Deaths	Mortality Ratio	Actual Deaths	Mortality Ratio
Male										
0–19	$ 531	84.0%	$ 1,433	101.3%	$ 1,393	72.1%	$ 274	81.5%	$ 3,631	84.2%
20–29	12,434	73.2	19,203	85.8	21,739	88.0	4,741	85.3	58,117	83.4
30–39	73,394	77.4	97,745	75.5	82,006	80.9	17,193	83.9	270,338	78.1
40–49	108,900	91.2	133,352	88.3	101,193	101.0	25,661	106.0	369,106	93.5
50–59	80,236	94.7	105,665	109.1	71,554	110.8	14,638	97.4	272,092	104.2
60 and over	28,891	113.2	34,075	105.7	14,982	115.8	2,202	106.7	80,150	110.1
All Ages	$304,386	89.0%	$391,473	90.3%	$292,867	95.8%	$ 64,709	95.6%	$1,053,434	91.7%
Female										
0–19	$ 0	0.0%	$ 425	152.1%	$ 95	29.8%	$ 40	80.4%	$ 560	67.3%
20–29	2,605	140.4	1,786	65.1	2,849	108.6	356	79.6	7,595	99.0
30–39	9,747	75.5	12,602	69.0	13,178	81.5	1,688	70.1	37,214	74.8
40–49	11,405	60.4	23,200	97.2	20,717	98.0	4,710	99.9	60,032	87.5
50–59	14,114	109.3	22,037	126.8	18,435	112.8	3,615	107.2	58,201	116.4
60 and over	8,351	123.9	12,381	152.8	5,906	132.7	895	116.1	27,533	137.2
All Ages	$ 46,221	86.4%	$ 72,431	102.5%	$ 61,180	100.3%	$ 11,303	96.1%	$ 191,136	97.1%
Combined										
0–19	$ 531	65.1%	$ 1,858	109.7%	$ 1,488	66.1%	$ 314	81.3%	$ 4,191	81.4%
20–29	15,039	79.8	20,988	83.5	24,588	90.0	5,097	84.8	65,712	85.0
30–39	83,141	77.2	110,347	74.7	95,184	81.0	18,881	82.4	307,553	77.7
40–49	120,305	87.0	156,552	89.5	121,910	100.5	30,371	105.0	429,138	92.6
50–59	94,349	96.7	127,702	111.8	89,989	111.2	18,252	99.2	330,293	106.2
60 and over	37,242	115.4	46,456	115.1	20,889	120.1	3,097	109.3	107,684	116.0
All Ages	$350,607	88.6%	$463,903	92.0%	$354,047	96.5%	$ 76,012	95.7%	$1,244,570	92.5%

TABLE 13

MALE AND FEMALE NONMEDICAL 1982–87 EXPERIENCE BY ISSUE AGE AND POLICY YEAR
ISSUES OF 1972–86 STUDIED BETWEEN 1982 AND 1987 ANNIVERSARIES
EXPECTED DEATHS BASED ON 1975–80 BASIC TABLES
(ACTUAL DEATHS IN $1,000 UNITS)

Ages at Issue	Policy Years 1–2		Policy Years 3–5		Policy Years 6–10		Policy Years 11–15		Policy Years 1–15	
	Actual Deaths	Mortality Ratio	Actual Deaths	Mortality Ratio	Actual Deaths	Mortality Ratio	Actual Deaths	Mortality Ratio	Actual Deaths	Mortality Ratio
Male										
0–19	$ 24,830	78.0%	$ 27,822	85.4%	$ 35,978	90.1%	$ 30,743	101.8%	$ 119,372	88.7%
20–29	92,498	80.0	83,420	94.4	73,009	101.5	64,260	99.1	313,188	91.9
30–39	108,568	89.8	93,199	90.9	45,356	101.8	43,649	100.2	290,772	93.3
40–49	46,305	103.6	43,444	101.3	13,697	115.1	11,480	106.4	114,926	104.2
50–59	16,615	123.0	19,540	140.1	4,628	89.3	3,943	125.6	44,726	125.0
60 and over	4,117	88.6	3,233	56.3	1,099	69.6	434	85.9	8,884	71.2
All Ages	$292,933	88.4%	$270,658	94.6%	$173,766	99.2%	$154,509	101.0%	$ 891,867	94.3%
Female										
0–19	$ 11,370	82.2%	$ 8,763	80.6%	$ 9,685	86.7%	$ 6,128	85.5%	$ 35,946	83.5%
20–29	22,882	75.1	21,404	80.0	17,880	85.0	11,975	82.6	74,141	79.9
30–39	26,574	66.0	28,999	80.3	18,379	83.6	13,648	87.7	87,600	76.9
40–49	13,220	83.1	13,341	93.4	7,193	108.4	7,415	115.8	41,168	95.2
50–59	5,647	132.9	7,625	171.6	816	112.3	328	107.6	$14,416	148.2
60 and over	1,017	125.6	914	124.9	190	109.2	480	357.1	2,601	140.6
All Ages	$ 80,709	76.5%	$ 81,046	87.0%	$ 54,143	87.7%	$ 39,974	90.7%	$ 255,872	84.0%
Combined										
0–19	$ 36,199	79.3%	$ 36,585	84.2%	$ 45,662	89.4%	$ 36,871	98.6%	$ 155,317	87.5%
20–29	115,380	78.9	104,825	91.0	90,889	97.7	76,235	96.1	387,329	89.3
30–39	135,141	83.9	122,198	88.2	63,735	95.8	57,297	96.9	378,372	88.9
40–49	59,525	98.2	56,784	99.3	20,890	112.7	18,896	109.9	156,094	101.7
50–59	22,262	125.4	27,164	147.7	5,444	92.1	4,271	124.0	59,141	130.0
60 and over	5,134	94.1	4,147	64.0	1,289	73.5	914	142.8	11,485	80.1
All Ages	$373,642	85.5%	$351,704	92.7%	$227,909	96.2%	$194,484	98.7%	$1,147,739	91.8%

TABLE 14

MALE AND FEMALE 1982–87 EXPERIENCE BY ISSUE AGE AND POLICY YEAR
MEDICAL, PARAMEDICAL AND NONMEDICAL COMBINED
ISSUES OF 1972–86 STUDIED BETWEEN 1982 AND 1987 ANNIVERSARIES
EXPECTED DEATHS BASED ON 1975–80 BASIC TABLES
(ACTUAL DEATHS IN $1,000 UNITS)

Ages at Issue	Policy Years 1–2		Policy Years 3–5		Policy Years 6–10		Policy Years 11–15		Policy Years 1–15	
	Actual Deaths	Mortality Ratio	Actual Deaths	Mortality Ratio	Actual Deaths	Mortality Ratio	Actual Deaths	Mortality Ratio	Actual Deaths	Mortality Ratio
Male										
0–19	$ 26,665	78.8%	$ 30,675	85.2%	$ 40,076	88.3%	$ 34,118	100.2%	$ 131,534	88.1%
20–29	115,156	79.9	116,278	93.5	117,227	98.4	96,045	95.0	444,706	91.0
30–39	243,304	83.5	294,030	86.7	230,240	84.9	176,969	84.3	944,542	85.0
40–49	258,667	85.2	351,797	89.4	307,183	95.1	277,175	88.2	1,194,822	89.5
50–59	210,030	88.5	318,946	104.1	284,321	91.6	209,966	81.6	1,023,263	92.1
60 and over	104,802	94.5	147,683	88.9	122,651	93.7	69,423	85.6	444,560	90.9
All Ages	$ 958,622	85.5%	$1,259,409	92.2%	$1,101,698	91.8%	$ 863,696	86.6%	$4,183,426	89.3%
Female										
0–19	$ 11,452	79.2%	$ 9,700	82.9%	$ 10,327	84.6%	$ 6,510	83.7%	$ 37,988	82.3%
20–29	26,682	79.2	24,814	80.0	23,165	90.5	13,758	82.1	88,419	82.6
30–39	41,207	68.9	52,080	81.7	40,919	81.5	23,559	84.5	157,765	78.3
40–49	36,966	80.1	53,794	97.7	47,145	92.8	38,943	103.2	176,847	93.2
50–59	35,788	124.7	48,097	117.5	46,554	103.5	30,409	103.6	160,949	111.7
60 and over	21,818	108.3	38,864	142.6	33,579	148.9	18,299	124.7	112,660	133.0
All Ages	$ 173,912	85.7%	$ 227,349	99.0%	$ 201,389	97.8%	$ 131,477	98.0%	$ 734,628	95.0%
Combined										
0–19	$ 38,116	78.9%	$ 40,375	84.6%	$ 50,403	87.5%	$ 40,627	97.2%	$ 169,522	86.7%
20–29	141,838	79.8	141,092	90.8	140,391	97.0	109,803	93.2	533,125	89.5
30–39	284,510	81.0	346,110	85.9	271,159	84.4	200,527	84.3	1,102,307	83.9
40–49	295,633	84.5	405,590	90.4	354,328	94.8	316,118	89.8	1,371,669	90.0
50–59	245,818	92.4	367,043	105.6	330,976	93.1	240,375	83.8	1,184,212	94.3
60 and over	126,619	96.6	186,547	96.5	156,330	101.9	87,723	91.6	557,220	97.1
All Ages	$1,132,535	85.5%	$1,486,758	93.2%	$1,303,588	92.7%	$ 995,173	87.9%	$4,918,053	90.1%

Table 15 shows the ratios of mortality ratios for the 1982–87 experience in the same way as Table 6 for the 1986–87 experience, except that Table 15 shows these ratios of mortality ratios separately for male and female. For males, as expected, the ratios of the less exacting underwriting requirement to the more exacting generally exceed 100 percent as in Table 6, except where the comparisons are distorted by small amounts of data. For females, the results are the opposite of what would be expected; the ratios of mortality ratios are generally less than 100 percent except for issue ages 50 and over (however, the amount of nonmedical data at issue ages 50 and over is quite small), and for issue ages under 20, where the amount of medical and paramedical data is also quite small.

III. SMOKER-NONSMOKER EXPERIENCE

Tables 16–21 present smoker-nonsmoker experience for issues of 1980 through 1986. Tables 16 and 17 show the experience between 1986 and 1987 anniversaries separately for medical, paramedical and nonmedical, but for males and females combined, by issue age and policy year, respectively. Tables 18 and 19 show the experience between 1982 and 1987 anniversaries but are otherwise identical to Tables 16 and 17. Tables 20 and 21 show the 1982–87 experience subdivided by sex, but not by type of underwriting.

For 1986–87 experience combined, the mortality ratio for nonsmokers is 69.2 percent, compared to 146.2 percent for smokers. For medical experience, the respective ratios are 60.8 percent and 141.2 percent; for paramedical, 73.8 percent and 151.0 percent; and for nonmedical, 72.7 percent and 145.5 percent.

By issue age (Tables 16 and 18), the adverse effect of smoking is most apparent at ages 50 and over, where some mortality ratios for smokers are as high as 2½ times those for nonsmokers. By policy year (Tables 17 and 19), the mortality ratios for smokers are generally more than twice those of nonsmokers, except for policy year 1.

TABLE 15

Summary of Male and Female 1982–87 Mortality Ratios Medical, Paramedical and Nonmedical Separately Issues of 1972–86 Studied Between 1982 and 1987 Anniversaries Expected Deaths Based on 1975–80 Basic Tables

Ages at Issue	Policy Years 1–2			Policy Years 3–5			Policy Years 6–10			Policy Years 11–15			Policy Years 1–15		
	Mortality Ratios														
	Medical	Para-medical	Non-medical	Medical	Para-medical	Non-medical	Medical	Para-medical	Non-medical	Medical	Para-medical	Non-medical	Medical	Para-medical	Non-medical
Male															
0–19	97.5%	84.0%	78.0%	68.2%	101.3%	85.4%	76.6%	72.1%	90.1%	88.9%	81.5%	101.8%	81.6%	84.2%	88.7%
20–29	83.1	73.2	80.0	100.6	85.8	94.4	100.5	88.0	101.5	88.7	85.3	99.1	93.5	83.4	91.9
30–39	81.8	77.4	89.8	96.2	75.5	90.9	81.6	80.9	101.8	79.9	83.9	100.2	84.5	78.1	93.3
40–49	73.5	91.2	103.6	87.9	88.3	101.3	90.9	101.0	115.1	85.8	106.0	106.4	85.6	93.5	104.2
50–59	81.4	94.7	123.0	99.0	109.1	140.1	86.5	110.8	89.3	80.1	97.4	125.6	86.7	104.2	125.0
60 and over	89.1	113.2	88.6	86.3	105.7	56.3	91.6	115.8	69.6	85.0	106.7	85.9	88.1	110.1	71.2
All Ages	80.5%	89.0%	88.4%	92.5%	90.3%	94.6%	88.2%	95.8%	99.2%	83.0%	95.6%	101.0%	86.4%	91.7%	94.3%
Female															
0–19	9.1%	0.0%	82.2%	97.7%	152.1%	80.6%	75.2%	29.8%	86.7%	61.1%	80.4%	85.5%	66.2%	67.3%	83.5%
20–29	120.9	140.4	75.1	119.3	65.1	80.0	128.8	108.6	85.0	76.3	79.6	82.6	109.5	99.0	79.9
30–39	73.1	75.5	66.0	116.0	69.0	80.3	78.1	81.5	83.6	82.4	70.1	87.7	87.7	74.8	76.9
40–49	118.0	60.4	83.1	103.5	97.2	93.4	83.1	98.0	108.4	100.8	99.9	115.8	98.4	87.5	95.2
50–59	140.6	109.3	132.9	95.7	126.8	171.6	97.8	112.8	112.3	103.1	107.2	107.6	104.6	116.4	148.2
60 and over	99.1	123.9	125.6	137.7	152.8	124.9	153.3	132.7	109.2	122.9	116.1	357.1	131.3	137.2	140.6
All Ages	111.2%	86.4%	76.5%	113.0%	102.5%	87.0%	103.4%	100.3%	87.7%	102.3%	96.1%	90.7%	106.6%	97.1%	84.0%
Combined															
0–19	76.5%	65.1%	79.3%	74.5%	109.7%	84.2%	76.4%	66.1%	89.4%	85.1%	81.3%	98.6%	78.9%	81.4%	87.5%
20–29	86.3	79.8	78.9	102.4	83.5	91.0	102.7	90.0	97.7	88.0	84.8	96.1	94.7	85.0	89.3
30–39	81.1	77.2	83.9	97.7	74.7	88.2	81.3	81.0	95.8	80.1	82.4	96.9	84.8	77.7	88.9
40–49	76.7	87.0	98.2	89.1	89.5	99.3	90.2	100.5	112.7	87.1	105.0	109.9	86.7	92.6	101.7
50–59	85.9	96.7	125.4	98.7	111.8	147.7	87.7	111.2	92.1	82.3	99.2	124.0	88.4	106.2	130.0
60 and over	90.4	115.4	94.1	92.8	115.1	64.0	99.9	120.1	73.5	90.7	109.3	142.8	94.0	116.0	80.1
All Ages	83.1%	88.6%	85.5%	94.4%	92.0%	92.7%	89.8%	96.5%	96.2%	84.8%	95.7%	98.7%	88.3%	92.5%	91.8%

TABLE 15—*Continued*

Ages at Issue	Policy Years 1–2			Policy Years 3–5			Policy Years 6–10			Policy Years 11–15			Policy Years 1–15		
	Ratio of Mortality Ratios														
	Para to Med	Non to Para	Non to Med	Para to Med	Non to Para	Non to Med	Para to Med	Non to Para	Non to Med	Para to Med	Non to Para	Non to Med	Para to Med	Non to Para	Non to Med
Male															
0–19	0.86	0.93	0.80	1.49	0.84	1.25	0.94	1.25	1.18	0.92	1.25	1.14	1.03	1.05	1.09
20–29	0.88	1.09	0.96	0.85	1.10	0.94	0.88	1.15	1.01	0.96	1.16	1.12	0.89	1.10	0.98
30–39	0.95	1.16	1.10	0.79	1.20	0.95	0.99	1.26	1.25	1.05	1.19	1.25	0.92	1.20	1.10
40–49	1.24	1.14	1.41	1.00	1.15	1.15	1.11	1.14	1.27	1.24	1.00	1.24	1.09	1.12	1.22
50–59	1.16	1.30	1.51	1.10	1.28	1.41	1.28	0.81	1.03	1.22	1.29	1.57	1.20	1.20	1.44
60 and over	1.27	0.78	0.99	1.22	0.53	0.65	1.26	0.60	0.76	1.25	0.80	1.01	1.25	0.65	0.81
All Ages	1.11	0.99	1.10	0.98	1.05	1.02	1.09	1.04	1.13	1.15	1.06	1.22	1.06	1.03	1.09
Female															
0–19	0.00	0.00	9.05	1.56	0.53	0.82	0.40	2.91	1.15	1.31	1.06	1.40	1.02	1.24	1.26
20–29	1.16	0.53	0.62	0.55	1.23	0.67	0.84	0.78	0.66	1.04	1.04	1.08	0.90	0.81	0.73
30–39	1.03	0.87	0.90	0.59	1.16	0.69	1.04	1.02	1.07	0.85	1.25	1.06	0.85	1.03	0.88
40–49	0.51	1.38	0.70	0.94	0.96	0.90	1.18	1.11	1.30	0.99	1.16	1.15	0.89	1.09	0.97
50–59	0.78	1.22	0.95	1.32	1.35	1.79	1.15	1.00	1.15	1.04	1.00	1.04	1.11	1.27	1.42
60 and over	1.25	1.01	1.27	1.11	0.82	0.91	0.87	0.82	0.71	0.95	3.07	2.91	1.04	1.02	1.07
All Ages	0.78	0.88	0.69	0.91	0.85	0.77	0.97	0.87	0.85	0.94	0.94	0.89	0.91	0.87	0.79
Combined															
0–19	0.85	1.22	1.04	1.47	0.77	1.13	0.87	1.35	1.17	0.96	1.21	1.16	1.03	1.07	1.11
20–29	0.92	0.99	0.91	0.82	1.09	0.89	0.88	1.09	0.95	0.96	1.13	1.09	0.90	1.05	0.94
30–39	0.95	1.09	1.03	0.76	1.18	0.90	1.00	1.18	1.18	1.03	1.18	1.21	0.92	1.14	1.05
40–49	1.13	1.13	1.28	1.00	1.11	1.11	1.11	1.12	1.25	1.21	1.05	1.26	1.07	1.10	1.17
50–59	1.13	1.30	1.46	1.13	1.32	1.50	1.27	0.83	1.05	1.20	1.25	1.51	1.20	1.22	1.47
60 and over	1.28	0.82	1.04	1.24	0.56	0.69	1.20	0.61	0.74	1.20	1.31	1.58	1.23	0.69	0.85
All Ages	1.07	0.97	1.03	0.98	1.01	0.98	1.08	1.00	1.07	1.13	1.03	1.16	1.05	0.99	1.04

Key: Med = medical
Para = paramedical
Non = nonmedical.

TABLE 16

SMOKER-NONSMOKER 1986–87 EXPERIENCE BY ISSUE AGE
SEPARATELY FOR MEDICAL, PARAMEDICAL AND NONMEDICAL; MALES AND FEMALES COMBINED
ISSUES OF 1980–86 STUDIED BETWEEN 1986 AND 1987 ANNIVERSARIES
EXPECTED DEATHS BASED ON 1975–80 BASIC TABLES
(EXPOSURES IN $1,000,000 UNITS; ACTUAL DEATHS IN $1,000 UNITS)

Ages at Issue	Nonsmoker			Smoker			Ratio of Smoker/Nonsmoker Mortality Ratios
	Exposure	Actual Deaths	Mortality Ratio	Exposure	Actual Deaths	Mortality Ratio	
Medical							
0–19	$ 201	$ 0	0.0%	$ 100	$ 250	366.0%	0.00
20–29	2,866	2,588	136.3	441	555	190.3	1.40
30–39	18,531	8,271	44.7	2,831	2,931	97.8	2.19
40–49	18,250	18,382	51.4	3,033	6,703	107.8	2.10
50–59	9,812	21,771	59.1	1,796	10,257	144.2	2.44
60 and over	3,179	21,058	82.7	594	9,132	205.8	2.49
All Ages	$ 52,838	$ 72,070	60.8%	$ 8,794	$ 29,828	141.2%	2.32
Paramedical							
0–19	$ 165	$ 125	108.6%	$ 46	$ 0	0.0%	0.00
20–29	6,787	2,302	52.6	961	559	91.4	1.74
30–39	37,755	23,840	69.8	6,483	7,232	117.3	1.68
40–49	24,514	30,593	71.2	5,322	12,304	126.4	1.77
50–59	8,422	22,724	77.9	2,021	14,210	201.0	2.58
60 and over	2,030	13,053	88.7	445	6,187	192.8	2.17
All Ages	$ 79,673	$ 92,637	73.8%	$ 15,278	$ 40,492	151.0%	2.05

TABLE 16—*Continued*

Ages at Issue	Nonsmoker			Smoker			Ratio of Smoker/Nonsmoker Mortality Ratios
	Exposure	Actual Deaths	Mortality Ratio	Exposure	Actual Deaths	Mortality Ratio	
Nonmedical							
0–19	$ 10,540	$ 5,253	89.0%	$ 2,089	$ 1,167	101.6%	1.14
20–29	55,647	23,425	72.1	11,603	8,430	123.1	1.71
30–39	57,282	30,918	69.3	13,293	12,734	117.9	1.70
40–49	12,499	15,919	76.3	3,679	9,873	158.9	2.08
50–59	2,286	6,411	85.2	715	7,282	307.6	3.61
60 and over	416	1,230	40.6	82	1,220	202.7	4.99
All Ages	$138,670	$ 83,156	72.7%	$ 31,461	$ 40,706	145.5%	2.00
Combined							
0–19	$ 10,906	$ 5,378	87.6%	$ 2,235	$ 1,417	113.4%	1.29
20–29	65,300	28,315	73.0	13,005	9,544	123.2	1.69
30–39	113,568	63,029	64.8	22,607	22,897	114.7	1.77
40–49	55,263	64,894	65.2	12,034	28,880	130.3	2.00
50–59	20,519	50,906	69.2	4,532	31,749	191.8	2.77
60 and over	5,625	35,341	81.8	1,121	16,539	200.5	2.45
All Ages	$271,181	$247,863	69.2%	$ 55,534	$111,026	146.2%	2.11

TABLE 17

SMOKER-NONSMOKER 1986–87 EXPERIENCE BY POLICY YEAR
SEPARATELY FOR MEDICAL, PARAMEDICAL AND NONMEDICAL; MALES AND FEMALES COMBINED
ISSUES OF 1980–86 STUDIED BETWEEN 1986 AND 1987 ANNIVERSARIES
EXPECTED DEATHS BASED ON 1975–80 BASIC TABLES
(EXPOSURES IN $1,000,000 UNITS; ACTUAL DEATHS IN $1,000 UNITS)

Year of Issue	Policy Year	Nonsmoker			Smoker			Ratio of Smoker/Nonsmoker Mortality Ratios
		Exposure	Actual Deaths	Mortality Ratio	Exposure	Actual Deaths	Mortality Ratio	
				Medical				
1986	1	$ 13,270	$ 6,790	37.9%	$ 2,072	$ 1,606	55.3%	1.46
1985	2	10,260	15,000	81.1	1,494	2,267	84.3	1.04
1984	3	9,151	15,117	70.4	1,437	5,873	172.7	2.45
1983	4	9,226	13,319	53.0	1,404	6,534	162.7	3.07
1982	5	5,960	10,808	60.8	1,171	7,287	203.1	3.34
1981	6	3,329	7,773	66.9	729	3,296	124.2	1.87
1980	7	1,643	3,263	53.2	487	2,965	158.7	2.98
1980–86	1–7	$ 52,838	$ 72,070	60.8%	$ 8,794	$ 29,828	141.2%	2.32
				Paramedical				
1986	1	$ 24,567	$ 17,401	72.6%	$ 4,397	$ 4,910	106.5%	1.47
1985	2	17,929	20,287	84.6	3,167	8,521	188.9	2.32
1984	3	13,960	17,620	69.2	2,596	7,301	142.2	2.05
1983	4	10,865	18,190	77.4	2,191	7,757	147.8	1.91
1982	5	7,373	10,268	60.3	1,798	9,209	204.5	3.39
1981	6	3,661	6,701	79.3	816	1,564	75.1	0.95
1980	7	1,319	2,170	69.9	311	1,230	168.4	2.41
1980–86	1–7	$ 79,673	$ 92,637	73.8%	$ 15,278	$ 40,492	151.0%	2.05

TABLE 17—*Continued*

Year of Issue	Policy Year	Nonsmoker			Smoker			Ratio of Smoker/Nonsmoker Mortality Ratios
		Exposure	Actual Deaths	Mortality Ratio	Exposure	Actual Deaths	Mortality Ratio	
				Nonmedical				
1986	1	$ 43,560	$ 18,332	68.4%	$ 9,911	$ 6,766	106.9%	1.56
1985	2	29,598	17,302	80.1	6,286	9,696	198.4	2.48
1984	3	25,242	16,358	71.3	5,516	7,205	135.7	1.90
1983	4	22,254	16,335	70.0	5,148	8,708	150.2	2.14
1982	5	13,090	11,296	79.6	3,383	6,131	146.6	1.84
1981	6	4,333	3,101	64.3	1,041	2,004	155.2	2.41
1980	7	592	432	60.7	178	196	110.7	1.82
1980–86	1–7	$138,670	$ 83,156	72.7%	$ 31,461	$ 40,706	145.5%	2.00
				Combined				
1986	1	$ 81,397	$ 42,523	61.9%	$ 16,380	$ 13,282	95.9%	1.55
1985	2	57,787	52,589	82.1	10,947	20,484	169.5	2.06
1984	3	48,353	49,095	70.3	9,550	20,379	147.2	2.09
1983	4	42,346	47,844	66.5	8,743	22,999	152.7	2.30
1982	5	26,423	32,372	66.1	6,352	22,627	184.4	2.79
1981	6	11,323	17,575	70.6	2,586	6,864	113.9	1.61
1980	7	3,553	5,865	58.9	976	4,391	158.2	2.68
1980–86	1–7	$271,181	$247,863	69.2%	$ 55,534	$111,026	146.2%	2.11

TABLE 18

Smoker-Nonsmoker 1982–87 Experience by Issue Age
Separately for Medical, Paramedical and Nonmedical; Males and Females Combined
Issues of 1980–86 Studied Between 1982 and 1987 Anniversaries
Expected Deaths Based on 1975–80 Basic Tables
(Exposures in $1,000,000 Units; Actual Deaths in $1,000 Units)

Ages at Issue	Nonsmoker			Smoker			Ratio of Smoker/Nonsmoker Mortality Ratios
	Exposure	Actual Deaths	Mortality Ratio	Exposure	Actual Deaths	Mortality Ratio	
Medical							
0–19	$ 1,014	$ 75	13.5%	$ 319	$ 275	136.6%	10.12
20–29	11,633	7,205	94.2	1,734	1,745	155.5	1.65
30–39	83,852	56,842	76.8	12,358	18,352	160.3	2.09
40–49	79,682	85,824	61.9	13,165	35,838	152.1	2.46
50–59	39,435	96,983	74.2	6,985	37,609	158.7	2.14
60 and over	10,825	57,730	76.7	1,836	20,091	161.3	2.10
All Ages	$226,442	$304,658	71.3%	$ 36,397	$113,910	157.1%	2.20
Paramedical							
0–19	$ 590	$ 435	110.3%	$ 126	$ 40	44.2%	0.40
20–29	21,818	9,064	64.6	3,183	2,578	127.2	1.97
30–39	117,589	58,245	59.0	20,516	22,956	127.3	2.16
40–49	67,710	74,058	66.8	15,692	36,781	137.8	2.06
50–59	24,966	56,590	72.7	6,309	38,296	193.6	2.66
60 and over	5,650	31,532	88.4	1,333	16,496	201.5	2.28
All Ages	$238,324	$229,924	68.1%	$ 47,158	$117,147	156.6%	2.30

TABLE 18—*Continued*

Ages at Issue	Nonsmoker			Smoker			Ratio of Smoker/Nonsmoker Mortality Ratios
	Exposure	Actual Deaths	Mortality Ratio	Exposure	Actual Deaths	Mortality Ratio	
				Nonmedical			
0–19	$ 34,959	$ 14,663	76.1%	$ 5,876	$ 3,204	98.4%	1.29
20–29	155,315	60,697	67.4	33,470	23,246	118.5	1.76
30–39	158,958	81,736	70.9	38,231	35,749	123.3	1.74
40–49	36,672	38,462	70.5	11,001	27,180	163.1	2.31
50–59	6,303	17,747	96.2	2,093	16,092	265.0	2.75
60 and over	1,049	3,315	48.5	207	3,032	227.5	4.69
All Ages	$393,255	$216,621	71.2%	$ 90,877	$108,503	142.9%	2.01
				Combined			
0–19	$ 36,563	$ 15,173	75.1%	$ 6,321	$ 3,519	99.1%	1.32
20–29	188,766	76,966	68.9	38,386	27,569	121.1	1.76
30–39	360,399	196,822	68.3	71,105	77,057	131.8	1.93
40–49	184,065	198,344	65.2	39,858	99,799	149.1	2.29
50–59	70,704	171,320	75.5	15,387	91,996	185.7	2.46
60 and over	17,523	92,577	78.6	3,375	39,619	180.3	2.29
All Ages	$858,021	$751,203	70.3%	$174,432	$339,559	152.1%	2.16

TABLE 19

SMOKER-NONSMOKER 1982–87 EXPERIENCE BY POLICY YEAR
SEPARATELY FOR MEDICAL, PARAMEDICAL AND NONMEDICAL; MALES AND FEMALES COMBINED
ISSUES OF 1980–86 STUDIED BETWEEN 1982 AND 1987 ANNIVERSARIES
EXPECTED DEATHS BASED ON 1975–80 BASIC TABLES
(EXPOSURES IN $1,000,000 UNITS; ACTUAL DEATHS IN $1,000 UNITS)

Policy Year	Nonsmoker			Smoker			Ratio of Smoker/Nonsmoker Mortality Ratios
	Exposure	Actual Deaths	Mortality Ratio	Exposure	Actual Deaths	Mortality Ratio	
				Medical			
1	$ 70,185	$ 55,700	63.6%	$ 10,927	$ 18,113	130.8%	2.06
2	60,860	76,637	75.4	9,036	22,811	150.4	1.99
3	46,450	74,696	74.1	6,916	24,002	156.7	2.11
4	29,076	60,385	81.1	4,761	21,768	172.0	2.12
5	13,174	22,956	58.8	2,928	18,605	208.7	3.55
6	5,053	11,021	63.7	1,342	5,646	119.9	1.88
7	1,643	3,263	53.2	487	2,965	158.7	2.98
1–7	$226,442	$304,658	71.3%	$ 36,397	$113,910	157.1%	2.20
				Paramedical			
1	$ 82,743	$ 53,223	65.4%	$ 15,331	$ 23,227	142.1%	2.17
2	63,637	60,416	72.1	12,091	29,837	170.6	2.37
3	45,110	48,771	63.9	8,944	25,027	149.0	2.33
4	27,694	39,376	72.9	5,955	20,979	162.5	2.23
5	12,963	17,982	64.4	3,327	13,998	182.8	2.84
6	4,859	7,985	72.6	1,199	2,848	99.5	1.37
7	1,319	2,170	69.9	311	1,230	168.4	2.41
1–7	$238,324	$229,924	68.1%	$ 47,158	$117,147	156.6%	2.30

TABLE 19—*Continued*

Policy Year	Nonsmoker			Smoker			Ratio of Smoker/Nonsmoker Mortality Ratios
	Exposure	Actual Deaths	Mortality Ratio	Exposure	Actual Deaths	Mortality Ratio	
Nonmedical							
1	$144,767	$ 63,274	69.9%	$ 33,210	$ 25,547	118.1%	1.69
2	106,435	57,943	73.8	23,787	30,317	161.3	2.18
3	73,701	44,879	68.4	16,755	22,918	141.6	2.07
4	44,521	31,796	71.9	10,758	18,745	159.2	2.21
5	18,249	14,676	75.8	4,919	8,666	147.9	1.95
6	4,990	3,621	65.5	1,269	2,114	140.4	2.14
7	592	432	60.7	178	196	110.7	1.82
1–7	$393,255	$216,621	71.2%	$ 90,877	$108,503	142.9%	2.01
Combined							
1	$297,695	$172,197	66.4%	$ 59,469	$ 66,886	129.0%	1.94
2	230,932	194,996	73.9	44,914	82,965	161.3	2.18
3	165,262	168,346	69.3	32,616	71,947	148.9	2.15
4	101,291	131,557	76.2	21,474	61,492	164.7	2.16
5	44,386	55,614	64.4	11,173	41,269	184.0	2.86
6	14,902	22,627	66.9	3,810	10,608	116.9	1.75
7	3,553	5,865	58.9	976	4,391	158.2	2.68
1–7	$858,021	$751,203	70.3%	$174,432	$339,559	152.1%	2.16

TABLE 20

SMOKER-NONSMOKER 1982–87 EXPERIENCE BY ISSUE AGE
SEPARATELY FOR MALES AND FEMALES; MEDICAL, PARAMEDICAL AND NONMEDICAL COMBINED
ISSUES OF 1980–86 STUDIED BETWEEN 1982 AND 1987 ANNIVERSARIES
EXPECTED DEATHS BASED ON 1975–80 BASIC TABLES
(EXPOSURES IN $1,000,000 UNITS; ACTUAL DEATHS IN $1,000 UNITS)

Ages at Issue	Nonsmoker			Smoker			Ratio of Smoker/Nonsmoker Mortality Ratios
	Exposure	Actual Deaths	Mortality Ratio	Exposure	Actual Deaths	Mortality Ratio	
Male							
0–19	$ 20,288	$ 11,333	76.5%	$ 3,474	$ 2,660	101.9%	1.33
20–29	124,796	62,467	70.6	25,358	23,132	128.3	1.82
30–39	274,796	167,568	69.8	54,695	66,238	135.5	1.94
40–49	153,572	175,078	65.3	32,096	87,921	153.1	2.34
50–59	59,439	150,064	73.7	12,078	77,420	182.2	2.47
60 and over	13,459	76,780	76.1	2,312	30,367	172.1	2.26
All Ages	$646,350	$643,291	70.2%	$130,013	$287,739	153.8%	2.19
Female							
0–19	$ 16,276	$ 3,840	71.1%	$ 2,847	$ 859	91.6%	1.29
20–29	63,970	14,499	62.6	13,028	4,437	93.8	1.50
30–39	85,603	29,254	60.7	16,410	10,819	113.1	1.86
40–49	30,493	23,266	64.6	7,762	11,878	124.9	1.93
50–59	11,265	21,256	90.7	3,309	14,576	206.7	2.28
60 and over	4,065	15,797	93.9	1,063	9,252	213.5	2.27
All Ages	$211,671	$107,912	70.5%	$ 44,420	$ 51,820	143.4%	2.03

TABLE 21

SMOKER-NONSMOKER 1982–87 EXPERIENCE BY POLICY YEAR
SEPARATELY FOR MALES AND FEMALES; MEDICAL, PARAMEDICAL AND NONMEDICAL COMBINED
ISSUES OF 1980–86 STUDIED BETWEEN 1982 AND 1987 ANNIVERSARIES
EXPECTED DEATHS BASED ON 1975–80 BASIC TABLES
(EXPOSURES IN $1,000,000 UNITS; ACTUAL DEATHS IN $1,000 UNITS)

Policy Year	Nonsmoker			Smoker			Ratio of Smoker/Nonsmoker Mortality Ratios
	Exposure	Actual Deaths	Mortality Ratio	Exposure	Actual Deaths	Mortality Ratio	
				Male			
1	$220,538	$145,950	66.7%	$ 43,620	$ 54,823	127.6%	1.91
2	173,915	169,450	75.1	33,403	70,391	164.1	2.18
3	125,891	142,892	68.0	24,431	62,594	154.1	2.27
4	77,258	116,274	78.1	16,153	51,851	165.6	2.12
5	33,949	44,086	59.5	8,545	34,795	183.9	3.09
6	11,841	19,272	64.9	3,050	9,464	119.8	1.84
7	2,958	5,367	60.7	811	3,820	154.6	2.55
1–7	$646,350	$643,291	70.2%	$130,013	$287,739	153.8%	2.19
				Female			
1	$ 77,157	$ 26,248	64.5%	$ 15,849	$ 12,063	135.9%	2.11
2	57,017	25,546	66.7	11,511	12,574	146.9	2.20
3	39,370	25,454	77.9	8,185	9,353	121.9	1.56
4	24,034	15,283	64.0	5,321	9,641	159.8	2.50
5	10,436	11,528	94.4	2,629	6,474	184.4	1.95
6	3,062	3,355	80.9	760	1,144	97.3	1.20
7	595	498	44.8	166	571	187.4	4.18
1–7	$211,671	$107,912	70.5%	$ 44,420	$ 51,820	143.4%	2.03

For the 1982–87 experience (Tables 18–21), the mortality ratios are as follows:

	Nonsmoker	Smoker	Ratio
Medical	71.3%	157.1%	2.20
Paramedical	68.1	156.6	2.30
Nonmedical	71.2	142.9	2.01
Male	70.2	153.8	2.19
Female	70.5	143.4	2.03
Total	70.3%	152.1%	2.16

The ratio of smoker-to-nonsmoker mortality ratios is remarkably consistent. The lower ratio for nonmedical reflects the younger age distribution, where the ratio of smoker-to-nonsmoker mortality is somewhat lower than at older ages. The lower ratios for females may be due to lighter smoking on average among females than males.

The proportion of nonsmoker to total exposure is 83.2 percent for males and 82.7 percent for females. This is a somewhat higher proportion than may have been expected, perhaps due to nonadmission of smoking habits by some smokers. Those who did not admit smoking may have been among the lighter smokers. The inclusion of some of the lighter smokers in the nonsmoker instead of the smoker group would have increased the mortality ratio for smokers more than that for nonsmokers.

Note that the nonsmoker-smoker data are only on 1980–86 issues and are heavily concentrated in the earlier policy years. However, it does not appear likely that the overall ratio of smoker-to-nonsmoker mortality ratios will change greatly as the experience matures.

IV. ULTIMATE EXPERIENCE (POLICY YEARS 16 AND OVER)

The experience between 1986 and 1987 anniversaries for policy years 16 and over is shown in Tables 22–25. Table 22 presents the total experience with mortality ratios based on four different tables. The mortality ratio based on the 1975–80 Ultimate Basic Tables is 90.8 percent for all ages. This compares to 89.8 percent for the 1985–86 experience and 91.1 percent for the 1984–85 experience. (Note that the company mix changed somewhat each year.) The ratios by attained age group are quite similar for ages 40–84. However, for attained ages 25–39, the ratios exceeded 100 percent, indicating an increase in mortality from the 1975–80 period from which mortality rates for expected deaths were obtained. This same mortality pattern appears in the 1985–86 experience and to a lesser extent, in the 1984–85 experience. Part of this extra mortality at younger ages could be attributed to AIDS deaths.

TABLE 22

1986–1987 ULTIMATE EXPERIENCE BY ATTAINED AGE
MALE AND FEMALE LIVES COMBINED
ISSUES OF 1971 AND PRIOR STUDIED BETWEEN 1986 AND 1987 ANNIVERSARIES
POLICY YEARS 16 AND OVER
(EXPOSURES IN $1,000,000 UNITS; ACTUAL DEATHS IN $1,000 UNITS)

			Mortality Ratios			
Attained Ages	Exposure	Actual Deaths	1965–70 Ultimate Tables	1975–80 Ultimate Tables	1980 CSO Tables	1979–81 U.S. Life Tables
15–19	$ 1,369	$ 936	85.9%	77.7%	48.8%	65.2%
20–24	1,719	1,632	101.6	87.2	59.1	64.0
25–29	2,084	2,231	115.4	105.5	68.2	70.3
30–34	3,321	4,522	120.8	137.4	77.4	82.7
35–39	7,215	10,290	86.7	112.5	60.0	63.7
40–44	11,140	19,840	66.9	92.8	50.8	52.3
45–49	12,155	35,119	66.4	89.8	55.8	53.1
50–54	12,932	59,600	63.8	86.8	59.5	53.0
55–59	13,926	111,803	67.9	93.6	67.0	60.0
60–64	13,195	169,654	69.0	92.7	70.6	62.9
65–69	9,412	185,699	68.0	89.0	69.2	64.9
70–74	5,950	189,124	71.9	90.4	71.3	70.3
75–79	3,698	183,458	71.6	89.2	69.1	75.4
80–84	1,704	138,256	77.7	93.6	74.0	83.6
85–89	708	76,980	69.8	82.0	64.5	76.5
90–95	181	35,819	92.3	101.2	80.2	99.0
All Ages ..	$100,709	$1,224,966	71.0%	90.8%	68.4%	68.0%

Table 22 also presents mortality ratios based on the 1965–70 Ultimate Basic Tables, the 1980 CSO Tables and the 1979–81 U.S. Population Life Tables (Whites and Non-Whites Combined). The mortality ratios based on the 1980 CSO and the 1979–81 U.S. Population Tables are remarkably similar (68.4 percent and 68.0 percent, respectively). By attained age, the CSO mortality ratios are lower than the population mortality ratios through attained age 44, are higher for ages 45–74, and then are lower again for ages 75 and over.

Tables 23–25 show the experience between 1982 and 1987 anniversaries for policy years 16 and over subdivided in three ways. The mortality ratio for fully paid-up policies (reduced paid-up policies are not included) is 93.7 percent compared to 91.1 percent for premium-paying policies. This lower mortality ratio for premium-paying policies has been a characteristic of the experience for many years.

The mortality ratios for medical (89.0 percent) and nonmedical (102.3 percent) issues are also presented in Tables 23–25. This large difference in mortality ratios exists for virtually each attained-age group. This result may be due more to lapsation antiselection among nonmedical policies than to the more rigorous initial selection applied to medical policies. As a result of higher lapse rates (generally by the better risks), the nonmedical exposure may contain an increasingly higher proportion of poorer risks than the medical experience.

Mortality ratios for males and females are also presented in Tables 23–25. However, the female mortality ratios used to calculate the female-to-male ratio of mortality ratios in the last column are based on the 1975–80 Ultimate Male Basic Table, so that male and female mortality ratios can be compared on the same basis. The female ultimate mortality ratio is 90.5 percent (down from 92.5 percent for the 1985–86 experience). As a result, the ratio of female-to-male mortality dropped to 61.2 percent from 62.5 percent. This ratio varies from less than 50 percent at attained ages 15–34, due to the relatively low accidental death rate of females at these young ages (where accidents are the primary cause of death), up to close to 70 percent at attained ages 40–54, down to about 60 percent at attained ages 55–84 where females are less subject to coronary artery disease.

The latest prior individual life experience studies, for various items, are in the following *TSA Reports:*

Study	TSA Reports No.
Standard Ordinary	Published Annually
Cause of Death	1983
Large Amounts	1985-86-87
Term Conversions	1982
Guaranteed Insurability Option	1982
Substandard	1979
Group Conversions	1979
Waiver of Premium	1978
Accidental Death Benefits	1977

TABLE 23

COMPARISONS OF 1982–87 ULTIMATE EXPERIENCE BY ATTAINED AGE
MALE AND FEMALE LIVES COMBINED
EXPERIENCE BETWEEN 1982 AND 1987 ANNIVERSARIES
POLICY YEARS 16 AND OVER
(ACTUAL DEATHS SHOWN IN $1,000 UNITS)

Attained Ages	Premium-Paying		Paid-Up		Ratio of Premium-Paying to Paid-Up Mortality Ratios
	Actual Deaths	Mortality Ratio	Actual Deaths	Mortality Ratio	
15–19	$ 4,936	82.2%	$ 80	105.9%	0.78
20–24	7,806	84.2	644	81.4	1.03
25–29	9,803	97.2	1,506	100.1	0.97
30–34	17,405	115.0	2,320	124.9	0.92
35–39	45,573	99.4	2,555	108.9	0.91
40–44	95,848	89.9	3,887	108.0	0.83
45–49	174,828	86.9	6,623	100.3	0.87
50–54	321,101	89.2	15,251	101.6	0.88
55–59	576,151	92.6	33,222	100.7	0.92
60–64	811,344	91.7	61,667	92.1	1.00
65–69	765,995	88.5	139,814	92.9	0.95
70–74	774,082	89.9	180,780	94.2	0.95
75–79	728,690	91.7	204,915	94.0	0.98
80–84	545,080	93.2	181,191	92.3	1.01
85–89	272,669	92.3	143,884	92.0	1.00
90–95	104,259	100.9	76,937	94.3	1.07
All Ages	$4,255,569	91.1%	$1,055,276	93.7%	0.97

TABLE 24

COMPARISONS OF 1982–87 ULTIMATE EXPERIENCE BY ATTAINED AGE
MALE AND FEMALE LIVES COMBINED
EXPERIENCE BETWEEN 1982 AND 1987 ANNIVERSARIES
POLICY YEARS 16 AND OVER
(ACTUAL DEATHS SHOWN IN $1,000 UNITS)

Attained Ages	Medical		Nonmedical		Ratio of Nonmedical to Medical Mortality Ratios
	Actual Deaths	Mortality Ratio	Actual Deaths	Mortality Ratio	
15–19	$ 216	39.0%	$ 4,228	86.4%	2.21
20–24	814	60.6	6,165	87.4	1.44
25–29	1,563	85.4	7,642	104.8	1.23
30–34	2,880	117.5	13,109	116.9	0.99
35–39	7,243	95.3	32,339	100.9	1.06
40–44	23,791	82.5	58,602	94.5	1.15
45–49	67,127	83.2	83,869	92.5	1.11
50–54	163,223	82.8	110,825	98.9	1.19
55–59	362,523	88.1	134,729	106.3	1.21
60–64	578,453	88.5	123,988	109.9	1.24
65–69	603,070	86.7	65,291	108.2	1.25
70–74	628,940	89.5	41,719	108.2	1.21
75–79	580,761	90.3	35,864	104.0	1.15
80–84	428,712	91.6	22,918	97.9	1.07
85–89	230,017	91.2	8,727	93.4	1.02
90–95	91,622	100.0	3,496	104.5	1.04
All Ages	$3,770,955	89.0%	$753,512	102.3%	1.15

TABLE 25

COMPARISONS OF 1982–87 ULTIMATE EXPERIENCE BY ATTAINED AGE
EXPERIENCE BETWEEN 1982 AND 1987 ANNIVERSARIES
POLICY YEARS 16 AND OVER
(ACTUAL DEATHS SHOWN IN $1,000 UNITS)

Attained Ages	Male		Female		Ratio of Female to Male Mortality Ratios
	Actual Deaths	Mortality Ratio	Actual Deaths	Mortality Ratio	
15–19	$ 4,202	81.1%	$ 970	85.0%	0.42
20–24	7,374	83.8	1,372	82.0	0.37
25–29	9,809	98.9	2,112	113.2	0.49
30–34	17,498	119.4	2,814	102.9	0.49
35–39	43,044	102.6	5,883	81.8	0.60
40–44	92,276	93.5	9,725	73.7	0.68
45–49	171,601	89.7	15,024	79.2	0.69
50–54	313,655	89.5	26,533	88.7	0.68
55–59	572,860	93.0	44,494	87.1	0.61
60–64	817,821	91.6	63,511	89.9	0.59
65–69	831,382	88.0	65,323	92.1	0.57
70–74	848,717	89.3	76,395	97.1	0.58
75–79	797,612	91.9	76,577	86.9	0.55
80–84	586,906	93.6	73,395	88.8	0.62
85–89	313,933	92.0	50,950	93.9	0.73
90–95	128,758	98.6	25,548	104.5	0.79
All Ages	$5,557,449	91.2%	$540,627	90.5%	0.61

APPENDIX A

Percentages of Total Exposures Between 1986 and 1987 Anniversaries Contributed by Each Company

Company	First Fifteen Policy Years							16th and Subsequent
	Medical	Paramedical	Nonmedical	Male	Female	Nonsmoker	Smoker	
New York Life	15.2%	16.2%	16.3%	14.7%	18.2%	—	—	13.4%
Equitable	11.1	6.5	8.6	11.2	10.7	18.8%	19.8%	7.3
State Farm Life	8.9	10.1	15.5	8.4	11.5	11.4	14.2	3.8
Prudential	8.3	14.6	20.7	8.1	9.0	9.0	9.4	24.0
Massachusetts Mutual	8.2	10.1	3.0	8.4	6.5	13.0	7.5	5.0
New England Life	7.3	4.5	2.9	7.6	5.6	12.7	16.0	2.7
Phoenix Mutual	6.7	2.1	0.7	6.9	5.3	—	—	1.5
Northwestern Mutual	6.2	3.0	2.0	6.3	5.1	4.9	3.4	8.5
Connecticut Mutual	5.9	5.4	3.6	6.0	5.3	9.3	5.3	3.6
Metropolitan	4.4	8.1	10.4	4.3	5.1	4.3	3.8	8.9
Aetna	3.3	3.6	2.5	3.3	2.8	4.8	7.7	1.4
John Hancock	3.0	7.0	2.3	3.1	3.1	3.7	3.3	6.7
Travelers	2.9	2.6	1.9	2.9	2.8	5.2	6.6	1.6
Mutual of New York	2.4	2.4	3.0	2.4	2.9	—	—	3.8
Franklin Life	2.3	1.1	3.9	2.3	2.6	—	—	1.9
Penn Mutual	2.0	0.7	0.6	2.1	1.7	—	—	2.7
Sun Life	0.8	0.5	1.1	0.8	0.8	1.6	1.8	0.7
Provident Mutual	0.6	1.0	0.8	0.6	0.5	0.6	—	1.5
Lincoln National	0.5	0.5	0.2	0.6	0.5	0.7	1.2	1.0

REPORT OF THE AVIATION AND HAZARDOUS SPORTS EXPERIENCE COMMITTEE

AVIATION STATISTICS

This report covers statistics obtained from United States and Canadian governmental sources, both civilian and military, supplemented by publications of the aviation industry. The emphasis in the report is primarily on the 1985 and 1986 data that have become available. Data from earlier periods (where included) are for comparison and for indication of trends.

UNITED STATES CIVIL AVIATION

United States Civil Aviation can be divided into two types: Commercial Air Carriers and General Aviation. Commercial Air Carriers can be divided into Certificated Route Air Carriers, Air Taxi, Commuter Air Carriers, Supplemental Air Carriers, Commercial Operators, Commercial Operators of Large Aircraft, and Air Travel Clubs. Definitions of what constitutes a particular aviation type or activity are formulated by the Civil Aeronautics Board or the Federal Aviation Administration. This report covers the mortality experience of Certificated Route Air Carriers and General Aviation.

Pilots engaged in air carrier flying may not, under government regulations, fly more than 100 hours per month or more than 1,000 hours per year in domestic operations. Pilots in international operations are generally limited to 120 hours per month or 300 hours every 90 days depending upon the size of the flight crew. Certificated Route Air Carrier pilots, in particular, under a union-negotiated contractual obligation, are allowed to fly a maximum of 700 to 800 hours per year. Some air carriers have no such union obligation and generally require pilots to fly the maximum annual number of regulation hours.

Certificated Route Air Carriers (Passenger/Cargo)

Certificated Route Air Carriers hold certificates of public convenience and necessity issued by the Civil Aeronautics Board authorizing the performance of service over specified routes and a limited amount of nonscheduled service. They are divided into two groups: passenger/cargo and all cargo.

As defined by the Civil Aeronautics Board, "domestic" operations are, in general, within the 50 states of the United States, including intra-Alaska and intra-Hawaii operations. "International" (technically, "international and territorial") operations are, in general, outside the territory of the United

States and include the operations between the United States and foreign countries and the United States and its territories and possessions.

Table 1 shows the recent aviation fatality rates of the United States Certificated Route Air Carriers for scheduled service for passengers, first pilots, all pilots and copilots, and other crew members in domestic and international flying. Lives exposed as "All Pilots and Copilots" and "Other Crew Members" include persons who may do the less-than-normal amounts of flying because of supervisory duties or other reasons. Helicopter airlines that are also Certificated Route Air Carriers are excluded from the experience in Table 1.

TABLE 1

UNITED STATES CERTIFICATED ROUTE AIR CARRIERS (PASSENGER/CARGO) AVIATION DEATH RATES*

Years	Passenger Rate per 1,000 Scheduled Passenger-Hours†	First-Pilot Rate per 1,000 Scheduled Airplane-Hours†	All Pilot and Copilot Rate per 1,000 Life-Years‡	Other Crew Member Rate per 1,000 Life-Years‡
		Domestic Operations		
1977–1981	0.0001 (9)	0.0002 (5)§	Not Available	Not Available
1982–1986	0.0001 (10)	0.0002 (8)		
1985	0.0002 (2)	0.0003 (2)§		
1986	0.0000 (1)§	0.0001 (1)§		
		International Operations		
1977–1981	0.0001 (1)	0.0003 (1)§	Not Available	Not Available
1982–1986	0.0000 (2)	0.0002 (1)§		
1985	0.0002 (1)	0.0012 (1)§		
1986	0.0000 (0)§	0.0000 (0)§		
		Domestic and International Operations		
1977–1981	0.0001 (10)	0.0002 (6)	0.0842 (7)	0.1391 (5)
1982–1986	0.0001 (12)	0.0002 (9)	0.1178 (9)	0.0794 (9)
1985	0.0002 (3)	0.0004 (3)§	0.1907 (3)	0.2029 (3)
1986	0.0000 (1)	0.0001 (1)§	0.0571 (1)§	0.0136 (1)§

*Number of fatal accidents is shown in parenthesis.
†Based on scheduled operations only; experience of helicopter carriers is excluded.
‡Based on all operations, scheduled and nonscheduled; experience of helicopter carriers is excluded.
§Based on five or fewer fatalities.

In some prior studies, mortality rates of crew members have been given separately for domestic and international operations. A review of the exposure information revealed that the split into domestic and international has not always been accurate. Therefore, the rates for this study are given for combined domestic and international operations.

The exposure figures in Table 1 are taken from the *FAA Statistical Handbook of Aviation* (Tables 6.3, 6.4, 6.7, and 6.8 in the 1986 edition) and the annual report of the Air Transport Association of America. The numbers for accidents and fatalities are taken from Safety Information Bulletins published annually by the National Transportation Safety Board.

Certificated Route Air Carriers (All-Cargo)

Carriers in this class hold temporary certificates of public convenience and necessity issued by the Civil Aeronautics Board authorizing the operation of scheduled air freight express and mail transportation over specified routes as well as nonscheduled flights that may include passengers.

Prior studies showed that there had been no pilot fatalities in scheduled service in the period 1973–1982. There was one fatal accident in each of 1983, 1984, 1985, and 1986. The 1983 and 1986 accidents each had three fatalities—the entire crew of the airplanes. The 1984 accident involved the death of four people: the entire crew and one passenger. The 1985 accident claimed the lives of the crew of two.

Unfortunately, all-cargo exposure is no longer available, so it is not possible to calculate fatality rates.

AIR CARRIERS OF COUNTRIES OTHER THAN THE UNITED STATES

The general conditions in aviation technology unique to any country influence the hazards of flying in that country. Each country has its own aviation regulations and methods of enforcement. These regulations may differ for domestic and international operations, the latter being affected by international agreements relating to the crossing of international boundaries.

World Air Transport Statistics, a publication of the International Air Transport Association (IATA), reports on the operations of association members. IATA member airlines numbered 160 on December 31, 1986. Of the 160 members, 127 reported data to the IATA. The reporting IATA members carried 57 percent of the world's passenger air traffic in 1986 and 1985. United States membership has fluctuated in recent years and stood at 11 passenger/cargo air carrier members in 1986 and 10 in 1985. Of the 1986 members, however, three did not report statistics to IATA.

Table 2 gives passenger fatality rates per 1,000 scheduled passenger hours. The results for the 1977–81 and 1982–86 periods show that the safety record of airlines in countries other than the United States is similar to that in the 1975–1984 period but continues to be less favorable than that of the United States scheduled airlines.

In 1986, 38 percent of the scheduled passenger hours reported to IATA were flown by the United States members. This is an increase from 35 percent in 1984 and 28 percent in 1982. United States IATA members also accounted for 64 percent of the scheduled airlines passenger hours flown by all United States Certificated Route Air Carriers in 1986. This is about the same as 66 percent in 1984 and an increase from 49 percent in 1982. The combined international and domestic schedules experience of all United States Certificated Route Air Carriers (passenger/cargo) is included in Table 2 for comparison. The information required for Table 2 was taken from *World Air Transport Statistics* and Table 1.

TABLE 2

SCHEDULED AIR CARRIERS (PASSENGERS/CARGO)
OF UNITED STATES AND OTHER COUNTRIES
PASSENGER DEATH RATES PER 1,000 SCHEDULED PASSENGER-HOURS*

Years	Members Reporting to IATA		All United States Air Carriers
	Countries Other Than the United States	United States	
1977–1981	0.0005 (1,674)	0.0002 (329)	0.0001 (402)
1982–1986	0.0004 (1,676)	0.0001 (152)	0.0001 (393)
1985	0.0008 (724)	0.0000 (21)	0.0002 (174)
1986	0.0002 (227)	0.0000 (0)	0.0000 (0)

*Number of fatalities is shown in parentheses.

UNITED STATES GENERAL AVIATION

General Aviation is divided into 11 use categories: Aerial Application, Aerial Observation, Commuter Air Carrier, Demand Air Taxi, Business Transportation, Executive Corporate Transportation, Instructional Flying, Personal Flying, Rental Aircraft, Other Work Use, and Other. The flying time in General Aviation during 1986 was 3.76 times that of the Certificated Route Air Carriers (passenger/cargo) domestic flights. This is a decline from the figures of 6.14 in 1982 and 5.24 in 1984. The decrease in this ratio reflects the increase in hours flown by Certificated Route Air Carriers and a decrease in hours reported for General Aviation.

Prior to 1977, the FAA collected statistics on General Aviation by sending a registration to all General Aviation aircraft owners each January requesting such information as the number of hours flown and the primary use of each aircraft. Beginning in 1977, a sample of approximately 14 percent of all registered General Aviation aircraft was selected as a basis for determining how many hours were flown by all aircraft according to primary use.

Death rates for General Aviation in Table 3 are expressed per 1,000 aircraft hours. Some distortion in death rates by type of flying may occur because the methods used for assigning deaths are not entirely consistent with those used for assigning aircraft hours. Although it might be helpful to relate deaths to average hours flown in a year by pilots in each category of General Aviation, such data cannot be estimated reliably from information supplied by the National Transportation Safety Board and the FAA. Only fixed-wing aircraft are included.

TABLE 3

GENERAL AVIATION FLYING BY KIND
PILOT AVIATION DEATH RATES PER 1,000 AIRCRAFT HOURS*

Years	Pleasure	Instruction	Business	Corporate	Aerial Application	Air Taxi
1977–1981	0.029 (1,828)	0.007 (206)	0.007 (293)	0.004 (97)	0.010 (109)	0.011 (220)
1982–1986	0.033 (1,760)	0.005 (115)	0.009 (293)	0.001 (28)	0.008 (75)	0.010 (125)
1985	0.029 (310)	0.005 (20)	0.008 (52)	0.003 (10)	0.005 (9)	0.012 (24)
1986	0.030 (289)	0.004 (18)	0.010 (56)	0.001 (3)	0.010 (17)	0.011 (24)

*Number of fatalities is shown in parentheses.

The six categories of Pleasure, Instruction, Business, Corporate, Aerial Application, and Air Taxi made up 91 percent of the total General Aviation flying hours during the period 1982–86.

In the five-year period 1982–86, Pleasure flying accounted for about 31 percent of pilots' flying time in General Aviation. Death rates in this category are probably overstated because there is a tendency for pilots to understate the amount of time they spend Pleasure flying and overreport the amount of time they spend on other flying. In Table 3, Rental hours are included in Pleasure hours on the assumption that most pilots renting planes do so for pleasure purposes.

Instruction flying in the 1982–86 period represents about 13 percent of the total hours in General Aviation. The experience under flight training of civilians included the death of either the instructor or the student, depending on who was acting as pilot when the accident occurred. Practice flying not under the supervision of an instructor, either in the air or on the ground, is not included in the Instruction category.

The combined Business and Corporate categories account for approximately 33 percent of the total General Aviation hours in the 1982–86 period. Business flying is done by nonprofessional pilots flying for business reasons. Corporate flying is done by professional pilots receiving a direct salary or compensation for piloting an aircraft (not for public hire) operated by a corporation or business firm for the transportation of personnel and/or cargo and furtherance of the company's business.

Air Taxi flying accounted for approximately 8 percent of the total General Aviation hours in 1982–86. This type of flying included scheduled and nonscheduled passenger and cargo flying by professional pilots other than Corporate that is not done by Certificated Route Air Carriers, Charter Air Carriers, or Commercial Operators. Table 3 includes both scheduled and nonscheduled Air Taxi flying.

Aerial Application, which accounted for approximately 6 percent of General Aviation flying during 1982–86, includes firefighting operations and the distribution of chemicals or seeds in agricultural, reforestation, and insect control. Pilot fatality rates in this category have traditionally been higher than those in other commercial activities, but in the years after 1975 have shown improvement. For example, the pilot death rate for the years 1971–74 was 0.018.

The exposure data in Table 3 were taken from the *FAA Statistical Handbook of Aviation* (Table 8.3 in the 1986 edition). The number of fatalities was supplied by the National Transportation Safety Board in response to a special request.

CANADIAN CIVIL FLYING

Canadian airlines aviation fatality rates are not available for the publication of this report. Statistics Canada has discontinued the publication that was used in the past to complete this table, and the committee has not been able to locate an appropriate source of data for passenger-hours and airplane-hours.

The fatality rates among Canadian civil pilots, by class of license, are shown in Table 4 for 1975–79, 1980–84, 1985, and 1986, based on figures furnished by Transport Canada. Note that many pilots holding licenses may be inactive and that pilots holding airline transport licenses are not necessarily flying for scheduled airlines, because they may engage in other types of flying.

TABLE 4

CANADIAN CIVIL PILOTS BY CLASS OF LICENSES
1975–1986 AVIATION FATALITY RATES

Class of License	Period	Life-Years of Exposure	Aviation Fatalities	Rate per 1000 Life-Years of Exposure
Glider	1975–79	13,117	6	0.46
	1980–84	21,020	0	0.00
	1985	4,621	1	0.22
	1986	4,727	0	0.00
Private (excluding students)	1975–79	176,237	182	1.03
	1980–84	201,612	136	0.67
	1985	37,790	14	0.37
	1986	35,845	24	0.67
Commercial	1975–79	37,122	124	3.34
	1980–84	41,563	73	1.76
	1985	7,967	7	0.88
	1986	7,053	11	1.56
Senior Commercial	1975–79	4,779	17	3.56
	1980–84	6,443	10	1.55
	1985	1,212	1	0.83
	1986	1,164	0	0.00
Airline Transport	1975–79	20,621	39	1.89
	1980–84	29,897	32	1.07
	1985	6,472	0	0.00
	1986	6,649	4	0.60

Source: Superintendent, Statistics Analysis, Canadian Aviation, Safety Board, Ottawa, Ontario K1G 3T8.

UNITED STATES MILITARY

The data for this portion of the study are not available at this time. Because of cutbacks and other changes, source data have not been located that can be utilized. In the next report, data will be brought up-to-date where feasible.

CANADIAN MILITARY

Aviation fatality rates among Canadian regular military forces, excluding reserves, are shown in Table 5 by age, rank, and functional classification.

TABLE 5

CANADIAN REGULAR FORCES
1985–1986 AVIATION FATALITY RATES PER 1,000 LIFE-YEARS OF EXPOSURE*

	1985		1986	
	Pilots	Crew	Pilots	Crew
Age Group				
Under 25	0.0 (0)	0.7 (1)	0.0 (0)	0.0 (0)
25–29	0.4 (2)	0.5 (2)	0.2 (1)	0.0 (0)
30–34	0.9 (3)	0.0 (0)	0.0 (0)	0.0 (0)
35–39	0.8 (2)	0.3 (1)	0.5 (1)	0.3 (1)
40 and over	0.3 (1)	0.3 (1)	0.3 (1)	0.0 (0)
All	0.4 (8)	0.3 (5)	0.2 (3)	0.1 (1)
Rank				
Lieutenant and lower rank	0.3 (1)	0.4 (4)	0.0 (0)	0.1 (1)
Captain	0.5 (5)	0.3 (1)	0.3 (3)	0.0 (0)
Major	0.6 (2)	0.0 (0)	0.0 (0)	0.0 (0)
Lieutenant and higher rank	0.0 (0)	0.0 (0)	0.0 (0)	0.0 (0)
All	0.4 (8)	0.3 (5)	0.2 (3)	0.1 (1)
Functional Classification†				
Fighter	0.0 (0)	0.0 (0)	0.3 (1)	0.0 (0)
Training	0.1 (1)	0.0 (0)	0.0 (0)	0.0 (0)
Transport	1.3 (6)	0.5 (4)	0.5 (2)	0.1 (1)
Maritime	0.0 (0)	0.0 (0)	0.0 (0)	0.0 (0)
Helicopter	0.2 (1)	0.2 (1)	0.0 (0)	0.0 (0)
Others	0.0 (0)	0.0 (0)	0.0 (0)	0.0 (0)
All	0.3 (8)	0.3 (5)	0.1 (34)	0.1 (1)

*The number of fatalities is shown in parentheses.

†The fatality rates by functional classification are understated because some pilots and crew members fly more than one type of aircraft. The extent of understatements in total can be determined by comparing the fatality rates of the "All" categories.

Note: The 1974–78 and 1980–84 data are available in prior reports. Care should be taken in comparing data and in developing trends.

Source: Director, Personnel Information Services, National Defense, National Defense Headquarters, Ottawa, Canada K1A OK2.

The average number of flying hours for all pilots combined has remained steady over the five-year period at approximately 280 hours per year and shows little variation by age group. Crew members average about 337 hours per year. There is some variation by functional classification, but this cannot be determined accurately because of duplicate counting in different functions. Pilots and crew members flying more than one type of aircraft are counted in each function in which flying is done.

The extent of overstatement by type of aircraft is unknown. The adjusted average annual flying time for pilots and crew in the transport and maritime categories is considerably higher than for that in the categories of fighter, training, and helicopter over five years. The former group averages 335 hours per year and the latter approximately 159 hours per year.

INTERCOMPANY EXPERIENCE

No intercompany experience was collected for the period 1985–86 because of the lack of company participation in providing meaningful data. However, efforts are being made to rejuvenate this portion of the report by collecting the exposure and deaths through the annual contributions to the Individual Life Insurance Experience Studies. As those data are collected, they will be reported.

HAZARDOUS SPORTS

As indicated in the previous report, the intercompany experience on hazardous sports has been discontinued because of a lack of exposure data. Here again, this portion of the report is being rejuvenated through the collection of data through the annual contributions to the Individual Life Insurance Experience Studies.

Also, efforts are being made to locate and obtain, from governmental and association sources, data that could be used to report the mortality for various hazardous sports.

Although some organizations do have accurate data on deaths, the reported exposures may be suspect.

REPORT OF THE ANNUITY EXPERIENCE COMMITTEE

GROUP ANNUITY MORTALITY

This report presents the 1987 and 1988 calendar-year experience of retired individuals who are covered under insured pension plans in the United States and Canada. Data for calendar-years 1983 through 1986 are also included to provide a comparison with 1987 and 1988 experience and to provide information on mortality improvement over time.

The report includes the experience of contracts providing insurer-guaranteed annuity benefits to ongoing pension plans and the experience of contracts covering closed groups of lives for which purchases are made by a single payment at issue (single-premium closeout business); it also includes contracts that do not contain insurer guarantees of future payments (for example, disbursed-payment arrangements).

The total data reported in this study include all annuities in payment status that are to continue for the future lifetime of the annuitant. With respect to joint and survivor annuities, only the primary annuitant is counted in the exposure and death statistics.

Data collection is generally done during the six months in the year following the experience year. It is possible that deaths will be reported subsequent to the gathering of data. If an insurance carrier submits data early in the year, that carrier will be expected to have a relatively high level of late reported deaths. If a carrier submits data later in the year, that carrier will have a relatively low level of late reported deaths. Although the level of late reporting might range from 1 percent to 3 percent for data submitted 6 months after the end of the experience year, no adjustment is made to the study results for the lag in the reporting of deaths. However, results for years prior to 1987 reflect some level of late reported deaths. Results for years 1987 and 1988 will reflect late reported deaths in the next report.

Ten major pension insurers submitted data in sufficient detail to allow the committee to break the total experience into subsets based on a single parameter or a combination of parameters (note that because of the timing of data submission, data from only nine insurers were included for the 1988 exposure year). The committee believes that the tables in this report produce data cells small enough to be relatively homogeneous, large enough to be credible, and in a format that facilitates data analysis.

FORMAT OF STUDY

The format is the same as that of the Group Annuity Mortality Report of 1985 and 1986 calendar-year experience. The following summary describes the tables.

Tables 1 and 2 summarize 1987 and 1988 exposure and deaths in five-year age groups, males and females by lives and income.

Tables 3–21 present summaries of 1987, 1988, and combined 1987 and 1988 ratios of actual to expected (A/E) mortality in five-year age groups for males and females, by lives and income.

Specifically, in Tables 3–8, A/E ratios are summarized by retirement class: prior to normal retirement date (NRD), on or after NRD, no stated NRD, and past NRD with no payment. In Tables 9 and 10, A/E ratios are summarized by benefit class: life annuity, life annuity with period certain, and modified cash refund annuity. In Tables 11 and 12, A/E ratios are summarized by survivor status: benefit elected is single life annuity or joint life annuity. In Tables 13 and 14, A/E ratios are summarized by years since retirement: 0–1, 2–5, 6–10, and 11 and more years). Table 15 presents the ratio of female to male mortality. In Tables 16 through 21, A/E ratios are summarized by guaranteed versus nonguaranteed status (guarantee status occurs when future benefit payments are guaranteed by an insurer).

Tables 22–33 are comparisons of A/E ratios from one exposure period to the next exposure period. Changes in A/E ratios for males and females by lives and income are summarized for the following classification groups: retirement class, benefit class, survivor class, years since retirement, and five-year age groups.

Specifically, Tables 22–25 present a comparison between 1988 and 1987 exposure years for male lives, male income, female lives, and female income in five-year age groups. Tables 26–29 present a comparison between the combined 1987–1988 and 1985–1986 exposure periods. Tables 30–33 summarize A/E ratios for exposure years 1983 through 1988 for males and females by lives and income in five-year age groups. The tables also provide annual improvement factors from one exposure year to the next, along with an arithmetic average of annual improvement factors over the period from 1983 to 1988.

Charts I–IV are histograms of A/E ratios from 1983 to 1988.

The mortality table used for expected deaths is the 1983 Group Annuity Mortality (GAM) Table without projection. Expected deaths for females are based on the female mortality tables (as opposed to the male mortality table with the standard six-year setback), except for Table 15, which is based on male mortality with no age setback.

Each of the tables displays exposure and A/E ratio. The amount of exposure provides a key to the credibility of the data in each classification age cell and for the classification group in total. Caution is advised in drawing any conclusions for experience at the very low or very high ages, because exposures are rather limited.

PRINCIPAL OBSERVATIONS

Comparing 1985–1986 calendar-year data against 1987–1988 calendar-year data did not reveal any distortions or unreasonable results for total experience or experience by class. The only major trend exhibited is, as expected, mortality improvement for both males and females over the last two years.

Exposure has increased steadily from the 1985/1986 exposure period to the 1987/1988 exposure period: the increase was 8.3 percent for male lives, 24.3 percent for male income, 11.2 percent for female lives, and 26.5 percent for female income. The increase in exposure is likely due to the increase in the number of insurers submitting data (from eight to ten insurers) as well as to the addition of new contracts. The trends of the increases in exposure indicate that new contracts are leading to a higher level of income (relative to older contracts) as well as a higher proportion of females.

The overall male A/E mortality ratio improved by 0.08 from the 1985/1986 exposure period to the 1987/1988 exposure period (A/E ratios of 1.20 versus 1.12, respectively; see Table 26) based on lives. The improvement based on income was 0.09 (A/E ratios of 1.11 versus 1.02, respectively; see Table 27). An examination of Table 30 reveals that most of the improvement occurred from 1985 to 1986.

The overall female A/E mortality ratio improved by 0.07 from the 1985/1986 exposure period to the 1987/1988 exposure period (A/E ratios of 1.26 versus 1.19, respectively; see Table 28) based on lives. The improvement based on income was 0.09 (A/E ratios of 1.26 versus 1.17, respectively; see Table 29). As with improvement factors for males, most of the improvement for females occurred from 1985 to 1986.

Overall A/E ratios for males are lower based on income than on number of lives (1.12 versus 1.02, respectively; see Tables 26 and 27) for the 1987/1988 exposure period. This phenomenon occurs for every five-year age group. The same phenomenon occurs for female A/E ratios (1.19 versus

1.17 overall; see Tables 28 and 29), although it is not quite as extreme as it is for male A/E ratios. As we concluded in the 1985/1986 report, the data support the notion that higher-income individuals exhibit lower mortality.

A/E ratios for individuals who retire prior to NRD are generally higher than those for individuals who retire on or after NRD for the 1987/1988 exposure period. This is true overall for males and females (based on lives and income; see Tables 7 and 8). Apparently, pension plans are being selected against based on retirement age.

Some selection may also occur based on benefit elected. Examination of Tables 10 and 12 reveals that female annuitants appear to be selecting against pension plans when electing life versus life and certain annuities or when electing single life annuities versus joint life annuities (based on lives and income). However, examination of Tables 9 and 11 reveals that the opposite is true for male annuitants (based on lives and income). Results are *not* consistent across the five-year age groups for males and females.

It is difficult to reach any conclusions about mortality experience based on number of years since retirement. Mortality would be expected to be lower for individuals who recently retired. However, examination of Tables 13 and 14 shows that A/E ratios vary widely within each age group when results from one "years since retirement" category are compared with those from the next. It is inappropriate to compare overall results because categories with the longest period since retirement would have a bias toward the older ages.

As expected, females are living longer than males. The ratio of female mortality to male mortality averages 0.59 (based on lives) and 0.61 (based on income) for the 1987/1988 exposure period (Table 15). Results for the 1985/1986 exposure period were similar. The ratio of female mortality to male mortality tends to increase as age increases.

Mortality has improved in each of the last five years for males based on lives and on income (Tables 30 and 31). The average improvement has been 0.029 based on number of lives and 0.035 based on income from 1983 to 1988. The largest improvement occurred from 1985 to 1986 (0.097 improvement based on income).

Female mortality has also generally improved over the last five years based on number of lives and based on income (Tables 32 and 33). Mortality improvement has averaged 0.022 based on lives and 0.029 based on income. Female mortality has improved considerably from 1985 to 1986 (0.086 based on income) and again from 1987 to 1988 (0.06 based on income).

CONTRIBUTING COMPANIES

The following companies have contributed experience for the investigation covered by this report:

Aetna Life Insurance Company
CIGNA
Equitable Life Assurance Society
John Hancock Mutual Life Insurance Company
Lincoln National Life Insurance Company
Pacific Mutual Life Insurance Company
Principal Mutual Life Insurance Company
Prudential Insurance Company of America
Sun Life Assurance Company of Canada
Travelers Insurance Company

TABLE 1

SUMMARY OF EXPOSURES AND ACTUAL DEATHS FOR CALENDAR-YEAR 1987

Attained Age	Males		Females		Total	
	Exposure	Deaths	Exposure	Deaths	Exposure	Deaths
			Lives			
Under 55...	5,601.91	70.00	3,614.15	32.00	9,216.06	102.00
55–59	47,303.94	598.00	17,781.62	134.00	65,085.56	732.00
60–64	129,028.29	2,138.00	53,226.99	533.00	182,255.28	2,671.00
65–69	238,848.85	5,773.00	101,240.19	1,356.00	340,089.04	7,129.00
70–74	223,665.17	8,714.00	98,442.35	2,054.00	322,107.52	10,768.00
75–79	157,461.29	9,443.00	74,752.64	2,525.00	232,213.93	11,968.00
80–84	83,820.45	7,671.00	43,600.05	2,452.00	127,420.50	10,123.00
85–89	34,094.97	4,590.00	18,036.28	1,677.00	52,131.25	6,267.00
90–94	9,836.78	1,921.00	5,395.54	825.00	15,232.32	2,746.00
95 and over.	1,966.60	497.00	1,177.17	219.00	3,143.77	716.00
Total	931,628.25	41,415.00	417,266.98	11,807.00	1,348,895.23	53,222.00
			Income			
Under 55...	$ 34,032,523	$ 281,713	$ 9,323,406	$ 63,440	$ 43,355,929	$ 345,153
55–59	210,158,576	1,976,367	41,923,217	218,100	252,081,793	2,194,467
60–64	638,269,146	8,498,365	123,415,175	1,301,471	761,684,321	9,799,836
65–69	924,007,779	18,416,216	193,074,584	2,407,175	1,117,082,363	20,823,391
70–74	651,936,536	22,480,815	145,406,529	2,867,298	797,343,065	25,348,113
75–79	366,368,818	20,325,685	89,994,886	2,994,881	456,363,704	23,320,566
80–84	162,622,551	13,977,077	44,337,143	2,267,803	206,959,694	16,244,880
85–89	58,678,939	7,079,850	16,239,936	1,478,707	74,918,875	8,558,557
90–94	14,831,974	2,883,031	4,354,890	650,698	19,186,864	3,533,729
95 and over.	2,509,387	627,800	867,658	153,281	3,377,045	781,081
Total	$3,063,416,229	$96,546,919	$668,937,424	$14,402,854	$3,732,353,653	$110,949,773

TABLE 2

SUMMARY OF EXPOSURES AND ACTUAL DEATHS FOR CALENDAR-YEAR 1988

Attained Age	Males		Females		Total	
	Exposure	Deaths	Exposure	Deaths	Exposure	Deaths
			Lives			
Under 55	5,971.65	92.00	3,756.80	22.00	9,728.45	114.00
55–59	49,424.32	683.00	18,162.87	141.00	67,587.19	824.00
60–64	132,778.58	2,252.00	53,788.54	513.00	186,567.12	2,765.00
65–69	235,874.82	5,587.00	102,022.53	1,295.00	337,897.35	6,882.00
70–74	221,164.05	8,388.00	99,853.21	2,116.00	321,017.26	10,504.00
75–79	162,202.31	9,530.00	78,542.78	2,630.00	240,745.09	12,160.00
80–84	88,225.65	8,012.00	47,418.51	2,583.00	135,644.16	10,595.00
85–89	35,929.54	4,707.00	20,142.57	1,879.00	56,072.11	6,586.00
90–94	10,484.98	2,002.00	5,926.74	845.00	16,411.72	2,847.00
95 and over	2,148.48	566.00	1,361.69	278.00	3,510.17	844.00
Total	944,204.38	41,819.00	430,976.24	12,302.00	1,375,180.62	54,121.00
			Income			
Under 55	$ 42,347,224	$ 319,621	$ 10,357,046	$ 63,914	$ 52,704,270	$ 383,535
55–59	238,147,305	2,645,844	46,379,080	312,534	284,526,385	2,958,378
60–64	713,734,376	9,860,876	136,887,308	1,025,299	850,621,684	10,886,175
65–69	979,519,612	19,394,332	213,005,243	2,313,370	1,192,524,855	21,707,702
70–74	698,620,860	23,199,041	159,795,293	3,119,522	858,416,153	26,318,563
75–79	405,723,211	21,453,790	101,625,827	3,229,133	507,349,038	24,682,923
80–84	183,466,257	15,200,593	51,292,736	2,617,384	234,758,993	17,817,977
85–89	63,754,909	7,835,225	19,030,705	1,740,079	82,785,614	9,575,304
90–94	16,434,294	3,018,058	4,882,865	672,501	21,317,159	3,690,559
95 and over	2,768,344	707,521	1,026,083	199,027	3,794,427	906,548
Total	$3,344,516,392	$103,634,901	$744,282,186	$15,292,763	$4,088,798,578	$118,927,664

TABLE 3

EXPERIENCE BY RETIREMENT CLASS FOR CALENDAR-YEAR 1987
EXPECTED MORTALITY BASIS—1983 GROUP ANNUITY MORTALITY

Attained Age	Prior to NRD		On/After NRD		No Stated NRD		Past NRD With No Payment		Total	
	Exposure	A/E Ratio	Exposure	A/E Ratio	Exposure	A/E Ratio	Exposure	A/E Ratio	Exposure	A/E Ratio
Male Lives										
Under 55	3,380.91	1.95	728.72	3.20	1,488.95	4.93	3.33	0.00	5,601.91	2.90
55–59	29,927.02	1.58	4,108.04	1.42	13,260.55	2.05	8.33	0.00	47,303.94	1.70
60–64	84,996.99	1.29	14,783.66	1.55	29,128.78	1.69	118.86	3.40	129,028.29	1.41
65–69	111,511.54	1.13	77,945.17	1.22	48,499.09	1.36	893.05	0.29	238,848.85	1.21
70–74	79,515.29	1.13	93,161.36	1.12	50,392.86	1.30	595.66	1.21	223,665.17	1.16
75–79	39,436.09	1.13	75,668.42	1.06	42,074.95	1.18	281.83	0.93	157,461.29	1.11
80–84	13,618.57	1.04	43,818.71	1.01	26,282.17	1.10	101.00	1.81	83,820.45	1.05
85–89	4,005.10	1.02	19,497.19	1.01	10,544.63	1.07	48.00	1.46	34,094.97	1.03
90–94	777.75	1.17	5,720.38	1.02	3,317.65	1.10	21.00	1.55	9,836.78	1.06
95 and over	156.64	0.88	1,155.72	0.85	652.24	1.11	2.00	2.01	1,966.60	0.94
Total	367,325.90	1.14	336,587.37	1.07	225,641.92	1.21	2,073.06	1.10	931,628.25	1.13
Male Income										
Under 55	$ 20,292,513	1.41	$ 4,026,044	2.76	$ 9,702,995	2.57	$ 10,970	0.00	$ 34,032,523	1.88
55–59	135,613,974	1.07	13,823,420	1.58	60,696,359	1.61	24,823	0.00	210,158,576	1.26
60–64	397,704,863	1.00	68,333,751	1.22	171,937,894	1.40	292,638	6.80	638,269,146	1.14
65–69	402,743,824	0.96	295,473,676	0.99	223,654,465	1.12	2,135,814	0.05	924,007,779	1.01
70–74	214,376,198	1.01	260,886,377	0.98	175,311,917	1.16	1,362,044	1.51	651,936,536	1.04
75–79	83,612,596	1.06	176,023,757	0.96	106,249,477	1.12	482,988	0.92	366,368,818	1.03
80–84	22,390,099	0.96	86,424,904	0.95	53,497,349	1.07	310,199	2.21	162,622,551	0.99
85–89	5,636,682	0.93	34,067,732	0.92	18,915,140	0.96	59,385	2.27	58,678,939	0.93
90–94	1,077,811	0.96	9,031,542	1.05	4,354,248	1.19	368,373	0.19	14,831,974	1.06
95 and over	288,399	0.33	1,475,321	0.92	743,958	1.15	1,709	3.82	2,509,387	0.90
Total	$1,283,736,959	1.00	$949,566,524	0.97	$825,063,803	1.14	$5,048,943	0.98	$3,063,416,229	1.03

TABLE 4

EXPERIENCE BY RETIREMENT CLASS FOR CALENDAR-YEAR 1987
EXPECTED MORTALITY BASIS—1983 GROUP ANNUITY MORTALITY

Attained Age	Prior to NRD		On/After NRD		No Stated NRD		Past NRD With No Payment		Total	
	Exposure	A/E Ratio	Exposure	A/E Ratio	Exposure	A/E Ratio	Exposure	A/E Ratio	Exposure	A/E Ratio
Female Lives										
Under 55......	2,497.01	4.78	482.30	5.40	633.84	7.75	1.00	0.00	3,614.15	5.37
55–59	12,826.67	2.10	1,653.81	2.90	3,287.39	2.61	13.75	21.98	17,781.62	2.29
60–64	36,204.13	1.77	7,457.44	2.06	9,479.46	1.90	85.96	0.00	53,226.99	1.83
65–69	44,217.95	1.44	36,563.87	1.61	20,124.13	1.48	334.24	1.04	101,240.19	1.51
70–74	29,891.98	1.31	44,922.93	1.23	23,424.95	1.34	202.49	0.61	98,442.35	1.28
75–79	15,811.33	1.16	38,213.00	1.07	20,560.31	1.15	168.00	1.70	74,752.64	1.11
80–84	5,762.57	1.12	23,335.27	1.07	14,333.71	1.10	168.50	2.25	43,600.05	1.09
85–89	1,884.50	1.23	10,224.44	1.10	5,861.34	1.18	66.00	1.89	18,036.28	1.14
90–94	456.67	1.32	3,236.77	1.13	1,681.60	1.26	20.50	0.39	5,395.54	1.18
95 and over....	95.09	0.69	730.48	0.79	350.60	0.95	1.00	0.00	1,177.17	0.83
Total	149,647.90	1.33	166,820.31	1.14	99,737.33	1.21	1,061.44	1.59	417,266.98	1.20
Female Income										
Under 55......	$ 6,656,771	3.44	$ 1,060,331	7.21	$ 1,603,009	4.60	$ 3,295	0.00	$ 9,323,406	4.02
55–59	31,136,079	1.37	3,018,010	2.24	7,751,434	2.11	17,694	8.55	41,923,217	1.57
60–64	86,253,903	2.05	12,885,730	1.52	24,200,458	1.72	75,084	0.00	123,415,175	1.93
65–69	82,272,626	1.41	65,721,078	1.53	44,558,019	1.30	522,861	1.03	193,074,584	1.42
70–74	40,440,615	1.25	64,579,144	1.19	40,118,068	1.25	268,702	0.35	145,406,529	1.22
75–79	16,086,582	1.24	46,316,093	1.04	27,258,299	1.12	333,912	1.78	89,994,886	1.10
80–84	4,352,527	1.02	23,947,063	0.97	15,741,803	1.02	295,750	1.51	44,337,143	1.00
85–89	1,202,600	1.22	9,540,487	1.09	5,403,647	1.13	93,202	2.42	16,239,936	1.12
90–94	348,633	1.10	2,648,860	1.05	1,327,579	1.41	29,818	0.38	4,354,890	1.16
95 and over....	86,737	0.47	547,605	0.76	233,007	0.89	309	0.00	867,658	0.76
Total	$268,837,073	1.41	$230,264,401	1.12	$168,195,323	1.19	$1,640,627	1.47	$668,937,424	1.21

TABLE 5

EXPERIENCE BY RETIREMENT CLASS FOR CALENDAR-YEAR 1988
EXPECTED MORTALITY BASIS—1983 GROUP ANNUITY MORTALITY

Attained Age	Prior to NRD		On/After NRD		No Stated NRD		Past NRD With No Payment		Total	
	Exposure	A/E Ratio	Exposure	A/E Ratio	Exposure	A/E Ratio	Exposure	A/E Ratio	Exposure	A/E Ratio
					Male Lives					
Under 55	3,784.97	2.49	574.12	3.09	1,610.56	6.44	2.00	0.00	5,971.65	3.63
55–59	29,651.51	1.68	4,155.96	1.54	15,607.53	2.28	9.32	0.00	49,424.32	1.85
60–64	83,700.34	1.41	14,998.93	1.37	33,979.86	1.56	99.45	1.60	132,778.58	1.44
65–69	107,517.55	1.10	74,754.25	1.20	52,581.90	1.33	1,021.12	0.70	235,874.82	1.18
70–74	77,698.94	1.10	89,185.57	1.13	53,659.80	1.17	619.74	1.22	221,164.05	1.13
75–79	41,148.57	1.10	76,732.40	1.05	43,989.67	1.13	331.67	1.02	162,202.31	1.08
80–84	13,703.59	1.12	45,367.47	1.00	29,046.51	1.07	108.08	0.64	88,225.65	1.04
85–89	3,870.01	1.03	20,396.83	1.00	11,619.70	1.02	43.00	0.54	35,929.54	1.01
90–94	723.00	1.02	6,094.92	1.04	3,651.06	1.05	16.00	0.68	10,484.98	1.04
95 and over	122.32	0.50	1,323.24	1.02	698.92	0.98	4.00	2.07	2,148.48	0.97
Total	361,920.80	1.14	333,583.69	1.06	246,445.51	1.15	2,254.38	0.92	944,204.38	1.11
					Male Income					
Under 55	$ 25,773,869	1.50	$ 5,714,231	0.75	$ 10,854,777	2.87	$ 4,347	0.00	$ 42,347,224	1.77
55–59	144,810,360	1.26	21,609,706	1.46	71,694,016	1.94	33,223	0.00	238,147,305	1.48
60–64	423,435,025	1.12	82,111,065	1.13	207,920,784	1.32	267,502	1.20	713,734,376	1.18
65–69	418,350,485	0.97	297,885,912	0.97	260,447,211	1.09	2,836,004	0.39	979,519,612	1.00
70–74	221,646,974	0.97	270,486,448	0.98	205,036,716	1.07	1,450,722	0.90	698,620,860	1.00
75–79	92,055,321	0.99	188,603,789	0.97	124,494,916	1.00	569,185	1.68	405,723,211	0.98
80–84	23,976,626	0.94	94,867,315	0.96	64,332,089	0.97	290,227	0.08	183,466,257	0.96
85–89	5,493,279	0.93	36,739,516	0.92	21,469,889	1.00	52,225	0.28	63,754,909	0.95
90–94	754,496	0.87	10,066,361	1.01	5,255,790	1.08	357,647	0.16	16,434,294	1.01
95 and over	302,699	0.21	1,673,807	1.00	786,629	1.08	5,209	2.88	2,768,344	0.91
Total	$1,356,599,134	1.01	$1,009,758,150	0.97	$972,292,817	1.07	$5,866,291	0.59	$3,344,516,392	1.01

TABLE 6

EXPERIENCE BY RETIREMENT CLASS FOR CALENDAR-YEAR 1988
EXPECTED MORTALITY BASIS—1983 GROUP ANNUITY MORTALITY

Attained Age	Prior to NRD		On/After NRD		No Stated NRD		Past NRD With No Payment		Total	
	Exposure	A/E Ratio	Exposure	A/E Ratio	Exposure	A/E Ratio	Exposure	A/E Ratio	Exposure	A/E Ratio
Female Lives										
Under 55	2,564.19	3.38	433.34	3.02	758.77	4.81	0.50	0.00	3,756.80	3.63
55–59	12,462.13	2.05	1,787.78	2.34	3,898.88	3.37	14.08	0.00	18,162.87	2.36
60–64	35,482.24	1.62	7,468.64	2.01	10,760.49	1.99	77.17	0.00	53,788.54	1.74
65–69	43,775.34	1.32	35,698.24	1.47	22,138.72	1.60	410.23	0.86	102,022.53	1.43
70–74	30,727.63	1.27	43,572.08	1.32	25,325.93	1.29	227.57	1.09	99,853.21	1.30
75–79	16,868.36	1.14	39,217.37	1.07	22,291.63	1.13	165.42	0.96	78,542.78	1.10
80–84	6,230.68	1.12	25,098.02	1.05	15,924.39	1.05	165.42	0.91	47,418.51	1.06
85–89	1,892.17	1.18	11,275.19	1.12	6,906.21	1.17	69.00	0.89	20,142.57	1.14
90–94	442.00	0.86	3,482.00	1.11	1,978.74	1.13	24.00	0.64	5,926.74	1.10
95 and over	93.17	0.69	855.01	0.97	410.51	0.79	3.00	0.00	1,361.69	0.89
Total	150,537.91	1.25	168,887.67	1.14	110,394.27	1.18	1,156.39	0.87	430,976.24	1.18
Female Income										
Under 55	$ 7,086,624	3.92	$ 1,127,448	1.56	$ 2,139,876	4.21	$ 3,098	0.00	$ 10,357,046	3.73
55–59	32,167,454	1.72	4,647,528	1.01	9,531,746	3.65	32,352	0.00	46,379,080	2.04
60–64	90,926,535	1.26	16,076,332	1.78	29,807,946	1.50	76,495	0.00	136,887,308	1.37
65–69	88,984,012	1.11	70,250,019	1.37	53,070,206	1.28	701,006	0.62	213,005,243	1.24
70–74	44,018,448	1.08	67,383,773	1.23	48,060,748	1.30	332,324	0.35	159,795,293	1.21
75–79	18,223,764	1.21	50,311,410	1.04	32,822,838	1.00	267,815	0.82	101,625,827	1.05
80–84	4,849,674	0.99	27,176,649	0.99	18,939,626	0.99	326,787	1.32	51,292,736	0.99
85–89	1,177,016	1.04	10,902,607	1.07	6,851,597	1.22	99,485	0.74	19,030,705	1.12
90–94	268,184	1.11	2,937,398	1.06	1,640,723	1.09	36,560	0.80	4,882,865	1.07
95 and over	89,358	0.35	630,642	0.88	304,510	0.77	1,573	0.00	1,026,083	0.79
Total	$287,791,069	1.16	$251,443,806	1.11	$203,169,816	1.16	$1,877,495	0.89	$744,282,186	1.13

TABLE 7

EXPERIENCE BY RETIREMENT CLASS FOR CALENDAR-YEARS 1987 AND 1988
EXPECTED MORTALITY BASIS—1983 GROUP ANNUITY MORTALITY

Attained Age	Prior to NRD		On/After NRD		No Stated NRD		Past NRD With No Payment		Total	
	Exposure	A/E Ratio	Exposure	A/E Ratio	Exposure	A/E Ratio	Exposure	A/E Ratio	Exposure	A/E Ratio
Male Lives										
Under 55	7,165.88	2.23	1,302.84	3.15	3,099.51	5.71	5.33	0.00	11,573.56	3.27
55–59	59,578.53	1.63	8,264.00	1.48	28,868.08	2.17	17.65	0.00	96,728.26	1.78
60–64	168,697.33	1.35	29,782.59	1.46	63,108.64	1.62	218.31	2.57	261,806.87	1.43
65–69	219,029.09	1.12	152,699.42	1.21	101,080.99	1.34	1,914.17	0.51	474,723.67	1.19
70–74	157,214.23	1.12	182,346.93	1.13	104,052.66	1.23	1,215.40	1.21	444,829.22	1.15
75–79	80,584.66	1.11	152,400.82	1.05	86,064.62	1.15	613.50	0.98	319,663.60	1.10
80–84	27,322.16	1.08	89,186.18	1.01	55,328.68	1.08	209.08	1.21	172,046.10	1.04
85–89	7,875.11	1.02	39,894.02	1.01	22,164.38	1.05	91.00	1.03	70,024.51	1.02
90–94	1,500.75	1.10	11,815.30	1.03	6,968.71	1.07	37.00	1.18	20,321.76	1.05
95 and over	278.96	0.71	2,478.96	0.94	1,351.16	1.04	6.00	2.05	4,115.08	0.96
Total	729,246.70	1.14	670,171.06	1.07	472,087.43	1.18	4,327.44	1.01	1,875,832.63	1.12
Male Income										
Under 55	$ 46,066,382	1.46	$ 9,740,275	1.60	$ 20,557,773	2.72	$ 15,317	0.00	$ 76,379,747	1.82
55–59	280,424,334	1.17	35,433,126	1.51	132,390,375	1.79	58,046	0.00	448,305,881	1.38
60–64	821,139,888	1.06	150,444,816	1.18	379,858,678	1.36	560,140	4.11	1,352,003,522	1.16
65–69	821,094,309	0.97	593,359,588	0.98	484,101,676	1.10	4,971,818	0.24	1,903,527,391	1.00
70–74	436,023,172	0.99	531,372,825	0.98	380,348,633	1.11	2,812,766	1.20	1,350,557,396	1.02
75–79	175,667,917	1.02	364,627,546	0.97	230,744,393	1.05	1,052,173	1.33	772,092,029	1.01
80–84	46,366,725	0.95	181,292,219	0.95	117,829,438	1.01	600,426	1.18	346,088,808	0.97
85–89	11,129,961	0.93	70,807,248	0.92	40,385,029	0.98	111,610	1.35	122,433,848	0.94
90–94	1,832,307	0.92	19,097,903	1.03	9,610,038	1.13	726,020	0.18	31,266,268	1.03
95 and over	591,098	0.27	3,149,128	0.96	1,530,587	1.11	6,918	3.12	5,277,731	0.91
Total	$2,640,336,093	1.00	$1,959,324,674	0.97	$1,797,356,620	1.10	$10,915,234	0.78	$6,407,932,621	1.02

TABLE 8

EXPERIENCE BY RETIREMENT CLASS FOR CALENDAR-YEARS 1987 AND 1988
EXPECTED MORTALITY BASIS—1983 GROUP ANNUITY MORTALITY

Attained Age	Prior to NRD		On/After NRD		No Stated NRD		Past NRD With No Payment		Total	
	Exposure	A/E Ratio	Exposure	A/E Ratio	Exposure	A/E Ratio	Exposure	A/E Ratio	Exposure	A/E Ratio
					Female Lives					
Under 55......	5,061.20	4.08	915.64	4.28	1,392.61	6.14	1.50	0.00	7,370.95	4.50
55–59	25,288.80	2.08	3,441.59	2.61	7,186.27	3.03	27.83	10.89	35,944.49	2.32
60–64	71,686.37	1.69	14,926.08	2.04	20,239.95	1.95	163.13	0.00	107,015.53	1.79
65–69	87,993.29	1.38	72,262.11	1.54	42,262.85	1.54	744.47	0.94	203,262.72	1.47
70–74	60,619.61	1.29	88,495.01	1.28	48,750.88	1.31	430.06	0.86	198,295.56	1.29
75–79	32,679.69	1.15	77,430.37	1.07	42,851.94	1.14	333.42	1.34	153,295.42	1.11
80–84	11,993.25	1.12	48,433.29	1.06	30,258.10	1.07	333.92	1.59	91,018.56	1.07
85–89	3,776.67	1.21	21,499.63	1.11	12,767.55	1.17	135.00	1.38	38,178.85	1.14
90–94	898.67	1.09	6,718.77	1.12	3,660.34	1.19	44.50	0.53	11,322.28	1.14
95 and over....	188.26	0.69	1,585.49	0.89	761.11	0.86	4.00	0.00	2,538.86	0.86
Total	300,185.81	1.29	335,707.98	1.14	210,131.60	1.20	2,217.83	1.22	848,243.22	1.19
					Female Income					
Under 55......	$ 13,743,395	3.68	$ 2,187,779	4.28	$ 3,742,885	4.38	$ 6,393	0.00	$ 19,680,452	3.87
55–59	63,303,533	1.55	7,665,538	1.50	17,283,180	2.96	50,046	3.04	88,302,297	1.82
60–64	177,180,438	1.65	28,962,062	1.66	54,008,404	1.60	151,579	0.00	260,302,483	1.64
65–69	171,256,638	1.25	135,971,097	1.45	97,628,225	1.29	1,223,867	0.80	406,079,827	1.33
70–74	84,459,063	1.16	131,962,917	1.21	88,178,816	1.28	601,026	0.35	305,201,822	1.22
75–79	34,310,346	1.22	96,627,503	1.04	60,081,137	1.06	601,727	1.35	191,620,713	1.08
80–84	9,202,201	1.00	51,123,712	0.98	34,681,429	1.01	622,537	1.41	95,629,879	1.00
85–89	2,379,616	1.13	20,443,094	1.08	12,255,244	1.18	192,687	1.55	35,270,641	1.12
90–94	616,817	1.10	5,586,258	1.05	2,968,302	1.23	66,378	0.62	9,237,755	1.11
95 and over....	176,095	0.41	1,178,247	0.83	537,517	0.82	1,882	0.00	1,893,741	0.77
Total	$556,628,142	1.28	$481,708,207	1.11	$371,365,139	1.17	$3,518,122	1.16	$1,413,219,610	1.17

TABLE 9

EXPERIENCE BY BENEFIT CLASS FOR CALENDAR-YEARS 1987 AND 1988
EXPECTED MORTALITY BASIS—1983 GROUP ANNUITY MORTALITY

Attained Age	Life		Life and Certain		Modified Cash Refund		Total	
	Exposure	A/E Ratio	Exposure	A/E Ratio	Exposure	A/E Ratio	Exposure	A/E Ratio
				Male Lives				
Under 55	8,457.54	3.52	1,584.85	2.58	1,531.17	2.59	11,573.56	3.27
55–59	73,885.57	1.78	11,651.14	1.91	11,191.55	1.62	96,728.26	1.78
60–64	186,464.26	1.43	36,061.87	1.58	39,280.74	1.25	261,806.87	1.43
65–69	317,556.34	1.24	79,560.38	1.13	77,606.95	1.08	474,723.67	1.19
70–74	284,193.06	1.19	83,997.08	1.07	76,639.08	1.09	444,829.22	1.15
75–79	200,988.79	1.11	62,334.11	1.09	56,340.70	1.04	319,663.60	1.10
80–84	115,114.39	1.05	29,613.43	1.04	27,318.28	1.04	172,046.10	1.04
85–89	50,520.33	1.01	8,660.10	1.02	10,844.08	1.06	70,024.51	1.02
90–94	15,364.29	1.02	1,553.55	1.23	3,403.92	1.12	20,321.76	1.05
95 and over	3,356.92	0.92	240.40	1.12	517.76	1.10	4,115.08	0.96
Total	1,255,901.49	1.13	315,256.91	1.10	304,674.23	1.07	1,875,832.63	1.12
				Male Income				
Under 55	$ 50,716,235	1.96	$ 9,445,477	1.28	$ 16,218,035	1.63	$ 76,379,747	1.82
55–59	341,519,242	1.35	43,499,479	1.67	63,287,160	1.31	448,305,881	1.38
60–64	991,814,747	1.17	151,729,947	1.30	208,458,828	1.01	1,352,003,522	1.16
65–69	1,321,527,026	1.03	278,267,359	0.99	303,733,006	0.92	1,903,527,391	1.00
70–74	887,566,161	1.05	244,910,640	0.99	218,080,595	0.95	1,350,557,396	1.02
75–79	491,239,231	1.01	155,655,170	0.99	125,197,628	0.99	772,092,029	1.01
80–84	231,267,194	0.96	62,476,271	0.96	52,345,343	1.03	346,088,808	0.97
85–89	88,729,609	0.94	15,757,815	0.88	17,946,424	1.01	122,433,848	0.94
90–94	24,182,388	1.00	2,423,827	1.06	4,660,053	1.22	31,266,268	1.03
95 and over	4,294,244	0.93	415,303	0.67	568,184	0.88	5,277,731	0.91
Total	$4,432,856,077	1.03	$964,581,288	1.00	$1,010,495,256	0.99	$6,407,932,621	1.02

TABLE 10

EXPERIENCE BY BENEFIT CLASS FOR CALENDAR-YEARS 1987 AND 1988
EXPECTED MORTALITY BASIS—1983 GROUP ANNUITY MORTALITY

Attained Age	Life		Life and Certain		Modified Cash Refund		Total	
	Exposure	A/E Ratio	Exposure	A/E Ratio	Exposure	A/E Ratio	Exposure	A/E Ratio
				Female Lives				
Under 55	5,351.71	4.55	1,007.41	3.07	1,011.83	5.67	7,370.95	4.50
55–59	26,725.29	2.33	4,387.27	2.89	4,831.93	1.75	35,944.49	2.32
60–64	74,979.89	1.76	14,281.42	1.74	17,754.22	1.92	107,015.53	1.79
65–69	137,580.60	1.46	28,861.30	1.47	36,820.82	1.50	203,262.72	1.47
70–74	131,124.87	1.29	30,389.99	1.23	36,780.70	1.31	198,295.56	1.29
75–79	103,560.70	1.10	23,131.12	1.18	26,603.60	1.09	153,295.42	1.11
80–84	64,728.37	1.07	11,761.19	1.03	14,529.00	1.10	91,018.56	1.07
85–89	28,706.95	1.13	3,794.63	1.17	5,677.27	1.18	38,178.85	1.14
90–94	8,803.88	1.13	737.96	1.29	1,780.44	1.12	11,322.28	1.14
95 and over	2,113.86	0.86	123.67	0.79	301.33	0.89	2,538.86	0.86
Total..........	583,676.12	1.18	118,475.96	1.21	146,091.14	1.21	848,243.22	1.19
				Female Income				
Under 55	$ 14,553,780	4.15	$ 2,589,300	1.22	$ 2,537,372	4.84	$ 19,680,452	3.87
55–59	67,165,739	1.86	9,822,760	2.40	11,313,798	1.08	88,302,297	1.82
60–64	185,904,237	1.62	32,256,359	1.71	42,141,887	1.67	260,302,483	1.64
65–69	275,364,639	1.31	57,907,130	1.44	72,808,058	1.30	406,079,827	1.33
70–74	200,097,751	1.23	48,316,378	1.21	56,787,693	1.15	305,201,822	1.22
75–79	128,640,185	1.07	29,608,330	1.17	33,372,198	1.01	191,620,713	1.08
80–84	68,626,784	1.00	12,151,890	0.93	14,851,205	1.05	95,629,879	1.00
85–89	27,664,692	1.11	3,067,944	1.17	4,538,005	1.18	35,270,641	1.12
90–94	7,555,063	1.08	564,186	1.69	1,118,506	1.01	9,237,755	1.11
95 and over	1,626,159	0.77	95,699	0.67	171,883	0.80	1,893,741	0.77
Total..........	$977,199,029	1.16	$196,379,976	1.22	$239,640,605	1.15	$1,413,219,610	1.17

TABLE 11

EXPERIENCE BY SURVIVOR STATUS FOR CALENDAR-YEARS 1987 AND 1988
EXPECTED MORTALITY BASIS—1983 GROUP ANNUITY MORTALITY

Attained Age	Single Life		Joint Life		Total	
	Exposure	A/E Ratio	Exposure	A/E Ratio	Exposure	A/E Ratio
			Males Lives			
Under 55	7,400.77	7.40	4,172.79	11.07	11,573.56	8.22
55–59	62,403.71	1.71	34,324.55	1.89	96,728.26	1.78
60–64	164,957.39	1.43	96,849.48	1.42	261,806.87	1.43
65–69	320,469.51	1.22	154,254.16	1.15	474,723.67	1.19
70–74	332,899.08	1.17	111,930.14	1.07	444,829.22	1.15
75–79	267,120.34	1.11	52,543.26	1.03	319,663.60	1.10
80–84	150,663.24	1.06	21,382.86	0.90	172,046.10	1.04
85–89	61,781.83	1.03	8,242.68	0.92	70,024.51	1.02
90–94	18,411.03	1.06	1,910.73	0.94	20,321.76	1.05
95 and over	3,848.45	0.96	266.63	0.98	4,115.08	0.96
Total	1,389,955.35	1.12	485,877.28	1.09	1,875,832.63	1.12
			Male Income			
Under 55	$ 45,027,678	3.43	$ 31,352,069	5.65	$ 76,379,747	4.00
55–59	261,959,883	1.16	186,345,998	1.69	448,305,881	1.38
60–64	737,997,361	1.14	614,006,161	1.18	1,352,003,522	1.16
65–69	1,066,510,949	1.02	837,016,442	0.98	1,903,527,391	1.00
70–74	881,830,947	1.06	468,726,449	0.95	1,350,557,396	1.02
75–79	586,212,710	1.03	185,879,319	0.93	772,092,029	1.01
80–84	279,531,813	1.00	66,556,995	0.88	346,088,808	0.97
85–89	99,721,219	0.97	22,712,629	0.83	122,433,848	0.94
90–94	25,815,642	1.07	5,450,626	0.86	31,266,268	1.03
95 and over	4,750,840	0.91	526,891	0.92	5,277,731	0.91
Total	$3,989,359,042	1.03	$2,418,573,579	0.99	$6,407,932,621	1.02

TABLE 12

EXPERIENCE BY SURVIVOR STATUS FOR CALENDAR-YEARS 1987 AND 1988
EXPECTED MORTALITY BASIS—1983 GROUP ANNUITY MORTALITY

Attained Age	Single Life		Joint Life		Total	
	Exposure	A/E Ratio	Exposure	A/E Ratio	Exposure	A/E Ratio
Female Lives						
Under 55	6,798.67	4.56	572.28	15.30	7,370.95	5.03
55–59	31,405.35	2.23	4,539.14	2.95	35,944.49	2.32
60–64	95,143.88	1.78	11,871.65	1.82	107,015.53	1.79
65–69	187,261.55	1.47	16,001.17	1.42	203,262.72	1.47
70–74	187,760.16	1.28	10,535.40	1.36	198,295.56	1.29
75–79	149,369.85	1.11	3,925.57	0.87	153,295.42	1.11
80–84	89,846.25	1.07	1,172.31	1.00	91,018.56	1.07
85–89	37,760.93	1.14	417.92	1.50	38,178.85	1.14
90–94	11,235.02	1.14	87.26	0.61	11,322.28	1.14
95 and over	2,515.28	0.86	23.58	0.50	2,538.86	0.86
Total	799,096.94	1.18	49,146.28	1.32	848,243.22	1.19
Female Income						
Under 55	$ 18,016,997	3.39	$ 1,663,455	37.44	$ 19,680,452	5.08
55–59	75,935,809	1.78	12,366,488	2.06	88,302,297	1.82
60–64	225,939,472	1.49	34,363,011	2.59	260,302,483	1.64
65–69	366,479,090	1.33	39,600,737	1.30	406,079,827	1.33
70–74	284,667,622	1.22	20,534,200	1.21	305,201,822	1.22
75–79	185,181,661	1.08	6,439,052	0.99	191,620,713	1.08
80–84	93,966,688	0.99	1,663,191	1.30	95,629,879	1.00
85–89	34,709,539	1.12	561,102	1.23	35,270,641	1.12
90–94	9,121,618	1.12	116,137	0.44	9,237,755	1.11
95 and over	1,874,320	0.78	19,421	0.39	1,893,741	0.77
Total	$1,295,892,816	1.15	$117,326,794	1.45	$1,413,219,610	1.17

TABLE 13

EXPERIENCE BY YEARS SINCE RETIREMENT FOR CALENDAR-YEARS 1987 AND 1988
EXPECTED MORTALITY BASIS—1983 GROUP ANNUITY MORTALITY

Attained Age	Years Since Retirement									
	0–1		2–5		6–10		11 and Over		Total	
	Exposure	A/E Ratio	Exposure	A/E Ratio	Exposure	A/E Ratio	Exposure	A/E Ratio	Exposure	A/E Ratio
Male Lives										
Under 55	4,859.38	11.75	5,216.91	8.34	1,156.97	3.02	340.30	2.07	11,573.56	8.22
55–59	41,899.01	1.82	50,562.04	1.73	3,379.25	1.76	887.96	2.40	96,728.26	1.78
60–64	84,738.88	1.39	126,006.39	1.36	47,302.54	1.60	3,759.06	2.18	261,806.87	1.43
65–69	73,092.23	1.20	232,607.78	1.13	127,498.98	1.23	41,524.68	1.44	474,723.67	1.19
70–74	18,651.87	1.04	74,848.11	1.09	234,777.64	1.13	116,551.60	1.23	444,829.22	1.15
75–79	9,768.56	1.00	25,372.15	1.15	50,423.94	1.06	234,098.95	1.10	319,663.60	1.10
80–84	4,491.29	0.93	11,029.12	1.11	12,485.00	1.03	144,040.69	1.04	172,046.10	1.04
85–89	1,648.87	0.83	3,808.55	1.04	4,441.96	0.99	60,125.13	1.03	70,024.51	1.02
90–94	487.78	0.92	1,023.49	1.09	1,110.24	1.07	17,700.25	1.05	20,321.76	1.05
95 and over	141.19	0.58	199.00	0.76	294.50	0.84	3,480.39	1.00	4,115.08	0.96
Total	239,779.06	1.20	530,673.54	1.16	482,871.02	1.14	622,509.01	1.09	1,875,832.63	1.12
Male Income										
Under 55	$ 35,510,832	4.02	$ 34,411,951	5.13	$ 5,234,203	1.41	$ 1,222,761	0.74	$ 76,379,747	4.00
55–59	226,952,395	1.37	203,693,766	1.37	14,046,507	1.35	3,613,213	2.28	448,305,881	1.38
60–64	541,891,085	1.06	675,872,922	1.17	117,282,875	1.41	16,956,640	1.83	1,352,003,522	1.16
65–69	342,404,053	0.87	1,003,521,496	0.97	465,254,567	1.08	92,347,275	1.41	1,903,527,391	1.00
70–74	78,997,868	0.92	284,158,787	0.92	689,549,106	1.04	297,851,635	1.08	1,350,557,396	1.02
75–79	32,488,346	0.79	78,188,889	1.03	127,347,402	0.98	534,067,392	1.02	772,092,029	1.01
80–84	11,205,250	0.74	27,537,994	1.00	27,431,419	1.00	279,914,145	0.98	346,088,808	0.97
85–89	4,202,572	0.66	9,374,266	0.87	8,904,208	0.93	99,952,802	0.96	122,433,848	0.94
90–94	1,351,903	0.56	2,796,129	0.83	1,835,834	1.20	25,282,402	1.07	31,266,268	1.03
95 and over	533,582	0.19	394,075	0.63	464,345	0.80	3,885,729	1.08	5,277,731	0.91
Total	$1,275,537,886	0.96	$2,319,950,275	1.01	$1,457,350,466	1.05	$1,355,093,994	1.02	$6,407,932,621	1.02

TABLE 14

EXPERIENCE BY YEARS SINCE RETIREMENT FOR CALENDAR-YEARS 1987 AND 1988
EXPECTED MORTALITY BASIS—1983 GROUP ANNUITY MORTALITY

Attained Age	Years Since Retirement									
	0–1		2–5		6–10		11 and Over		Total	
	Exposure	A/E Ratio	Exposure	A/E Ratio	Exposure	A/E Ratio	Exposure	A/E Ratio	Exposure	A/E Ratio
Female Lives										
Under 55	2,590.44	3.10	3,437.92	6.43	1,042.17	5.57	300.42	2.25	7,370.95	5.03
55–59	14,377.21	2.49	18,730.84	2.07	2,432.77	2.84	403.67	5.40	35,944.49	2.32
60–64	32,795.80	1.87	51,035.94	1.68	20,501.07	1.80	2,682.72	2.78	107,015.53	1.79
65–69	33,671.74	1.49	98,962.73	1.43	52,730.11	1.49	17,898.14	1.57	203,262.72	1.47
70–74	10,174.46	1.26	41,444.45	1.28	96,061.63	1.27	50,615.02	1.33	198,295.56	1.29
75–79	5,204.33	0.95	14,922.50	1.09	26,149.18	1.10	107,019.41	1.12	153,295.42	1.11
80–84	2,426.40	0.74	6,626.56	1.04	6,549.11	1.10	75,416.49	1.08	91,018.56	1.07
85–89	1,070.65	0.87	2,663.47	1.11	2,548.62	1.15	31,896.11	1.15	38,178.85	1.14
90–94	276.37	0.78	785.91	1.39	612.67	1.11	9,647.33	1.13	11,322.28	1.14
95 and over	92.69	0.32	213.00	1.02	167.75	0.54	2,065.42	0.90	2,538.86	0.86
Total	102,680.09	1.30	238,823.32	1.32	208,795.08	1.25	297,944.73	1.13	848,243.22	1.19
Female Income										
Under 55	$ 7,698,046	4.44	$ 8,995,710	5.80	$ 2,417,711	5.53	$ 568,985	2.00	$ 19,680,452	5.08
55–59	40,988,062	1.73	41,707,741	1.75	4,882,580	2.89	723,914	3.43	88,302,297	1.82
60–64	100,629,616	1.79	125,206,590	1.47	29,929,355	1.73	4,536,922	2.22	260,302,483	1.64
65–69	83,526,599	1.25	214,447,833	1.31	86,562,540	1.42	21,542,855	1.32	406,079,827	1.33
70–74	23,212,925	1.29	76,590,306	1.23	145,055,606	1.22	60,342,985	1.17	305,201,822	1.22
75–79	9,876,774	0.82	23,412,781	1.19	35,400,541	1.11	122,930,617	1.07	191,620,713	1.08
80–84	4,048,554	0.61	9,784,360	1.04	7,965,586	1.04	73,831,379	1.01	95,629,879	1.00
85–89	1,769,694	0.90	3,437,561	0.99	2,682,557	1.15	27,380,829	1.15	35,270,641	1.12
90–94	376,432	0.70	923,944	1.17	653,485	1.50	7,283,894	1.09	9,237,755	1.11
95 and over	148,553	0.14	174,583	0.52	156,860	0.69	1,413,745	0.92	1,893,741	0.77
Total	$272,275,255	1.25	$504,681,409	1.27	$315,706,821	1.23	$320,556,125	1.08	$1,413,219,610	1.17

TABLE 15

COMPARISON OF MALE AND FEMALE MORTALITY EXPERIENCE
FOR CALENDAR-YEARS 1987 AND 1988
EXPECTED MORTALITY BASIS—1983 GROUP ANNUITY MORTALITY

Attained Age	Exposure		A/E Ratio		Ratio of Female to Male Mortality
	Male	Female	Male*	Female	
		Lives			
Under 55	11,573.56	7,370.95	8.22	2.35	0.42
55–59	96,728.26	35,944.49	1.78	1.02	0.58
60–64	261,806.87	107,015.53	1.43	0.83	0.58
65–69	474,723.67	203,262.72	1.19	0.65	0.54
70–74	444,829.22	198,295.56	1.15	0.63	0.55
75–79	319,663.60	153,295.42	1.10	0.62	0.56
80–84	172,046.10	91,018.56	1.04	0.63	0.61
85–89	70,024.51	38,178.85	1.02	0.72	0.70
90–94	20,321.76	11,322.28	1.05	0.80	0.76
95 and over	4,115.08	2,538.86	0.96	0.73	0.76
Total..........	1,875,832.63	848,243.22	1.12	0.66	0.59
		Income			
Under 55	$ 76,379,747	$ 19,680,452	4.00	2.46	0.64
55–59	448,305,881	88,302,297	1.38	0.80	0.58
60–64	1,352,003,522	260,302,483	1.16	0.76	0.66
65–69	1,903,527,391	406,079,827	1.00	0.59	0.58
70–74	1,350,557,396	305,201,822	1.02	0.59	0.58
75–79	772,092,029	191,620,713	1.01	0.60	0.60
80–84	346,088,808	95,629,879	0.97	0.59	0.60
85–89	122,433,848	35,270,641	0.94	0.70	0.75
90–94	31,266,268	9,237,755	1.03	0.78	0.76
95 and over	5,277,731	1,893,741	0.91	0.67	0.73
Total..........	$6,407,932,621	$1,413,219,610	1.02	0.63	0.61

*Expected deaths for both males and females using male mortality.

TABLE 16

EXPERIENCE BY GUARANTEED STATUS FOR CALENDAR-YEAR 1987
EXPECTED MORTALITY BASIS—1983 GROUP ANNUITY MORTALITY

	Guaranteed		Nonguaranteed		Total	
Attained Age	Exposure	A/E Ratio	Exposure	A/E Ratio	Exposure	A/E Ratio
			Male Lives			
Under 55......	3,558.46	2.09	2,043.45	4.31	5,601.91	2.90
55–59	27,674.94	1.58	19,629.00	1.86	47,303.94	1.70
60–64	81,197.43	1.40	47,830.86	1.42	129,028.29	1.41
65–69	171,369.69	1.19	67,479.16	1.25	238,848.85	1.21
70–74	175,998.43	1.15	47,666.74	1.20	223,665.17	1.16
75–79	130,404.22	1.09	27,057.07	1.16	157,461.29	1.11
80–84	70,764.20	1.05	13,056.25	1.04	83,820.45	1.05
85–89	29,151.67	1.04	4,943.30	0.99	34,094.97	1.03
90–94	8,521.84	1.07	1,314.94	1.01	9,836.78	1.06
95 and over....	1,709.70	0.95	256.90	0.84	1,966.60	0.94
Total	700,350.58	1.11	231,277.67	1.18	931,628.25	1.13
			Male Income			
Under 55......	$ 19,731,888	1.85	$ 14,300,635	1.93	$ 34,032,523	1.88
55–59	110,755,546	1.26	99,403,030	1.25	210,158,576	1.26
60–64	343,479,035	1.19	294,790,111	1.07	638,269,146	1.14
65–69	597,059,183	0.99	326,948,596	1.03	924,007,779	1.01
70–74	467,899,537	1.02	184,036,999	1.11	651,936,536	1.04
75–79	279,160,261	1.01	87,208,557	1.09	366,368,818	1.03
80–84	128,870,464	0.99	33,752,087	0.98	162,622,551	0.99
85–89	47,870,171	0.94	10,808,768	0.89	58,678,939	0.93
90–94	12,269,284	1.07	2,562,690	1.03	14,831,974	1.06
95 and over....	2,059,159	0.91	450,228	0.90	2,509,387	0.90
Total	$2,009,154,528	1.02	$1,054,261,701	1.06	$3,063,416,229	1.03

TABLE 17

EXPERIENCE BY GUARANTEED STATUS FOR CALENDAR-YEAR 1987
EXPECTED MORTALITY BASIS—1983 GROUP ANNUITY MORTALITY

Attained Age	Guaranteed		Nonguaranteed		Total	
	Exposure	A/E Ratio	Exposure	A/E Ratio	Exposure	A/E Ratio
Female Lives						
Under 55......	2,510.48	5.64	1,103.67	4.80	3,614.15	5.37
55–59	11,291.38	2.25	6,490.24	2.35	17,781.62	2.29
60–64	37,119.01	1.78	16,107.98	1.95	53,226.99	1.83
65–69	76,146.34	1.52	25,093.85	1.48	101,240.19	1.51
70–74	80,272.13	1.29	18,170.22	1.21	98,442.35	1.28
75–79	62,893.89	1.14	11,858.75	0.98	74,752.64	1.11
80–84	37,070.02	1.09	6,530.03	1.08	43,600.05	1.09
85–89	15,559.15	1.14	2,477.13	1.17	18,036.28	1.14
90–94	4,704.17	1.19	691.37	1.10	5,395.54	1.18
95 and over....	1,022.60	0.85	154.57	0.65	1,177.17	0.83
Total	328,589.17	1.20	88,677.81	1.20	417,266.98	1.20
Female Income						
Under 55......	$ 6,293,569	3.78	$ 3,029,837	4.54	$ 9,323,406	4.02
55–59	24,326,957	1.72	17,596,260	1.37	41,923,217	1.57
60–64	76,901,189	1.69	46,513,986	2.33	123,415,175	1.93
65–69	135,578,764	1.46	57,495,820	1.33	193,074,584	1.42
70–74	112,188,481	1.21	33,218,048	1.28	145,406,529	1.22
75–79	70,825,327	1.13	19,169,559	1.00	89,994,886	1.10
80–84	35,320,510	1.00	9,016,633	0.97	44,337,143	1.00
85–89	12,938,109	1.14	3,301,827	1.06	16,239,936	1.12
90–94	3,527,836	1.21	827,054	0.92	4,354,890	1.16
95 and over....	697,453	0.82	170,205	0.48	867,658	0.76
Total	$478,598,195	1.20	$190,339,229	1.24	$668,937,424	1.21

TABLE 18

EXPERIENCE BY GUARANTEED STATUS FOR CALENDAR-YEAR 1988
EXPECTED MORTALITY BASIS—1983 GROUP ANNUITY MORTALITY

Attained Age	Guaranteed		Nonguaranteed		Total	
	Exposure	A/E Ratio	Exposure	A/E Ratio	Exposure	A/E Ratio
Male Lives						
Under 55	3,623.83	2.99	2,347.82	4.63	5,971.65	3.63
55–59	27,645.11	1.78	21,779.21	1.95	49,424.32	1.85
60–64	81,522.24	1.44	51,256.34	1.44	132,778.58	1.44
65–69	166,338.53	1.18	69,536.29	1.19	235,874.82	1.18
70–74	172,857.28	1.13	48,306.77	1.14	221,164.05	1.13
75–79	134,089.20	1.07	28,113.11	1.15	162,202.31	1.08
80–84	74,676.56	1.04	13,549.09	1.05	88,225.65	1.04
85–89	30,729.86	1.01	5,199.68	1.00	35,929.54	1.01
90–94	9,004.01	1.04	1,480.97	1.03	10,484.98	1.04
95 and over	1,874.74	1.03	273.74	0.62	2,148.48	0.97
Total	702,361.36	1.09	241,843.02	1.16	944,204.38	1.11
Male Income						
Under 55	$ 22,173,615	1.61	$ 20,173,609	1.94	$ 42,347,224	1.77
55–59	120,549,865	1.48	117,597,440	1.48	238,147,305	1.48
60–64	378,567,504	1.15	335,166,872	1.21	713,734,376	1.18
65–69	615,052,546	1.01	364,467,066	0.99	979,519,612	1.00
70–74	501,912,997	1.01	196,707,863	0.98	698,620,860	1.00
75–79	310,826,050	0.97	94,897,161	1.03	405,723,211	0.98
80–84	146,055,236	0.94	37,411,021	1.02	183,466,257	0.96
85–89	51,917,865	0.94	11,837,044	1.00	63,754,909	0.95
90–94	13,296,001	1.03	3,138,293	0.93	16,434,294	1.01
95 and over	2,261,155	0.99	507,189	0.60	2,768,344	0.91
Total	$2,162,612,834	1.00	$1,181,903,558	1.04	$3,344,516,392	1.01

TABLE 19

EXPERIENCE BY GUARANTEED STATUS FOR CALENDAR-YEAR 1988
EXPECTED MORTALITY BASIS—1983 GROUP ANNUITY MORTALITY

Attained Age	Guaranteed		Nonguaranteed		Total	
	Exposure	A/E Ratio	Exposure	A/E Ratio	Exposure	A/E Ratio
Female Lives						
Under 55......	2,653.13	3.33	1,103.67	4.32	3,756.80	3.63
55–59	11,760.43	2.58	6,402.44	1.95	18,162.87	2.36
60–64	37,776.78	1.80	16,011.76	1.60	53,788.54	1.74
65–69	77,088.33	1.46	24,934.20	1.33	102,022.53	1.43
70–74	81,532.52	1.31	18,320.69	1.23	99,853.21	1.30
75–79	66,585.36	1.10	11,957.42	1.09	78,542.78	1.10
80–84	40,718.67	1.06	6,699.84	1.04	47,418.51	1.06
85–89	17,452.15	1.14	2,690.42	1.15	20,142.57	1.14
90–94	5,186.68	1.11	740.06	1.02	5,926.74	1.10
95 and over....	1,195.11	0.92	166.58	0.69	1,361.69	0.89
Total	341,949.16	1.18	89,027.08	1.17	430,976.24	1.18
Female Income						
Under 55......	$ 7,137,024	4.12	$ 3,220,022	2.85	$ 10,357,046	3.73
55–59	28,459,562	2.34	17,919,518	1.56	46,379,080	2.04
60–64	87,509,537	1.42	49,377,771	1.28	136,887,308	1.37
65–69	149,975,357	1.31	63,029,886	1.07	213,005,243	1.24
70–74	124,335,368	1.22	35,459,925	1.18	159,795,293	1.21
75–79	81,506,951	1.05	20,118,876	1.05	101,625,827	1.05
80–84	41,544,049	0.98	9,748,687	1.06	51,292,736	0.99
85–89	15,372,942	1.14	3,657,763	1.04	19,030,705	1.12
90–94	3,923,716	1.06	959,149	1.08	4,882,865	1.07
95 and over....	824,168	0.87	201,915	0.45	1,026,083	0.79
Total	$540,588,674	1.14	$203,693,512	1.10	$744,282,186	1.13

TABLE 20

EXPERIENCE BY GUARANTEED STATUS FOR CALENDAR-YEARS 1987 AND 1988
EXPECTED MORTALITY BASIS—1983 GROUP ANNUITY MORTALITY

Attained Age	Guaranteed		Nonguaranteed		Total	
	Exposure	A/E Ratio	Exposure	A/E Ratio	Exposure	A/E Ratio
			Male Lives			
Under 55......	7,182.29	2.54	4,391.27	4.48	11,573.56	3.27
55–59	55,320.05	1.68	41,408.21	1.91	96,728.26	1.78
60–64	162,719.67	1.42	99,087.20	1.43	261,806.87	1.43
65–69	337,708.22	1.18	137,015.45	1.22	474,723.67	1.19
70–74	348,855.71	1.14	95,973.51	1.17	444,829.22	1.15
75–79	264,493.42	1.08	55,170.18	1.16	319,663.60	1.10
80–84	145,440.76	1.04	26,605.34	1.05	172,046.10	1.04
85–89	59,881.53	1.02	10,142.98	1.00	70,024.51	1.02
90–94	17,525.85	1.05	2,795.91	1.02	20,321.76	1.05
95 and over....	3,584.44	0.99	530.64	0.73	4,115.08	0.96
Total	1,402,711.94	1.10	473,120.69	1.17	1,875,832.63	1.12
			Male Income			
Under 55......	$ 41,905,503	1.72	$ 34,474,244	1.94	$ 76,379,747	1.82
55–59	231,305,411	1.37	217,000,470	1.38	448,305,881	1.38
60–64	722,046,539	1.17	629,956,983	1.14	1,352,003,522	1.16
65–69	1,212,111,729	1.00	691,415,662	1.01	1,903,527,391	1.00
70–74	969,812,534	1.01	380,744,862	1.04	1,350,557,396	1.02
75–79	589,986,311	0.99	182,105,718	1.06	772,092,029	1.01
80–84	274,925,700	0.97	71,163,108	1.00	346,088,808	0.97
85–89	99,788,036	0.94	22,645,812	0.95	122,433,848	0.94
90–94	25,565,285	1.05	5,700,983	0.98	31,266,268	1.03
95 and over....	4,320,314	0.95	957,417	0.74	5,277,731	0.91
Total	$4,171,767,362	1.01	$2,236,165,259	1.05	$6,407,932,621	1.02

TABLE 21

EXPERIENCE BY GUARANTEED STATUS FOR CALENDAR-YEARS 1987 AND 1988
EXPECTED MORTALITY BASIS—1983 GROUP ANNUITY MORTALITY

Attained Age	Guaranteed		Nonguaranteed		Total	
	Exposure	A/E Ratio	Exposure	A/E Ratio	Exposure	A/E Ratio
			Female Lives			
Under 55	5,163.61	4.46	2,207.34	4.56	7,370.95	4.50
55–59	23,051.81	2.42	12,892.68	2.15	35,944.49	2.32
60–64	74,895.79	1.79	32,119.74	1.78	107,015.53	1.79
65–69	153,234.67	1.49	50,028.05	1.40	203,262.72	1.47
70–74	161,804.65	1.30	36,490.91	1.22	198,295.56	1.29
75–79	129,479.25	1.12	23,816.17	1.03	153,295.42	1.11
80–84	77,788.69	1.07	13,229.87	1.06	91,018.56	1.07
85–89	33,011.30	1.14	5,167.55	1.16	38,178.85	1.14
90–94	9,890.85	1.15	1,431.43	1.06	11,322.28	1.14
95 and over	2,217.71	0.89	321.15	0.67	2,538.86	0.86
Total	670,538.33	1.19	177,704.89	1.19	848,243.22	1.19
			Female Income			
Under 55	$ 13,430,593	3.96	$ 6,249,859	3.68	$ 19,680,452	3.87
55–59	52,786,519	2.05	35,515,778	1.47	88,302,297	1.82
60–64	164,410,726	1.55	95,891,757	1.79	260,302,483	1.64
65–69	285,554,121	1.38	120,525,706	1.19	406,079,827	1.33
70–74	236,523,849	1.21	68,677,973	1.23	305,201,822	1.22
75–79	152,332,278	1.09	39,288,435	1.03	191,620,713	1.08
80–84	76,864,559	0.99	18,765,320	1.02	95,629,879	1.00
85–89	28,311,051	1.14	6,959,590	1.05	35,270,641	1.12
90–94	7,451,552	1.14	1,786,203	1.01	9,237,755	1.11
95 and over	1,521,621	0.85	372,120	0.46	1,893,741	0.77
Total	$1,019,186,869	1.17	$394,032,741	1.17	$1,413,219,610	1.17

TABLE 22

SUMMARY OF GROUP ANNUITY MORTALITY EXPERIENCE BY MALE LIVES
EXPECTED MORTALITY BASIS—1983 GROUP ANNUITY MORTALITY

	1987		1988		Change in A/E Ratios
	Exposure	A/E Ratio	Exposure	A/E Ratio	
Total	931,628	1.13	944,204	1.11	−0.02
By Retirement Class					
Prior to NRD	367,326	1.14	361,921	1.14	0.00
On/After NRD	336,587	1.07	333,584	1.06	−0.01
No Stated NRD	225,642	1.21	246,446	1.15	−0.06
Past NRD/No Payment	2,073	1.10	2,254	0.92	−0.18
By Benefit Class					
Life	618,689	1.14	637,212	1.12	−0.02
Life and Certain	159,124	1.10	156,133	1.10	0.00
Modified Cash Refund	153,815	1.10	150,859	1.05	−0.05
By Survivor Class					
Single Life	696,845	1.13	693,110	1.11	−0.02
Joint Life	234,783	1.09	251,094	1.09	0.00
By Years Since Retirement					
0–1	126,217	1.18	113,562	1.21	0.03
2–5	260,880	1.15	269,793	1.18	0.03
6–10	240,549	1.15	242,322	1.13	−0.02
11+	303,982	1.10	318,527	1.07	−0.03
By Attained Age					
Under 55	5,602	2.90	5,972	3.63	0.73
55–59	47,304	1.70	49,424	1.85	0.15
60–64	129,028	1.41	132,779	1.44	0.03
65–69	238,849	1.21	235,875	1.18	−0.03
70–74	223,665	1.16	221,164	1.13	−0.03
75–79	157,461	1.11	162,202	1.08	−0.03
80–84	83,820	1.05	88,226	1.04	−0.01
85–89	34,095	1.03	35,930	1.01	−0.02
90–94	9,837	1.06	10,485	1.04	−0.02
95 and Over	1,967	0.94	2,148	0.97	0.03
Comparison of Female/ Male		0.59		0.59	0.00

TABLE 23

SUMMARY OF GROUP ANNUITY MORTALITY EXPERIENCE BY MALE INCOME
EXPECTED MORTALITY BASIS—1983 GROUP ANNUITY MORTALITY

	1987		1988		Change in A/E Ratios
	Exposure	A/E Ratio	Exposure	A/E Ratio	
Total	$3,063,416,229	1.03	$3,344,516,392	1.01	−0.02
By Retirement Class					
Prior to NRD	$1,283,736,959	1.00	$1,356,599,134	1.01	0.01
On/After NRD	949,566,524	0.97	1,009,758,150	0.97	0.00
No Stated NRD	825,063,803	1.14	972,292,817	1.07	−0.07
Past NRD/No Payment	5,048,943	0.98	5,866,291	0.59	−0.39
By Benefit Class					
Life	$2,101,781,301	1.03	$2,331,074,776	1.03	0.00
Life and Certain	470,508,319	1.00	494,072,969	1.00	0.00
Modified Cash Refund	491,126,609	1.04	519,368,647	0.94	−0.10
By Survivor Class					
Single Life	$1,931,101,299	1.04	$2,058,257,743	1.02	−0.02
Joint Life	1,132,314,930	0.99	1,286,258,649	0.98	−0.01
By Years Since Retirement					
0–1	$ 653,284,079	0.95	$ 622,253,807	0.97	0.02
2–5	1,068,560,661	0.99	1,251,389,614	1.03	0.04
6–10	700,905,670	1.07	756,444,796	1.03	−0.04
11+	640,665,819	1.05	714,428,175	1.00	−0.05
By Attained Age					
Under 55	$ 34,032,523	1.88	$ 42,347,224	1.77	−0.11
55–59	210,158,576	1.26	238,147,305	1.48	0.22
60–64	638,269,146	1.14	713,734,376	1.18	0.04
65–69	924,007,779	1.01	979,519,612	1.00	−0.01
70–74	651,936,536	1.04	698,620,860	1.00	−0.04
75–79	366,368,818	1.03	405,723,211	0.98	−0.05
80–84	162,622,551	0.99	183,466,257	0.96	−0.03
85–89	58,678,939	0.93	63,754,909	0.95	0.02
90–94	14,831,974	1.06	16,434,294	1.01	−0.05
95 and Over	2,509,387	0.90	2,768,344	0.91	0.01
Comparison of Female/ Male		0.63		0.60	−0.03

TABLE 24

SUMMARY OF GROUP ANNUITY MORTALITY EXPERIENCE BY FEMALE LIVES
EXPECTED MORTALITY BASIS—1983 GROUP ANNUITY MORTALITY

	1987		1988		Change in A/E Ratios
	Exposure	A/E Ratio	Exposure	A/E Ratio	
Total	417,267	1.20	430,976	1.18	−0.02
By Retirement Class					
Prior to NRD	149,648	1.33	150,538	1.25	−0.08
On/After NRD	166,820	1.14	168,888	1.14	0.00
No Stated NRD	99,737	1.21	110,394	1.18	−0.03
Past NRD/No Payment	1,061	1.59	1,156	0.87	−0.72
By Benefit Class					
Life	286,898	1.19	296,778	1.17	−0.02
Life and Certain	58,023	1.24	60,453	1.18	−0.06
Modified Cash Refund	72,346	1.23	73,745	1.20	−0.03
By Survivor Class					
Single Life	394,053	1.20	405,044	1.17	−0.03
Joint Life	23,214	1.38	25,932	1.28	−0.10
By Years Since Retirement					
0–1	53,979	1.37	48,701	1.23	−0.14
2–5	117,254	1.30	121,569	1.33	0.03
6–10	102,447	1.27	106,348	1.23	−0.04
11+	143,587	1.14	154,358	1.12	−0.02
By Attained Age					
Under 55	3,614	5.37	3,757	3.63	−1.74
55–59	17,782	2.29	18,163	2.36	0.07
60–64	53,227	1.83	53,789	1.74	−0.09
65–69	101,240	1.51	102,023	1.43	−0.08
70–74	98,442	1.28	99,853	1.30	0.02
75–79	74,753	1.11	78,543	1.10	−0.01
80–84	43,600	1.09	47,419	1.06	−0.03
85–89	18,036	1.14	20,143	1.14	0.00
90–94	5,396	1.18	5,927	1.10	−0.08
95 and Over	1,177	0.83	1,362	0.89	0.06

TABLE 25

SUMMARY OF GROUP ANNUITY MORTALITY EXPERIENCE BY FEMALE INCOME
EXPECTED MORTALITY BASIS—1983 GROUP ANNUITY MORTALITY

	1987		1988		Change in A/E Ratios
	Exposure	A/E Ratio	Exposure	A/E Ratio	
Total	$668,937,424	1.21	$744,282,186	1.13	−0.08
By Retirement Class					
Prior to NRD	$268,837,073	1.41	$287,791,069	1.16	−0.25
On/After NRD	230,264,401	1.12	251,443,806	1.11	−0.01
No Stated NRD	168,195,323	1.19	203,169,816	1.16	−0.03
Past NRD/No Payment	1,640,627	1.47	1,877,495	0.89	−0.58
By Benefit Class					
Life	$461,058,559	1.19	$516,140,470	1.14	−0.05
Life and Certain	92,519,203	1.32	103,860,773	1.14	−0.18
Modified Cash Refund	115,359,662	1.20	124,280,943	1.10	−0.10
By Survivor Class					
Single Life	$615,652,587	1.18	$680,240,229	1.13	−0.05
Joint Life	53,284,837	1.81	64,041,957	1.16	−0.65
By Years Since Retirement					
0–1	$136,484,624	1.42	$135,790,631	1.08	−0.34
2–5	233,378,967	1.27	271,302,442	1.27	0.00
6–10	148,977,259	1.28	166,729,562	1.19	−0.09
11+	150,096,574	1.10	170,459,551	1.06	−0.04
By Attained Age					
Under 55	$ 9,323,406	4.02	$ 10,357,046	3.73	−0.29
55–59	41,923,217	1.57	46,379,080	2.04	0.47
60–64	123,415,175	1.93	136,887,308	1.37	−0.56
65–69	193,074,584	1.42	213,005,243	1.24	−0.18
70–74	145,406,529	1.22	159,795,293	1.21	−0.01
75–79	89,994,886	1.10	101,625,827	1.05	−0.05
80–84	44,337,143	1.00	51,292,736	0.99	−0.01
85–89	16,239,936	1.12	19,030,705	1.12	0.00
90–94	4,354,890	1.16	4,882,865	1.07	−0.09
95 and Over	867,658	0.76	1,026,083	0.79	0.03

TABLE 26

COMPARISON OF 1988–87 WITH 1986–85 GROUP ANNUITY MORTALITY EXPERIENCE BY MALE LIVES
EXPECTED MORTALITY BASIS—1983 GROUP ANNUITY MORTALITY

	1985–86		1987–88		Change in A/E Ratios
	Exposure	A/E Ratio	Exposure	A/E Ratio	
Total	1,731,887	1.20	1,875,833	1.12	−0.08
By Retirement Class					
Prior to NRD	688,837	1.21	729,247	1.14	−0.07
On/After NRD	591,855	1.15	670,171	1.07	−0.08
No Stated NRD	447,764	1.25	472,087	1.18	−0.07
Past NRD/No Payment	3,431	0.96	4,327	1.01	0.05
By Benefit Class					
Life	1,099,672	1.22	1,255,901	1.13	−0.09
Life and Certain	322,075	1.17	315,257	1.10	−0.07
Modified Cash Refund	310,140	1.15	304,674	1.07	−0.08
By Survivor Class					
Single Life	1,344,803	1.20	1,389,955	1.12	−0.08
Joint Life	387,085	1.18	485,877	1.09	−0.09
By Years Since Retirement					
0–1	224,474	1.39	239,779	1.20	−0.19
2–5	495,269	1.27	530,674	1.16	−0.11
6–10	469,701	1.19	482,871	1.14	−0.05
11+	542,444	1.15	622,509	1.09	−0.06
By Attained Age					
Under 55	8,633	3.41	11,574	3.27	−0.14
55–59	87,402	1.98	96,728	1.78	−0.20
60–64	245,969	1.58	261,807	1.43	−0.15
65–69	452,089	1.32	474,724	1.19	−0.13
70–74	423,736	1.22	444,829	1.15	−0.07
75–79	283,219	1.17	319,664	1.10	−0.07
80–84	149,978	1.10	172,046	1.04	−0.06
85–89	60,104	1.07	70,025	1.02	−0.05
90–94	17,493	1.09	20,322	1.05	−0.04
95 and Over	3,263	0.93	4,115	0.96	0.03
Comparison of Female/ Male		0.58		0.59	0.01

TABLE 27

COMPARISON OF 1988–87 WITH 1986–85 GROUP ANNUITY MORTALITY EXPERIENCE BY MALE INCOME
EXPECTED MORTALITY BASIS—1983 GROUP ANNUITY MORTALITY

	1985–86		1987–88		Change in A/E Ratios
	Exposure	A/E Ratio	Exposure	A/E Ratio	
Total	$5,153,766,061	1.11	$6,407,932,621	1.02	−0.09
By Retirement Class					
Prior to NRD	$2,129,167,573	1.08	$2,640,336,093	1.00	−0.08
On/After NRD	1,571,792,007	1.05	1,959,324,674	0.97	−0.08
No Stated NRD	1,445,143,739	1.20	1,797,356,620	1.10	−0.10
Past NRD/No Payment	7,662,742	0.80	10,915,234	0.78	−0.02
By Benefit Class					
Life	$3,392,712,656	1.12	$4,432,856,077	1.03	−0.09
Life and Certain	873,202,053	1.10	964,581,288	1.00	−0.10
Modified Cash Refund	887,851,352	1.06	1,010,495,256	0.99	−0.07
By Survivor Class					
Single Life	$3,432,604,062	1.12	$3,989,359,042	1.03	−0.09
Joint Life	1,721,161,999	1.07	2,418,573,579	0.99	−0.08
By Years Since Retirement					
0–1	$1,010,611,789	1.16	$1,275,537,886	0.96	−0.20
2–5	1,804,023,032	1.13	2,319,950,275	1.01	−0.12
6–10	1,264,646,786	1.09	1,457,350,466	1.05	−0.04
11+	1,074,484,454	1.09	1,355,093,994	1.02	−0.07
By Attained Age					
Under 55	$ 49,839,419	2.21	$ 76,379,747	1.82	−0.39
55–59	321,767,628	1.68	448,305,881	1.38	−0.30
60–64	1,064,744,662	1.26	1,352,003,522	1.16	−0.10
65–69	1,567,252,932	1.14	1,903,527,391	1.00	−0.14
70–74	1,128,312,550	1.11	1,350,557,396	1.02	−0.09
75–79	622,456,740	1.07	772,092,029	1.01	−0.06
80–84	273,825,778	1.03	346,088,808	0.97	−0.06
85–89	97,931,850	0.98	122,433,848	0.94	−0.04
90–94	23,811,818	1.10	31,266,268	1.03	−0.07
95 and Over	3,822,684	0.93	5,277,731	0.91	−0.02
Comparison of Female/ Male		0.61		0.61	0.00

TABLE 28

COMPARISON OF 1987–88 WITH 1986–85 GROUP ANNUITY MORTALITY EXPERIENCE
BY FEMALE LIVES
EXPECTED MORTALITY BASIS—1983 GROUP ANNUITY MORTALITY

	1985–86		1987–88		Change in A/E Ratios
	Exposure	A/E Ratio	Exposure	A/E Ratio	
Total	762,736	1.26	848,243	1.19	−0.07
By Retirement Class					
Prior to NRD	271,830	1.35	300,186	1.29	−0.06
On/After NRD	286,492	1.24	335,708	1.14	−0.10
No Stated NRD	202,714	1.23	210,132	1.20	−0.03
Past NRD/No Payment	1,701	1.38	2,218	1.22	−0.16
By Benefit Class					
Life	506,796	1.28	583,676	1.18	−0.10
Life and Certain	113,179	1.19	118,476	1.21	0.02
Modified Cash Refund	142,762	1.27	146,091	1.21	−0.06
By Survivor Class					
Single Life	727,581	1.26	799,097	1.18	−0.08
Joint Life	35,156	1.46	49,146	1.32	−0.14
By Years Since Retirement					
0–1	96,298	1.56	102,680	1.30	−0.26
2–5	212,058	1.45	238,823	1.32	−0.13
6–10	206,708	1.29	208,795	1.25	−0.04
11+	247,672	1.18	297,945	1.13	−0.05
By Attained Age					
Under 55	6,048	3.83	7,371	4.50	0.67
55–59	33,729	2.37	35,944	2.32	−0.05
60–64	101,063	1.91	107,016	1.79	−0.12
65–69	189,201	1.58	203,263	1.47	−0.11
70–74	184,051	1.35	198,296	1.29	−0.06
75–79	134,016	1.18	153,295	1.11	−0.07
80–84	74,226	1.12	91,019	1.07	−0.05
85–89	29,743	1.19	38,179	1.14	−0.05
90–94	8,853	1.20	11,322	1.14	−0.06
95 and Over	1,806	0.92	2,539	0.86	−0.06

TABLE 29

COMPARISON OF 1987–88 WITH 1986–85 GROUP ANNUITY MORTALITY EXPERIENCE
BY FEMALE INCOME
EXPECTED MORTALITY BASIS—1983 GROUP ANNUITY MORTALITY

	1985–86		1987–88		Change in A/E Ratios
	Exposure	A/E Ratio	Exposure	A/E Ratio	
Total	$1,117,058,261	1.26	$1,413,219,610	1.17	−0.09
By Retirement Class					
Prior to NRD	$ 436,404,843	1.33	$ 556,628,142	1.28	−0.05
On/After NRD	367,840,600	1.23	481,708,207	1.11	−0.12
No Stated NRD	310,198,857	1.25	371,365,139	1.17	−0.08
Past NRD/No Payment	2,613,961	1.32	3,518,122	1.16	−0.16
By Benefit Class					
Life	$ 741,285,598	1.25	$ 977,199,029	1.16	−0.09
Life and Certain	167,697,480	1.21	196,379,976	1.22	0.01
Modified Cash Refund	208,075,183	1.36	239,640,605	1.15	−0.21
By Survivor Class					
Single Life	$1,038,510,547	1.25	$1,295,892,816	1.15	−0.10
Joint Life	78,547,714	1.52	117,326,794	1.45	−0.07
By Years Since Retirement					
0–1	$ 215,695,919	1.42	$ 272,275,255	1.25	−0.17
2–5	381,852,852	1.44	504,681,409	1.27	−0.17
6–10	277,805,627	1.28	315,706,821	1.23	−0.05
11+	241,703,863	1.14	320,556,125	1.08	−0.06
By Attained Age					
Under 55	$ 14,728,293	2.24	$ 19,680,452	3.87	1.63
55–59	69,492,070	2.07	88,302,297	1.82	−0.25
60–64	208,456,099	1.69	260,302,483	1.64	−0.05
65–69	322,346,511	1.48	406,079,827	1.33	−0.15
70–74	250,167,590	1.33	305,201,822	1.22	−0.11
75–79	149,126,796	1.14	191,620,713	1.08	−0.06
80–84	70,062,715	1.05	95,629,879	1.00	−0.05
85–89	24,950,298	1.18	35,270,641	1.12	−0.06
90–94	6,479,765	1.23	9,237,755	1.11	−0.12
95 and Over	1,248,124	0.89	1,893,741	0.77	−0.12

TABLE 30

SUMMARY OF MORTALITY IMPROVEMENT FOR MALE LIVES
FOR CALENDAR-YEARS 1983 TO 1988
EXPECTED MORTALITY BASIS—1983 GROUP ANNUITY MORTALITY

	A/E Ratio						Annual Improvement Factors					
Attained Age	1988	1987	1986	1985	1984	1983	1988 to 1987	1987 to 1986	1986 to 1985	1985 to 1984	1984 to 1983	Arithmetic Average
Under 55.....	3.63	2.90	2.87	4.00	3.36	3.63	−0.253	−0.009	0.283	−0.192	0.073	−0.019
55–59........	1.85	1.70	1.92	2.04	2.14	2.23	−0.091	0.118	0.057	0.045	0.042	0.034
60–64........	1.44	1.41	1.51	1.64	1.68	1.75	−0.023	0.066	0.081	0.022	0.042	0.038
65–69........	1.18	1.21	1.26	1.39	1.37	1.41	0.021	0.040	0.096	−0.013	0.029	0.035
70–74........	1.13	1.16	1.13	1.31	1.31	1.32	0.027	−0.026	0.131	0.002	0.012	0.029
75–79........	1.08	1.11	1.10	1.25	1.24	1.28	0.020	−0.006	0.117	−0.005	0.034	0.032
80–84........	1.04	1.05	1.06	1.14	1.14	1.13	0.006	0.013	0.069	−0.003	−0.005	0.016
85–89........	1.01	1.03	0.99	1.15	1.15	1.15	0.025	−0.042	0.140	0.000	−0.001	0.025
90–94........	1.04	1.06	1.01	1.18	1.18	1.15	0.020	−0.046	0.139	0.001	−0.023	0.018
95 and over...	0.97	0.94	0.81	1.06	1.08	1.06	−0.036	−0.161	0.239	0.019	−0.021	0.008
Total	1.11	1.13	1.13	1.27	1.27	1.29	0.016	0.000	0.113	0.001	0.016	0.029

TABLE 31

SUMMARY OF MORTALITY IMPROVEMENT FOR MALE INCOME
FOR CALENDAR-YEARS 1983 TO 1988
EXPECTED MORTALITY BASIS—1983 GROUP ANNUITY MORTALITY

Attained Age	A/E Ratio						Annual Improvement Factors					
	1988	1987	1986	1985	1984	1983	1988 to 1987	1987 to 1986	1986 to 1985	1985 to 1984	1984 to 1983	Arithmetic Average
Under 55	1.77	1.88	1.78	2.73	2.63	2.46	0.060	−0.054	0.346	−0.039	−0.067	0.049
55–59........	1.48	1.26	1.68	1.69	1.76	1.86	−0.177	0.249	0.007	0.043	0.050	0.035
60–64........	1.18	1.14	1.21	1.31	1.27	1.37	−0.037	0.063	0.073	−0.032	0.072	0.028
65–69........	1.00	1.01	1.09	1.20	1.19	1.27	0.008	0.078	0.087	−0.004	0.061	0.046
70–74........	1.00	1.04	1.03	1.19	1.22	1.21	0.038	−0.013	0.139	0.022	−0.011	0.035
75–79........	0.98	1.03	1.01	1.14	1.14	1.18	0.047	−0.018	0.112	0.004	0.031	0.035
80–84........	0.96	0.99	1.03	1.03	1.03	1.07	0.034	0.038	0.001	−0.006	0.041	0.022
85–89........	0.95	0.93	0.93	1.05	1.09	1.10	−0.019	−0.005	0.115	0.039	0.009	0.028
90–94........	1.01	1.06	1.00	1.21	1.19	1.13	0.054	−0.066	0.174	−0.012	−0.061	0.018
95 and over...	0.91	0.90	0.77	1.09	0.98	1.17	−0.005	−0.168	0.289	−0.116	0.164	0.033
Total	1.01	1.03	1.05	1.17	1.17	1.21	0.018	0.023	0.097	0.005	0.029	0.035

TABLE 32

SUMMARY OF MORTALITY IMPROVEMENT FOR FEMALE LIVES FOR CALENDAR-YEARS 1983 TO 1988 EXPECTED MORTALITY BASIS—1983 GROUP ANNUITY MORTALITY

Attained Age	A/E Ratio						Annual Improvement Factors					
	1988	1987	1986	1985	1984	1983	1988 to 1987	1987 to 1986	1986 to 1985	1985 to 1984	1984 to 1983	Arithmetic Average
Under 55	3.63	5.37	4.00	3.65	4.87	3.04	0.324	−0.344	−0.095	0.250	−0.604	−0.094
55–59	2.36	2.29	2.11	2.62	2.69	2.72	−0.032	−0.084	0.197	0.024	0.011	0.023
60–64	1.74	1.83	1.75	2.06	1.77	2.00	0.049	−0.045	0.148	−0.160	0.114	0.021
65–69	1.43	1.51	1.50	1.65	1.63	1.67	0.053	−0.005	0.091	−0.016	0.025	0.029
70–74	1.30	1.28	1.30	1.40	1.41	1.37	−0.014	0.018	0.072	0.005	−0.033	0.010
75–79	1.10	1.11	1.13	1.24	1.22	1.19	0.009	0.016	0.087	−0.012	−0.031	0.014
80–84	1.06	1.09	1.06	1.18	1.16	1.19	0.031	−0.024	0.097	−0.015	0.022	0.022
85–89	1.14	1.14	1.12	1.25	1.28	1.21	−0.002	−0.015	0.105	0.018	−0.053	0.010
90–94	1.10	1.18	1.16	1.24	1.26	1.13	0.068	−0.019	0.069	0.015	−0.116	0.003
95 and over	0.89	0.83	0.93	0.90	0.94	1.03	−0.078	0.114	−0.035	0.039	0.091	0.026
Total	1.18	1.20	1.20	1.33	1.32	1.32	0.022	0.000	0.095	−0.004	−0.004	0.022

TABLE 33

SUMMARY OF MORTALITY IMPROVEMENT FOR FEMALE INCOME FOR CALENDAR-YEARS 1983 TO 1988

EXPECTED MORTALITY BASIS—1983 GROUP ANNUITY MORTALITY

Attained Age	A/E Ratio						Annual Improvement Factors					
	1988	1987	1986	1985	1984	1983	1988 to 1987	1987 to 1986	1986 to 1985	1985 to 1984	1984 to 1983	Arithmetic Average
Under 55	3.73	4.02	2.19	2.30	3.47	1.96	0.072	−0.836	0.047	0.338	−0.768	−0.229
55–59	2.04	1.57	1.94	2.22	2.03	2.77	−0.300	0.191	0.125	−0.090	0.265	0.038
60–64	1.37	1.93	1.67	1.71	1.75	1.86	0.289	−0.157	0.026	0.020	0.058	0.047
65–69	1.24	1.42	1.38	1.59	1.65	1.48	0.130	−0.033	0.136	0.036	−0.118	0.030
70–74	1.21	1.22	1.25	1.42	1.32	1.30	0.010	0.025	0.116	−0.073	−0.016	0.012
75–79	1.05	1.10	1.09	1.18	1.17	1.17	0.046	−0.009	0.077	−0.011	−0.005	0.019
80–84	0.99	1.00	1.02	1.08	1.15	1.20	0.001	0.028	0.052	0.060	0.038	0.036
85–89	1.12	1.12	1.17	1.19	1.31	1.17	−0.003	0.042	0.015	0.092	−0.114	0.006
90–94	1.07	1.16	1.17	1.30	1.23	1.23	0.080	0.005	0.106	−0.062	0.002	0.026
95 and over	0.79	0.76	0.90	0.88	0.83	1.14	−0.041	0.161	−0.020	−0.061	0.270	0.062
Total	1.13	1.21	1.21	1.32	1.33	1.32	0.060	0.001	0.086	0.011	−0.012	0.029

CHART I

SUMMARY OF MORTALITY IMPROVEMENT FOR MALES LIVES
FOR CALENDAR-YEARS 1983 THROUGH 1988
EXPECTED MORTALITY BASIS—1983 GROUP ANNUITY MORTALITY

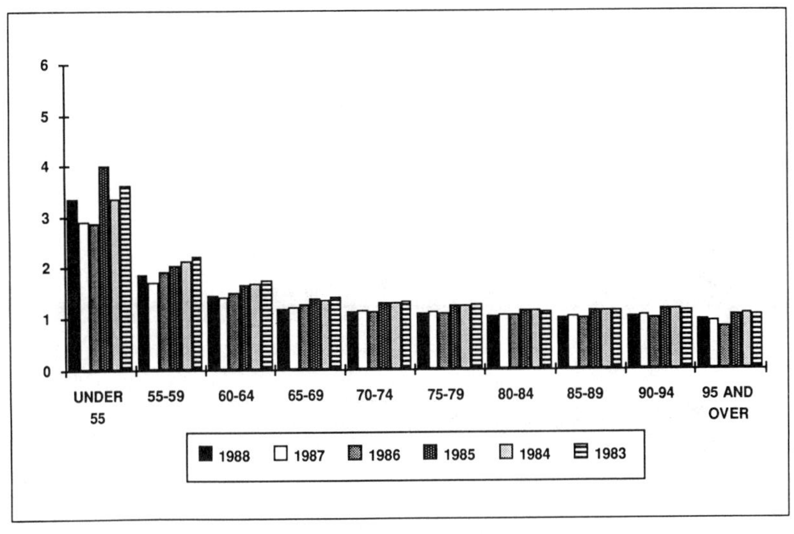

CHART II

SUMMARY OF MORTALITY IMPROVEMENT FOR MALE INCOME
FOR CALENDAR-YEARS 1983 THROUGH 1988
EXPECTED MORTALITY BASIS—1983 GROUP ANNUITY MORTALITY

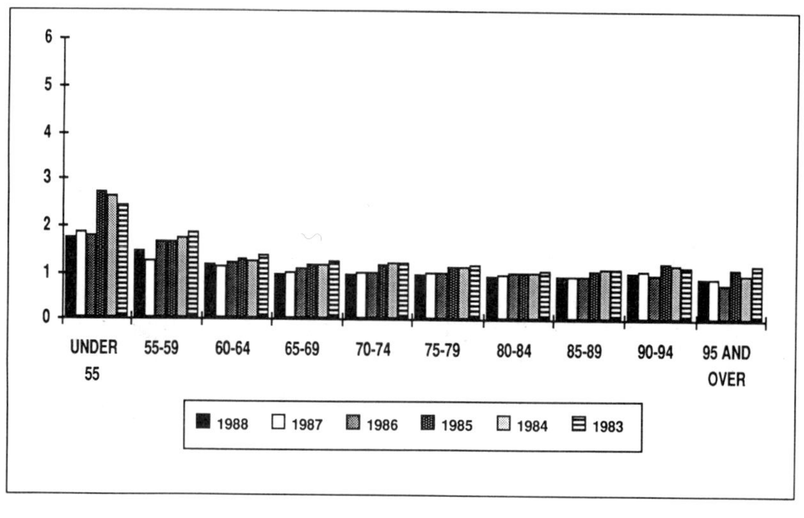

CHART III

SUMMARY OF MORTALITY IMPROVEMENT FOR FEMALE LIVES
FOR CALENDAR-YEARS 1983 THROUGH 1988
EXPECTED MORTALITY BASIS—1983 GROUP ANNUITY MORTALITY

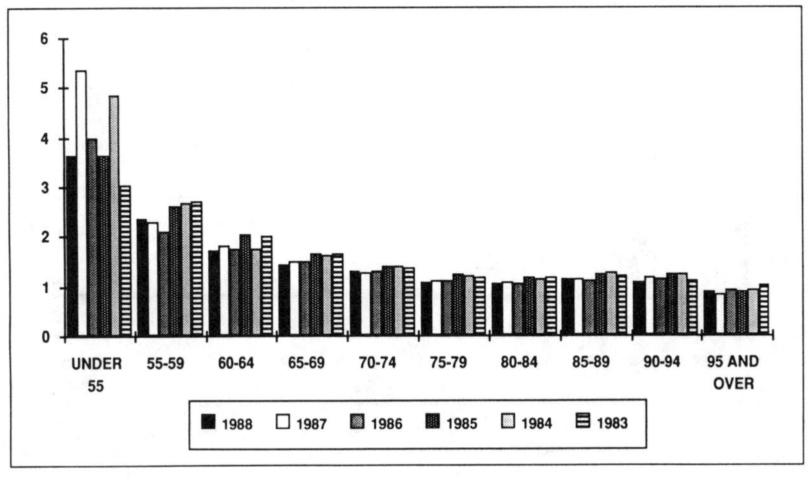

CHART IV

SUMMARY OF MORTALITY IMPROVEMENT FOR FEMALE INCOME
FOR CALENDAR-YEARS 1983 THROUGH 1988
EXPECTED MORTALITY BASIS—1983 GROUP ANNUITY MORTALITY

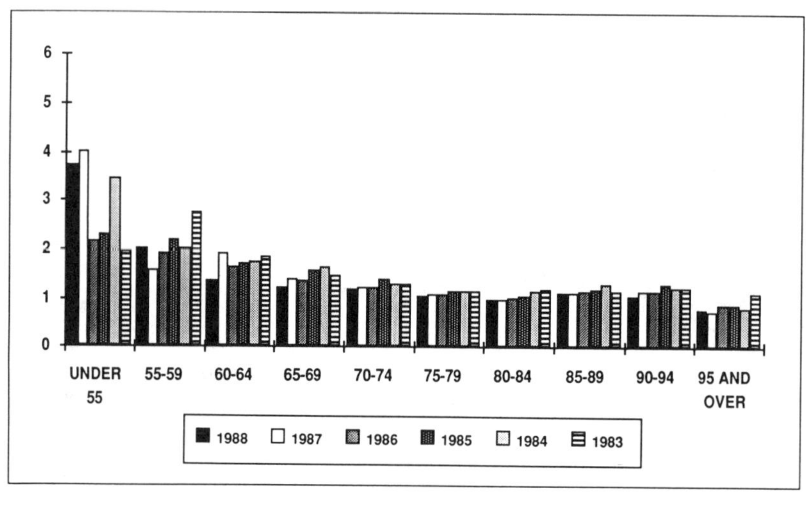

REPORT OF THE LONG-TERM-CARE EXPERIENCE COMMITTEE

1985 NATIONAL NURSING HOME SURVEY UTILIZATION DATA

I. INTRODUCTION

This report presents results of tabulations from the 1985 National Nursing Home Survey (NNHS). The tabulations are designed to estimate nursing home admission rates, average lengths-of-stay, and continuance tables, which together are referred to as utilization data. The purpose of this report is to establish a complete "baseline" set of utilization data that can be used in actuarial models and as a basis of comparison with other experience.

This is not an attempt to develop utilization data that are directly appropriate for the pricing or reserving of long-term-care (LTC) insurance products, although the data could be used as a basis from which such rates can be derived. In particular, the rates apply to the general population, not an insured population. Also, the general population experience relates to a largely uninsured environment under which nursing home residents had to pay for their own care or impoverish themselves before Medicaid would pay. Further, the rates do not reflect the effect of policy provisions that limit benefits to nursing home residents who meet certain criteria, such as the failure of activities of daily living (ADLs), medical necessity, or a prior hospital stay. Finally, these rates are for 1985 and reflect the conditions at that time. Through time, changes in the nursing home bed supply, the general level of health of succeeding cohorts of the population, and the availability of spouses and nonworking children as caregivers will influence future utilization rates.

Nevertheless, three sets of tabulations of admission rates and length-of-stay distributions have been made in a manner that is useful for those who are interested in LTC insurance. The first two sets include all patients in the survey. The first set is based on the "stay" concept, and the second set is based on the "benefit period" concept. Under the stay concept, each admission and discharge is treated independently, while under the benefit period concept, stays that are interrupted only because the patient transferred from one nursing home to another or from one nursing home to a hospital and then to another nursing home are treated as one benefit period. The benefit period concept is more appropriate for measuring the effects of deductible periods and lifetime maximums.

These first two sets of tabulations are representative of the general U.S. population and thus include persons with types of conditions that would preclude being issued insurance and persons with a diagnosis that would not be covered under LTC insurance policies. The third set of rates was compiled excluding these patients. In particular, this set excludes the experience of patients whose only condition is mental (although Alzheimer's Disease and other organic brain syndrome are included), is congenital, or involves substance abuse. The mentally retarded, who represent a significant proportion of patients under age 65, are excluded.

Each set of utilization data has been calculated independently. Thus, each set of admission rates, average lengths-of-stay, and continuance tables has been calculated from the basic data to be consistent within each set. Other subsets are also possible, such as including only those admissions that follow a three-day hospital stay or only those where the patient fails three ADLs, and so on, but these subsets are not included in this report.

II. THE 1985 NATIONAL NURSING HOME SURVEY

The 1985 National Nursing Home Survey was a nationwide (excluding Alaska and Hawaii) sample survey conducted by the National Center for Health Statistics (NCHS) between August 1985 and January 1986, with an average date of interview of October 11, 1985. It is the third and most recent in a series of periodic surveys of nursing and related care homes and their residents, discharges, and staffs. The first survey was conducted in 1973–74, and the second was conducted in 1977. The 1985 survey contains many more questions than the prior surveys, so that the analysis done here is not possible with the earlier surveys.

Data from the 1985 resident survey and the 1985 discharge survey were used in this report. The surveys cover all types of nursing homes without regard to the level of care they provide, whether they participate in the Medicare or Medicaid program, or whether they are licensed. It does not include homes for the aged, community care facilities, congregate living facilities, adult foster homes, or other residential facilities without nursing care.

The survey was based on a stratified two-stage probability sample. In the first stage, a stratified random sample of facilities was selected from four components: (1) the base, a national inventory maintained by the National

Center for Health Facilities, called the 1982 National Master Facility Inventory (NMFI); (2) the 1982 Complement Survey, which identified homes missed in the NMFI; (3) hospital-based homes identified by the Health Care Financing Administration (HCFA); and (4) homes opened for business between 1982 and June 1, 1984. This frame resulted in an universe of 20,479 nursing and related care facilities. The strata in the selection process were certified versus not certified and number of beds, with large certified homes being the most likely to be selected. This selection process resulted in 1,079 facilities being surveyed.

In the second stage, random samples of residents and discharges were selected from each of the chosen facilities. This process resulted in 5,243 current residents and 6,023 discharged residents from the 1,079 facilities included in the survey. Each of the responses was given a weight that reflected the probability with which the facility was chosen and the proportion of residents chosen from each facility, so that the total weighted responses represented the 48 contiguous states and the District of Columbia.

Information was obtained from each chosen facility through a Facility Questionnaire, from (or about) the chosen residents through a Current Resident Questionnaire, and from the sample of patients discharged through a Discharged Resident Questionnaire. Each questionnaire included questions seeking detailed information on the characteristics of the residents and the facilities. These surveys are referred to as simply the facility survey, the resident survey, and the discharge survey.

The Current Resident Questionnaire included questions on:

- Basic demographic information, such as current age, sex, race, marital status.
- Information on the date of admission and residence before the most recent admission to the nursing home. Up to eight prior stays in the patient's current facility and up to three stays in up to three different facilities are recorded. Thus, information is contained on a possible 18 stays in all.
- Current condition of the patient, including a primary and up to seven secondary diagnoses.
- Information on the primary and up to seven secondary diagnoses at the time of admission.
- Information on the patient's ability to perform Activities of Daily Living (ADLs).

- Information on therapies currently being received and sources of funds for payment.

The Discharged Resident Questionnaire contains much of the same information as the Current Resident Questionnaire, plus the date of discharge and residence after leaving the facility. The discharge survey, however, does not have detailed information on the patient's ability to perform ADLs. It only asks whether the patient was bedfast, chairfast, or continent at the time of discharge.

III. METHODOLOGY AND RESULTS

The nursing home admission rates developed in this report are by sex and single years of age, from age 30 through age 110. The length-of-stay distributions were developed by sex for seven age groups. The lengths-of-stay were grouped into intervals of varying length for up to 15 years.

A. Admission Rates

The admission rates (or incidence rates) are calculated relative to the noninstitutionalized population (that is, as a percentage of those exposed to the risk of institutionalization) and not relative to the total population (that is, including the institutionalized). A rigorous actuarial model should use rates relative to the exposed population. Occasionally models are constructed that use admission rates calculated relative to the total population, on the theory that such rates can be applied in a manner consistent with their derivation by applying them to the total number of policies in-force, including those already in a nursing home. But this theory assumes that the proportion institutionalized is the same for both the population from which the rates were derived and the population to which the rates are applied. Problems with this assumption can readily be seen, because an insured population always starts off at issue as 100 percent noninstitutionalized and then gradually moves to a lower percentage. These observations are especially applicable at advanced ages where very high proportions of the population are confined.

The admission rates based on total admissions could, theoretically, have been based on the total population, because new admissions could come from those already institutionalized, if they are first discharged before the end of the observation period. This was not done, however, because the emphasis of this report is on nontransfer admissions.

To calculate admission rates, the number of admissions during the one-year period prior to the date of the interview (in both the resident survey and the discharge survey) is divided by the average exposed population during that period (estimated as the mid-year noninstitutionalized population), resulting in central admission rates. Because the average date of interview was October 11, 1985, the mid-year population is April 12 (182 days earlier). The estimation of this population is discussed in Appendix A.

Three sets of rates were calculated. Each set uses the same population for the denominator, but differs in the number of admissions reflected in the numerator. The first set uses all surveyed admissions, regardless of whether the admission was preceded by a recent discharge from another nursing home (that is, a transfer); this set is labeled "All Stays, Stay Concept." The second set, labeled "All Stays, Benefit Period Concept," excludes admissions for which the patient's residence prior to admission was (1) a Personal Care Facility (PCF), an Intermediate Care Facility (ICF), or a Skilled Nursing Facility (SNF), or (2) any type of health facility and the patient's residence immediately prior to that was a nursing home. The primary application of the second type of exclusion is hospital episodes that interrupt a longer nursing home stay.

According to these criteria, 28 percent of nursing home admissions were transfers from another nursing home. A much higher percentage, 62 percent, of nursing home admissions were transfers from another health facility. Of these, 17 percent were directly from a nursing home (PCF, ICF, or SNF), 72 percent were from short-term general hospitals, and 11 percent were from another type of facility (mostly mental or government). Of those who were admitted from a short-term hospital, roughly 25 percent were in a nursing home before that; that is, these were really continuous nursing home stays.

In the first set of tabulations (under the stay concept), the gross admission rate over all ages and both sexes was 0.53 percent; 0.01 percent under age 30, 0.13 percent for ages 30–64, 2.85 percent for ages 65–84, and 18.99 percent for ages 85 and over. Under age 65 the rates were higher for males than for females, while for ages over 65 the rates were higher (by more than 20 percent) for females than for males. The average length-of-stay was 405 days, ranging from 437 days for ages 30–64 to 400 days for ages 65–84.

Of the 1.249 million admissions tabulated when all admissions were counted, 345,000 were considered transfers, leaving 904,000 admissions in the second set of tabulations, which used the benefit period concept. By excluding transfers, 27.6 percent of the admissions were eliminated from the calculation. There was no significant variation in the reduction by age. By excluding transfers, the resulting admission rate over all ages and both sexes combined was 0.38 percent; 0.01 percent under age 30, 0.10 percent for ages 30–64, 2.08 percent for ages 65–84, and 13.27 percent for ages 85 and over. Although the average admission rate excluding transfers is 28 percent lower than the total, the average length-of-stay (whose calculation is discussed in Sections C and D) increased by 44 percent from 405 days to 583 days.

Utilization rates based on all admissions from a general population may be much different from those based on covered conditions from an insured population. Rates that are more appropriate for insurance purposes than the total rates from the general population can be obtained by using only those admissions that are for covered conditions. For this report, a third set of utilization rates was calculated, labeled "Insurable Stays, Benefit Period Concept," which excludes those admissions and stays for diagnoses that are indicative of persons (1) who are never insured (congenital malformations, perinatal conditions, and mental retardation) or (2) whose condition is not covered (nonorganic mental disorders and substance abuse).

The insured population can vary greatly from one insurer to another, depending on the marketing strategies and underwriting rules. In addition, claims experience can vary by claims administration procedures. There is no way to adjust general population data to reflect these differences. A possible adjustment in the calculation of the rates, although quite small, would be to subtract from the population in the denominator the number of noncovered admissions that are excluded from the numerator. To the extent that these persons would be excluded from the population anyway (because they are institutionalized), however, this would be an overadjustment. For this report, no adjustment was made to the denominator.

Admissions were excluded only if the patient had no covered diagnosis. Thus, a patient's record was included in the calculations if his or her primary diagnosis was for a mental condition but he or she had a secondary condition of hypertensive heart disease. In general, the exclusion process can be described as one in which only those who clearly would not be covered by insurance were excluded. Most insurance companies should be able to obtain a stronger effect through underwriting and claims administration.

The exclusions in this analysis resulted in a 6 percent decrease in admission rates and a 5 percent decrease in the average length-of-stay. The effect was the strongest at the youngest ages. For the age group 30–64, the decrease in the admission rates was 18 percent and the decrease in the average length-of-stay was 8 percent. For the age group 85 and over, the decrease in the admission rates was 4 percent and in the average length-of-stay was only 1 percent.

The admission rates calculated from the survey data by single year of age were smoothed by using a Whittaker-Henderson Type B graduation formula with the corresponding population at each age as the weights. With this graduation formula, the graduated rates times the population reproduces the actual total number of admissions and the actual average age at admission. The admission rate of an age group, however, such as for ages 65–74, is not necessarily preserved. Also, the graduated rates were modified slightly at the high ages (that is, over age 100), where the graduated rate was not allowed to go more than 25 percent of the distance from the rate at the previous age to 100 percent. The graduated rates are shown in Tables 1–3.

B. Prevalence Rates

Another measure of utilization often found in the literature is the prevalence rate. Whereas the incidence rate is the rate of admission over a one-year period for the exposed population, the prevalence rate is the fraction of the total population that is resident in a nursing home at a point in time. Thus, the prevalence rate differs from the incidence rate in both the numerator and the denominator. The numerator of the prevalence rate is the number of residents on a particular day. In the 1985 NNHS, this was, on average, October 11, 1985. The denominator is the total population (including the institutionalized) on that same date. For the calculation of incidence rates from the NNHS, the denominator is the noninstitutionalized population 182 days earlier (April 12, 1985).

The number of nursing home residents by age and sex, and the corresponding prevalence rates, both ungraduated and graduated, are shown in Table 4. The rates are very small under age 45, where less than 1 person per 1000 is confined in a nursing home, for both males and females. After age 65, the rates increase almost exponentially, practically doubling every 5 years between age 65 and 90. The rates for females are generally much higher than the rates for males. For every 1000 males in the population, 6 are confined at age 65, 48 at age 80, and 258 at age 95. For every 1000 females in the population, 8 are confined at age 65, 73 at age 80, and 368 at age 95. It is estimated that more than 50 percent of those over age 100 are confined in nursing homes.

Many analysts of the NNHS have related incidence rates and prevalence rates. They observe that the incidence rate times the average length-of-stay

TABLE 1

MALE ADMISSIONS, ADMISSION RATES, AND AVERAGE LENGTH-OF-STAY (GRADUATED) FROM THE 1985 NNHS

Age	All Stays Stay Concept			All Stays Benefit Period Concept			Insurable Stays Benefit Period Concept		
	Admissions		Average Length of Stay	Admissions		Average Length of Stay	Admissions		Average Length of Stay
	Number	Rate		Number	Rate		Number	Rate	
<30...	11,828	.01%	417	9,968	.01%	941	6,116	.01%	825
30...	1,215	.06	419	977	.05	947	273	.01	830
31...	1,215	.06	419	946	.04	945	234	.01	828
32...	1,164	.06	419	864	.04	942	198	.01	825
33...	1,085	.05	418	751	.04	939	172	.01	822
34...	1,004	.05	418	639	.03	934	162	.01	818
35...	951	.05	417	564	.03	928	172	.01	813
36...	964	.05	416	562	.03	920	208	.01	807
37...	1,042	.06	414	632	.03	912	269	.01	800
38...	1,150	.06	412	752	.04	902	351	.02	793
39...	995	.07	410	708	.05	892	358	.02	785
40...	1,134	.08	408	879	.06	880	490	.03	776
41...	1,302	.09	405	1,091	.07	869	684	.05	767
42...	1,512	.10	402	1,352	.09	856	947	.06	757
43...	1,555	.12	399	1,460	.11	844	1,115	.08	748
44...	1,686	.13	396	1,633	.13	832	1,322	.10	738
45...	1,835	.15	393	1,800	.15	821	1,512	.12	729
46...	1,976	.16	389	1,933	.16	812	1,657	.14	720
47...	2,018	.17	386	1,935	.16	804	1,677	.14	712
48...	1,961	.17	384	1,811	.16	798	1,579	.14	705
49...	1,938	.17	381	1,693	.15	793	1,483	.13	699
50...	1,923	.17	379	1,565	.14	791	1,384	.13	693
51...	1,898	.18	378	1,433	.13	790	1,288	.12	689
52...	1,982	.19	377	1,402	.13	790	1,287	.12	685
53...	2,174	.20	376	1,477	.14	791	1,382	.13	681
54...	2,438	.22	376	1,638	.15	792	1,551	.14	678
55...	2,727	.24	376	1,852	.17	793	1,754	.16	674
56...	3,018	.27	377	2,092	.19	792	1,964	.18	670
57...	3,352	.30	378	2,371	.21	790	2,191	.20	666
58...	3,580	.33	379	2,569	.24	785	2,328	.22	660
59...	3,837	.36	380	2,773	.26	777	2,464	.23	653
60...	4,166	.39	382	3,008	.28	767	2,628	.24	644
61...	4,349	.42	383	3,117	.30	753	2,691	.26	634
62...	4,488	.44	385	3,176	.31	735	2,726	.27	622
63...	4,787	.47	386	3,330	.33	715	2,860	.28	608
64...	4,910	.50	386	3,351	.34	692	2,896	.30	593
65...	5,024	.55	386	3,364	.37	667	2,941	.32	577
66...	5,378	.62	385	3,543	.41	641	3,151	.36	561
67...	6,056	.72	382	3,953	.47	614	3,590	.43	543
68...	6,762	.86	379	4,412	.56	587	4,096	.52	525
69...	7,738	1.05	373	5,088	.69	561	4,816	.65	507

TABLE 1—*Continued*

Age	All Stays Stay Concept			All Stays Benefit Period Concept			Insurable Stays Benefit Period Concept		
	Admissions		Average Length of Stay	Admissions		Average Length of Stay	Admissions		Average Length of Stay
	Number	Rate		Number	Rate		Number	Rate	
70....	9,014	1.28%	367	6,011	.85%	535	5,776	.82%	489
71....	10,422	1.57	358	7,074	1.06	510	6,868	1.03	471
72....	11,864	1.90	348	8,198	1.31	486	8,010	1.28	453
73....	13,250	2.28	338	9,301	1.60	463	9,120	1.57	436
74....	14,502	2.71	326	10,309	1.92	441	10,126	1.89	419
75....	15,570	3.17	315	11,171	2.27	422	10,978	2.24	404
76....	16,370	3.67	304	11,820	2.65	405	11,611	2.60	390
77....	16,927	4.20	295	12,273	3.04	390	12,044	2.99	378
78....	17,238	4.76	287	12,537	3.46	379	12,285	3.39	369
79....	17,135	5.36	282	12,501	3.91	370	12,227	3.82	361
80....	17,019	6.00	278	12,465	4.39	365	12,164	4.29	356
81....	16,491	6.69	277	12,138	4.93	362	11,814	4.80	353
82....	16,019	7.46	278	11,862	5.53	361	11,512	5.36	352
83....	15,364	8.33	280	11,452	6.21	361	11,079	6.00	352
84....	14,777	9.31	284	11,087	6.99	363	10,688	6.73	353
85....	14,030	10.44	288	10,585	7.88	365	10,170	7.57	355
86....	13,154	11.74	292	9,966	8.90	368	9,543	8.52	356
87....	12,050	13.23	296	9,150	10.05	370	8,737	9.60	358
88....	10,888	14.93	299	8,271	11.34	371	7,880	10.81	358
89....	9,660	16.86	302	7,327	12.79	371	6,970	12.16	357
90....	8,981	19.01	303	6,791	14.38	369	6,457	13.67	355
91....	7,908	21.41	303	5,955	16.12	366	5,663	15.33	352
92....	6,947	24.07	301	5,206	18.03	361	4,957	17.17	346
93....	5,724	26.98	298	4,267	20.11	354	4,070	19.19	339
94....	4,450	30.17	294	3,299	22.37	345	3,155	21.39	331
95....	3,589	33.64	289	2,648	24.82	335	2,539	23.80	321
96....	2,863	37.38	282	2,103	27.46	323	2,022	26.41	309
97....	2,190	41.41	274	1,602	30.30	310	1,546	29.23	296
98....	1,502	45.72	266	1,096	33.34	295	1,060	32.27	281
99....	1,192	50.32	256	866	36.59	279	841	35.52	265
100....	577	55.20	246	419	40.04	261	408	38.99	249
101....	363	60.36	235	263	43.70	243	256	42.67	230
102....	224	65.81	223	162	47.56	223	158	46.57	211
103....	134	71.54	210	97	51.63	202	95	50.69	191
104....	80	77.55	196	58	55.90	180	57	55.02	169
105....	46	83.16	182	33	60.38	156	33	59.57	150
106....	25	87.37	167	19	65.06	150	19	64.34	150
107....	14	90.53	151	10	69.95	150	10	69.32	150
108....	7	92.90	150	5	75.04	150	5	74.52	150
109....	4	94.67	150	3	80.34	150	3	79.93	150
110....	2	96.00	150	2	85.25	150	2	84.95	150
30–64..	77,333	0.07	388	58,136	0.06	800	46,255	0.04	678
65–84..	252,919	2.44	313	180,557	1.74	427	174,897	1.69	404
85+...	106,603	16.44	294	80,203	12.37	359	76,657	11.82	346
Total ..	448,682	0.38%	324	328,865	0.28%	492	303,925	0.26%	440

TABLE 2

FEMALE ADMISSIONS, ADMISSION RATES, AND AVERAGE LENGTH-OF-STAY (GRADUATED) FROM THE 1985 NNHS

Age	All Stays Stay Concept			All Stays Benefit Period Concept			Insurable Stays Benefit Period Concept		
	Admissions		Average Length of Stay	Admissions		Average Length of Stay	Admissions		Average Length of Stay
	Number	Rate		Number	Rate		Number	Rate	
<30...	4,245	.00%	438	3,912	.00%	908	1,868	.00%	1,096
30...	352	.02	431	357	.02	898	104	.00	1,098
31...	377	.02	429	359	.02	899	125	.01	1,101
32...	407	.02	427	350	.02	901	148	.01	1,105
33...	441	.02	425	334	.02	904	170	.01	1,109
34...	473	.02	423	313	.02	908	189	.01	1,114
35...	499	.03	421	295	.02	914	207	.01	1,120
36...	528	.03	420	295	.02	920	233	.01	1,125
37...	552	.03	418	312	.02	927	267	.01	1,132
38...	556	.03	417	340	.02	936	306	.02	1,138
39...	439	.03	416	296	.02	945	274	.02	1,144
40...	457	.03	416	336	.02	956	313	.02	1,150
41...	494	.03	416	379	.03	967	352	.02	1,156
42...	554	.04	418	423	.03	979	389	.03	1,162
43...	573	.04	420	418	.03	991	378	.03	1,166
44...	641	.05	423	440	.03	1,004	390	.03	1,170
45...	735	.06	427	477	.04	1,017	414	.03	1,172
46...	849	.07	433	530	.04	1,029	451	.04	1,172
47...	941	.08	439	579	.05	1,040	487	.04	1,171
48...	992	.09	447	616	.05	1,051	515	.04	1,167
49...	1,054	.09	455	676	.06	1,059	564	.05	1,162
50...	1,104	.10	464	743	.07	1,066	618	.05	1,153
51...	1,132	.10	474	804	.07	1,071	665	.06	1,143
52...	1,207	.11	484	901	.08	1,074	740	.07	1,129
53...	1,323	.12	493	1,025	.09	1,073	838	.07	1,113
54...	1,462	.13	503	1,157	.10	1,070	941	.08	1,094
55...	1,611	.14	511	1,279	.11	1,063	1,039	.09	1,073
56...	1,810	.15	518	1,421	.12	1,053	1,158	.10	1,049
57...	2,081	.18	523	1,597	.13	1,039	1,313	.11	1,024
58...	2,374	.20	526	1,773	.15	1,021	1,484	.13	996
59...	2,773	.24	526	2,020	.17	1,000	1,736	.15	966
60...	3,344	.28	525	2,394	.20	975	2,124	.18	936
61...	3,966	.34	521	2,825	.24	947	2,579	.22	904
62...	4,713	.41	514	3,379	.30	917	3,142	.27	872
63...	5,745	.50	507	4,179	.36	885	3,912	.34	839
64...	6,684	.60	498	4,949	.45	853	4,628	.42	808
65...	7,629	.72	488	5,751	.54	821	5,351	.51	778
66...	8,773	.86	478	6,712	.66	790	6,214	.61	750
67...	10,119	1.01	469	7,821	.78	762	7,222	.72	725
68...	11,220	1.16	461	8,708	.90	737	8,051	.83	703
69...	12,276	1.32	455	9,509	1.02	715	8,830	.95	684

TABLE 2—*Continued*

Age	All Stays Stay Concept: Admissions Number	Admissions Rate	Average Length of Stay	All Stays Benefit Period Concept: Admissions Number	Admissions Rate	Average Length of Stay	Insurable Stays Benefit Period Concept: Admissions Number	Admissions Rate	Average Length of Stay
70....	13,506	1.49%	449	10,391	1.15%	697	9,713	1.07%	669
71....	14,740	1.68	446	11,232	1.28	683	10,583	1.21	656
72....	16,049	1.90	444	12,108	1.44	671	11,498	1.36	646
73....	17,559	2.18	443	13,139	1.63	662	12,557	1.56	639
74....	19,368	2.53	442	14,420	1.89	655	13,839	1.81	633
75....	21,518	2.98	443	15,985	2.22	650	15,374	2.13	628
76....	24,030	3.54	444	17,842	2.63	646	17,173	2.53	624
77....	26,694	4.22	445	19,819	3.14	642	19,082	3.02	621
78....	29,561	5.02	446	21,935	3.73	638	21,124	3.59	618
79....	31,812	5.95	448	23,568	4.41	634	22,701	4.24	615
80....	34,404	6.99	448	25,418	5.16	630	24,487	4.97	612
81....	35,974	8.15	449	26,465	6.00	625	25,497	5.78	609
82....	37,573	9.44	450	27,472	6.90	618	26,466	6.65	604
83....	38,480	10.85	450	27,905	7.87	611	26,879	7.58	599
84....	38,730	12.38	451	27,801	8.89	603	26,772	8.56	594
85....	38,376	14.03	451	27,228	9.95	594	26,206	9.58	588
86....	37,311	15.77	451	26,145	11.05	585	25,143	10.63	583
87....	34,848	17.60	451	24,112	12.18	577	23,161	11.70	577
88....	32,949	19.46	450	22,523	13.30	569	21,601	12.76	571
89....	28,655	21.34	449	19,369	14.42	562	18,539	13.80	566
90....	25,385	23.19	447	16,987	15.52	556	16,224	14.82	561
91....	21,858	24.99	444	14,501	16.58	550	13,817	15.80	556
92....	19,036	26.72	440	12,536	17.60	544	11,919	16.73	550
93....	15,223	28.36	436	9,964	18.57	539	9,455	17.62	544
94....	11,532	29.91	430	7,513	19.49	534	7,117	18.46	538
95....	8,567	31.36	424	5,562	20.36	528	5,263	19.26	532
96....	6,342	32.70	417	4,110	21.19	523	3,885	20.03	525
97....	4,498	33.94	409	2,913	21.99	518	2,753	20.78	518
98....	3,079	35.08	401	1,998	22.76	513	1,888	21.51	510
99....	1,968	36.12	393	1,281	23.51	508	1,211	22.24	503
100....	1,212	37.08	385	793	24.27	503	751	22.97	496
101....	823	37.96	377	543	25.03	498	515	23.73	488
102....	547	38.77	369	364	25.81	494	346	24.52	481
103....	356	39.50	361	239	26.61	489	228	25.34	473
104....	225	40.18	353	154	27.43	485	147	26.20	466
105....	139	40.79	344	97	28.29	480	93	27.10	458
106....	84	41.34	336	60	29.17	476	57	28.05	450
107....	49	41.83	328	36	30.09	472	34	29.04	443
108....	28	42.26	320	21	31.04	467	20	30.07	435
109....	16	42.62	311	12	32.01	463	12	31.15	427
110....	8	42.93	303	6	33.02	459	6	32.27	419
30–64..	53,243	0.03	491	38,574	0.02	966	33,194	0.02	976
65–84..	450,017	3.14	450	334,000	2.33	651	319,412	2.23	630
85+...	293,114	20.14	444	199,065	13.68	563	190,390	13.08	564
Total ..	800,618	0.66%	450	575,552	0.48%	643	544,865	0.45%	630

TABLE 3

TOTAL ADMISSIONS, ADMISSION RATES, AND AVERAGE LENGTH-OF-STAY (GRADUATED) FROM THE 1985 NNHS

	All Stays Stay Concept			All Stays Benefit Period Concept			Insurable Stays Benefit Period Concept		
	Admissions		Average Length of Stay	Admissions		Average Length of Stay	Admissions		Average Length of Stay
Age	Number	Rate		Number	Rate		Number	Rate	
<30...	15,923	.01%	418	13,725	.01%	886	7,922	.01%	907
30...	1,591	.04	418	1,380	.03	885	376	.01	910
31...	1,638	.04	418	1,377	.03	884	364	.01	909
32...	1,610	.04	418	1,278	.03	882	355	.01	907
33...	1,542	.04	417	1,115	.03	881	354	.01	905
34...	1,472	.04	417	943	.02	879	365	.01	903
35...	1,438	.04	417	824	.02	877	398	.01	899
36...	1,489	.04	416	819	.02	875	464	.01	895
37...	1,609	.04	416	922	.02	872	559	.01	891
38...	1,731	.05	415	1,089	.03	870	663	.02	886
39...	1,445	.05	415	1,006	.03	867	610	.02	881
40...	1,570	.05	415	1,197	.04	865	748	.03	875
41...	1,729	.06	415	1,419	.05	864	953	.03	869
42...	1,967	.07	415	1,701	.06	862	1,250	.04	863
43...	2,053	.08	415	1,829	.07	862	1,450	.05	857
44...	2,309	.09	416	2,077	.08	862	1,732	.07	851
45...	2,627	.11	417	2,350	.10	863	2,012	.08	846
46...	2,940	.12	418	2,585	.11	865	2,236	.09	841
47...	3,081	.13	420	2,635	.11	868	2,281	.10	836
48...	3,032	.13	422	2,499	.11	872	2,156	.09	833
49...	3,013	.13	425	2,380	.11	877	2,044	.09	830
50...	2,995	.13	428	2,262	.10	883	1,944	.09	827
51...	2,968	.14	431	2,156	.10	889	1,868	.09	825
52...	3,115	.14	435	2,208	.10	895	1,937	.09	823
53...	3,427	.15	438	2,414	.11	900	2,145	.10	821
54...	3,847	.17	442	2,734	.12	904	2,451	.11	819
55...	4,308	.19	445	3,111	.14	907	2,794	.12	815
56...	4,828	.21	448	3,537	.16	906	3,158	.14	810
57...	5,450	.24	450	4,021	.17	903	3,552	.15	804
58...	5,977	.26	451	4,401	.19	896	3,848	.17	795
59...	6,634	.30	452	4,837	.22	885	4,211	.19	784
60...	7,536	.33	451	5,426	.24	869	4,746	.21	771
61...	8,345	.38	450	5,943	.27	850	5,263	.24	755
62...	9,225	.43	448	6,534	.30	827	5,871	.27	737
63...	10,539	.49	445	7,471	.34	801	6,784	.31	718
64...	11,588	.56	441	8,269	.40	773	7,543	.36	697
65...	12,650	.64	438	9,112	.46	744	8,314	.42	676
66...	14,176	.75	434	10,300	.55	716	9,400	.50	656
67...	16,248	.88	430	11,875	.64	690	10,873	.59	636
68...	18,074	1.03	426	13,232	.76	665	12,207	.70	619
69...	20,097	1.21	422	14,684	.88	644	13,689	.82	603

TABLE 3—*Continued*

Age	All Stays Stay Concept			All Stays Benefit Period Concept			Insurable Stays Benefit Period Concept		
	Admissions		Average Length of Stay	Admissions		Average Length of Stay	Admissions		Average Length of Stay
	Number	Rate		Number	Rate		Number	Rate	
70....	22,542	1.40%	418	16,413	1.02%	625	15,478	.96%	590
71....	25,084	1.63	414	18,219	1.18	609	17,370	1.13	577
72....	27,734	1.89	411	20,139	1.37	596	19,370	1.32	567
73....	30,578	2.21	406	22,247	1.61	583	21,525	1.55	557
74....	33,657	2.59	402	24,573	1.89	573	23,843	1.83	549
75....	36,955	3.05	398	27,084	2.23	564	26,293	2.17	542
76....	40,391	3.59	395	29,689	2.64	556	28,802	2.56	535
77....	43,745	4.22	392	32,204	3.11	549	31,209	3.01	530
78....	47,029	4.95	390	34,632	3.64	544	33,529	3.53	526
79....	49,226	5.76	388	36,233	4.24	539	35,054	4.10	522
80....	51,669	6.66	388	38,001	4.90	536	36,745	4.74	520
81....	52,616	7.65	389	38,654	5.62	533	37,358	5.43	518
82....	53,617	8.75	392	39,311	6.42	530	37,973	6.20	517
83....	53,750	9.97	394	39,275	7.28	527	37,913	7.03	515
84....	53,371	11.32	398	38,801	8.23	524	37,421	7.93	514
85....	52,261	12.81	401	37,741	9.25	521	36,353	8.91	513
86....	50,343	14.44	405	36,069	10.35	518	34,685	9.95	512
87....	46,838	16.20	408	33,269	11.51	515	31,928	11.04	510
88....	43,750	18.06	410	30,801	12.72	511	29,491	12.18	508
89....	38,318	20.00	411	26,743	13.96	508	25,542	13.33	506
90....	34,445	21.98	410	23,843	15.21	504	22,718	14.50	502
91....	29,837	23.98	408	20,498	16.48	500	19,492	15.67	498
92....	26,023	25.99	405	17,758	17.74	495	16,862	16.84	493
93....	20,965	28.00	400	14,225	19.00	489	13,496	18.02	487
94....	15,982	29.99	394	10,795	20.25	483	10,240	19.21	480
95....	12,138	31.95	387	8,173	21.51	476	7,757	20.42	472
96....	9,169	33.90	380	6,164	22.79	468	5,857	21.65	463
97....	6,639	35.82	372	4,463	24.08	460	4,249	22.92	454
98....	4,549	37.71	364	3,064	25.40	452	2,923	24.23	445
99....	3,094	39.59	356	2,091	26.75	444	2,001	25.59	435
100....	1,788	41.44	349	1,215	28.16	436	1,166	27.02	425
101....	1,199	43.29	341	821	29.63	427	790	28.53	415
102....	790	45.13	333	545	31.17	419	527	30.11	406
103....	511	46.97	326	357	32.77	411	346	31.79	396
104....	325	48.81	319	229	34.45	403	223	33.56	386
105....	202	50.66	312	144	36.21	394	141	35.42	377
106....	122	52.50	305	89	38.04	386	87	37.37	367
107....	72	54.35	299	53	39.96	378	52	39.42	357
108....	42	56.20	293	31	41.95	370	31	41.56	348
109....	24	58.06	287	18	44.02	362	18	43.80	338
110....	13	59.92	281	10	46.17	354	10	46.14	328
30–64..	130,666	0.13	437	96,753	0.10	861	79,482	0.08	792
65–84..	703,210	2.85	400	514,678	2.08	567	494,368	2.00	544
85+...	399,440	18.99	403	279,207	13.27	504	266,985	12.69	499
Total ..	1,249,239	0.53%	405	904,364	0.38%	583	848,757	0.36%	556

TABLE 4

NURSING HOME RESIDENTS AND PREVALENCE RATES AS OF OCTOBER 11, 1985 FROM THE 1985 NNHS BY AGE AND SEX

	Male				Female				Total			
	Ungraduated		Graduated		Ungraduated		Graduated		Ungraduated		Graduated	
Age	Residents	Rate	Rate	Residents	Residents	Rate	Rate	Residents	Residents	Rate	Rate	Residents
<30....	7,128	.01%	.01%	8,325	3,580	.01%	.01%	3,964	10,708	.01%	.01%	12,289
30....	1,173	.05	.05	1,156	739	.03	.03	540	1,912	.04	.04	1,696
31....	1,826	.08	.06	1,218	1,013	.05	.03	590	2,839	.07	.04	1,808
32....	1,854	.09	.06	1,256	352	.02	.03	641	2,206	.05	.05	1,897
33....	1,777	.09	.06	1,274	658	.03	.04	696	2,435	.06	.05	1,970
34....	2,057	.10	.06	1,275	1,059	.05	.04	758	3,116	.08	.05	2,033
35....	698	.04	.07	1,255	554	.03	.04	818	1,252	.03	.05	2,074
36....	293	.02	.07	1,257	929	.05	.05	901	1,222	.03	.06	2,159
37....	0	.00	.07	1,266	1,300	.07	.05	996	1,300	.04	.06	2,263
38....	882	.04	.07	1,353	437	.02	.06	1,159	1,319	.03	.06	2,513
39....	1,895	.12	.07	1,124	1,738	.11	.07	1,054	3,633	.11	.07	2,178
40....	3,762	.26	.07	1,045	761	.05	.07	1,062	4,523	.15	.07	2,107
41....	1,624	.11	.07	1,079	1,399	.09	.08	1,174	3,023	.10	.08	2,253
42....	0	.00	.08	1,162	1,142	.07	.09	1,329	1,142	.04	.08	2,491
43....	473	.03	.08	1,135	292	.02	.09	1,338	765	.03	.09	2,473
44....	494	.04	.09	1,125	1,804	.14	.10	1,327	2,298	.09	.09	2,452
45....	1,386	.11	.09	1,179	1,009	.08	.11	1,347	2,395	.10	.10	2,526
46....	1,541	.13	.11	1,293	1,371	.11	.11	1,396	2,912	.12	.11	2,689
47....	874	.07	.12	1,444	2,703	.22	.12	1,446	3,577	.15	.12	2,890
48....	1,447	.13	.14	1,579	2,167	.19	.12	1,455	3,614	.16	.13	3,034
49....	934	.08	.16	1,754	1,200	.10	.13	1,491	2,134	.09	.14	3,244
50....	3,134	.28	.18	1,971	2,138	.19	.14	1,556	5,272	.23	.16	3,528
51....	2,097	.19	.20	2,145	977	.09	.15	1,607	3,074	.14	.17	3,752
52....	1,115	.10	.22	2,340	2,042	.19	.16	1,718	3,157	.15	.19	4,057
53....	2,694	.25	.24	2,601	1,231	.11	.17	1,926	3,925	.18	.21	4,526
54....	2,539	.23	.26	2,893	2,902	.25	.19	2,219	5,441	.24	.23	5,112
55....	5,175	.46	.28	3,158	1,756	.15	.22	2,553	6,931	.30	.25	5,711
56....	3,940	.35	.30	3,359	2,900	.25	.25	2,945	6,840	.30	.28	6,305
57....	5,294	.47	.32	3,587	2,303	.19	.29	3,455	7,597	.33	.31	7,042
58....	1,691	.15	.34	3,732	2,607	.22	.34	3,985	4,298	.19	.34	7,717
59....	4,311	.40	.36	3,867	5,848	.50	.39	4,545	10,159	.45	.37	8,412

TABLE 4—*Continued*

Age	Male				Female				Total			
	Ungraduated		Graduated		Ungraduated		Graduated		Ungraduated		Graduated	
	Residents	Rate	Rate	Residents	Residents	Rate	Rate	Residents	Residents	Rate	Rate	Residents
60....	3,089	.29%	.39%	4,141	2,932	.25%	.44%	5,258	6,021	.27%	.42%	9,399
61....	3,042	.29	.41	4,404	6,707	.57	.50	5,946	9,749	.43	.46	10,351
62....	4,743	.46	.45	4,612	6,495	.56	.56	6,515	11,238	.52	.51	11,127
63....	6,796	.66	.49	5,050	6,082	.53	.63	7,286	12,878	.59	.57	12,336
64....	6,234	.62	.55	5,463	10,339	.91	.70	7,927	16,573	.78	.63	13,390
65....	4,775	.51	.61	5,738	9,390	.87	.77	8,350	14,165	.70	.70	14,088
66....	4,066	.46	.69	6,066	10,065	.97	.85	8,827	14,131	.74	.78	14,893
67....	8,623	1.01	.78	6,670	8,824	.86	.94	9,600	17,447	.93	.87	16,270
68....	6,899	.85	.89	7,211	9,012	.91	1.05	10,368	15,911	.88	.98	17,579
69....	6,527	.86	1.02	7,750	14,607	1.54	1.18	11,174	21,134	1.24	1.11	18,923
70....	9,407	1.31	1.17	8,453	10,783	1.17	1.34	12,352	20,190	1.23	1.27	20,805
71....	7,723	1.13	1.35	9,240	18,572	2.06	1.54	13,865	26,295	1.66	1.46	23,105
72....	9,883	1.53	1.56	10,034	17,475	2.01	1.80	15,649	27,358	1.81	1.69	25,683
73....	14,109	2.34	1.80	10,805	17,314	2.07	2.12	17,721	31,423	2.18	1.98	28,526
74....	9,055	1.62	2.07	11,529	15,730	1.97	2.52	20,111	24,785	1.83	2.33	31,640
75....	13,383	2.61	2.38	12,222	25,128	3.31	3.01	22,852	38,511	3.03	2.76	35,074
76....	13,534	2.88	2.74	12,856	27,270	3.79	3.61	25,928	40,804	3.43	3.26	38,783
77....	16,070	3.77	3.15	13,413	26,271	3.88	4.32	29,232	42,341	3.84	3.87	42,645
78....	13,459	3.51	3.62	13,893	32,224	5.08	5.16	32,730	45,683	4.49	4.58	46,622
79....	13,461	3.92	4.15	14,259	36,039	6.10	6.14	36,265	49,500	5.30	5.41	50,523
80....	16,145	5.29	4.76	14,539	41,043	7.51	7.26	39,679	57,188	6.71	6.36	54,218
81....	15,667	5.84	5.45	14,623	41,674	8.30	8.53	42,784	57,341	7.45	7.45	57,407
82....	14,102	6.02	6.23	14,601	46,651	10.18	9.94	45,564	60,753	8.77	8.68	60,165
83....	12,387	6.08	7.10	14,461	45,121	10.82	11.50	47,953	57,508	9.27	10.06	62,414
84....	13,588	7.68	8.08	14,296	48,736	12.94	13.20	49,702	62,324	11.26	11.56	63,998
85....	14,165	9.35	9.16	13,888	45,675	13.55	15.04	50,697	59,840	12.24	13.22	64,584
86....	9,603	7.50	10.36	13,273	42,947	14.37	16.99	50,775	52,550	12.31	15.00	64,047
87....	9,974	9.34	11.67	12,452	51,918	19.91	19.05	49,682	61,892	16.84	16.90	62,134
88....	11,254	13.03	13.08	11,299	45,475	20.22	21.19	47,663	56,729	18.22	18.94	58,962
89....	9,055	13.11	14.61	10,086	50,804	26.62	23.40	44,650	59,859	23.03	21.06	54,736

TABLE 4—*Continued*

Age	Male				Female				Total			
	Ungraduated		Graduated		Ungraduated		Graduated		Ungraduated		Graduated	
	Residents	Rate	Rate	Residents	Residents	Rate	Rate	Residents	Residents	Rate	Rate	Residents
90	10,277	17.68%	16.24%	9,441	41,008	25.29%	25.65%	41,595	51,285	23.28%	23.17%	51,036
91	9,648	20.19	17.97	8,588	44,358	32.60	27.92	37,991	54,006	29.37	25.33	46,579
92	8,862	23.38	19.80	7,505	34,092	30.70	30.19	33,523	42,954	28.84	27.54	41,027
93	9,201	31.98	21.71	6,246	27,306	31.09	32.44	28,493	36,507	31.31	29.80	34,740
94	3,381	16.38	23.72	4,894	24,655	36.38	34.66	23,492	28,036	31.71	32.11	28,386
95	6,014	39.41	25.80	3,938	22,066	43.62	36.84	18,633	28,080	42.65	34.28	22,571
96	3,572	31.92	27.97	3,130	15,957	42.43	38.95	14,650	19,529	40.02	36.43	17,779
97	2,299	28.24	30.22	2,460	10,321	38.58	40.99	10,966	12,620	36.17	38.48	13,426
98	992	18.45	32.54	1,749	6,466	35.35	42.96	7,859	7,458	31.51	40.60	9,609
99	811	19.91	34.93	1,423	4,932	35.06	44.85	6,309	5,743	31.66	42.63	7,732
100	1,481	65.21	37.41	849	5,951	63.23	46.66	4,391	7,432	63.61	44.86	5,241
101	190	12.28	39.95	618	3,198	47.95	48.37	3,226	3,388	41.24	46.78	3,844
102	261	25.17	42.57	441	1,167	25.18	49.99	2,317	1,428	25.18	48.64	2,758
103	0	.00	45.27	308	1,922	60.84	51.52	1,628	1,922	50.07	50.41	1,935
104	384	86.88	48.03	212	566	26.86	52.96	1,116	950	37.27	52.11	1,328
105	297	106.07	50.87	142	476	34.67	54.30	746	773	46.76	53.72	888
106	0	.00	53.79	93	262	29.94	55.55	486	262	25.00	55.26	579
107	0	.00	56.77	60	259	47.79	56.70	307	259	39.97	56.71	368
108	0	.00	59.83	37	0	.00	57.76	189	0	.00	58.09	226
109	0	.00	62.97	23	0	.00	58.72	113	0	.00	59.40	137
110	0	.00	66.17	13	0	.00	59.59	65	0	.00	60.61	78
30–64 ..	80,884	0.16	0.16	78,550	79,886	0.16	0.16	80,962	160,770	0.16	0.16	159,512
65–84 ..	222,863	2.07	2.07	222,659	501,929	3.32	3.32	500,705	724,792	2.80	2.80	723,364
85+ ...	111,721	14.22	14.40	113,171	481,781	23.45	23.44	481,560	593,502	20.90	20.94	594,731
Total ...	422,596	0.35%	0.35%	422,705	1,067,176	0.87%	0.87%	1,067,191	1,489,772	0.62%	0.62%	1,489,896

produces a rate with the same units of measure as the prevalence rate, as follows:

$$\text{(residents admitted per year)/(population)} * \text{(average years of residence)} = \text{(residents)/(population)}$$

Using this relationship, analysts have often tabulated two of these factors and then calculated the third. Among these factors, the prevalence rate can be estimated most accurately from the NNHS; the admission rates are second; and average lengths-of-stay are the least accurate. The prevalence rate is accurate because it is based on a count of the current number of residents, which is precisely the purpose of the Current Resident Survey.

The relationship between incidence rates and prevalence rates is much more complicated than implied by this equation. A more rigorous analysis of the relationship between incidence rates and prevalence rates should take into account several other factors. First, as noted earlier, the populations used in calculating the two rates are different. Thus, the relationship should include a factor (on the left side of the equation) that is equal to the population used in the incidence rate calculation divided by the population used in the prevalence rate calculation. Because this factor is unitless, its need is often not recognized.

Second, the resident population is not made up of admissions in the current year, but of admissions over all prior years. To obtain an estimate of current residents, the admissions in past years should be multiplied by the probability that they are still residents on the date on which prevalence is measured. The number of admissions in past years reflects changes through time in admission rates and the size of the population. The approximation does not reflect these trends; thus, the accuracy of the estimate depends on the stability of admission rates and the population through time. In addition, the probability of a past admission still being a resident depends on the distribution by length-of-stay for each prior age through time, whereas the approximation relies on the average length-of-stay for the current age in the current year. In general, the incidence rate times the average length-of-stay does not accurately reflect the number of current residents with long stays. To the extent that the population is growing and admission rates are increasing, the incidence rate times the average length-of-stay will overestimate the prevalence rate.

Nevertheless, this relationship is a useful concept, because the average length-of-stay is only about one and one-half years. Thus, the distortions resulting from the inaccurate estimate of current residents with long stays are small. Similarly, the difference between the total population and the noninstitutionalized population is small except for advanced ages. If it is impossible to obtain an accurate measure of one factor, then the relationship can be used to roughly estimate the third. Many analysts use the relationship to estimate the average length-of-stay, which is the most difficult to obtain from the data. The use of this relationship generally results in an underestimate of the average length-of-stay. Because the NCHS publishes data on prevalence rates and average lengths-of-stay, some analysts use it to estimate incidence rates. In this report, however, each of the three factors (admission rate, prevalence rate, and average length-of-stay) was tabulated independently.

The relationship was used as a check for reasonableness. This check was done for the two sets of rates using all stays (under the stay concept and the benefit period concept), but not for the rates for insurable stays. The results of this comparison are shown in Table 5. In general, the relationship based on the rates under the stay concept seems to be closer than that based on the benefit period concept. This is to be expected, because the shorter the average length-of-stay, the more accurate the approximation.

C. Discharge Rates

The distribution by length-of-stay was obtained by a mortality table construction method, in which the period of observation was the one-year period ending with the date of the interview. Each record in both the discharge survey and the resident survey was tabulated by age at admission (summarized into seven age groups) and duration since admission or duration at discharge. Durations were grouped as follows: For the first 30 days, by day; for the second through the 60th month, by month; from the sixth through the 15th year, by year. (Results for each of the first 30 days are not shown in the attached tables.) Discharge rates were not calculated for durations of more than 15 years because of the sparsity of data. The calculations were performed independently for males, females, and males and females combined, as well as for all stays under the stay concept, all stays under the benefit period concept, and insurable stays under the benefit period concept.

The contribution of each record to the exposure in the study was determined as the difference between (1) the earlier of the date of discharge or the date of the interview and (2) the later of the date of admission or one year prior to the date of the interview. The exposure was not adjusted to include the time from discharge to the end of the observation period, as would be done under the Balducci Hypothesis. If the total contribution to

TABLE 5

COMPARISON OF PREVALENCE RATES AND ADMISSION RATES FROM THE 1985 NNHS

Age	Prevalence Rate (1)	All Stays Stay Concept: Admission Rate (2)	ALOS (Year) (3)	Estimated Prevalence (2)*(3)	(2)*(3) /(1)	All Stays Benefit Period Concept: Admission Rate (4)	ALOS (Year) (5)	Estimated Prevalence (4)*(5)	(4)*(5) /(1)
<30...	.01%	.01%	1.15	.02%	149.19%	.01%	2.43	.03%	272.22%
30...	.04	.04	1.15	.04	109.45	.03	2.42	.08	200.83
31...	.04	.04	1.15	.05	105.85	.03	2.42	.08	188.23
32...	.05	.04	1.14	.05	99.20	.03	2.42	.08	166.35
33...	.05	.04	1.14	.04	91.36	.03	2.41	.07	139.49
34...	.05	.04	1.14	.04	84.63	.02	2.41	.06	114.24
35...	.05	.04	1.14	.04	80.55	.02	2.40	.05	97.20
36...	.06	.04	1.14	.05	79.36	.02	2.40	.05	91.66
37...	.06	.04	1.14	.05	80.40	.02	2.39	.06	96.69
38...	.06	.05	1.14	.05	82.19	.03	2.38	.07	108.32
39...	.07	.05	1.14	.06	83.60	.03	2.38	.08	121.68
40...	.07	.05	1.14	.06	84.65	.04	2.37	.10	134.62
41...	.08	.06	1.14	.07	86.48	.05	2.37	.11	147.75
42...	.08	.07	1.14	.07	91.21	.06	2.36	.13	163.95
43...	.09	.08	1.14	.09	99.79	.07	2.36	.16	184.42
44...	.09	.09	1.14	.10	110.84	.08	2.36	.19	206.49
45...	.10	.11	1.14	.12	121.18	.10	2.36	.23	224.21
46...	.11	.12	1.15	.14	126.74	.11	2.37	.25	230.26
47...	.12	.13	1.15	.15	125.09	.11	2.38	.26	220.96
48...	.13	.13	1.16	.15	117.99	.11	2.39	.26	200.84
49...	.14	.13	1.16	.16	109.00	.11	2.40	.25	177.69
50...	.16	.13	1.17	.16	100.87	.10	2.42	.25	157.18
51...	.17	.14	1.18	.16	94.94	.10	2.44	.24	142.15
52...	.19	.14	1.19	.17	91.38	.10	2.45	.25	133.34
53...	.21	.15	1.20	.19	90.05	.11	2.47	.27	130.30
54...	.23	.17	1.21	.21	90.51	.12	2.48	.30	131.73
55...	.25	.19	1.22	.23	92.01	.14	2.48	.34	135.42
56...	.28	.21	1.23	.26	93.86	.16	2.48	.39	139.24
57...	.31	.24	1.23	.29	95.54	.17	2.47	.43	141.49
58...	.34	.26	1.24	.33	96.74	.19	2.45	.48	141.40
59...	.37	.30	1.24	.37	97.83	.22	2.42	.52	139.71
60...	.42	.33	1.24	.41	99.18	.24	2.38	.57	137.57
61...	.46	.38	1.23	.46	100.80	.27	2.33	.62	135.62
62...	.51	.43	1.23	.52	102.55	.30	2.27	.68	134.15
63...	.57	.49	1.22	.59	104.59	.34	2.19	.75	133.50
64...	.63	.56	1.21	.67	107.28	.40	2.12	.84	134.06
65...	.70	.64	1.20	.77	110.85	.46	2.04	.94	135.79
66...	.78	.75	1.19	.89	115.18	.55	1.96	1.07	138.18
67...	.87	.88	1.18	1.04	119.64	.64	1.89	1.22	140.30
68...	.98	1.03	1.17	1.20	123.38	.76	1.82	1.38	141.13
69...	1.11	1.21	1.16	1.39	125.91	.88	1.76	1.55	140.37

TABLE 5—*Continued*

Age	Prevalence Rate (1)	All Stays — Stay Concept: Admission Rate (2)	ALOS (Year) (3)	Estimated Prevalence (2)*(3)	(2)*(3) /(1)	Benefit Period Concept: Admission Rate (4)	ALOS (Year) (5)	Estimated Prevalence (4)*(5)	(4)*(5) /(1)
70....	1.27%	1.40%	1.15	1.61%	126.90%	1.02%	1.71	1.75%	138.15%
71....	1.46	1.63	1.14	1.85	126.56	1.18	1.67	1.97	135.15
72....	1.69	1.89	1.12	2.12	125.38	1.37	1.63	2.24	132.07
73....	1.98	2.21	1.11	2.46	123.91	1.61	1.60	2.57	129.41
74....	2.33	2.59	1.10	2.85	122.34	1.89	1.57	2.97	127.16
75....	2.76	3.05	1.09	3.33	120.69	2.23	1.54	3.45	125.13%
76....	3.26	3.59	1.08	3.88	118.97	2.64	1.52	4.02	123.08
77....	3.87	4.22	1.07	4.53	117.17	3.11	1.50	4.68	120.87
78....	4.58	4.95	1.07	5.28	115.28	3.64	1.49	5.42	118.42
79....	5.41	5.76	1.06	6.13	113.30	4.24	1.48	6.26	115.74
80....	6.36	6.66	1.06	7.09	111.35	4.90	1.47	7.19	112.91
81....	7.45	7.65	1.07	8.17	109.53	5.62	1.46	8.20	110.02
82....	8.68	8.75	1.07	9.39	108.08	6.42	1.45	9.31	107.19
83....	10.06	9.97	1.08	10.77	107.08	7.28	1.44	10.51	104.50
84....	11.56	11.32	1.09	12.34	106.66	8.23	1.44	11.81	102.10
85....	13.22	12.81	1.10	14.09	106.62	9.25	1.43	13.20	99.87
86....	15.00	14.44	1.11	16.02	106.83	10.35	1.42	14.68	97.84
87....	16.90	16.20	1.12	18.10	107.10	11.51	1.41	16.22	95.97
88....	18.94	18.06	1.12	20.28	107.06	12.72	1.40	17.81	94.05
89....	21.06	20.00	1.12	22.50	106.80	13.96	1.39	19.42	92.21
90....	23.17	21.98	1.12	24.69	106.59	15.21	1.38	21.02	90.72
91....	25.33	23.98	1.12	26.82	105.86	16.48	1.37	22.57	89.08
92....	27.54	25.99	1.11	28.82	104.65	17.74	1.36	24.05	87.32
93....	29.80	28.00	1.10	30.69	102.99	19.00	1.34	25.46	85.45
94....	32.11	29.99	1.08	32.39	100.87	20.25	1.32	26.79	83.43
95....	34.28	31.95	1.06	33.92	98.96	21.51	1.30	28.04	81.79
96....	36.43	33.90	1.04	35.30	96.89	22.79	1.28	29.22	80.21
97....	38.48	35.82	1.02	36.54	94.95	24.08	1.26	30.36	78.89
98....	40.60	37.71	1.00	37.65	92.75	25.40	1.24	31.45	77.48
99....	42.63	39.59	.98	38.66	90.70	26.75	1.22	32.53	76.32
100....	44.86	41.44	.96	39.59	88.25	28.16	1.19	33.61	74.92
101....	46.78	43.29	.93	40.44	86.43	29.63	1.17	34.69	74.14
102....	48.64	45.13	.91	41.23	84.77	31.17	1.15	35.78	73.56
103....	50.41	46.97	.89	41.97	83.24	32.77	1.13	36.88	73.16
104....	52.11	48.81	.87	42.66	81.88	34.45	1.10	38.00	72.93
105....	53.72	50.66	.86	43.32	80.63	36.21	1.08	39.13	72.84
106....	55.26	52.50	.84	43.94	79.51	38.04	1.06	40.27	72.88
107....	56.71	54.35	.82	44.52	78.51	39.96	1.04	41.41	73.02
108....	58.09	56.20	.80	45.08	77.61	41.95	1.01	42.56	73.26
109....	59.40	58.06	.79	45.61	76.79	44.02	.99	43.70	73.56
110....	60.61	59.92	.77	46.12	76.10	46.17	.97	44.83	73.96
30–64..	0.16	0.13	1.20	0.16	99.67	0.10	2.36	0.23	145.44
65–84..	2.80	2.85	1.10	3.12	111.66	2.08	1.55	3.24	115.75
85+...	20.94	18.99	1.10	20.94	99.99	13.27	1.38	18.31	87.45
Total ..	0.62%	0.53%	1.11	0.58%	94.58%	0.38%	1.60	0.61%	98.67%

exposure of any record spanned two or more durational groups, the appropriate exposure was placed into each interval.

The discharges were also tabulated by sex, age group at admission, and duration interval at discharge. The discharge rates were then calculated by dividing the discharges in each interval by the corresponding exposure. Under the stay concept, all discharges were counted in determining the discharge rate. Under the benefit period concept, those discharges that transferred to another nursing home (either immediately or after a hospital stay) were excluded from the discharges. They were treated like a withdrawal from observation. A total of 39 percent of the discharges ended in a hospital stay followed by readmission to the same or another nursing home or a direct transfer to another home. Excluding these discharges resulted in lower discharge rates and longer lengths-of-stay, the longer length-of-stay offsetting the lower admission rate. By excluding transfers from the discharges, the only discharges that were counted were deaths and recoveries.

The discharge rates were then smoothed by the separate application of the Whittaker-Henderson Type B graduation formula within each set of equally spaced duration cells. Finally, because discharge rates were only calculated up to duration 15 years, it was assumed that the rate after the 15th year was the same as the rate in the 15th year.

Discharge rates were then used to calculate the proportion of nursing home admissions still resident at the end of each interval. This is equivalent to the lx column of a life table with a radix of 1.0. The results of these calculations are shown in Table 6 for all stays under the stay concept, Table 7 for all stays under the benefit period concept, and Table 8 for insurable stays under the benefit period concept.

As mentioned earlier, the distribution by length-of-stay is not as accurately estimated from the NNHS as are the distributions by incidence rates and number of residents on October 11, 1985 (the average date of interview). Therefore, the distributions by length-of-stay were adjusted based on the number of residents on October 11, 1985 tabulated from the survey. An estimate of the number of residents on this date was made from the incidence rates and the fractions shown in Tables 6–8. The total number of residents was estimated separately for the stay concept and for the benefit period concept, while the number of residents without the excluded conditions was estimated for the benefit period concept.

Under each concept, the number of admissions in the U.S. (excluding Alaska and Hawaii) was calculated for each year back to 1970, by applying the admission rates to the July 1 noninstitutionalized population in each year.

TABLE 6

PROPORTION OF ADMISSIONS STILL RESIDENT AT THE END OF THE PERIOD SHOWN; ALL STAYS; STAY CONCEPT; UNADJUSTED 1985 NNHS EXPERIENCE

Days from Admission	Age at Admission						
	<45	45–54	55–64	65–74	75–84	85–94	95+
				Males			
0	1.0000	1.0000	1.0000	1.0000	1.0000	1.0000	1.0000
10	.8747	.8420	.9054	.8635	.8491	.8577	.8721
20	.7800	.7441	.7996	.7840	.7298	.7359	.7698
30	.7243	.6748	.7315	.6971	.6298	.6622	.7036
60	.5620	.4720	.5818	.5540	.4724	.5337	.4936
90	.4545	.3612	.4744	.4545	.3747	.4420	.3719
121	.3805	.2964	.3955	.3832	.3107	.3748	.2963
151	.3278	.2563	.3362	.3306	.2666	.3241	.2463
182	.2888	.2306	.2908	.2908	.2349	.2848	.2114
212	.2588	.2133	.2555	.2601	.2109	.2536	.1856
243	.2348	.2012	.2276	.2358	.1920	.2284	.1657
273	.2147	.1921	.2053	.2162	.1765	.2075	.1496
304	.1973	.1847	.1872	.2001	.1632	.1899	.1361
334	.1818	.1780	.1723	.1866	.1515	.1748	.1248
365	.1680	.1716	.1597	.1750	.1410	.1618	.1151
547	.1084	.1292	.1096	.1279	.0938	.1091	.0814
730	.0715	.0909	.0825	.0986	.0633	.0794	.0648
912	.0500	.0659	.0695	.0764	.0402	.0560	.0446
1095	.0429	.0471	.0601	.0576	.0261	.0364	.0227
1277	.0416	.0353	.0480	.0438	.0193	.0242	.0105
1460	.0408	.0254	.0338	.0361	.0152	.0168	.0065
1642	.0366	.0173	.0238	.0319	.0118	.0107	.0058
1825	.0334	.0119	.0192	.0242	.0093	.0068	.0057
2190	.0220	.0092	.0106	.0072	.0033	.0018	.0009
2555	.0135	.0077	.0066	.0025	.0009	.0003	.0003
2920	.0081	.0067	.0044	.0009	.0002	.0000	.0002
3285	.0049	.0061	.0030	.0004	.0000	.0000	.0001
3650	.0031	.0056	.0021	.0002	.0000	.0000	.0001
4015	.0021	.0051	.0013	.0001	.0000	.0000	.0001
4380	.0016	.0042	.0008	.0001	.0000	.0000	.0001
4745	.0014	.0030	.0004	.0000	.0000	.0000	.0000
5110	.0012	.0018	.0002	.0000	.0000	.0000	.0000
5475	.0011	.0008	.0001	.0000	.0000	.0000	.0000
5840	.0010	.0004	.0000	.0000	.0000	.0000	.0000
6205	.0009	.0002	.0000	.0000	.0000	.0000	.0000
6570	.0008	.0001	.0000	.0000	.0000	.0000	.0000
6935	.0007	.0000	.0000	.0000	.0000	.0000	.0000
7300	.0006	.0000	.0000	.0000	.0000	.0000	.0000
7665	.0006	.0000	.0000	.0000	.0000	.0000	.0000
8030	.0005	.0000	.0000	.0000	.0000	.0000	.0000
8395	.0005	.0000	.0000	.0000	.0000	.0000	.0000
8760	.0004	.0000	.0000	.0000	.0000	.0000	.0000
9125	.0004	.0000	.0000	.0000	.0000	.0000	.0000

TABLE 6—*Continued*

Days from Admission	Age at Admission						
	<45	45–54	55–64	65–74	75–84	85–94	95+
				Females			
0	1.0000	1.0000	1.0000	1.0000	1.0000	1.0000	1.0000
10	.8648	.9363	.9095	.8995	.8900	.8798	.8926
20	.8048	.8426	.8192	.7864	.7839	.7854	.8349
30	.7434	.7491	.7363	.6958	.7064	.7212	.7813
60	.6521	.5378	.5872	.5430	.5684	.5902	.6266
90	.5747	.4149	.4917	.4486	.4761	.5021	.5226
121	.5083	.3386	.4282	.3878	.4122	.4407	.4500
151	.4509	.2884	.3846	.3471	.3664	.3966	.3975
182	.4008	.2536	.3535	.3188	.3325	.3638	.3580
212	.3570	.2283	.3303	.2984	.3065	.3385	.3272
243	.3188	.2089	.3120	.2828	.2858	.3181	.3023
273	.2855	.1933	.2967	.2699	.2688	.3010	.2814
304	.2566	.1800	.2829	.2584	.2543	.2861	.2632
334	.2317	.1682	.2700	.2476	.2415	.2726	.2469
365	.2104	.1572	.2575	.2369	.2301	.2601	.2322
547	.1378	.1031	.1899	.1707	.1772	.1965	.1648
730	.1008	.0759	.1437	.1209	.1409	.1461	.1133
912	.0693	.0666	.1082	.0908	.1124	.1082	.0681
1095	.0538	.0607	.0823	.0699	.0863	.0820	.0438
1277	.0481	.0556	.0709	.0569	.0651	.0628	.0344
1460	.0394	.0473	.0679	.0487	.0501	.0459	.0284
1642	.0225	.0295	.0625	.0412	.0380	.0319	.0226
1825	.0128	.0145	.0521	.0307	.0260	.0236	.0159
2190	.0094	.0094	.0340	.0142	.0133	.0079	.0097
2555	.0075	.0067	.0204	.0073	.0055	.0025	.0016
2920	.0064	.0051	.0117	.0040	.0019	.0007	.0000
3285	.0057	.0042	.0066	.0023	.0006	.0001	.0000
3650	.0052	.0036	.0039	.0013	.0002	.0000	.0000
4015	.0046	.0032	.0024	.0007	.0001	.0000	.0000
4380	.0037	.0030	.0017	.0004	.0000	.0000	.0000
4745	.0025	.0028	.0013	.0002	.0000	.0000	.0000
5110	.0014	.0027	.0011	.0001	.0000	.0000	.0000
5475	.0005	.0026	.0009	.0000	.0000	.0000	.0000
5840	.0002	.0025	.0008	.0000	.0000	.0000	.0000
6205	.0001	.0024	.0007	.0000	.0000	.0000	.0000
6570	.0000	.0023	.0006	.0000	.0000	.0000	.0000
6935	.0000	.0023	.0005	.0000	.0000	.0000	.0000
7300	.0000	.0022	.0005	.0000	.0000	.0000	.0000
7665	.0000	.0021	.0004	.0000	.0000	.0000	.0000
8030	.0000	.0021	.0004	.0000	.0000	.0000	.0000
8395	.0000	.0020	.0003	.0000	.0000	.0000	.0000
8760	.0000	.0019	.0003	.0000	.0000	.0000	.0000
9125	.0000	.0019	.0002	.0000	.0000	.0000	.0000

TABLE 6—*Continued*

Days from Admission	Age at Admission						
	<45	45–54	55–64	65–74	75–84	85–94	95+
				Total			
0.........	1.0000	1.0000	1.0000	1.0000	1.0000	1.0000	1.0000
10.........	.8715	.8830	.9072	.8849	.8763	.8741	.8868
20.........	.7888	.7873	.8084	.7854	.7658	.7722	.8164
30.........	.7315	.7143	.7336	.6963	.6807	.7055	.7593
60.........	.5939	.5046	.5833	.5472	.5366	.5750	.5913
90.........	.4958	.3874	.4815	.4509	.4424	.4860	.4822
121.........	.4236	.3173	.4102	.3862	.3782	.4232	.4082
151.........	.3688	.2730	.3585	.3411	.3328	.3774	.3557
182.........	.3260	.2437	.3200	.3085	.2994	.3429	.3170
212.........	.2915	.2234	.2902	.2840	.2739	.3159	.2873
243.........	.2629	.2086	.2665	.2649	.2537	.2941	.2636
273.........	.2386	.1971	.2471	.2493	.2370	.2759	.2438
304.........	.2175	.1876	.2307	.2358	.2228	.2601	.2267
334.........	.1990	.1790	.2164	.2238	.2102	.2460	.2118
365.........	.1827	.1708	.2036	.2126	.1989	.2332	.1984
547.........	.1188	.1231	.1450	.1545	.1469	.1722	.1408
730.........	.0817	.0895	.1094	.1132	.1119	.1275	.0998
912.........	.0566	.0714	.0865	.0861	.0850	.0934	.0618
1095.........	.0461	.0569	.0695	.0658	.0633	.0687	.0388
1277.........	.0426	.0464	.0578	.0523	.0476	.0513	.0289
1460.........	.0373	.0360	.0491	.0442	.0368	.0372	.0237
1642.........	.0270	.0235	.0414	.0380	.0281	.0254	.0194
1825.........	.0203	.0143	.0344	.0285	.0200	.0183	.0139
2190.........	.0141	.0106	.0205	.0113	.0096	.0059	.0070
2555.........	.0103	.0085	.0125	.0052	.0037	.0018	.0014
2920.........	.0079	.0071	.0078	.0026	.0012	.0005	.0001
3285.........	.0062	.0062	.0049	.0014	.0003	.0001	.0000
3650.........	.0050	.0055	.0031	.0008	.0001	.0000	.0000
4015.........	.0040	.0049	.0020	.0004	.0000	.0000	.0000
4380.........	.0032	.0044	.0013	.0002	.0000	.0000	.0000
4745.........	.0025	.0039	.0008	.0001	.0000	.0000	.0000
5110.........	.0019	.0034	.0005	.0001	.0000	.0000	.0000
5475.........	.0013	.0029	.0003	.0000	.0000	.0000	.0000
5840.........	.0010	.0024	.0002	.0000	.0000	.0000	.0000
6205.........	.0007	.0020	.0001	.0000	.0000	.0000	.0000
6570.........	.0005	.0017	.0001	.0000	.0000	.0000	.0000
6935.........	.0003	.0014	.0001	.0000	.0000	.0000	.0000
7300.........	.0002	.0012	.0000	.0000	.0000	.0000	.0000
7665.........	.0002	.0010	.0000	.0000	.0000	.0000	.0000
8030.........	.0001	.0009	.0000	.0000	.0000	.0000	.0000
8395.........	.0001	.0007	.0000	.0000	.0000	.0000	.0000
8760.........	.0001	.0006	.0000	.0000	.0000	.0000	.0000
9125.........	.0000	.0005	.0000	.0000	.0000	.0000	.0000

TABLE 7

PROPORTION OF ADMISSIONS STILL RESIDENT AT THE END OF THE PERIOD SHOWN; ALL STAYS; BENEFIT PERIOD CONCEPT; UNADJUSTED 1985 NNHS EXPERIENCE

Days from Admission	Age at Admission						
	<45	45–54	55–64	65–74	75–84	85–94	95+
				Males			
0.........	1.0000	1.0000	1.0000	1.0000	1.0000	1.0000	1.0000
10.........	.9146	.9218	.9466	.8974	.8844	.8854	.9238
20.........	.8641	.8612	.8670	.8404	.7942	.7816	.8136
30.........	.8251	.8523	.8168	.7709	.7145	.7139	.7694
60.........	.7275	.6959	.7044	.6472	.5842	.6152	.5863
90.........	.6499	.5949	.6252	.5600	.4967	.5395	.4650
121.........	.5878	.5276	.5680	.4973	.4360	.4806	.3816
151.........	.5381	.4816	.5256	.4514	.3924	.4339	.3224
182.........	.4981	.4495	.4930	.4174	.3600	.3966	.2791
212.........	.4659	.4263	.4672	.3918	.3350	.3662	.2467
243.........	.4397	.4088	.4458	.3721	.3149	.3414	.2219
273.........	.4182	.3949	.4274	.3565	.2981	.3208	.2024
304.........	.4001	.3830	.4109	.3436	.2834	.3035	.1869
334.........	.3845	.3721	.3956	.3324	.2702	.2890	.1745
365.........	.3707	.3613	.3808	.3221	.2580	.2764	.1643
547.........	.2981	.2868	.2978	.2629	.1958	.2214	.1333
730.........	.2338	.2179	.2450	.2116	.1461	.1718	.1200
912.........	.2009	.1889	.2309	.1830	.1032	.1198	.0854
1095.........	.1934	.1698	.2253	.1595	.0719	.0801	.0419
1277.........	.1921	.1429	.2018	.1311	.0541	.0567	.0239
1460.........	.1918	.1254	.1720	.1088	.0426	.0420	.0200
1642.........	.1910	.1214	.1562	.0975	.0329	.0298	.0194
1825.........	.1907	.0929	.1420	.0820	.0258	.0227	.0178
2190.........	.1420	.0820	.1117	.0369	.0167	.0107	.0027
2555.........	.1124	.0716	.0869	.0170	.0101	.0007	.0010
2920.........	.0926	.0617	.0666	.0081	.0057	.0000	.0005
3285.........	.0780	.0521	.0503	.0040	.0031	.0000	.0003
3650.........	.0660	.0431	.0374	.0021	.0017	.0000	.0002
4015.........	.0551	.0346	.0273	.0011	.0009	.0000	.0002
4380.........	.0447	.0269	.0194	.0006	.0005	.0000	.0002
4745.........	.0346	.0202	.0135	.0004	.0003	.0000	.0001
5110.........	.0249	.0145	.0091	.0002	.0002	.0000	.0001
5475.........	.0163	.0099	.0060	.0002	.0001	.0000	.0001
5840.........	.0107	.0068	.0039	.0001	.0001	.0000	.0000
6205.........	.0070	.0046	.0026	.0001	.0001	.0000	.0000
6570.........	.0046	.0032	.0017	.0000	.0000	.0000	.0000
6935.........	.0030	.0022	.0011	.0000	.0000	.0000	.0000
7300.........	.0020	.0015	.0007	.0000	.0000	.0000	.0000
7665.........	.0013	.0010	.0005	.0000	.0000	.0000	.0000
8030.........	.0008	.0007	.0003	.0000	.0000	.0000	.0000
8395.........	.0006	.0005	.0002	.0000	.0000	.0000	.0000
8760.........	.0004	.0003	.0001	.0000	.0000	.0000	.0000
9125.........	.0002	.0002	.0001	.0000	.0000	.0000	.0000

TABLE 7—*Continued*

Days from Admission	Age at Admission						
	<45	45–54	55–64	65–74	75–84	85–94	95+
	Females						
0.........	1.0000	1.0000	1.0000	1.0000	1.0000	1.0000	1.0000
10.........	.9225	.9776	.9246	.9211	.9315	.9159	.9134
20.........	.8562	.8999	.8441	.8346	.8551	.8418	.8658
30.........	.8226	.8390	.8047	.7697	.7824	.7896	.8149
60.........	.7892	.6791	.6854	.6482	.6742	.6727	.7360
90.........	.7509	.5800	.6040	.5669	.5973	.5925	.6664
121.........	.7100	.5165	.5474	.5113	.5414	.5362	.6055
151.........	.6686	.4746	.5077	.4727	.4999	.4959	.5524
182.........	.6284	.4460	.4795	.4454	.4685	.4665	.5065
212.........	.5907	.4256	.4592	.4258	.4441	.4443	.4669
243.........	.5563	.4100	.4441	.4113	.4245	.4269	.4327
273.........	.5258	.3970	.4324	.4000	.4084	.4127	.4030
304.........	.4992	.3850	.4226	.3908	.3945	.4004	.3769
334.........	.4765	.3731	.4138	.3826	.3823	.3892	.3539
365.........	.4574	.3609	.4053	.3750	.3712	.3785	.3333
547.........	.3950	.2838	.3528	.3247	.3163	.3160	.2468
730.........	.3325	.2392	.3129	.2651	.2720	.2570	.1917
912.........	.2450	.2248	.2736	.2176	.2345	.2104	.1485
1095.........	.1943	.2216	.2375	.1860	.1998	.1745	.1185
1277.........	.1819	.2122	.2199	.1609	.1682	.1404	.0954
1460.........	.1731	.1967	.2103	.1393	.1399	.1072	.0797
1642.........	.1441	.1807	.1953	.1239	.1145	.0820	.0713
1825.........	.1127	.1569	.1851	.1149	.0916	.0681	.0573
2190.........	.0990	.1271	.1486	.0789	.0559	.0377	.0443
2555.........	.0900	.1033	.1155	.0541	.0323	.0154	.0248
2920.........	.0839	.0846	.0881	.0370	.0180	.0046	.0069
3285.........	.0786	.0703	.0667	.0255	.0099	.0010	.0000
3650.........	.0702	.0596	.0509	.0176	.0054	.0002	.0000
4015.........	.0571	.0519	.0398	.0123	.0030	.0000	.0000
4380.........	.0401	.0467	.0322	.0087	.0018	.0000	.0000
4745.........	.0224	.0431	.0274	.0062	.0011	.0000	.0000
5110.........	.0084	.0407	.0243	.0046	.0007	.0000	.0000
5475.........	.0014	.0390	.0223	.0034	.0005	.0000	.0000
5840.........	.0002	.0373	.0204	.0025	.0004	.0000	.0000
6205.........	.0000	.0357	.0187	.0019	.0003	.0000	.0000
6570.........	.0000	.0342	.0171	.0014	.0002	.0000	.0000
6935.........	.0000	.0328	.0157	.0010	.0001	.0000	.0000
7300.........	.0000	.0314	.0143	.0008	.0001	.0000	.0000
7665.........	.0000	.0300	.0131	.0006	.0001	.0000	.0000
8030.........	.0000	.0288	.0120	.0004	.0001	.0000	.0000
8395.........	.0000	.0276	.0110	.0003	.0000	.0000	.0000
8760.........	.0000	.0264	.0101	.0002	.0000	.0000	.0000
9125.........	.0000	.0253	.0092	.0002	.0000	.0000	.0000

TABLE 7—*Continued*

Days from Admission	Age at Admission						
	<45	45–54	55–64	65–74	75–84	85–94	95+
	Total						
0	1.0000	1.0000	1.0000	1.0000	1.0000	1.0000	1.0000
10	.9170	.9444	.9364	.9115	.9149	.9072	.9164
20	.8623	.8772	.8564	.8369	.8337	.8245	.8510
30	.8337	.8512	.8121	.7704	.7585	.7678	.8052
60	.7590	.6929	.6962	.6480	.6433	.6557	.7003
90	.6945	.5922	.6159	.5645	.5628	.5769	.6160
121	.6389	.5262	.5591	.5063	.5052	.5201	.5477
151	.5912	.4817	.5182	.4650	.4629	.4784	.4919
182	.5505	.4509	.4880	.4352	.4311	.4470	.4461
212	.5159	.4287	.4652	.4134	.4064	.4228	.4081
243	.4865	.4119	.4472	.3969	.3867	.4035	.3764
273	.4615	.3983	.4323	.3840	.3702	.3876	.3495
304	.4402	.3863	.4192	.3733	.3561	.3740	.3264
334	.4218	.3749	.4071	.3640	.3435	.3619	.3063
365	.4058	.3635	.3954	.3552	.3320	.3507	.2887
547	.3346	.2886	.3258	.3006	.2739	.2905	.2174
730	.2679	.2310	.2774	.2437	.2268	.2341	.1728
912	.2123	.2079	.2497	.2039	.1867	.1851	.1313
1095	.1861	.1925	.2272	.1756	.1526	.1468	.0979
1277	.1802	.1694	.2063	.1493	.1257	.1153	.0771
1460	.1744	.1518	.1870	.1274	.1035	.0878	.0660
1642	.1564	.1449	.1722	.1137	.0836	.0663	.0605
1825	.1360	.1145	.1613	.1017	.0665	.0543	.0487
2190	.1110	.0976	.1284	.0615	.0411	.0292	.0281
2555	.0953	.0825	.0997	.0379	.0240	.0110	.0136
2920	.0841	.0693	.0761	.0239	.0134	.0029	.0047
3285	.0742	.0579	.0575	.0153	.0074	.0005	.0008
3650	.0642	.0483	.0434	.0100	.0040	.0001	.0000
4015	.0529	.0404	.0330	.0067	.0022	.0000	.0000
4380	.0404	.0339	.0255	.0045	.0013	.0000	.0000
4745	.0276	.0286	.0202	.0031	.0008	.0000	.0000
5110	.0160	.0244	.0165	.0022	.0005	.0000	.0000
5475	.0073	.0212	.0140	.0015	.0004	.0000	.0000
5840	.0033	.0183	.0119	.0011	.0003	.0000	.0000
6205	.0015	.0159	.0101	.0008	.0002	.0000	.0000
6570	.0007	.0137	.0085	.0006	.0001	.0000	.0000
6935	.0003	.0119	.0073	.0004	.0001	.0000	.0000
7300	.0001	.0103	.0062	.0003	.0001	.0000	.0000
7665	.0001	.0089	.0052	.0002	.0000	.0000	.0000
8030	.0000	.0077	.0044	.0001	.0000	.0000	.0000
8395	.0000	.0067	.0038	.0001	.0000	.0000	.0000
8760	.0000	.0058	.0032	.0001	.0000	.0000	.0000
9125	.0000	.0050	.0027	.0000	.0000	.0000	.0000

TABLE 8

PROPORTION OF ADMISSIONS STILL RESIDENT AT THE END OF THE PERIOD SHOWN; INSURABLE STAYS; BENEFIT PERIOD CONCEPT; UNADJUSTED 1985 NNHS EXPERIENCE

Days from Admission	Age at Admission						
	<45	45–54	55–64	65–74	75–84	85–94	95+
				Males			
0	1.0000	1.0000	1.0000	1.0000	1.0000	1.0000	1.0000
10	.8595	.9029	.9410	.8935	.8826	.8839	.9294
20	.8332	.8281	.8530	.8356	.7927	.7792	.8401
30	.8016	.8172	.7976	.7616	.7121	.7154	.7939
60	.6772	.6794	.6750	.6324	.5840	.6110	.6039
90	.5862	.5907	.5897	.5427	.4973	.5322	.4756
121	.5188	.5324	.5286	.4790	.4367	.4717	.3861
151	.4684	.4932	.4834	.4329	.3929	.4245	.3217
182	.4304	.4662	.4488	.3992	.3602	.3871	.2743
212	.4014	.4471	.4213	.3740	.3349	.3571	.2386
243	.3790	.4327	.3986	.3549	.3145	.3326	.2111
273	.3610	.4210	.3790	.3399	.2973	.3124	.1897
304	.3461	.4102	.3616	.3277	.2824	.2956	.1728
334	.3331	.3995	.3455	.3171	.2689	.2814	.1592
365	.3210	.3880	.3303	.3074	.2565	.2692	.1484
547	.2549	.2944	.2480	.2502	.1930	.2162	.1169
730	.2077	.2067	.1988	.1985	.1420	.1679	.1057
912	.1884	.1725	.1864	.1690	.0991	.1159	.0754
1095	.1844	.1533	.1779	.1446	.0682	.0758	.0368
1277	.1837	.1303	.1492	.1153	.0507	.0522	.0209
1460	.1834	.1182	.1225	.0926	.0393	.0379	.0176
1642	.1827	.1153	.1147	.0811	.0296	.0266	.0170
1825	.1824	.0799	.1134	.0674	.0234	.0203	.0155
2190	.1397	.0679	.0846	.0298	.0148	.0074	.0024
2555	.1071	.0563	.0639	.0134	.0088	.0000	.0009
2920	.0818	.0455	.0486	.0062	.0049	.0000	.0004
3285	.0620	.0358	.0367	.0030	.0027	.0000	.0003
3650	.0463	.0276	.0274	.0015	.0014	.0000	.0002
4015	.0340	.0207	.0199	.0008	.0007	.0000	.0002
4380	.0245	.0151	.0140	.0004	.0004	.0000	.0001
4745	.0171	.0109	.0093	.0002	.0002	.0000	.0001
5110	.0116	.0076	.0058	.0002	.0001	.0000	.0001
5475	.0076	.0052	.0033	.0001	.0001	.0000	.0001
5840	.0049	.0036	.0019	.0001	.0000	.0000	.0000
6205	.0032	.0025	.0011	.0000	.0000	.0000	.0000
6570	.0021	.0017	.0006	.0000	.0000	.0000	.0000
6935	.0014	.0012	.0004	.0000	.0000	.0000	.0000
7300	.0009	.0008	.0002	.0000	.0000	.0000	.0000
7665	.0006	.0006	.0001	.0000	.0000	.0000	.0000
8030	.0004	.0004	.0001	.0000	.0000	.0000	.0000
8395	.0003	.0003	.0000	.0000	.0000	.0000	.0000
8760	.0002	.0002	.0000	.0000	.0000	.0000	.0000
9125	.0001	.0001	.0000	.0000	.0000	.0000	.0000

TABLE 8—*Continued*

Days from Admission	Age at Admission						
	<45	45–54	55–64	65–74	75–84	85–94	95+
				Females			
0.........	1.0000	1.0000	1.0000	1.0000	1.0000	1.0000	1.0000
10.........	.8884	.9727	.9229	.9266	.9322	.9139	.9092
20.........	.7935	.9126	.8401	.8390	.8531	.8403	.8592
30.........	.7458	.8514	.8044	.7706	.7794	.7881	.8059
60.........	.7222	.6854	.6771	.6436	.6687	.6705	.7285
90.........	.7012	.5839	.5924	.5592	.5903	.5900	.6592
121.........	.6820	.5202	.5350	.5019	.5336	.5335	.5979
151.........	.6644	.4799	.4958	.4624	.4918	.4932	.5444
182.........	.6478	.4546	.4688	.4346	.4602	.4637	.4982
212.........	.6319	.4366	.4497	.4148	.4358	.4415	.4585
243.........	.6164	.4236	.4360	.4002	.4163	.4241	.4243
273.........	.6011	.4141	.4260	.3891	.4002	.4098	.3948
304.........	.5859	.4072	.4177	.3800	.3864	.3975	.3690
334.........	.5707	.4021	.4099	.3721	.3743	.3862	.3462
365.........	.5558	.3972	.4019	.3647	.3633	.3755	.3258
547.........	.4962	.3306	.3419	.3156	.3087	.3135	.2391
730.........	.4775	.2638	.2925	.2550	.2641	.2566	.1869
912.........	.4012	.2383	.2524	.2049	.2266	.2122	.1485
1095.........	.3028	.2334	.2190	.1728	.1916	.1778	.1197
1277.........	.2681	.2198	.2037	.1502	.1603	.1446	.0960
1460.........	.2508	.1961	.1975	.1316	.1331	.1104	.0799
1642.........	.2018	.1880	.1932	.1175	.1089	.0835	.0717
1825.........	.1503	.1866	.1921	.1087	.0876	.0696	.0575
2190.........	.1307	.1636	.1343	.0739	.0525	.0399	.0445
2555.........	.1127	.1384	.0964	.0497	.0298	.0176	.0249
2920.........	.0954	.1145	.0712	.0334	.0163	.0060	.0069
3285.........	.0788	.0939	.0540	.0225	.0087	.0016	.0000
3650.........	.0628	.0776	.0421	.0154	.0047	.0003	.0000
4015.........	.0479	.0655	.0339	.0108	.0026	.0001	.0000
4380.........	.0346	.0575	.0281	.0077	.0015	.0000	.0000
4745.........	.0233	.0521	.0241	.0057	.0009	.0000	.0000
5110.........	.0144	.0485	.0215	.0044	.0006	.0000	.0000
5475.........	.0080	.0460	.0197	.0036	.0005	.0000	.0000
5840.........	.0045	.0436	.0181	.0029	.0003	.0000	.0000
6205.........	.0025	.0413	.0166	.0023	.0003	.0000	.0000
6570.........	.0014	.0392	.0152	.0019	.0002	.0000	.0000
6935.........	.0008	.0371	.0139	.0015	.0001	.0000	.0000
7300.........	.0004	.0352	.0128	.0012	.0001	.0000	.0000
7665.........	.0002	.0334	.0117	.0010	.0001	.0000	.0000
8030.........	.0001	.0316	.0107	.0008	.0001	.0000	.0000
8395.........	.0001	.0300	.0099	.0006	.0000	.0000	.0000
8760.........	.0000	.0284	.0090	.0005	.0000	.0000	.0000
9125.........	.0000	.0269	.0083	.0004	.0000	.0000	.0000

TABLE 8—*Continued*

Days from Admission	Age at Admission						
	<45	45–54	55–64	65–74	75–84	85–94	95+
	Total						
0	1.0000	1.0000	1.0000	1.0000	1.0000	1.0000	1.0000
10	.8719	.9323	.9326	.9133	.9146	.9054	.9150
20	.8178	.8639	.8471	.8376	.8317	.8228	.8538
30	.7881	.8366	.8010	.7674	.7556	.7673	.8056
60	.7057	.6872	.6760	.6393	.6392	.6531	.6998
90	.6424	.5929	.5911	.5529	.5581	.5731	.6137
121	.5935	.5319	.5322	.4933	.5000	.5159	.5435
151	.5553	.4918	.4905	.4513	.4575	.4740	.4860
182	.5253	.4650	.4602	.4213	.4256	.4425	.4388
212	.5012	.4460	.4376	.3995	.4008	.4184	.3997
243	.4816	.4324	.4200	.3832	.3810	.3992	.3673
273	.4649	.4225	.4055	.3705	.3646	.3834	.3399
304	.4500	.4138	.3928	.3602	.3504	.3699	.3166
334	.4362	.4052	.3808	.3512	.3379	.3579	.2963
365	.4229	.3957	.3689	.3428	.3264	.3467	.2786
547	.3533	.3113	.2943	.2896	.2681	.2874	.2074
730	.3085	.2327	.2421	.2321	.2205	.2327	.1658
912	.2683	.2016	.2161	.1905	.1803	.1850	.1284
1095	.2337	.1848	.1951	.1616	.1459	.1474	.0964
1277	.2219	.1618	.1736	.1366	.1193	.1163	.0756
1460	.2104	.1459	.1571	.1164	.0979	.0882	.0646
1642	.1798	.1417	.1516	.1034	.0787	.0659	.0593
1825	.1476	.1058	.1506	.0921	.0631	.0541	.0477
2190	.1204	.0912	.1094	.0549	.0382	.0294	.0275
2555	.0975	.0762	.0805	.0331	.0219	.0117	.0133
2920	.0781	.0622	.0601	.0204	.0120	.0033	.0046
3285	.0615	.0498	.0453	.0128	.0065	.0007	.0008
3650	.0473	.0395	.0346	.0082	.0035	.0001	.0000
4015	.0353	.0314	.0267	.0054	.0019	.0000	.0000
4380	.0255	.0251	.0208	.0037	.0011	.0000	.0000
4745	.0177	.0204	.0164	.0026	.0007	.0000	.0000
5110	.0117	.0171	.0130	.0019	.0004	.0000	.0000
5475	.0073	.0147	.0105	.0014	.0003	.0000	.0000
5840	.0045	.0127	.0084	.0010	.0002	.0000	.0000
6205	.0028	.0109	.0067	.0008	.0002	.0000	.0000
6570	.0018	.0094	.0054	.0006	.0001	.0000	.0000
6935	.0011	.0081	.0043	.0004	.0001	.0000	.0000
7300	.0007	.0070	.0035	.0003	.0001	.0000	.0000
7665	.0004	.0061	.0028	.0002	.0000	.0000	.0000
8030	.0003	.0052	.0022	.0002	.0000	.0000	.0000
8395	.0002	.0045	.0018	.0001	.0000	.0000	.0000
8760	.0001	.0039	.0014	.0001	.0000	.0000	.0000
9125	.0001	.0034	.0012	.0001	.0000	.0000	.0000

No trend was assumed in the admission rates through time. It was assumed that the admissions in each year were made uniformly throughout each calendar year. The fraction of each year's admissions still confined on October 11, 1985 was estimated by applying the appropriate fractions from Tables 6–8. This was done as follows: All the estimated admissions on October 11 were counted. For each of the 30 days prior to October 11, the number of admissions still confined on October 11 was estimated by multiplying the estimated number of admissions times the appropriate "proportion of residents still resident." Similar calculations were made for the estimated number of admissions in monthly intervals for the prior 59 months and then in yearly intervals for the prior 10 years.

In general, the resulting estimates of the number of nursing home residents were slightly below the actual as tabulated from the NNHS. The discharge rates were then adjusted downward by applying a constant factor (producing higher proportions of admissions still resident at each duration, and thus longer stays) until the estimated residents matched the tabulated. The results of these calculations are shown in Tables 9–11 for the three sets of utilization data.

This adjustment added several percentage points to the proportion still resident at each duration. For example, compare, for admissions between ages 75 and 84, the proportions still resident at 1 year and at 5 years after admission for total (male and female) insurable stays under the benefit period concept (Tables 8 and 11). Before adjustment, the proportions are 33 percent and 6 percent still resident after 1 year and 5 years, respectively; after adjustment, the proportions are 36 percent and 8 percent, respectively. The longer the stay, the greater the relative adjustment, because the adjustment factor was applied to the rates of discharge between intervals (that is, the rates calculated from the raw data). Thus, the adjusted proportions still resident at each succeeding interval become progressively greater.

D. Continuance Tables and Average Length-of-Stay

For pricing, the distribution of days by length-of-stay is more important than the distribution of residents by length-of-stay. The number of days in each interval was estimated as the average number of residents in the life table (that is, the average of the lx at the beginning and at the end of the interval, taking into account that discharges can only occur at integral days) times the number of days in the interval. The number of days above each threshold was then calculated by summing from the end of the life table

TABLE 9

PROPORTION OF ADMISSIONS STILL RESIDENT AT THE END OF THE PERIOD SHOWN; ALL STAYS; STAY CONCEPT; ADJUSTED TO MATCH 1985 NNHS RESIDENTS

Days from Admission	Age at Admission						
	<45	45–54	55–64	65–74	75–84	85–94	95+
	Males						
0.........	1.0000	1.0000	1.0000	1.0000	1.0000	1.0000	1.0000
10.........	.9004	.8739	.9250	.8913	.8797	.8867	.8983
20.........	.8230	.7932	.8391	.8263	.7812	.7864	.8146
30.........	.7766	.7347	.7826	.7536	.6961	.7240	.7591
60.........	.6399	.5614	.6569	.6322	.5595	.6136	.5813
90.........	.5438	.4579	.5617	.5431	.4687	.5309	.4688
121.........	.4744	.3934	.4884	.4761	.4058	.4675	.3940
151.........	.4228	.3517	.4309	.4248	.3606	.4179	.3418
182.........	.3833	.3240	.3852	.3847	.3269	.3781	.3038
212.........	.3521	.3049	.3485	.3528	.3008	.3456	.2747
243.........	.3264	.2913	.3186	.3270	.2796	.3186	.2515
273.........	.3044	.2810	.2941	.3057	.2618	.2957	.2323
304.........	.2851	.2725	.2737	.2878	.2463	.2760	.2159
334.........	.2676	.2647	.2566	.2725	.2325	.2589	.2018
365.........	.2515	.2572	.2419	.2592	.2198	.2437	.1895
547.........	.1788	.2060	.1804	.2030	.1600	.1792	.1447
730.........	.1294	.1567	.1446	.1656	.1178	.1399	.1211
912.........	.0978	.1219	.1264	.1357	.0827	.1065	.0904
1095.........	.0868	.0938	.1128	.1088	.0591	.0761	.0536
1277.........	.0848	.0748	.0945	.0879	.0467	.0554	.0295
1460.........	.0835	.0579	.0719	.0755	.0388	.0417	.0203
1642.........	.0767	.0429	.0548	.0686	.0318	.0293	.0186
1825.........	.0713	.0320	.0463	.0553	.0265	.0207	.0183
2190.........	.0522	.0264	.0301	.0248	.0131	.0088	.0061
2555.........	.0364	.0229	.0212	.0120	.0056	.0030	.0031
2920.........	.0249	.0206	.0156	.0062	.0022	.0008	.0019
3285.........	.0171	.0191	.0117	.0034	.0008	.0002	.0014
3650.........	.0122	.0181	.0088	.0020	.0003	.0000	.0011
4015.........	.0092	.0166	.0064	.0012	.0001	.0000	.0009
4380.........	.0076	.0144	.0044	.0008	.0000	.0000	.0008
4745.........	.0065	.0113	.0028	.0006	.0000	.0000	.0007
5110.........	.0059	.0077	.0016	.0004	.0000	.0000	.0007
5475.........	.0054	.0044	.0008	.0003	.0000	.0000	.0007
5840.........	.0050	.0024	.0004	.0002	.0000	.0000	.0001
6205.........	.0046	.0014	.0002	.0002	.0000	.0000	.0000
6570.........	.0043	.0008	.0001	.0001	.0000	.0000	.0000
6935.........	.0039	.0004	.0000	.0001	.0000	.0000	.0000
7300.........	.0036	.0002	.0000	.0001	.0000	.0000	.0000
7665.........	.0034	.0001	.0000	.0000	.0000	.0000	.0000
8030.........	.0031	.0001	.0000	.0000	.0000	.0000	.0000
8395.........	.0029	.0000	.0000	.0000	.0000	.0000	.0000
8760.........	.0026	.0000	.0000	.0000	.0000	.0000	.0000
9125.........	.0024	.0000	.0000	.0000	.0000	.0000	.0000

TABLE 9—*Continued*

Days from Admission	Age at Admission						
	<45	45–54	55–64	65–74	75–84	85–94	95+
	Females						
0	1.0000	1.0000	1.0000	1.0000	1.0000	1.0000	1.0000
10	.8924	.9497	.9283	.9203	.9127	.9045	.9148
20	.8435	.8743	.8552	.8283	.8263	.8275	.8681
30	.7926	.7973	.7866	.7525	.7615	.7739	.8240
60	.7162	.6208	.6616	.6228	.6447	.6636	.6960
90	.6495	.5094	.5771	.5378	.5625	.5858	.6053
121	.5906	.4359	.5186	.4805	.5032	.5296	.5393
151	.5382	.3851	.4771	.4409	.4593	.4880	.4898
182	.4912	.3486	.4468	.4128	.4260	.4563	.4516
212	.4491	.3213	.4238	.3920	.3998	.4314	.4212
243	.4114	.2999	.4054	.3759	.3786	.4110	.3960
273	.3776	.2824	.3897	.3624	.3609	.3937	.3745
304	.3476	.2671	.3756	.3504	.3456	.3783	.3555
334	.3211	.2533	.3622	.3389	.3320	.3643	.3382
365	.2980	.2404	.3490	.3273	.3197	.3512	.3224
547	.2144	.1730	.2751	.2535	.2607	.2822	.2468
730	.1679	.1363	.2213	.1937	.2179	.2238	.1843
912	.1254	.1230	.1773	.1548	.1826	.1770	.1240
1095	.1029	.1143	.1432	.1263	.1486	.1426	.0880
1277	.0942	.1067	.1274	.1075	.1192	.1158	.0727
1460	.0807	.0941	.1231	.0952	.0971	.0906	.0626
1642	.0521	.0651	.1155	.0835	.0782	.0683	.0523
1825	.0336	.0376	.1001	.0664	.0583	.0540	.0398
2190	.0266	.0273	.0729	.0384	.0359	.0257	.0277
2555	.0224	.0211	.0500	.0237	.0194	.0120	.0095
2920	.0198	.0172	.0332	.0153	.0095	.0051	.0021
3285	.0181	.0147	.0219	.0101	.0044	.0018	.0004
3650	.0169	.0131	.0147	.0067	.0020	.0005	.0001
4015	.0153	.0121	.0104	.0044	.0009	.0001	.0000
4380	.0129	.0113	.0079	.0028	.0005	.0000	.0000
4745	.0098	.0108	.0065	.0017	.0003	.0000	.0000
5110	.0063	.0104	.0056	.0010	.0002	.0000	.0000
5475	.0031	.0102	.0050	.0005	.0001	.0000	.0000
5840	.0015	.0099	.0045	.0002	.0001	.0000	.0000
6205	.0007	.0096	.0041	.0001	.0001	.0000	.0000
6570	.0004	.0094	.0037	.0001	.0001	.0000	.0000
6935	.0002	.0091	.0033	.0000	.0000	.0000	.0000
7300	.0001	.0089	.0030	.0000	.0000	.0000	.0000
7665	.0000	.0087	.0027	.0000	.0000	.0000	.0000
8030	.0000	.0085	.0024	.0000	.0000	.0000	.0000
8395	.0000	.0082	.0021	.0000	.0000	.0000	.0000
8760	.0000	.0080	.0019	.0000	.0000	.0000	.0000
9125	.0000	.0078	.0017	.0000	.0000	.0000	.0000

TABLE 9—*Continued*

Days from Admission	Age at Admission						
	<45	45–54	55–64	65–74	75–84	85–94	95+
				Total			
0.........	1.0000	1.0000	1.0000	1.0000	1.0000	1.0000	1.0000
10.........	.8978	.9071	.9265	.9086	.9017	.8999	.9101
20.........	.8303	.8290	.8464	.8275	.8112	.8166	.8529
30.........	.7826	.7681	.7844	.7529	.7397	.7607	.8058
60.........	.6670	.5911	.6582	.6263	.6168	.6503	.6658
90.........	.5805	.4834	.5680	.5398	.5318	.5713	.5694
121.........	.5141	.4147	.5020	.4790	.4712	.5133	.5008
151.........	.4620	.3692	.4524	.4351	.4268	.4697	.4503
182.........	.4199	.3381	.4141	.4025	.3932	.4359	.4118
212.........	.3850	.3160	.3839	.3774	.3669	.4091	.3815
243.........	.3554	.2996	.3593	.3575	.3456	.3869	.3568
273.........	.3296	.2867	.3388	.3409	.3278	.3681	.3357
304.........	.3067	.2757	.3211	.3264	.3123	.3515	.3173
334.........	.2862	.2658	.3055	.3134	.2985	.3366	.3009
365.........	.2678	.2563	.2913	.3011	.2859	.3228	.2859
547.........	.1915	.1985	.2236	.2346	.2256	.2547	.2189
730.........	.1431	.1548	.1793	.1841	.1825	.2015	.1673
912.........	.1075	.1298	.1493	.1486	.1472	.1581	.1152
1095.........	.0915	.1086	.1258	.1205	.1169	.1243	.0802
1277.........	.0861	.0927	.1090	.1007	.0937	.0990	.0638
1460.........	.0775	.0760	.0958	.0882	.0766	.0770	.0545
1642.........	.0602	.0545	.0839	.0783	.0619	.0573	.0467
1825.........	.0482	.0370	.0725	.0626	.0476	.0443	.0360
2190.........	.0367	.0296	.0496	.0329	.0282	.0208	.0219
2555.........	.0290	.0248	.0344	.0189	.0146	.0095	.0082
2920.........	.0236	.0217	.0242	.0116	.0069	.0040	.0022
3285.........	.0197	.0194	.0172	.0074	.0030	.0014	.0006
3650.........	.0166	.0177	.0123	.0048	.0013	.0004	.0003
4015.........	.0140	.0163	.0088	.0031	.0006	.0001	.0002
4380.........	.0118	.0150	.0063	.0020	.0003	.0000	.0002
4745.........	.0098	.0137	.0045	.0013	.0002	.0000	.0000
5110.........	.0079	.0123	.0033	.0007	.0001	.0000	.0000
5475.........	.0061	.0108	.0024	.0004	.0001	.0000	.0000
5840.........	.0047	.0094	.0017	.0002	.0001	.0000	.0000
6205.........	.0036	.0082	.0012	.0001	.0000	.0000	.0000
6570.........	.0028	.0072	.0009	.0001	.0000	.0000	.0000
6935.........	.0022	.0063	.0006	.0000	.0000	.0000	.0000
7300.........	.0017	.0055	.0005	.0000	.0000	.0000	.0000
7665.........	.0013	.0048	.0003	.0000	.0000	.0000	.0000
8030.........	.0010	.0042	.0002	.0000	.0000	.0000	.0000
8395.........	.0008	.0037	.0002	.0000	.0000	.0000	.0000
8760.........	.0006	.0032	.0001	.0000	.0000	.0000	.0000
9125.........	.0005	.0028	.0001	.0000	.0000	.0000	.0000

TABLE 10

PROPORTION OF ADMISSIONS STILL RESIDENT AT THE END OF THE PERIOD SHOWN; ALL STAYS; BENEFIT PERIOD CONCEPT; ADJUSTED TO MATCH 1985 NNHS RESIDENTS

Days from Admission	Age at Admission						
	<45	45–54	55–64	65–74	75–84	85–94	95+
	Males						
0	1.0000	1.0000	1.0000	1.0000	1.0000	1.0000	1.0000
10	.9212	.9279	.9508	.9053	.8932	.8941	.9297
20	.8743	.8716	.8770	.8522	.8090	.7973	.8272
30	.8379	.8633	.8301	.7872	.7340	.7335	.7858
60	.7468	.7176	.7250	.6710	.6109	.6402	.6137
90	.6734	.6218	.6501	.5878	.5268	.5678	.4969
121	.6143	.5570	.5954	.5272	.4675	.5107	.4149
151	.5665	.5124	.5544	.4825	.4245	.4651	.3557
182	.5278	.4809	.5229	.4491	.3922	.4282	.3118
212	.4963	.4581	.4976	.4237	.3672	.3981	.2785
243	.4707	.4408	.4767	.4041	.3469	.3732	.2527
273	.4495	.4270	.4586	.3885	.3299	.3525	.2323
304	.4316	.4152	.4423	.3756	.3150	.3351	.2160
334	.4162	.4043	.4271	.3643	.3015	.3203	.2027
365	.4024	.3935	.4125	.3540	.2890	.3075	.1919
547	.3294	.3183	.3290	.2937	.2243	.2508	.1583
730	.2635	.2473	.2751	.2406	.1714	.1987	.1437
912	.2292	.2169	.2604	.2105	.1246	.1427	.1052
1095	.2213	.1966	.2546	.1855	.0894	.0986	.0548
1277	.2200	.1679	.2301	.1549	.0689	.0719	.0327
1460	.2197	.1488	.1987	.1306	.0553	.0545	.0278
1642	.2188	.1444	.1818	.1180	.0436	.0398	.0270
1825	.2184	.1130	.1666	.1007	.0348	.0310	.0250
2190	.1672	.1008	.1339	.0497	.0236	.0160	.0055
2555	.1351	.0891	.1065	.0251	.0150	.0022	.0023
2920	.1132	.0777	.0837	.0130	.0090	.0002	.0013
3285	.0968	.0667	.0649	.0070	.0052	.0000	.0009
3650	.0831	.0560	.0495	.0039	.0030	.0000	.0006
4015	.0705	.0459	.0372	.0022	.0017	.0000	.0005
4380	.0583	.0365	.0274	.0013	.0010	.0000	.0005
4745	.0461	.0281	.0197	.0008	.0006	.0000	.0004
5110	.0342	.0208	.0138	.0006	.0004	.0000	.0004
5475	.0233	.0147	.0094	.0004	.0003	.0000	.0004
5840	.0159	.0105	.0065	.0003	.0002	.0000	.0000
6205	.0109	.0074	.0044	.0002	.0001	.0000	.0000
6570	.0074	.0053	.0030	.0001	.0001	.0000	.0000
6935	.0051	.0037	.0021	.0001	.0001	.0000	.0000
7300	.0035	.0026	.0014	.0001	.0001	.0000	.0000
7665	.0024	.0019	.0010	.0000	.0000	.0000	.0000
8030	.0016	.0013	.0007	.0000	.0000	.0000	.0000
8395	.0011	.0009	.0004	.0000	.0000	.0000	.0000
8760	.0007	.0007	.0003	.0000	.0000	.0000	.0000
9125	.0005	.0005	.0002	.0000	.0000	.0000	.0000

TABLE 10—*Continued*

Days from Admission	Age at Admission						
	<45	45–54	55–64	65–74	75–84	85–94	95+
				Females			
0.........	1.0000	1.0000	1.0000	1.0000	1.0000	1.0000	1.0000
10.........	.9285	.9794	.9304	.9272	.9368	.9223	.9201
20.........	.8669	.9076	.8556	.8468	.8659	.8536	.8759
30.........	.8356	.8509	.8189	.7860	.7979	.8047	.8284
60.........	.8044	.7017	.7072	.6719	.6965	.6951	.7546
90.........	.7685	.6075	.6299	.5943	.6233	.6188	.6890
121.........	.7300	.5463	.5756	.5407	.5697	.5648	.6310
151.........	.6908	.5055	.5372	.5031	.5295	.5257	.5801
182.........	.6526	.4775	.5098	.4765	.4989	.4970	.5358
212.........	.6166	.4574	.4899	.4572	.4750	.4753	.4973
243.........	.5835	.4420	.4751	.4428	.4558	.4582	.4638
273.........	.5541	.4291	.4636	.4317	.4398	.4442	.4345
304.........	.5283	.4172	.4539	.4225	.4260	.4320	.4086
334.........	.5062	.4053	.4452	.4144	.4139	.4208	.3856
365.........	.4875	.3931	.4367	.4068	.4028	.4102	.3650
547.........	.4261	.3153	.3845	.3564	.3478	.3475	.2769
730.........	.3637	.2694	.3443	.2957	.3028	.2874	.2196
912.........	.2748	.2545	.3044	.2467	.2642	.2392	.1737
1095.........	.2220	.2511	.2673	.2136	.2280	.2014	.1412
1277.........	.2091	.2413	.2490	.1869	.1946	.1649	.1157
1460.........	.1997	.2251	.2389	.1637	.1643	.1288	.0980
1642.........	.1688	.2082	.2233	.1471	.1367	.1007	.0886
1825.........	.1347	.1828	.2126	.1372	.1114	.0849	.0724
2190.........	.1196	.1509	.1740	.0977	.0714	.0501	.0574
2555.........	.1096	.1248	.1383	.0694	.0437	.0228	.0340
2920.........	.1027	.1041	.1081	.0493	.0259	.0081	.0115
3285.........	.0968	.0879	.0840	.0351	.0151	.0023	.0009
3650.........	.0872	.0756	.0657	.0252	.0089	.0005	.0001
4015.........	.0723	.0666	.0525	.0182	.0053	.0001	.0000
4380.........	.0525	.0604	.0433	.0133	.0033	.0000	.0000
4745.........	.0311	.0562	.0373	.0098	.0021	.0000	.0000
5110.........	.0133	.0533	.0335	.0074	.0015	.0000	.0000
5475.........	.0030	.0512	.0309	.0056	.0011	.0000	.0000
5840.........	.0007	.0492	.0285	.0043	.0008	.0000	.0000
6205.........	.0002	.0473	.0263	.0033	.0006	.0000	.0000
6570.........	.0000	.0455	.0242	.0025	.0004	.0000	.0000
6935.........	.0000	.0437	.0223	.0019	.0003	.0000	.0000
7300.........	.0000	.0420	.0206	.0015	.0002	.0000	.0000
7665.........	.0000	.0403	.0190	.0011	.0002	.0000	.0000
8030.........	.0000	.0388	.0175	.0009	.0001	.0000	.0000
8395.........	.0000	.0372	.0162	.0007	.0001	.0000	.0000
8760.........	.0000	.0358	.0149	.0005	.0001	.0000	.0000
9125.........	.0000	.0344	.0138	.0004	.0001	.0000	.0000

TABLE 10—*Continued*

Days from Admission	Age at Admission						
	<45	45–54	55–64	65–74	75–84	85–94	95+
	Total						
0	1.0000	1.0000	1.0000	1.0000	1.0000	1.0000	1.0000
10	.9234	.9488	.9414	.9183	.9215	.9144	.9228
20	.8727	.8864	.8672	.8489	.8459	.8374	.8621
30	.8459	.8623	.8258	.7868	.7755	.7843	.8193
60	.7762	.7147	.7173	.6717	.6672	.6790	.7212
90	.7155	.6192	.6412	.5920	.5904	.6038	.6413
121	.6628	.5557	.5868	.5359	.5347	.5492	.5759
151	.6173	.5125	.5473	.4957	.4936	.5086	.5219
182	.5782	.4823	.5180	.4665	.4624	.4779	.4772
212	.5448	.4604	.4957	.4450	.4380	.4541	.4398
243	.5162	.4439	.4781	.4286	.4184	.4351	.4083
273	.4918	.4304	.4634	.4158	.4021	.4193	.3815
304	.4709	.4184	.4505	.4052	.3880	.4058	.3583
334	.4528	.4071	.4386	.3958	.3753	.3936	.3380
365	.4371	.3957	.4270	.3871	.3638	.3824	.3202
547	.3660	.3201	.3573	.3320	.3048	.3217	.2467
730	.2984	.2609	.3082	.2739	.2563	.2638	.1998
912	.2410	.2369	.2798	.2325	.2144	.2127	.1553
1095	.2135	.2207	.2566	.2027	.1781	.1719	.1186
1277	.2073	.1962	.2348	.1745	.1490	.1377	.0952
1460	.2012	.1774	.2145	.1509	.1246	.1071	.0825
1642	.1820	.1699	.1989	.1359	.1025	.0828	.0762
1825	.1600	.1369	.1872	.1227	.0831	.0690	.0624
2190	.1329	.1183	.1521	.0781	.0539	.0396	.0381
2555	.1157	.1015	.1208	.0505	.0332	.0169	.0200
2920	.1031	.0865	.0945	.0333	.0198	.0054	.0079
3285	.0920	.0735	.0733	.0223	.0116	.0013	.0018
3650	.0806	.0623	.0567	.0152	.0067	.0003	.0001
4015	.0676	.0529	.0442	.0105	.0040	.0001	.0000
4380	.0529	.0450	.0349	.0074	.0024	.0000	.0000
4745	.0375	.0386	.0282	.0053	.0016	.0000	.0000
5110	.0230	.0334	.0235	.0038	.0011	.0000	.0000
5475	.0115	.0293	.0202	.0028	.0008	.0000	.0000
5840	.0057	.0257	.0174	.0021	.0006	.0000	.0000
6205	.0029	.0225	.0150	.0015	.0004	.0000	.0000
6570	.0014	.0197	.0129	.0011	.0003	.0000	.0000
6935	.0007	.0173	.0111	.0008	.0002	.0000	.0000
7300	.0004	.0151	.0096	.0006	.0002	.0000	.0000
7665	.0002	.0133	.0082	.0004	.0001	.0000	.0000
8030	.0001	.0116	.0071	.0003	.0001	.0000	.0000
8395	.0000	.0102	.0061	.0002	.0001	.0000	.0000
8760	.0000	.0089	.0053	.0002	.0000	.0000	.0000
9125	.0000	.0078	.0045	.0001	.0000	.0000	.0000

TABLE 11

PROPORTION OF ADMISSIONS STILL RESIDENT AT THE END OF THE PERIOD SHOWN; INSURABLE STAYS; BENEFIT PERIOD CONCEPT; ADJUSTED TO MATCH 1985 NNHS RESIDENTS

Days from Admission	Age at Admission						
	<45	45–54	55–64	65–74	75–84	85–94	95+
	Males						
0	1.0000	1.0000	1.0000	1.0000	1.0000	1.0000	1.0000
10	.8701	.9103	.9456	.9016	.8915	.8927	.9348
20	.8456	.8408	.8640	.8477	.8077	.7950	.8519
30	.8160	.8306	.8122	.7785	.7319	.7350	.8088
60	.6995	.7017	.6973	.6570	.6107	.6362	.6307
90	.6130	.6175	.6163	.5712	.5273	.5608	.5074
121	.5482	.5613	.5576	.5095	.4682	.5022	.4195
151	.4992	.5233	.5137	.4645	.4250	.4559	.3552
182	.4619	.4970	.4799	.4311	.3925	.4190	.3070
212	.4333	.4783	.4528	.4061	.3671	.3890	.2702
243	.4110	.4641	.4303	.3871	.3465	.3645	.2417
273	.3931	.4525	.4109	.3720	.3291	.3442	.2191
304	.3782	.4419	.3935	.3597	.3139	.3271	.2011
334	.3650	.4312	.3774	.3490	.3001	.3127	.1866
365	.3529	.4198	.3621	.3392	.2873	.3002	.1749
547	.2856	.3259	.2784	.2808	.2213	.2454	.1405
730	.2366	.2355	.2271	.2270	.1670	.1946	.1281
912	.2163	.1995	.2141	.1957	.1200	.1384	.0940
1095	.2121	.1789	.2051	.1697	.0852	.0938	.0487
1277	.2113	.1541	.1745	.1378	.0648	.0666	.0290
1460	.2110	.1409	.1456	.1126	.0514	.0496	.0247
1642	.2102	.1377	.1370	.0997	.0396	.0359	.0240
1825	.2100	.0984	.1356	.0842	.0319	.0280	.0221
2190	.1647	.0849	.1039	.0410	.0211	.0117	.0049
2555	.1293	.0715	.0806	.0203	.0132	.0009	.0020
2920	.1012	.0589	.0627	.0102	.0079	.0001	.0011
3285	.0786	.0474	.0487	.0053	.0045	.0000	.0008
3650	.0604	.0373	.0373	.0029	.0026	.0000	.0006
4015	.0457	.0287	.0280	.0016	.0014	.0000	.0005
4380	.0338	.0217	.0203	.0009	.0008	.0000	.0004
4745	.0245	.0160	.0141	.0006	.0005	.0000	.0004
5110	.0172	.0116	.0092	.0004	.0003	.0000	.0003
5475	.0117	.0083	.0056	.0002	.0002	.0000	.0003
5840	.0080	.0059	.0034	.0002	.0001	.0000	.0000
6205	.0054	.0042	.0021	.0001	.0001	.0000	.0000
6570	.0037	.0030	.0012	.0001	.0000	.0000	.0000
6935	.0025	.0021	.0008	.0001	.0000	.0000	.0000
7300	.0017	.0015	.0005	.0000	.0000	.0000	.0000
7665	.0012	.0011	.0003	.0000	.0000	.0000	.0000
8030	.0008	.0008	.0002	.0000	.0000	.0000	.0000
8395	.0005	.0006	.0001	.0000	.0000	.0000	.0000
8760	.0004	.0004	.0001	.0000	.0000	.0000	.0000
9125	.0003	.0003	.0000	.0000	.0000	.0000	.0000

TABLE 11—*Continued*

Days from Admission	Age at Admission						
	<45	45–54	55–64	65–74	75–84	85–94	95+
				Females			
0	1.0000	1.0000	1.0000	1.0000	1.0000	1.0000	1.0000
10	.8969	.9749	.9289	.9323	.9374	.9206	.9162
20	.8084	.9193	.8520	.8509	.8641	.8522	.8697
30	.7636	.8625	.8185	.7869	.7952	.8033	.8200
60	.7414	.7078	.6994	.6676	.6912	.6931	.7476
90	.7215	.6113	.6189	.5871	.6167	.6165	.6821
121	.7034	.5500	.5637	.5317	.5622	.5622	.6238
151	.6866	.5108	.5257	.4932	.5217	.5231	.5724
182	.6709	.4860	.4994	.4660	.4909	.4943	.5277
212	.6557	.4683	.4807	.4464	.4669	.4725	.4890
243	.6410	.4555	.4672	.4320	.4476	.4554	.4555
273	.6263	.4461	.4573	.4209	.4317	.4413	.4264
304	.6117	.4393	.4491	.4119	.4181	.4291	.4007
334	.5971	.4342	.4415	.4040	.4060	.4179	.3779
365	.5828	.4293	.4335	.3966	.3951	.4072	.3574
547	.5251	.3627	.3737	.3472	.3401	.3450	.2690
730	.5068	.2947	.3237	.2854	.2947	.2870	.2146
912	.4319	.2685	.2827	.2335	.2560	.2411	.1737
1095	.3336	.2634	.2481	.1996	.2195	.2049	.1425
1277	.2983	.2492	.2322	.1755	.1862	.1695	.1164
1460	.2805	.2244	.2256	.1554	.1570	.1323	.0983
1642	.2298	.2159	.2211	.1400	.1306	.1023	.0890
1825	.1753	.2144	.2199	.1303	.1068	.0866	.0727
2190	.1543	.1901	.1590	.0920	.0675	.0525	.0576
2555	.1347	.1631	.1178	.0643	.0406	.0255	.0342
2920	.1157	.1372	.0894	.0448	.0237	.0100	.0115
3285	.0972	.1145	.0695	.0314	.0136	.0032	.0009
3650	.0790	.0962	.0555	.0223	.0078	.0009	.0001
4015	.0618	.0825	.0455	.0161	.0046	.0002	.0000
4380	.0459	.0731	.0384	.0119	.0029	.0001	.0000
4745	.0321	.0669	.0334	.0091	.0019	.0000	.0000
5110	.0208	.0626	.0300	.0072	.0013	.0000	.0000
5475	.0123	.0596	.0277	.0059	.0010	.0000	.0000
5840	.0073	.0567	.0256	.0049	.0007	.0000	.0000
6205	.0043	.0540	.0236	.0040	.0006	.0000	.0000
6570	.0026	.0514	.0218	.0033	.0004	.0000	.0000
6935	.0015	.0490	.0202	.0027	.0003	.0000	.0000
7300	.0009	.0466	.0186	.0022	.0002	.0000	.0000
7665	.0005	.0444	.0172	.0018	.0002	.0000	.0000
8030	.0003	.0423	.0159	.0015	.0001	.0000	.0000
8395	.0002	.0402	.0147	.0012	.0001	.0000	.0000
8760	.0001	.0383	.0136	.0010	.0001	.0000	.0000
9125	.0001	.0365	.0125	.0008	.0001	.0000	.0000

TABLE 11—*Continued*

Days from Admission	Age at Admission						
	<45	45–54	55–64	65–74	75–84	85–94	95+
				Total			
0.........	1.0000	1.0000	1.0000	1.0000	1.0000	1.0000	1.0000
10.........	.8816	.9375	.9378	.9200	.9212	.9127	.9216
20.........	.8312	.8741	.8584	.8496	.8441	.8358	.8647
30.........	.8033	.8487	.8154	.7839	.7728	.7838	.8197
60.........	.7261	.7092	.6983	.6635	.6633	.6765	.7206
90.........	.6662	.6197	.6177	.5810	.5858	.6003	.6391
121.........	.6195	.5610	.5610	.5234	.5298	.5451	.5719
151.........	.5828	.5221	.5206	.4824	.4883	.5044	.5162
182.........	.5538	.4960	.4910	.4529	.4570	.4736	.4700
212.........	.5305	.4774	.4688	.4313	.4325	.4498	.4316
243.........	.5114	.4639	.4515	.4151	.4128	.4309	.3993
273.........	.4950	.4541	.4371	.4025	.3965	.4152	.3720
304.........	.4805	.4456	.4245	.3922	.3823	.4017	.3484
334.........	.4669	.4370	.4126	.3832	.3697	.3897	.3279
365.........	.4539	.4276	.4008	.3747	.3581	.3785	.3099
547.........	.3847	.3431	.3256	.3209	.2989	.3186	.2364
730.........	.3396	.2626	.2722	.2619	.2497	.2624	.1925
912.........	.2988	.2301	.2452	.2184	.2076	.2126	.1522
1095.........	.2631	.2125	.2232	.1878	.1710	.1725	.1169
1277.........	.2509	.1880	.2005	.1609	.1421	.1388	.0935
1460.........	.2389	.1710	.1829	.1389	.1185	.1077	.0810
1642.........	.2068	.1664	.1770	.1246	.0970	.0823	.0748
1825.........	.1725	.1273	.1760	.1120	.0791	.0688	.0612
2190.........	.1432	.1112	.1316	.0704	.0504	.0399	.0374
2555.........	.1182	.0944	.0997	.0447	.0306	.0177	.0196
2920.........	.0965	.0783	.0764	.0288	.0179	.0061	.0078
3285.........	.0776	.0640	.0591	.0189	.0103	.0017	.0018
3650.........	.0611	.0519	.0463	.0127	.0059	.0004	.0001
4015.........	.0469	.0420	.0366	.0087	.0035	.0001	.0000
4380.........	.0349	.0343	.0292	.0062	.0021	.0000	.0000
4745.........	.0250	.0284	.0235	.0045	.0013	.0000	.0000
5110.........	.0172	.0241	.0190	.0033	.0009	.0000	.0000
5475.........	.0112	.0211	.0156	.0026	.0007	.0000	.0000
5840.........	.0073	.0184	.0127	.0020	.0005	.0000	.0000
6205.........	.0048	.0161	.0104	.0015	.0004	.0000	.0000
6570.........	.0031	.0140	.0085	.0012	.0003	.0000	.0000
6935.........	.0020	.0123	.0070	.0009	.0002	.0000	.0000
7300.........	.0013	.0107	.0057	.0007	.0001	.0000	.0000
7665.........	.0009	.0094	.0047	.0005	.0001	.0000	.0000
8030.........	.0006	.0082	.0038	.0004	.0001	.0000	.0000
8395.........	.0004	.0071	.0031	.0003	.0001	.0000	.0000
8760.........	.0002	.0062	.0026	.0002	.0000	.0000	.0000
9125.........	.0002	.0055	.0021	.0002	.0000	.0000	.0000

back to the interval. (This is equivalent to the *Tx* column in a life table.) The results of these calculations are shown in Tables 12–17.

The average length-of-stay was calculated from these tables in a manner similar to that for life expectancy. The total number of days after the admission date (from the radix of 1.0 admissions) is the average length-of-stay. The averages derived in this manner are shown at the bottom of Tables 12–17. The averages for both the unadjusted and the adjusted discharge rates are shown. The adjusted averages (Tables 12–14) are significantly longer than the unadjusted (Tables 15–17). For example, compare, for admissions between 75 and 84, the average lengths-of-stay for total (male and female) for insurable stays under the benefit period concept. Before adjustment it is 458 days, and after adjustment it is 521 days.

The authors believe that the adjusted continuance tables and average lengths-of-stay are more accurate than the unadjusted, not only because the adjusted have been controlled to the reliable counts of residents on the survey date, but also because of the questionable reliability and the sparsity of data on long stays.

The average lengths-of-stay based on the adjusted continuance tables were graduated in the same manner as the admission rates, except that the graduated number of admissions was used as the weight in the average length-of-stay graduation and the ungraduated at each age of an interval was taken as the average length-of-stay over the whole interval. The graduated average lengths-of-stay are shown in Tables 1–3. The graduation process preserved the total number of days for all admissions.

TABLE 12

PROPORTION OF DAYS AFTER THE PERIOD SHOWN; ALL STAYS; STAY CONCEPT; UNADJUSTED 1985 NNHS EXPERIENCE

Days from Admission	Age at Admission						
	<45	45–54	55–64	65–74	75–84	85–94	95+
				Males			
0	1.0000	1.0000	1.0000	1.0000	1.0000	1.0000	1.0000
10	.9594	.9559	.9566	.9583	.9432	.9500	.9379
20	.9267	.9216	.9216	.9249	.8997	.9118	.8884
30	.8972	.8905	.8904	.8950	.8618	.8781	.8444
60	.8209	.8154	.8094	.8188	.7699	.7913	.7362
90	.7605	.7608	.7442	.7574	.6992	.7204	.6580
121	.7093	.7163	.6887	.7046	.6400	.6590	.5954
151	.6672	.6800	.6435	.6610	.5918	.6082	.5463
182	.6293	.6469	.6035	.6219	.5485	.5624	.5034
212	.5967	.6178	.5698	.5882	.5112	.5233	.4674
243	.5663	.5896	.5389	.5570	.4764	.4870	.4344
273	.5396	.5637	.5122	.5294	.4455	.4553	.4058
304	.5143	.5381	.4871	.5031	.4162	.4254	.3791
334	.4917	.5143	.4649	.4795	.3899	.3989	.3554
365	.4702	.4905	.4437	.4567	.3646	.3736	.3329
547	.3726	.3702	.3446	.3462	.2474	.2566	.2277
730	.3082	.2830	.2733	.2625	.1681	.1738	.1470
912	.2653	.2210	.2168	.1979	.1163	.1142	.0861
1095	.2322	.1761	.1678	.1482	.0832	.0737	.0495
1277	.2018	.1436	.1271	.1110	.0606	.0475	.0321
1460	.1717	.1193	.0963	.0815	.0430	.0294	.0232
1642	.1436	.1025	.0751	.0563	.0293	.0174	.0166
1825	.1184	.0910	.0591	.0350	.0187	.0098	.0102
2190	.0782	.0741	.0366	.0117	.0057	.0022	.0030
2555	.0525	.0606	.0236	.0045	.0014	.0003	.0017
2920	.0369	.0491	.0153	.0020	.0003	.0000	.0011
3285	.0275	.0388	.0097	.0010	.0000	.0000	.0008
3650	.0218	.0295	.0059	.0005	.0000	.0000	.0006
4015	.0180	.0209	.0034	.0003	.0000	.0000	.0005
4380	.0153	.0135	.0017	.0002	.0000	.0000	.0003
4745	.0131	.0077	.0008	.0001	.0000	.0000	.0002
5110	.0113	.0038	.0003	.0001	.0000	.0000	.0001
5475	.0096	.0017	.0001	.0001	.0000	.0000	.0000
5840	.0082	.0007	.0000	.0000	.0000	.0000	.0000
6205	.0069	.0003	.0000	.0000	.0000	.0000	.0000
6570	.0057	.0001	.0000	.0000	.0000	.0000	.0000
6935	.0046	.0001	.0000	.0000	.0000	.0000	.0000
7300	.0036	.0000	.0000	.0000	.0000	.0000	.0000
7665	.0027	.0000	.0000	.0000	.0000	.0000	.0000
8030	.0019	.0000	.0000	.0000	.0000	.0000	.0000
8395	.0012	.0000	.0000	.0000	.0000	.0000	.0000
8760	.0006	.0000	.0000	.0000	.0000	.0000	.0000
9125	.0000	.0000	.0000	.0000	.0000	.0000	.0000
ALOS*	251	227	242	245	179	205	165

*Average length-of-stay.

TABLE 12—*Continued*

Days from Admission	Age at Admission						
	<45	45–54	55–64	65–74	75–84	85–94	95+
	Females						
0	1.0000	1.0000	1.0000	1.0000	1.0000	1.0000	1.0000
10	.9648	.9572	.9707	.9644	.9658	.9670	.9618
20	.9360	.9209	.9465	.9358	.9385	.9405	.9302
30	.9088	.8894	.9249	.9109	.9142	.9166	.9007
60	.8361	.8117	.8694	.8477	.8515	.8539	.8233
90	.7721	.7541	.8242	.7971	.8001	.8016	.7601
121	.7138	.7070	.7843	.7529	.7550	.7549	.7048
151	.6638	.6690	.7501	.7154	.7166	.7148	.6581
182	.6179	.6351	.7181	.6802	.6811	.6771	.6151
212	.5784	.6058	.6893	.6486	.6496	.6435	.5774
243	.5420	.5784	.6614	.6179	.6195	.6109	.5416
273	.5105	.5541	.6359	.5896	.5921	.5812	.5094
304	.4813	.5306	.6107	.5617	.5655	.5521	.4784
334	.4558	.5095	.5874	.5358	.5411	.5253	.4503
365	.4320	.4891	.5645	.5102	.5171	.4989	.4230
547	.3257	.3947	.4512	.3839	.3964	.3669	.2920
730	.2500	.3301	.3665	.2942	.3014	.2673	.1988
912	.1969	.2782	.3026	.2292	.2259	.1940	.1390
1095	.1585	.2311	.2543	.1795	.1663	.1388	.1026
1277	.1264	.1883	.2158	.1405	.1214	.0969	.0769
1460	.0980	.1497	.1803	.1077	.0870	.0652	.0559
1642	.0784	.1210	.1468	.0797	.0608	.0428	.0388
1825	.0679	.1055	.1173	.0571	.0415	.0268	.0258
2190	.0538	.0879	.0732	.0291	.0180	.0085	.0087
2555	.0431	.0759	.0453	.0157	.0067	.0024	.0011
2920	.0342	.0672	.0289	.0087	.0022	.0005	.0000
3285	.0266	.0603	.0196	.0048	.0007	.0001	.0000
3650	.0197	.0545	.0142	.0026	.0002	.0000	.0000
4015	.0135	.0495	.0110	.0014	.0001	.0000	.0000
4380	.0083	.0449	.0089	.0007	.0000	.0000	.0000
4745	.0043	.0406	.0074	.0003	.0000	.0000	.0000
5110	.0018	.0365	.0062	.0001	.0000	.0000	.0000
5475	.0006	.0326	.0052	.0000	.0000	.0000	.0000
5840	.0002	.0289	.0043	.0000	.0000	.0000	.0000
6205	.0001	.0252	.0035	.0000	.0000	.0000	.0000
6570	.0000	.0217	.0028	.0000	.0000	.0000	.0000
6935	.0000	.0183	.0022	.0000	.0000	.0000	.0000
7300	.0000	.0150	.0017	.0000	.0000	.0000	.0000
7665	.0000	.0118	.0013	.0000	.0000	.0000	.0000
8030	.0000	.0087	.0009	.0000	.0000	.0000	.0000
8395	.0000	.0057	.0006	.0000	.0000	.0000	.0000
8760	.0000	.0028	.0003	.0000	.0000	.0000	.0000
9125	.0000	.0000	.0000	.0000	.0000	.0000	.0000
ALOS*	287	246	356	292	304	312	271

*Average length-of-stay.

TABLE 12—*Continued*

Days from Admission	Age at Admission						
	<45	45–54	55–64	65–74	75–84	85–94	95+
	Total						
0.........	1.0000	1.0000	1.0000	1.0000	1.0000	1.0000	1.0000
10.........	.9609	.9585	.9641	.9624	.9600	.9635	.9574
20.........	.9293	.9249	.9350	.9322	.9286	.9346	.9226
30.........	.9003	.8949	.9089	.9056	.9008	.9086	.8904
60.........	.8243	.8215	.8417	.8380	.8304	.8408	.8074
90.........	.7619	.7676	.7873	.7837	.7738	.7846	.7414
121.........	.7074	.7236	.7402	.7367	.7247	.7348	.6847
151.........	.6619	.6880	.7009	.6971	.6836	.6923	.6377
182.........	.6207	.6557	.6651	.6605	.6457	.6528	.5949
212.........	.5852	.6274	.6339	.6282	.6125	.6179	.5576
243.........	.5523	.6004	.6044	.5973	.5809	.5844	.5225
273.........	.5235	.5758	.5781	.5693	.5525	.5541	.4913
304.........	.4964	.5517	.5529	.5420	.5250	.5247	.4613
334.........	.4725	.5295	.5300	.5169	.4999	.4979	.4343
365.........	.4499	.5076	.5078	.4923	.4754	.4716	.4081
547.........	.3476	.4000	.4009	.3718	.3551	.3423	.2833
730.........	.2780	.3227	.3225	.2839	.2644	.2459	.1930
912.........	.2307	.2641	.2620	.2185	.1954	.1753	.1332
1095.........	.1953	.2169	.2136	.1684	.1433	.1233	.0965
1277.........	.1645	.1791	.1743	.1297	.1047	.0850	.0716
1460.........	.1362	.1485	.1410	.0978	.0750	.0564	.0520
1642.........	.1137	.1266	.1129	.0706	.0523	.0365	.0358
1825.........	.0976	.1131	.0892	.0482	.0353	.0225	.0232
2190.........	.0735	.0947	.0551	.0219	.0144	.0069	.0075
2555.........	.0564	.0806	.0345	.0110	.0050	.0019	.0012
2920.........	.0437	.0692	.0218	.0058	.0016	.0004	.0001
3285.........	.0338	.0594	.0139	.0032	.0005	.0001	.0000
3650.........	.0260	.0508	.0089	.0017	.0001	.0000	.0000
4015.........	.0197	.0432	.0057	.0009	.0001	.0000	.0000
4380.........	.0146	.0363	.0037	.0005	.0000	.0000	.0000
4745.........	.0107	.0302	.0024	.0002	.0000	.0000	.0000
5110.........	.0076	.0248	.0015	.0001	.0000	.0000	.0000
5475.........	.0054	.0201	.0010	.0000	.0000	.0000	.0000
5840.........	.0038	.0162	.0006	.0000	.0000	.0000	.0000
6205.........	.0026	.0130	.0004	.0000	.0000	.0000	.0000
6570.........	.0018	.0102	.0002	.0000	.0000	.0000	.0000
6935.........	.0012	.0079	.0002	.0000	.0000	.0000	.0000
7300.........	.0008	.0060	.0001	.0000	.0000	.0000	.0000
7665.........	.0005	.0043	.0001	.0000	.0000	.0000	.0000
8030.........	.0003	.0029	.0000	.0000	.0000	.0000	.0000
8395.........	.0002	.0018	.0000	.0000	.0000	.0000	.0000
8760.........	.0001	.0008	.0000	.0000	.0000	.0000	.0000
9125.........	.0000	.0000	.0000	.0000	.0000	.0000	.0000
ALOS*	260	247	292	274	258	282	243

*Average length-of-stay.

TABLE 13

PROPORTION OF DAYS AFTER THE PERIOD SHOWN;
ALL STAYS; BENEFIT PERIOD CONCEPT; UNADJUSTED 1985 NNHS EXPERIENCE

Days from Admission	Age at Admission						
	<45	45–54	55–64	65–74	75–84	85–94	95+
	Males						
0	1.0000	1.0000	1.0000	1.0000	1.0000	1.0000	1.0000
10	.9873	.9835	.9849	.9775	.9673	.9685	.9553
20	.9763	.9696	.9722	.9589	.9411	.9436	.9186
30	.9660	.9562	.9605	.9417	.9173	.9212	.8855
60	.9375	.9198	.9285	.8960	.8561	.8612	.7998
90	.9121	.8895	.9005	.8570	.8052	.8090	.7332
121	.8886	.8622	.8746	.8218	.7597	.7613	.6778
151	.8679	.8384	.8516	.7912	.7206	.7200	.6332
182	.8482	.8158	.8294	.7622	.6839	.6812	.5938
212	.8304	.7951	.8092	.7360	.6511	.6467	.5605
243	.8132	.7748	.7894	.7105	.6193	.6136	.5298
273	.7974	.7559	.7710	.6870	.5904	.5837	.5028
304	.7819	.7369	.7527	.6636	.5620	.5545	.4773
334	.7674	.7192	.7357	.6418	.5358	.5277	.4544
365	.7530	.7013	.7188	.6199	.5101	.5013	.4321
547	.6784	.6083	.6325	.5053	.3808	.3656	.3199
730	.6191	.5366	.5637	.4124	.2827	.2569	.2217
912	.5712	.4792	.5034	.3357	.2117	.1771	.1405
1095	.5271	.4275	.4446	.2680	.1620	.1228	.0926
1277	.4840	.3828	.3896	.2110	.1263	.0859	.0687
1460	.4409	.3447	.3418	.1641	.0986	.0588	.0521
1642	.3981	.3095	.3002	.1239	.0771	.0393	.0370
1825	.3552	.2775	.2616	.0880	.0603	.0251	.0223
2190	.2806	.2273	.1966	.0413	.0359	.0067	.0065
2555	.2236	.1833	.1457	.0201	.0205	.0004	.0036
2920	.1776	.1451	.1064	.0102	.0114	.0000	.0025
3285	.1394	.1124	.0764	.0054	.0063	.0000	.0018
3650	.1071	.0851	.0539	.0030	.0035	.0000	.0014
4015	.0800	.0629	.0374	.0018	.0021	.0000	.0010
4380	.0576	.0452	.0254	.0011	.0013	.0000	.0007
4745	.0398	.0317	.0170	.0007	.0008	.0000	.0005
5110	.0265	.0218	.0112	.0004	.0005	.0000	.0003
5475	.0172	.0148	.0073	.0003	.0004	.0000	.0001
5840	.0112	.0100	.0047	.0002	.0002	.0000	.0000
6205	.0072	.0067	.0031	.0001	.0002	.0000	.0000
6570	.0047	.0045	.0020	.0001	.0001	.0000	.0000
6935	.0030	.0030	.0013	.0000	.0001	.0000	.0000
7300	.0019	.0019	.0008	.0000	.0000	.0000	.0000
7665	.0011	.0012	.0005	.0000	.0000	.0000	.0000
8030	.0006	.0007	.0003	.0000	.0000	.0000	.0000
8395	.0003	.0004	.0001	.0000	.0000	.0000	.0000
8760	.0001	.0002	.0001	.0000	.0000	.0000	.0000
9125	.0000	.0000	.0000	.0000	.0000	.0000	.0000
ALOS*	813	636	711	463	317	331	236

*Average length-of-stay.

TABLE 13—*Continued*

Days from Admission	Age at Admission						
	<45	45–54	55–64	65–74	75–84	85–94	95+
	Females						
0.........	1.0000	1.0000	1.0000	1.0000	1.0000	1.0000	1.0000
10.........	.9869	.9879	.9881	.9825	.9811	.9790	.9765
20.........	.9761	.9774	.9782	.9680	.9652	.9615	.9566
30.........	.9657	.9679	.9690	.9549	.9507	.9453	.9379
60.........	.9359	.9427	.9439	.9197	.9119	.9016	.8858
90.........	.9075	.9218	.9221	.8896	.8780	.8638	.8387
121.........	.8796	.9029	.9021	.8619	.8466	.8289	.7945
151.........	.8542	.8864	.8843	.8375	.8188	.7980	.7556
182.........	.8294	.8706	.8671	.8140	.7921	.7682	.7189
212.........	.8069	.8561	.8512	.7923	.7677	.7410	.6862
243.........	.7851	.8417	.8355	.7708	.7437	.7140	.6549
273.........	.7651	.8283	.8207	.7507	.7215	.6889	.6269
304.........	.7456	.8148	.8057	.7304	.6993	.6637	.5998
334.........	.7275	.8022	.7916	.7112	.6786	.6400	.5752
365.........	.7097	.7896	.7773	.6917	.6578	.6163	.5513
547.........	.6154	.7246	.6997	.5860	.5468	.4902	.4349
730.........	.5326	.6722	.6314	.4966	.4511	.3858	.3454
912.........	.4682	.6256	.5712	.4244	.3692	.3013	.2766
1095.........	.4197	.5803	.5189	.3635	.2985	.2312	.2221
1277.........	.3779	.5363	.4723	.3113	.2390	.1740	.1787
1460.........	.3376	.4947	.4279	.2660	.1889	.1289	.1431
1642.........	.3018	.4565	.3863	.2265	.1477	.0949	.1124
1825.........	.2731	.4221	.3473	.1904	.1142	.0678	.0856
2190.........	.2255	.3646	.2788	.1318	.0663	.0292	.0440
2555.........	.1831	.3179	.2245	.0916	.0377	.0098	.0157
2920.........	.1440	.2798	.1827	.0641	.0213	.0025	.0028
3285.........	.1075	.2484	.1509	.0452	.0123	.0005	.0000
3650.........	.0740	.2221	.1267	.0322	.0073	.0001	.0000
4015.........	.0454	.1995	.1081	.0231	.0045	.0000	.0000
4380.........	.0236	.1796	.0933	.0168	.0030	.0000	.0000
4745.........	.0095	.1614	.0811	.0123	.0020	.0000	.0000
5110.........	.0026	.1444	.0704	.0090	.0014	.0000	.0000
5475.........	.0004	.1282	.0609	.0066	.0010	.0000	.0000
5840.........	.0001	.1128	.0521	.0048	.0007	.0000	.0000
6205.........	.0000	.0980	.0441	.0035	.0005	.0000	.0000
6570.........	.0000	.0838	.0367	.0025	.0004	.0000	.0000
6935.........	.0000	.0702	.0300	.0018	.0002	.0000	.0000
7300.........	.0000	.0572	.0238	.0012	.0002	.0000	.0000
7665.........	.0000	.0447	.0182	.0008	.0001	.0000	.0000
8030.........	.0000	.0328	.0130	.0005	.0001	.0000	.0000
8395.........	.0000	.0214	.0083	.0003	.0000	.0000	.0000
8760.........	.0000	.0105	.0040	.0001	.0000	.0000	.0000
9125.........	.0000	.0000	.0000	.0000	.0000	.0000	.0000
ALOS*	811	900	888	603	561	500	445

*Average length-of-stay.

TABLE 13—*Continued*

Days from Admission	Age at Admission						
	<45	45–54	55–64	65–74	75–84	85–94	95+
	Total						
0.........	1.0000	1.0000	1.0000	1.0000	1.0000	1.0000	1.0000
10.........	.9865	.9854	.9865	.9807	.9777	.9768	.9730
20.........	.9751	.9729	.9752	.9647	.9593	.9577	.9503
30.........	.9642	.9611	.9647	.9500	.9425	.9402	.9291
60.........	.9334	.9295	.9361	.9110	.8981	.8930	.8711
90.........	.9054	.9031	.9112	.8777	.8599	.8522	.8204
121.........	.8788	.8793	.8882	.8472	.8249	.8146	.7741
151.........	.8550	.8586	.8677	.8205	.7942	.7815	.7340
182.........	.8322	.8388	.8480	.7948	.7649	.7498	.6966
212.........	.8116	.8207	.8299	.7715	.7383	.7209	.6637
243.........	.7916	.8029	.8119	.7484	.7123	.6926	.6324
273.........	.7733	.7862	.7952	.7269	.6883	.6663	.6044
304.........	.7553	.7695	.7785	.7053	.6644	.6402	.5775
334.........	.7387	.7539	.7628	.6850	.6422	.6158	.5530
365.........	.7221	.7382	.7471	.6645	.6201	.5913	.5293
547.........	.6358	.6567	.6641	.5546	.5039	.4625	.4127
730.........	.5648	.5923	.5948	.4634	.4073	.3564	.3212
912.........	.5090	.5380	.5342	.3891	.3278	.2724	.2502
1095.........	.4626	.4877	.4790	.3254	.2624	.2056	.1967
1277.........	.4198	.4424	.4290	.2711	.2090	.1530	.1562
1460.........	.3778	.4024	.3835	.2248	.1647	.1120	.1228
1642.........	.3388	.3653	.3422	.1847	.1288	.0813	.0933
1825.........	.3044	.3319	.3036	.1483	.0999	.0572	.0671
2190.........	.2464	.2789	.2366	.0936	.0583	.0235	.0310
2555.........	.1978	.2338	.1839	.0603	.0332	.0073	.0115
2920.........	.1556	.1958	.1433	.0395	.0187	.0017	.0029
3285.........	.1184	.1639	.1124	.0264	.0107	.0003	.0004
3650.........	.0858	.1373	.0891	.0179	.0063	.0000	.0000
4015.........	.0583	.1151	.0714	.0123	.0039	.0000	.0000
4380.........	.0363	.0965	.0579	.0085	.0025	.0000	.0000
4745.........	.0203	.0809	.0474	.0060	.0017	.0000	.0000
5110.........	.0101	.0676	.0389	.0042	.0012	.0000	.0000
5475.........	.0046	.0562	.0319	.0029	.0008	.0000	.0000
5840.........	.0021	.0463	.0259	.0021	.0006	.0000	.0000
6205.........	.0010	.0377	.0208	.0014	.0004	.0000	.0000
6570.........	.0004	.0303	.0165	.0010	.0003	.0000	.0000
6935.........	.0002	.0239	.0129	.0007	.0002	.0000	.0000
7300.........	.0001	.0184	.0097	.0004	.0001	.0000	.0000
7665.........	.0000	.0136	.0071	.0003	.0001	.0000	.0000
8030.........	.0000	.0094	.0049	.0002	.0001	.0000	.0000
8395.........	.0000	.0058	.0030	.0001	.0000	.0000	.0000
8760.........	.0000	.0027	.0014	.0000	.0000	.0000	.0000
9125.........	.0000	.0000	.0000	.0000	.0000	.0000	.0000
ALOS*	775	728	789	543	472	451	388

*Average length-of-stay.

TABLE 14

PROPORTION OF DAYS AFTER THE PERIOD SHOWN;
INSURABLE STAYS; BENEFIT PERIOD CONCEPT; UNADJUSTED 1985 NNHS EXPERIENCE

Days from Admission	Age at Admission						
	<45	45–54	55–64	65–74	75–84	85–94	95+
				Males			
0	1.0000	1.0000	1.0000	1.0000	1.0000	1.0000	1.0000
10	.9860	.9821	.9815	.9757	.9665	.9675	.9528
20	.9741	.9672	.9661	.9556	.9398	.9419	.9131
30	.9626	.9531	.9520	.9372	.9154	.9187	.8771
60	.9315	.9144	.9140	.8886	.8529	.8568	.7836
90	.9049	.8815	.8813	.8475	.8007	.8034	.7114
121	.8808	.8515	.8515	.8107	.7540	.7549	.6518
151	.8600	.8249	.8254	.7788	.7139	.7131	.6045
182	.8404	.7992	.8005	.7488	.6763	.6739	.5632
212	.8228	.7756	.7780	.7217	.6427	.6391	.5289
243	.8058	.7520	.7561	.6954	.6102	.6058	.4977
273	.7902	.7299	.7360	.6711	.5806	.5757	.4709
304	.7748	.7076	.7162	.6470	.5516	.5463	.4458
334	.7604	.6867	.6979	.6244	.5249	.5193	.4235
365	.7462	.6656	.6799	.6018	.4987	.4927	.4022
547	.6726	.5574	.5897	.4834	.3676	.3561	.2971
730	.6137	.4796	.5204	.3883	.2692	.2463	.2059
912	.5634	.4210	.4605	.3110	.1989	.1660	.1302
1095	.5156	.3694	.4027	.2439	.1503	.1123	.0856
1277	.4684	.3249	.3510	.1888	.1159	.0767	.0635
1460	.4211	.2860	.3086	.1449	.0895	.0512	.0482
1642	.3742	.2493	.2717	.1083	.0693	.0331	.0341
1825	.3272	.2169	.2358	.0761	.0539	.0200	.0205
2190	.2444	.1703	.1735	.0348	.0314	.0042	.0060
2555	.1810	.1311	.1268	.0164	.0176	.0000	.0033
2920	.1325	.0990	.0914	.0080	.0095	.0000	.0023
3285	.0956	.0733	.0646	.0041	.0051	.0000	.0017
3650	.0678	.0533	.0444	.0022	.0027	.0000	.0013
4015	.0471	.0381	.0295	.0013	.0014	.0000	.0009
4380	.0321	.0268	.0189	.0007	.0008	.0000	.0007
4745	.0214	.0186	.0115	.0005	.0004	.0000	.0005
5110	.0141	.0128	.0067	.0003	.0002	.0000	.0003
5475	.0091	.0087	.0038	.0002	.0001	.0000	.0001
5840	.0059	.0059	.0022	.0001	.0001	.0000	.0000
6205	.0038	.0040	.0012	.0001	.0000	.0000	.0000
6570	.0025	.0027	.0007	.0000	.0000	.0000	.0000
6935	.0016	.0018	.0004	.0000	.0000	.0000	.0000
7300	.0010	.0012	.0002	.0000	.0000	.0000	.0000
7665	.0006	.0007	.0001	.0000	.0000	.0000	.0000
8030	.0003	.0004	.0001	.0000	.0000	.0000	.0000
8395	.0002	.0002	.0000	.0000	.0000	.0000	.0000
8760	.0001	.0001	.0000	.0000	.0000	.0000	.0000
9125	.0000	.0000	.0000	.0000	.0000	.0000	.0000
ALOS*	710	578	579	428	309	320	223

*Average length-of-stay.

TABLE 14—*Continued*

Days from Admission	Age at Admission						
	<45	45–54	55–64	65–74	75–84	85–94	95+
				Females			
0.........	1.0000	1.0000	1.0000	1.0000	1.0000	1.0000	1.0000
10.........	.9895	.9893	.9872	.9817	.9804	.9791	.9763
20.........	.9812	.9801	.9767	.9665	.9641	.9618	.9563
30.........	.9734	.9715	.9668	.9527	.9491	.9458	.9375
60.........	.9513	.9490	.9401	.9162	.9093	.9025	.8854
90.........	.9298	.9304	.9172	.8851	.8746	.8651	.8382
121.........	.9083	.9136	.8962	.8567	.8426	.8306	.7941
151.........	.8880	.8990	.8776	.8318	.8143	.8001	.7553
182.........	.8676	.8848	.8596	.8078	.7872	.7707	.7186
212.........	.8484	.8717	.8430	.7858	.7625	.7438	.6861
243.........	.8289	.8586	.8265	.7640	.7382	.7172	.6551
273.........	.8106	.8463	.8109	.7435	.7157	.6924	.6273
304.........	.7921	.8338	.7951	.7229	.6933	.6676	.6004
334.........	.7747	.8219	.7802	.7034	.6723	.6443	.5761
365.........	.7572	.8098	.7650	.6837	.6513	.6209	.5525
547.........	.6621	.7441	.6833	.5765	.5392	.4967	.4378
730.........	.5726	.6914	.6138	.4863	.4431	.3936	.3501
912.........	.4911	.6472	.5541	.4146	.3611	.3094	.2813
1095.........	.4272	.6050	.5024	.3553	.2908	.2389	.2259
1277.........	.3759	.5642	.4563	.3047	.2321	.1807	.1816
1460.........	.3279	.5271	.4121	.2603	.1829	.1345	.1455
1642.........	.2861	.4930	.3694	.2213	.1425	.0999	.1143
1825.........	.2542	.4594	.3269	.1857	.1095	.0725	.0870
2190.........	.2027	.3968	.2552	.1281	.0625	.0329	.0447
2555.........	.1581	.3428	.2044	.0891	.0349	.0121	.0160
2920.........	.1200	.2975	.1676	.0629	.0195	.0036	.0029
3285.........	.0881	.2603	.1401	.0453	.0111	.0009	.0000
3650.........	.0621	.2296	.1189	.0334	.0066	.0002	.0000
4015.........	.0418	.2040	.1022	.0251	.0041	.0000	.0000
4380.........	.0267	.1820	.0886	.0193	.0027	.0000	.0000
4745.........	.0161	.1624	.0771	.0151	.0019	.0000	.0000
5110.........	.0092	.1444	.0671	.0119	.0013	.0000	.0000
5475.........	.0051	.1275	.0580	.0093	.0010	.0000	.0000
5840.........	.0029	.1114	.0497	.0073	.0007	.0000	.0000
6205.........	.0016	.0962	.0421	.0057	.0005	.0000	.0000
6570.........	.0009	.0818	.0351	.0043	.0004	.0000	.0000
6935.........	.0005	.0682	.0287	.0033	.0002	.0000	.0000
7300.........	.0003	.0553	.0228	.0024	.0002	.0000	.0000
7665.........	.0001	.0430	.0174	.0017	.0001	.0000	.0000
8030.........	.0001	.0314	.0125	.0011	.0001	.0000	.0000
8395.........	.0000	.0203	.0080	.0007	.0000	.0000	.0000
8760.........	.0000	.0099	.0038	.0003	.0000	.0000	.0000
9125.........	.0000	.0000	.0000	.0000	.0000	.0000	.0000
ALOS*	995	1019	829	578	543	504	440

*Average length-of-stay.

TABLE 14—*Continued*

Days from Admission	Age at Admission						
	<45	45–54	55–64	65–74	75–84	85–94	95+
				Total			
0.........	1.0000	1.0000	1.0000	1.0000	1.0000	1.0000	1.0000
10.........	.9872	.9847	.9846	.9795	.9770	.9767	.9724
20.........	.9767	.9718	.9718	.9625	.9581	.9576	.9492
30.........	.9666	.9596	.9599	.9470	.9408	.9400	.9276
60.........	.9386	.9268	.9280	.9059	.8952	.8928	.8683
90.........	.9133	.8992	.9006	.8711	.8561	.8520	.8165
121.........	.8893	.8741	.8754	.8396	.8204	.8146	.7694
151.........	.8677	.8520	.8532	.8120	.7891	.7816	.7289
182.........	.8467	.8306	.8320	.7856	.7592	.7501	.6912
212.........	.8274	.8109	.8125	.7616	.7322	.7214	.6582
243.........	.8083	.7913	.7933	.7380	.7058	.6933	.6269
273.........	.7905	.7728	.7754	.7159	.6814	.6672	.5991
304.........	.7727	.7541	.7575	.6938	.6572	.6413	.5723
334.........	.7561	.7364	.7407	.6730	.6347	.6170	.5481
365.........	.7394	.7185	.7239	.6521	.6122	.5928	.5247
547.........	.6513	.6249	.6367	.5396	.4947	.4649	.4104
730.........	.5757	.5542	.5666	.4468	.3975	.3593	.3211
912.........	.5099	.4980	.5066	.3724	.3181	.2753	.2508
1095.........	.4527	.4470	.4522	.3097	.2532	.2080	.1971
1277.........	.4010	.4015	.4037	.2570	.2009	.1549	.1564
1460.........	.3511	.3612	.3601	.2120	.1576	.1135	.1230
1642.........	.3063	.3235	.3197	.1732	.1226	.0826	.0934
1825.........	.2690	.2896	.2797	.1382	.0945	.0586	.0672
2190.........	.2077	.2377	.2111	.0859	.0542	.0248	.0311
2555.........	.1578	.1936	.1610	.0546	.0303	.0081	.0115
2920.........	.1176	.1572	.1239	.0356	.0168	.0020	.0029
3285.........	.0857	.1278	.0960	.0238	.0094	.0004	.0004
3650.........	.0608	.1042	.0749	.0163	.0054	.0001	.0000
4015.........	.0419	.0856	.0588	.0115	.0033	.0000	.0000
4380.........	.0280	.0707	.0462	.0082	.0021	.0000	.0000
4745.........	.0181	.0587	.0364	.0060	.0014	.0000	.0000
5110.........	.0114	.0489	.0286	.0044	.0010	.0000	.0000
5475.........	.0071	.0405	.0224	.0033	.0007	.0000	.0000
5840.........	.0044	.0333	.0174	.0024	.0005	.0000	.0000
6205.........	.0027	.0271	.0134	.0018	.0003	.0000	.0000
6570.........	.0017	.0217	.0102	.0013	.0002	.0000	.0000
6935.........	.0010	.0171	.0077	.0009	.0002	.0000	.0000
7300.........	.0006	.0131	.0056	.0006	.0001	.0000	.0000
7665.........	.0004	.0097	.0039	.0004	.0001	.0000	.0000
8030.........	.0002	.0067	.0026	.0003	.0000	.0000	.0000
8395.........	.0001	.0041	.0015	.0002	.0000	.0000	.0000
8760.........	.0000	.0019	.0007	.0001	.0000	.0000	.0000
9125.........	.0000	.0000	.0000	.0000	.0000	.0000	.0000
ALOS*	797	693	691	512	458	449	380

*Average length-of-stay.

TABLE 15

PROPORTION OF DAYS AFTER THE PERIOD SHOWN;
ALL STAYS; STAY CONCEPT; ADJUSTED TO MATCH 1985 NNHS RESIDENTS

Days from Admission	Age at Admission						
	<45	45–54	55–64	65–74	75–84	85–94	95+
	Males						
0	1.0000	1.0000	1.0000	1.0000	1.0000	1.0000	1.0000
10	.9751	.9729	.9720	.9723	.9626	.9658	.9592
20	.9545	.9510	.9489	.9495	.9328	.9387	.9257
30	.9355	.9308	.9277	.9286	.9061	.9141	.8952
60	.8847	.8795	.8710	.8733	.8382	.8485	.8166
90	.8422	.8391	.8229	.8264	.7826	.7924	.7550
121	.8044	.8043	.7801	.7843	.7336	.7417	.7027
151	.7722	.7747	.7439	.7483	.6921	.6983	.6595
182	.7423	.7470	.7106	.7149	.6536	.6579	.6203
212	.7158	.7220	.6817	.6854	.6196	.6224	.5863
243	.6906	.6976	.6545	.6574	.5871	.5887	.5544
273	.6680	.6748	.6303	.6321	.5577	.5586	.5260
304	.6461	.6521	.6071	.6076	.5293	.5296	.4987
334	.6262	.6308	.5862	.5852	.5033	.5033	.4742
365	.6069	.6094	.5658	.5632	.4780	.4778	.4504
547	.5144	.4974	.4660	.4523	.3544	.3537	.3336
730	.4473	.4102	.3886	.3629	.2631	.2588	.2385
912	.3986	.3434	.3242	.2900	.1976	.1854	.1623
1095	.3587	.2915	.2665	.2305	.1515	.1311	.1110
1277	.3213	.2512	.2166	.1831	.1171	.0924	.0824
1460	.2843	.2190	.1765	.1436	.0889	.0635	.0652
1642	.2492	.1949	.1465	.1087	.0657	.0424	.0515
1825	.2169	.1769	.1224	.0779	.0466	.0277	.0382
2190	.1629	.1487	.0857	.0390	.0205	.0101	.0208
2555	.1241	.1249	.0611	.0211	.0081	.0031	.0142
2920	.0972	.1038	.0434	.0123	.0029	.0008	.0106
3285	.0789	.0846	.0303	.0076	.0010	.0002	.0083
3650	.0660	.0666	.0204	.0050	.0003	.0000	.0065
4015	.0567	.0499	.0131	.0034	.0001	.0000	.0051
4380	.0493	.0349	.0079	.0024	.0000	.0000	.0038
4745	.0431	.0225	.0044	.0017	.0000	.0000	.0027
5110	.0377	.0133	.0022	.0012	.0000	.0000	.0017
5475	.0327	.0075	.0011	.0009	.0000	.0000	.0007
5840	.0282	.0042	.0005	.0007	.0000	.0000	.0002
6205	.0240	.0023	.0003	.0005	.0000	.0000	.0000
6570	.0201	.0013	.0001	.0003	.0000	.0000	.0000
6935	.0165	.0007	.0001	.0002	.0000	.0000	.0000
7300	.0131	.0004	.0000	.0002	.0000	.0000	.0000
7665	.0101	.0002	.0000	.0001	.0000	.0000	.0000
8030	.0073	.0001	.0000	.0001	.0000	.0000	.0000
8395	.0046	.0001	.0000	.0000	.0000	.0000	.0000
8760	.0022	.0000	.0000	.0000	.0000	.0000	.0000
9125	.0000	.0000	.0000	.0000	.0000	.0000	.0000
ALOS*	416	377	379	374	276	305	254

*Average length-of-stay.

TABLE 15—*Continued*

Days from Admission	Age at Admission						
	<45	45–54	55–64	65–74	75–84	85–94	95+
	Females						
0.........	1.0000	1.0000	1.0000	1.0000	1.0000	1.0000	1.0000
10.........	.9764	.9747	.9809	.9763	.9766	.9767	.9732
20.........	.9566	.9529	.9648	.9567	.9574	.9576	.9505
30.........	.9377	.9334	.9501	.9392	.9398	.9399	.9290
60.........	.8858	.8831	.9109	.8929	.8931	.8921	.8710
90.........	.8389	.8429	.8774	.8539	.8529	.8505	.8213
121.........	.7948	.8082	.8468	.8185	.8163	.8121	.7762
151.........	.7560	.7790	.8198	.7875	.7842	.7782	.7368
182.........	.7194	.7520	.7940	.7578	.7538	.7457	.6996
212.........	.6871	.7282	.7704	.7307	.7263	.7161	.6663
243.........	.6565	.7053	.7472	.7039	.6995	.6871	.6340
273.........	.6294	.6846	.7256	.6790	.6749	.6603	.6045
304.........	.6036	.6644	.7042	.6542	.6505	.6337	.5757
334.........	.5806	.6459	.6842	.6310	.6280	.6090	.5491
365.........	.5586	.6277	.6643	.6078	.6055	.5843	.5230
547.........	.4544	.5392	.5621	.4891	.4890	.4567	.3921
730.........	.3743	.4733	.4806	.3981	.3921	.3542	.2916
912.........	.3136	.4177	.4153	.3274	.3113	.2737	.2207
1095.........	.2664	.3661	.3627	.2699	.2440	.2091	.1723
1277.........	.2255	.3184	.3187	.2224	.1902	.1570	.1355
1460.........	.1882	.2743	.2774	.1809	.1464	.1150	.1039
1642.........	.1603	.2394	.2379	.1443	.1110	.0831	.0772
1825.........	.1431	.2178	.2022	.1132	.0832	.0586	.0556
2190.........	.1179	.1897	.1452	.0703	.0451	.0263	.0242
2555.........	.0974	.1687	.1046	.0448	.0226	.0110	.0069
2920.........	.0797	.1521	.0772	.0289	.0109	.0040	.0015
3285.........	.0638	.1383	.0591	.0185	.0053	.0012	.0003
3650.........	.0492	.1262	.0470	.0116	.0027	.0003	.0001
4015.........	.0357	.1153	.0387	.0071	.0016	.0001	.0000
4380.........	.0239	.1052	.0327	.0041	.0010	.0000	.0000
4745.........	.0144	.0956	.0280	.0023	.0007	.0000	.0000
5110.........	.0077	.0864	.0240	.0012	.0005	.0000	.0000
5475.........	.0037	.0775	.0205	.0006	.0003	.0000	.0000
5840.........	.0018	.0688	.0173	.0003	.0003	.0000	.0000
6205.........	.0009	.0603	.0145	.0002	.0002	.0000	.0000
6570.........	.0004	.0521	.0119	.0001	.0001	.0000	.0000
6935.........	.0002	.0440	.0096	.0000	.0001	.0000	.0000
7300.........	.0001	.0362	.0076	.0000	.0001	.0000	.0000
7665.........	.0000	.0286	.0057	.0000	.0000	.0000	.0000
8030.........	.0000	.0212	.0040	.0000	.0000	.0000	.0000
8395.........	.0000	.0139	.0026	.0000	.0000	.0000	.0000
8760.........	.0000	.0069	.0012	.0000	.0000	.0000	.0000
9125.........	.0000	.0000	.0000	.0000	.0000	.0000	.0000
ALOS*	435	420	553	444	449	449	391

*Average length-of-stay.

TABLE 15—*Continued*

Days from Admission	Age at Admission <45	45–54	55–64	65–74	75–84	85–94	95+
				Total			
0	1.0000	1.0000	1.0000	1.0000	1.0000	1.0000	1.0000
10	.9753	.9752	.9768	.9750	.9731	.9745	.9707
20	.9547	.9546	.9575	.9543	.9513	.9538	.9461
30	.9355	.9358	.9399	.9356	.9315	.9347	.9230
60	.8837	.8875	.8927	.8864	.8795	.8832	.8615
90	.8391	.8492	.8526	.8447	.8354	.8387	.8097
121	.7987	.8162	.8165	.8071	.7956	.7978	.7634
151	.7637	.7882	.7852	.7744	.7611	.7620	.7236
182	.7311	.7622	.7559	.7435	.7285	.7278	.6862
212	.7023	.7389	.7298	.7156	.6993	.6969	.6530
243	.6749	.7162	.7046	.6884	.6710	.6669	.6210
273	.6504	.6953	.6818	.6634	.6451	.6394	.5919
304	.6269	.6745	.6595	.6387	.6196	.6122	.5636
334	.6057	.6552	.6389	.6158	.5961	.5871	.5377
365	.5852	.6359	.6187	.5931	.5729	.5622	.5123
547	.4873	.5376	.5173	.4773	.4545	.4350	.3852
730	.4146	.4616	.4375	.3866	.3592	.3338	.2865
912	.3609	.4003	.3724	.3147	.2825	.2546	.2149
1095	.3180	.3486	.3177	.2562	.2208	.1920	.1660
1277	.2795	.3052	.2712	.2085	.1720	.1428	.1298
1460	.2435	.2683	.2304	.1674	.1322	.1037	.0997
1642	.2134	.2400	.1947	.1312	.0999	.0741	.0739
1825	.1902	.2205	.1634	.1001	.0742	.0518	.0526
2190	.1533	.1916	.1148	.0585	.0388	.0228	.0230
2555	.1246	.1680	.0813	.0359	.0188	.0094	.0076
2920	.1017	.1478	.0579	.0227	.0087	.0034	.0023
3285	.0828	.1299	.0414	.0144	.0041	.0010	.0009
3650	.0670	.1138	.0297	.0091	.0021	.0003	.0005
4015	.0537	.0990	.0213	.0057	.0011	.0001	.0003
4380	.0424	.0854	.0153	.0034	.0007	.0000	.0001
4745	.0330	.0730	.0109	.0020	.0005	.0000	.0000
5110	.0253	.0617	.0078	.0011	.0004	.0000	.0000
5475	.0192	.0517	.0056	.0006	.0003	.0000	.0000
5840	.0145	.0429	.0039	.0003	.0002	.0000	.0000
6205	.0109	.0352	.0028	.0002	.0001	.0000	.0000
6570	.0081	.0285	.0019	.0001	.0001	.0000	.0000
6935	.0059	.0227	.0013	.0001	.0001	.0000	.0000
7300	.0042	.0175	.0009	.0000	.0000	.0000	.0000
7665	.0029	.0130	.0006	.0000	.0000	.0000	.0000
8030	.0019	.0091	.0004	.0000	.0000	.0000	.0000
8395	.0011	.0057	.0002	.0000	.0000	.0000	.0000
8760	.0005	.0026	.0001	.0000	.0000	.0000	.0000
9125	.0000	.0000	.0000	.0000	.0000	.0000	.0000
ALOS*	418	420	457	418	389	410	357

*Average length-of-stay.

TABLE 16

PROPORTION OF DAYS AFTER THE PERIOD SHOWN;
ALL STAYS; BENEFIT PERIOD CONCEPT; ADJUSTED TO MATCH 1985 NNHS RESIDENTS

Days from Admission	Age at Admission						
	<45	45–54	55–64	65–74	75–84	85–94	95+
				Males			
0.........	1.0000	1.0000	1.0000	1.0000	1.0000	1.0000	1.0000
10.........	.9889	.9857	.9867	.9802	.9714	.9720	.9612
20.........	.9793	.9736	.9756	.9635	.9483	.9496	.9291
30.........	.9702	.9619	.9652	.9481	.9271	.9292	.8999
60.........	.9449	.9298	.9366	.9068	.8720	.8743	.8232
90.........	.9221	.9027	.9113	.8711	.8253	.8259	.7624
121.........	.9009	.8779	.8876	.8384	.7831	.7813	.7107
151.........	.8820	.8562	.8664	.8097	.7465	.7422	.6684
182.........	.8639	.8354	.8459	.7823	.7118	.7053	.6306
212.........	.8475	.8163	.8271	.7575	.6806	.6722	.5982
243.........	.8315	.7974	.8086	.7332	.6503	.6402	.5680
273.........	.8167	.7798	.7914	.7107	.6225	.6111	.5414
304.........	.8022	.7621	.7742	.6883	.5951	.5827	.5160
334.........	.7886	.7455	.7582	.6672	.5697	.5564	.4930
365.........	.7750	.7287	.7422	.6461	.5447	.5304	.4706
547.........	.7040	.6406	.6596	.5344	.4173	.3955	.3560
730.........	.6465	.5712	.5926	.4424	.3185	.2854	.2547
912.........	.5992	.5147	.5332	.3651	.2451	.2026	.1696
1095.........	.5554	.4632	.4752	.2963	.1921	.1444	.1172
1277.........	.5125	.4183	.4206	.2376	.1531	.1035	.0895
1460.........	.4696	.3794	.3726	.1884	.1221	.0728	.0697
1642.........	.4269	.3434	.3303	.1458	.0975	.0500	.0515
1825.........	.3842	.3103	.2910	.1073	.0780	.0331	.0337
2190.........	.3091	.2574	.2236	.0554	.0488	.0101	.0133
2555.........	.2502	.2104	.1697	.0295	.0295	.0013	.0081
2920.........	.2018	.1692	.1271	.0163	.0175	.0001	.0057
3285.........	.1608	.1335	.0938	.0094	.0104	.0000	.0043
3650.........	.1258	.1031	.0682	.0056	.0062	.0000	.0033
4015.........	.0958	.0780	.0487	.0035	.0039	.0000	.0025
4380.........	.0708	.0576	.0343	.0022	.0025	.0000	.0019
4745.........	.0504	.0416	.0237	.0015	.0017	.0000	.0013
5110.........	.0348	.0295	.0162	.0010	.0012	.0000	.0008
5475.........	.0236	.0207	.0110	.0007	.0008	.0000	.0003
5840.........	.0159	.0145	.0074	.0005	.0006	.0000	.0000
6205.........	.0107	.0101	.0050	.0003	.0004	.0000	.0000
6570.........	.0071	.0070	.0033	.0002	.0003	.0000	.0000
6935.........	.0047	.0047	.0022	.0001	.0002	.0000	.0000
7300.........	.0030	.0032	.0014	.0001	.0001	.0000	.0000
7665.........	.0019	.0020	.0009	.0001	.0001	.0000	.0000
8030.........	.0011	.0012	.0005	.0000	.0000	.0000	.0000
8395.........	.0006	.0007	.0003	.0000	.0000	.0000	.0000
8760.........	.0002	.0003	.0001	.0000	.0000	.0000	.0000
9125.........	.0000	.0000	.0000	.0000	.0000	.0000	.0000
ALOS*	936	737	813	527	364	374	272

*Average length-of-stay.

TABLE 16—*Continued*

Days from Admission	Age at Admission						
	<45	45–54	55–64	65–74	75–84	85–94	95+
				Females			
0.........	1.0000	1.0000	1.0000	1.0000	1.0000	1.0000	1.0000
10.........	.9883	.9897	.9896	.9847	.9832	.9811	.9790
20.........	.9787	.9807	.9810	.9719	.9690	.9654	.9612
30.........	.9693	.9725	.9728	.9602	.9559	.9507	.9443
60.........	.9424	.9504	.9505	.9286	.9206	.9106	.8971
90.........	.9167	.9319	.9310	.9011	.8894	.8755	.8540
121.........	.8913	.9149	.9127	.8757	.8603	.8428	.8134
151.........	.8681	.9000	.8964	.8531	.8343	.8137	.7772
182.........	.8453	.8856	.8806	.8311	.8091	.7854	.7428
212.........	.8246	.8723	.8660	.8108	.7861	.7594	.7120
243.........	.8043	.8591	.8514	.7906	.7633	.7336	.6824
273.........	.7856	.8467	.8376	.7717	.7421	.7095	.6556
304.........	.7673	.8343	.8237	.7525	.7210	.6853	.6296
334.........	.7504	.8226	.8105	.7343	.7011	.6624	.6059
365.........	.7336	.8108	.7972	.7159	.6811	.6395	.5827
547.........	.6438	.7499	.7243	.6151	.5737	.5165	.4680
730.........	.5641	.6998	.6593	.5288	.4799	.4131	.3780
912.........	.5009	.6549	.6016	.4578	.3986	.3281	.3072
1095.........	.4521	.6110	.5507	.3971	.3276	.2563	.2502
1277.........	.4096	.5684	.5051	.3445	.2671	.1969	.2039
1460.........	.3685	.5280	.4614	.2982	.2153	.1491	.1652
1642.........	.3316	.4905	.4203	.2574	.1722	.1122	.1315
1825.........	.3016	.4565	.3815	.2199	.1364	.0822	.1017
2190.........	.2509	.3988	.3126	.1579	.0838	.0383	.0546
2555.........	.2052	.3511	.2570	.1137	.0507	.0146	.0214
2920.........	.1629	.3115	.2130	.0824	.0306	.0046	.0049
3285.........	.1231	.2783	.1788	.0601	.0188	.0012	.0004
3650.........	.0864	.2500	.1521	.0442	.0119	.0003	.0000
4015.........	.0546	.2254	.1311	.0328	.0078	.0001	.0000
4380.........	.0297	.2034	.1140	.0245	.0053	.0000	.0000
4745.........	.0131	.1833	.0996	.0184	.0038	.0000	.0000
5110.........	.0042	.1643	.0870	.0138	.0027	.0000	.0000
5475.........	.0010	.1462	.0756	.0104	.0020	.0000	.0000
5840.........	.0002	.1289	.0650	.0077	.0015	.0000	.0000
6205.........	.0001	.1122	.0552	.0057	.0011	.0000	.0000
6570.........	.0000	.0961	.0462	.0042	.0008	.0000	.0000
6935.........	.0000	.0807	.0379	.0030	.0005	.0000	.0000
7300.........	.0000	.0659	.0303	.0021	.0004	.0000	.0000
7665.........	.0000	.0516	.0232	.0015	.0002	.0000	.0000
8030.........	.0000	.0379	.0167	.0009	.0002	.0000	.0000
8395.........	.0000	.0248	.0107	.0005	.0001	.0000	.0000
8760.........	.0000	.0121	.0051	.0002	.0000	.0000	.0000
9125.........	.0000	.0000	.0000	.0000	.0000	.0000	.0000
ALOS*	915	1054	1023	690	633	560	502

*Average length-of-stay.

TABLE 16—*Continued*

Days from Admission	Age at Admission						
	<45	45–54	55–64	65–74	75–84	85–94	95+
	Total						
0	1.0000	1.0000	1.0000	1.0000	1.0000	1.0000	1.0000
10	.9881	.9874	.9882	.9830	.9803	.9792	.9761
20	.9780	.9767	.9783	.9688	.9640	.9621	.9559
30	.9683	.9665	.9690	.9558	.9489	.9462	.9369
60	.9409	.9388	.9436	.9207	.9087	.9030	.8845
90	.9156	.9153	.9212	.8902	.8737	.8652	.8382
121	.8915	.8939	.9002	.8621	.8413	.8300	.7954
151	.8698	.8751	.8815	.8373	.8126	.7988	.7581
182	.8489	.8570	.8633	.8133	.7851	.7686	.7229
212	.8299	.8404	.8465	.7913	.7599	.7411	.6917
243	.8113	.8239	.8299	.7695	.7352	.7140	.6619
273	.7942	.8085	.8144	.7491	.7124	.6887	.6350
304	.7773	.7931	.7988	.7287	.6896	.6635	.6090
334	.7617	.7785	.7841	.7093	.6683	.6399	.5853
365	.7461	.7639	.7693	.6898	.6470	.6162	.5622
547	.6640	.6873	.6908	.5843	.5342	.4902	.4467
730	.5952	.6255	.6242	.4954	.4389	.3848	.3543
912	.5402	.5727	.5654	.4217	.3594	.2997	.2810
1095	.4937	.5234	.5114	.3578	.2928	.2307	.2246
1277	.4506	.4788	.4621	.3026	.2376	.1753	.1809
1460	.4082	.4389	.4169	.2549	.1911	.1313	.1443
1642	.3686	.4017	.3755	.2131	.1528	.0976	.1115
1825	.3334	.3679	.3366	.1749	.1213	.0705	.0822
2190	.2730	.3132	.2684	.1160	.0748	.0315	.0406
2555	.2217	.2661	.2135	.0783	.0452	.0112	.0165
2920	.1765	.2258	.1702	.0536	.0273	.0032	.0049
3285	.1363	.1915	.1365	.0373	.0166	.0008	.0009
3650	.1007	.1623	.1103	.0263	.0104	.0002	.0001
4015	.0701	.1376	.0900	.0187	.0068	.0000	.0000
4380	.0453	.1167	.0741	.0134	.0046	.0000	.0000
4745	.0266	.0987	.0614	.0097	.0032	.0000	.0000
5110	.0142	.0833	.0510	.0070	.0023	.0000	.0000
5475	.0071	.0698	.0422	.0051	.0017	.0000	.0000
5840	.0035	.0581	.0347	.0037	.0012	.0000	.0000
6205	.0018	.0477	.0282	.0026	.0009	.0000	.0000
6570	.0009	.0387	.0226	.0019	.0006	.0000	.0000
6935	.0004	.0308	.0177	.0013	.0004	.0000	.0000
7300	.0002	.0238	.0136	.0009	.0003	.0000	.0000
7665	.0001	.0177	.0100	.0006	.0002	.0000	.0000
8030	.0000	.0124	.0069	.0004	.0001	.0000	.0000
8395	.0000	.0077	.0043	.0002	.0001	.0000	.0000
8760	.0000	.0036	.0020	.0001	.0000	.0000	.0000
9125	.0000	.0000	.0000	.0000	.0000	.0000	.0000
ALOS*	884	850	907	621	537	507	440

*Average length-of-stay.

TABLE 17

PROPORTION OF DAYS AFTER THE PERIOD SHOWN;
INSURABLE STAYS; BENEFIT PERIOD CONCEPT; ADJUSTED TO MATCH 1985 NNHS RESIDENTS

Days from Admission	Age at Admission						
	<45	45–54	55–64	65–74	75–84	85–94	95+
				Males			
0	1.0000	1.0000	1.0000	1.0000	1.0000	1.0000	1.0000
10	.9878	.9844	.9839	.9786	.9707	.9711	.9590
20	.9773	.9713	.9705	.9607	.9470	.9480	.9243
30	.9672	.9589	.9580	.9442	.9253	.9270	.8926
60	.9396	.9245	.9243	.9003	.8689	.8703	.8092
90	.9156	.8949	.8949	.8626	.8210	.8208	.7433
121	.8937	.8675	.8678	.8283	.7776	.7753	.6878
151	.8746	.8432	.8438	.7985	.7400	.7357	.6429
182	.8565	.8195	.8208	.7701	.7044	.6983	.6033
212	.8401	.7976	.7999	.7444	.6724	.6648	.5698
243	.8242	.7757	.7795	.7192	.6413	.6326	.5391
273	.8095	.7551	.7607	.6959	.6128	.6032	.5124
304	.7949	.7343	.7420	.6727	.5848	.5745	.4872
334	.7813	.7147	.7248	.6509	.5589	.5480	.4647
365	.7678	.6949	.7077	.6291	.5333	.5218	.4430
547	.6971	.5925	.6210	.5134	.4039	.3856	.3345
730	.6395	.5166	.5530	.4189	.3044	.2741	.2393
912	.5897	.4583	.4935	.3408	.2314	.1906	.1591
1095	.5420	.4063	.4359	.2721	.1793	.1328	.1098
1277	.4951	.3609	.3839	.2148	.1415	.0931	.0838
1460	.4480	.3209	.3406	.1683	.1117	.0640	.0652
1642	.4012	.2829	.3025	.1290	.0885	.0427	.0481
1825	.3544	.2490	.2653	.0941	.0704	.0269	.0314
2190	.2710	.1988	.2000	.0474	.0432	.0069	.0124
2555	.2056	.1561	.1498	.0245	.0256	.0006	.0076
2920	.1543	.1204	.1107	.0131	.0148	.0000	.0054
3285	.1143	.0914	.0803	.0073	.0084	.0000	.0040
3650	.0834	.0682	.0569	.0042	.0048	.0000	.0031
4015	.0598	.0502	.0391	.0026	.0027	.0000	.0023
4380	.0421	.0364	.0259	.0016	.0016	.0000	.0017
4745	.0292	.0261	.0166	.0011	.0009	.0000	.0012
5110	.0199	.0185	.0102	.0007	.0006	.0000	.0007
5475	.0134	.0131	.0062	.0005	.0004	.0000	.0003
5840	.0091	.0092	.0037	.0003	.0002	.0000	.0000
6205	.0061	.0064	.0022	.0002	.0001	.0000	.0000
6570	.0040	.0045	.0013	.0001	.0001	.0000	.0000
6935	.0027	.0030	.0008	.0001	.0000	.0000	.0000
7300	.0017	.0020	.0005	.0001	.0000	.0000	.0000
7665	.0011	.0013	.0003	.0000	.0000	.0000	.0000
8030	.0006	.0008	.0001	.0000	.0000	.0000	.0000
8395	.0003	.0004	.0001	.0000	.0000	.0000	.0000
8760	.0001	.0002	.0000	.0000	.0000	.0000	.0000
9125	.0000	.0000	.0000	.0000	.0000	.0000	.0000
ALOS*	820	667	669	488	355	361	258

*Average length-of-stay.

TABLE 17—*Continued*

Days from Admission	Age at Admission						
	<45	45–54	55–64	65–74	75–84	85–94	95+
				Females			
0	1.0000	1.0000	1.0000	1.0000	1.0000	1.0000	1.0000
10	.9905	.9908	.9889	.9840	.9826	.9813	.9789
20	.9829	.9828	.9797	.9706	.9680	.9657	.9610
30	.9758	.9754	.9711	.9584	.9546	.9511	.9441
60	.9554	.9556	.9474	.9257	.9184	.9115	.8968
90	.9356	.9390	.9268	.8974	.8865	.8768	.8538
121	.9156	.9238	.9078	.8714	.8568	.8445	.8131
151	.8968	.9105	.8908	.8483	.8303	.8158	.7770
182	.8778	.8974	.8742	.8259	.8048	.7879	.7428
212	.8598	.8854	.8589	.8054	.7814	.7622	.7121
243	.8417	.8733	.8436	.7849	.7583	.7368	.6827
273	.8245	.8619	.8292	.7656	.7369	.7130	.6561
304	.8072	.8504	.8145	.7462	.7154	.6892	.6304
334	.7908	.8393	.8006	.7278	.6953	.6667	.6069
365	.7743	.8281	.7865	.7091	.6751	.6441	.5840
547	.6841	.7667	.7098	.6070	.5665	.5231	.4710
730	.5988	.7166	.6436	.5199	.4722	.4210	.3826
912	.5206	.6739	.5862	.4494	.3908	.3364	.3119
1095	.4580	.6330	.5358	.3901	.3200	.2644	.2540
1277	.4068	.5934	.4906	.3389	.2601	.2041	.2068
1460	.3587	.5570	.4470	.2934	.2091	.1553	.1676
1642	.3164	.5234	.4047	.2531	.1665	.1179	.1335
1825	.2833	.4903	.3627	.2160	.1313	.0877	.1032
2190	.2290	.4281	.2906	.1550	.0795	.0428	.0554
2555	.1813	.3738	.2380	.1121	.0474	.0176	.0217
2920	.1400	.3276	.1986	.0821	.0283	.0062	.0049
3285	.1050	.2889	.1684	.0612	.0172	.0019	.0004
3650	.0759	.2565	.1446	.0464	.0109	.0006	.0000
4015	.0527	.2290	.1254	.0359	.0072	.0002	.0000
4380	.0350	.2051	.1095	.0282	.0050	.0001	.0000
4745	.0221	.1836	.0958	.0224	.0036	.0001	.0000
5110	.0134	.1637	.0838	.0180	.0026	.0000	.0000
5475	.0079	.1449	.0728	.0144	.0019	.0000	.0000
5840	.0047	.1270	.0626	.0114	.0014	.0000	.0000
6205	.0027	.1099	.0533	.0090	.0011	.0000	.0000
6570	.0016	.0937	.0446	.0070	.0008	.0000	.0000
6935	.0009	.0783	.0366	.0053	.0005	.0000	.0000
7300	.0005	.0636	.0293	.0039	.0004	.0000	.0000
7665	.0003	.0496	.0225	.0028	.0003	.0000	.0000
8030	.0002	.0363	.0162	.0019	.0002	.0000	.0000
8395	.0001	.0236	.0103	.0011	.0001	.0000	.0000
8760	.0000	.0115	.0050	.0005	.0000	.0000	.0000
9125	.0000	.0000	.0000	.0000	.0000	.0000	.0000
ALOS*	1107	1186	959	664	614	565	497

*Average length-of-stay.

TABLE 17—*Continued*

Days from Admission	Age at Admission						
	<45	45–54	55–64	65–74	75–84	85–94	95+
	Total						
0	1.0000	1.0000	1.0000	1.0000	1.0000	1.0000	1.0000
10	.9887	.9868	.9866	.9820	.9797	.9792	.9756
20	.9793	.9756	.9754	.9670	.9629	.9620	.9550
30	.9702	.9650	.9650	.9532	.9474	.9461	.9356
60	.9449	.9360	.9367	.9163	.9062	.9029	.8821
90	.9219	.9113	.9120	.8846	.8703	.8651	.8350
121	.8999	.8886	.8892	.8554	.8372	.8301	.7915
151	.8800	.8685	.8689	.8298	.8080	.7990	.7538
182	.8605	.8489	.8493	.8051	.7799	.7691	.7184
212	.8426	.8308	.8313	.7825	.7543	.7417	.6871
243	.8247	.8127	.8134	.7602	.7292	.7148	.6573
273	.8081	.7956	.7967	.7393	.7059	.6897	.6305
304	.7914	.7782	.7800	.7183	.6828	.6647	.6046
334	.7757	.7618	.7643	.6985	.6612	.6412	.5811
365	.7599	.7452	.7485	.6785	.6396	.6177	.5582
547	.6760	.6574	.6659	.5704	.5253	.4926	.4448
730	.6031	.5895	.5981	.4797	.4293	.3877	.3544
912	.5388	.5345	.5394	.4058	.3497	.3027	.2818
1095	.4824	.4841	.4858	.3427	.2835	.2333	.2251
1277	.4310	.4388	.4376	.2887	.2292	.1775	.1812
1460	.3812	.3984	.3939	.2422	.1836	.1331	.1445
1642	.3361	.3603	.3531	.2015	.1461	.0992	.1118
1825	.2980	.3256	.3127	.1645	.1153	.0723	.0824
2190	.2344	.2716	.2424	.1079	.0700	.0331	.0406
2555	.1817	.2250	.1896	.0721	.0417	.0124	.0165
2920	.1384	.1859	.1494	.0492	.0247	.0038	.0050
3285	.1032	.1536	.1184	.0344	.0149	.0010	.0009
3650	.0753	.1273	.0943	.0245	.0092	.0003	.0001
4015	.0535	.1061	.0754	.0178	.0059	.0001	.0000
4380	.0370	.0888	.0604	.0132	.0039	.0000	.0000
4745	.0249	.0746	.0484	.0099	.0027	.0000	.0000
5110	.0164	.0626	.0387	.0075	.0020	.0000	.0000
5475	.0106	.0524	.0308	.0057	.0014	.0000	.0000
5840	.0069	.0435	.0243	.0043	.0010	.0000	.0000
6205	.0045	.0357	.0190	.0032	.0007	.0000	.0000
6570	.0029	.0288	.0147	.0023	.0005	.0000	.0000
6935	.0018	.0229	.0112	.0017	.0004	.0000	.0000
7300	.0011	.0177	.0083	.0012	.0002	.0000	.0000
7665	.0007	.0131	.0059	.0008	.0002	.0000	.0000
8030	.0004	.0092	.0039	.0005	.0001	.0000	.0000
8395	.0002	.0057	.0024	.0003	.0001	.0000	.0000
8760	.0001	.0026	.0011	.0001	.0000	.0000	.0000
9125	.0000	.0000	.0000	.0000	.0000	.0000	.0000
ALOS*	904	805	798	586	521	505	431

*Average length-of-stay.

APPENDIX A

ESTIMATION OF THE NONINSTITUTIONALIZED POPULATION OF THE CONTIGUOUS UNITED STATES, INCLUDING THE ARMED FORCES OVERSEAS, ON APRIL 12, 1985, AND OF THE TOTAL POPULATION OF THE CONTIGUOUS UNITED STATES, INCLUDING THE ARMED FORCES OVERSEAS, ON OCTOBER 11, 1985

There are many estimates of the U.S. population, each of which represents a slightly different concept of types of persons included. The appropriate one must be determined to obtain meaningful admission rates. The most commonly quoted estimate is probably the Resident Population as counted by the Bureau of the Census every ten years and estimated (and projected) for other dates. This is the count on which congressional districts are determined. Other estimates include (1) the Total Population Including Armed Forces Overseas, (2) the Total Population Adjusted for Net Census Undercount, and (3) the Social Security Area Population, which includes the populations of Puerto Rico and other Outlying Areas controlled by the U.S. whose residents are covered by the Social Security program. Each of the these populations is progressively larger than the preceding one. A subset of the Resident Population is the Civilian Population, which excludes the Armed Forces stationed in the U.S. A subset of the Total Population Including Armed Forces Overseas is the Noninstitutionalized Population.

The desired population for the admission rates calculated in this report is the April 12, 1985 Noninstitutionalized Population (which includes the Armed Forces Overseas) Adjusted for Net Census Undercount and Excluding Alaska and Hawaii. The Armed Forces Overseas data were included in the desired population, because such a person who needed to be confined would likely be returned to the U.S. The adjustment for the net census undercount results in a more accurate estimate of the number of persons residing in the U.S. than the official count of residents, because (as the name of the adjustment implies) many persons are missed in the decennial census. Persons who were not counted by the census can be admitted to a nursing home, however, and be included in the National Nursing Home Survey (NNHS). Residents of Alaska and Hawaii could not be in the NNHS, so they were excluded from the desired population.

The desired population for the prevalence rates calculated in this report is the October 11, 1985 Total Population (Including Armed Forces Overseas) of the U.S. Adjusted for the Net Census Undercount and Excluding Alaska and Hawaii.

To estimate the desired noninstitutionalized population, the first step was to obtain an estimate of the July 1, 1984 total population from the Current Population Reports of the Bureau of the Census (P-25, No. 1045, issued January 1990). This provided an estimate by single year of age through age 99 and then the total for ages 100 and over. The population aged 100 and over was distributed by single year of age through age 110 according to the *Lx* column of the 1985 Life Table produced by the Office of the Actuary, Social Security Administration. In some cases, the population 99 and over was redistributed between age 99 and ages 100 and over to make a smoother progression through ages 98, 99, and 100.

Estimates of the resident populations of Alaska and Hawaii were obtained in age groups from the Bureau of the Census (P-25, No. 1044, issued August 1989). Within each age group, the population of each state was assumed to be distributed in proportion to the total U.S. population. These populations were subtracted from the total U.S. to obtain the total population of the 48 states plus Washington, D.C., that is, the contiguous U.S.

The Bureau of the Census publishes factors by age and sex to adjust estimates of the total population for the net census undercount (referred to as completeness-of-coverage estimates) and for the noninstitutionalized (P-25, No. 1045 has the factors for April 1, 1980). These factors were applied to the total population of the contiguous U.S. to obtain an estimate of the noninstitutionalized population including the undercount in this area. The factors are published by single year of age through age 99, with a single factor for ages 100 and over. For completeness of coverage, the aggregate factor for ages 100 and over was applied for each age. For the noninstitutionalized, the factor for each age 100 and over was taken as a percentage of the factor at the previous age. The percentage was calculated to produce the published aggregate factor for all ages 100 and over.

The above procedure was performed to obtain estimates of the noninstitutionalized population by sex on July 1 of 1984 and 1985. An estimate of the noninstitutionalized population on April 12, 1985 was obtained by linearly interpolating between the two July 1 populations. The resulting population estimate is shown in Table A1. The total population was obtained by summing the male and female populations.

The table on the next page summarizes the derivation of the April 12, 1985 noninstitutionalized population in broad age groups.

NONINSTITUTIONALIZED POPULATION OF THE CONTIGUOUS U.S.,
INCLUDING ARMED FORCES OVERSEAS
AND THE UNDERCOUNT, APRIL 12, 1985 (THOUSANDS)

Age Group	July 1, 1985 U.S. Population Including Armed Forces Overseas	Adjustments				April 12 Study Population
		Alaska and Hawaii	Undercount	Institu-tionalized	Change from April 12	
<65	210,739	−1,456	3,365	−1,233	−379	211,036
65–84 ..	25,847	−107	−19	−933	−102	24,686
85+ ...	2,693	−9	131	−699	−12	2,104
Total...	239,279	−1,572	3,477	−2,865	−493	237,826

The same procedure (except for the application of the noninstitutionalized factor) was followed to estimate the desired total population on July 1 of 1985 and 1986. An estimate of the desired population on October 11, 1985 was obtained by linearly interpolating between the two July 1 population estimates. The estimated population is also shown in Table A1. The following table summarizes the derivation of the October 11, 1985 total population in broad age groups.

TOTAL POPULATION OF THE CONTIGUOUS U.S.,
INCLUDING ARMED FORCES OVERSEAS
AND THE UNDERCOUNT, OCTOBER 11, 1985 (THOUSANDS)

Age Group	July 1, 1985 U.S. Population Including Armed Forces Overseas	Adjustments			October 11 Study Population
		Alaska and Hawaii	Undercount	Change to October 11	
<65	210,739	−1,456	3,365	487	213,135
65–84	25,847	−107	−19	154	25,875
85+	2,693	−9	131	25	2,840
Total........	239,279	−1,572	3,477	666	241,850

TABLE A1

POPULATION INCLUDING ARMED FORCES OVERSEAS OF CONTIGUOUS U.S. INCLUDING UNDERCOUNT

Age	Noninstitutionalized as of April 12, 1985			Total as of October 11, 1985		
	Male	Female	Total	Male	Female	Total
<30....	58,018,946	55,787,645	113,806,591	58,468,311	55,844,930	114,313,241
30....	2,152,017	2,092,942	4,244,959	2,202,965	2,117,828	4,320,793
31....	2,103,645	2,053,028	4,156,673	2,157,823	2,082,588	4,240,411
32....	2,047,533	2,000,079	4,047,612	2,100,803	2,033,359	4,134,162
33....	1,990,433	1,949,825	3,940,258	2,040,932	1,980,679	4,021,611
34....	1,930,135	1,900,732	3,830,867	1,983,450	1,933,893	3,917,343
35....	1,873,337	1,847,234	3,720,571	1,914,313	1,872,609	3,786,922
36....	1,863,566	1,843,911	3,707,477	1,886,951	1,852,710	3,739,661
37....	1,879,600	1,861,478	3,741,078	1,871,332	1,842,667	3,713,999
38....	1,869,836	1,851,560	3,721,396	1,967,142	1,934,449	3,901,591
39....	1,442,208	1,443,180	2,885,388	1,605,293	1,591,414	3,196,707
40....	1,462,284	1,462,816	2,925,100	1,465,299	1,458,139	2,923,438
41....	1,487,743	1,489,361	2,977,104	1,477,962	1,473,254	2,951,216
42....	1,511,583	1,511,425	3,023,008	1,539,612	1,532,357	3,071,969
43....	1,347,310	1,354,092	2,701,402	1,427,962	1,425,803	2,853,765
44....	1,269,647	1,278,291	2,547,938	1,313,771	1,316,604	2,630,375
45....	1,223,447	1,233,279	2,456,726	1,250,021	1,254,874	2,504,895
46....	1,207,643	1,219,001	2,426,644	1,223,039	1,229,829	2,452,868
47....	1,179,025	1,194,309	2,373,334	1,204,487	1,213,839	2,418,326
48....	1,130,297	1,148,118	2,278,415	1,155,691	1,168,882	2,324,573
49....	1,116,665	1,138,628	2,255,293	1,127,313	1,145,944	2,273,257
50....	1,102,367	1,125,391	2,227,758	1,118,852	1,138,612	2,257,464
51....	1,064,380	1,091,963	2,156,343	1,083,964	1,106,606	2,190,570
52....	1,061,048	1,098,565	2,159,613	1,063,595	1,095,045	2,158,640
53....	1,082,732	1,129,240	2,211,972	1,074,982	1,116,186	2,191,168
54....	1,105,452	1,156,410	2,261,862	1,099,322	1,148,735	2,248,057
55....	1,112,872	1,162,913	2,275,785	1,114,600	1,162,741	2,277,341
56....	1,107,428	1,172,673	2,280,101	1,110,672	1,168,239	2,278,911
57....	1,111,265	1,188,677	2,299,942	1,117,129	1,186,989	2,304,118
58....	1,081,733	1,177,254	2,258,987	1,097,097	1,185,316	2,282,413
59....	1,065,977	1,173,989	2,239,966	1,071,087	1,174,676	2,245,763
60....	1,072,808	1,188,935	2,261,743	1,074,831	1,188,467	2,263,298
61....	1,046,810	1,169,306	2,216,116	1,063,054	1,184,880	2,247,934
62....	1,016,454	1,145,372	2,161,826	1,025,455	1,154,470	2,179,925
63....	1,020,153	1,151,425	2,171,578	1,024,251	1,157,226	2,181,477
64....	975,095	1,109,320	2,084,415	1,000,718	1,135,981	2,136,699
65....	910,310	1,055,994	1,966,304	940,731	1,084,032	2,024,763
66....	864,231	1,022,548	1,886,779	882,441	1,039,064	1,921,505
67....	837,878	1,006,362	1,844,240	854,805	1,021,811	1,876,616
68....	784,409	966,455	1,750,864	809,525	991,323	1,800,848
69....	739,081	928,335	1,667,416	758,985	950,471	1,709,456
70....	703,461	905,183	1,608,644	720,131	923,859	1,643,990
71....	665,554	877,413	1,542,967	683,612	900,297	1,583,909
72....	624,366	843,744	1,468,110	644,177	871,340	1,515,517
73....	580,564	805,487	1,386,051	601,879	836,948	1,438,827
74....	535,622	764,272	1,299,894	557,382	798,858	1,356,240

TABLE A1—*Continued*

Age	Noninstitutionalized as of April 12, 1985			Total as of October 11, 1985		
	Male	Female	Total	Male	Female	Total
75	491,105	721,193	1,212,298	513,177	759,251	1,272,428
76	446,416	678,122	1,124,538	469,126	718,802	1,187,928
77	403,474	632,158	1,035,632	425,715	676,510	1,102,225
78	362,394	588,335	950,729	383,851	634,000	1,017,851
79	319,974	534,855	854,829	343,280	590,655	933,935
80	283,768	492,198	775,966	305,343	546,578	851,921
81	246,328	441,284	687,612	268,266	501,820	770,086
82	214,621	398,135	612,756	234,403	458,394	692,797
83	184,509	354,768	539,277	203,568	416,977	620,545
84	158,717	312,886	471,603	176,913	376,488	553,401
85	134,376	273,614	407,990	151,528	337,182	488,710
86	112,023	236,539	348,562	128,121	298,859	426,980
87	91,045	198,035	289,080	106,743	260,827	367,570
88	72,907	169,302	242,209	86,370	224,918	311,288
89	57,307	134,302	191,609	69,045	190,824	259,869
90	47,236	109,475	156,711	58,139	162,176	220,315
91	36,931	87,470	124,401	47,791	136,080	183,871
92	28,868	71,242	100,110	37,909	111,043	148,952
93	21,215	53,668	74,883	28,768	87,827	116,595
94	14,749	38,551	53,300	20,637	67,773	88,410
95	10,671	27,317	37,988	15,262	50,583	65,845
96	7,658	19,393	27,051	11,190	37,612	48,802
97	5,288	13,251	18,539	8,141	26,750	34,891
98	3,286	8,778	12,064	5,376	18,293	23,669
99	2,368	5,448	7,816	4,074	14,066	18,140
100	1,046	3,268	4,314	2,271	9,412	11,683
101	601	2,168	2,769	1,547	6,669	8,216
102	340	1,410	1,750	1,037	4,634	5,671
103	188	900	1,088	680	3,159	3,839
104	103	561	664	442	2,107	2,549
105	55	342	397	280	1,373	1,653
106	29	204	233	173	875	1,048
107	15	118	133	106	542	648
108	7	67	74	62	327	389
109	4	37	41	37	193	230
110	2	19	21	20	109	129
30–64 ..	48,114,528	49,114,722	97,229,250	49,055,770	49,765,890	98,821,660
65–84 ..	10,356,782	14,329,727	24,686,509	10,777,310	15,097,478	25,874,788
85+ ...	648,318	1,455,479	2,103,797	785,749	2,054,213	2,839,962
Total ...	117,138,574	120,687,573	237,826,147	119,087,140	122,762,511	241,849,651

REPORT OF THE COMMITTEE ON LIFE INSURANCE EXPECTED EXPERIENCE OF THE CANADIAN INSTITUTE OF ACTUARIES

MORTALITY UNDER CANADIAN STANDARD ORDINARY INSURANCE ISSUES STUDIED BETWEEN THE 1987 AND 1988 ANNIVERSARIES*

PREFACE

This report was prepared by the Committee on Life Insurance Expected Experience of the Canadian Institute of Actuaries. The Canadian Institute of Actuaries has given the Society of Actuaries permission to reproduce this report as part of the Society's expansion of its experience studies. Discussions of this report as well as of any experience study are encouraged. The Canadian Institute and the Society intend to cooperate in experience studies to benefit actuaries in both Canada and the United States.

---

1. INTRODUCTION

This is the 39th annual report submitted by the Committee on Life Insurance Expected Experience on the intercompany mortality experience for Canadian Standard Ordinary Life insurance policies. The CA 69–75 mortality tables are used to calculate the expected death claims separately for males and females. For data submitted without classification by sex, the male table was used.

2. TABLES

The following tables comprise the results of the 1987–88 mortality study:

- Table 1 The total experience analyzed for the select period by groups of duration and by groups of ages at issue; for the ultimate period by groups of attained ages.
- Table 2 Table 1 classified by: (a) males and (b) females.
- Table 3 Table 1 (select period only) classified by: (a) medical males, (b) medical females, (c) nonmedical males, (d) nonmedical females, (e) paramedical males, and (f) paramedical females.
- Table 4 Mortality ratios by amount for policy years 1980–81 through 1987–88.
- Table 5 The variation of the experience of the individual companies from the overall mortality ratio for the total intercompany experience.

Table 6 Various classes in broad groups of policy years and ages at issue or attained ages.
Table 7 Cause of death.
Table 8 Smoking habits.
Table 9 Type of insurance.

Additional detailed data, showing mortality ratios by quinquennial age groupings, are available and can be obtained by writing to the Chairman of the Committee on Life Insurance Expected Experience of the CIA.

3. COMMENTS ON DATA FROM CONTRIBUTING COMPANIES

The 1987–88 study is based on the data of 16 contributing companies. Five companies are temporarily unable to submit data.

Contributors	Exposures
Canada Life	4.40%
Confederation Life	3.40
Crown Life	3.22
Equitable Life	0.67
Great-West Life	5.48
Imperial Life	1.81
Industrial-Alliance	12.27
London Life	17.29
Manufacturers Life	3.84
Metropolitan Life	4.77
Mutual Life	15.32
North American Life	4.70
North-West Life	0.69
Prudential Assurance	1.73
Sun Life	12.73
Transamerica	7.68
Total exposures	100.00%

A comparison of total exposures and death claims with previous years is as follows:

	1985–86 Study	1986–87 Study	1987–88 Study
Exposures			
By Number	6,942,570	6,929,713	6,163,896
By Amount ('000)	158,094,377	164,875,777	170,782,585
Death Claims			
By Number	36,296	35,901	33,144
By Amount ('000)	285,830	285,047	283,049

4. COMMENTS

In Table 1, the column entitled S.D. provides estimates of the standard deviation of the ratios of actual to expected numbers of deaths. These numbers measure the degree of confidence which may be placed in the ratios experienced. The formula used to calculate the standard deviations is as follows:

$$\text{S.D.} = \frac{(\text{actual \# of deaths})^{1/2}}{\text{expected \# of deaths}}$$

In Table 2, the average sum assured for the exposures has been steadily increasing as follows:

	1983–84	1984–85	1985–86	1986–87	1987–88
Males	21,539	23,400	25,700	26,493	30,927
Females	13,335	14,910	17,448	18,836	22,033
Combined	18,829	20,488	22,770	23,792	27,707

The following shows the trend in the average amount of claims over the last five years:

	1983–84	1984–85	1985–86	1986–87	1987–88
Average Claim	6,833	8,271	7,875	7,940	8,540

In Table 3, we note that paramedical results for males are slightly better than medical, which in turn are better than nonmedical.

In Table 4, the mortality rates generally have declined over the last eight years.

In Table 7, percentage of death claims (by amount) for the main cause of death groupings:

	Policy Years		
	1–5	6–15	16 and over
Motor Vehicle and Other Accidents and Homicides	24.0% 21.9 22.4	11.7% 15.6 12.6	3.2% (87–88) 4.0 (86–87) 3.8 (85–86)
Diseases of the Heart and Circulatory System	18.1% 17.0 18.6	21.6% 21.4 25.0	32.1% (87–88) 38.4 (86–87) 32.0 (85–86)
Malignant Neoplasms	27.7% 32.7 28.8	35.3% 37.9 32.4	27.8% (87–88) 27.6 (86–87) 24.1 (85–86)

This is the first year that AIDS has been included in the study.

In Table 8, the following select ratios for smokers and nonsmokers were extracted from the 1987–88 study (with the comparable ratios from the previous year shown in brackets).

	A/E %	Expected Deaths ('000)
Males (by amount)		
Smokers	95.2 (96.6)	$26,631 (19,501)
Nonsmokers	52.1 (59.9)	72,352 (58,808)
Nonclassified	70.3 (78.6)	110,832 (112,601)
Females (by amount)		
Smokers	103.4 (86.6)	$5,088 (4,360)
Nonsmokers	54.6 (51.5)	12,952 (10,267)
Nonclassified	72.2 (76.8)	19,207 (19,434)
	(Smoker A/E)/(Nonsmokers A/E) %	
Male	211.1 (215.0)	182.7 (161.3)
Female	205.7 (198.1)	189.4 (168.2)

The unclassified data fell from 50.9% of total exposures (by amount) in the last study to 46.6% in the 1987–88 study.

In Table 9, the ratio of actual to expected for term-riders is less than for term, which in turn is less than for permanent in both the current and previous study years.

THIS REPORT WAS PREPARED AT THE UNIVERSITY OF WATERLOO BY:

W.H. AITKEN
M.A. BENNETT
R.L. BROWN
V. BORCHERT

THE REPORT WAS APPROVED BY THE COMMITTEE ON LIFE INSURANCE EXPECTED EXPERIENCE

M.A. BENNETT
J.V. CASTELLINO
A.G. JARDIN (VICE-CHAIRMAN)
J.A. MEREU
W.A. RAMSEY
R.A. WILLIS
R.W. WILSON

TABLE 1

CANADIAN STANDARD ORDINARY EXPERIENCE BETWEEN POLICY ANNIVERSARIES IN 1987 AND 1988
MALES AND FEMALES COMBINED—EXPECTED CA 69–75 TABLES

	Ratio A/E			Actual Deaths		Exposures		Expected Deaths	
	Number	S.D.	Amount	Number	Amount*	Number	Amount*	Number	Amount*
Policy Years 1 to 15 from 16 Companies									
Select Experience by Policy Year									
1	78.7	3.98	68.3	391	21,345	491,483	31,078,602	496.95	31,261.90
2	104.3	4.39	55.0	564	17,242	465,315	27,352,180	540.72	31,354.24
3	77.6	3.75	51.2	428	16,355	435,552	23,729,664	551.86	31,920.95
4	95.2	4.07	60.6	547	17,071	399,678	18,270,416	574.48	28,156.51
5	98.0	4.02	79.8	595	21,020	367,100	15,104,725	607.19	26,324.70
6–10	84.9	2.10	73.8	1,640	51,047	1,073,357	31,967,438	1,932.33	69,182,71
11–15	81.9	2.20	79.7	1,379	22,999	695,937	10,360,020	1,684.44	28,861.17
By Issue Age									
0–4	57.5	4.88	52.2	139	2,442	527,404	8,719,767	241.68	4,678.33
5–29	76.0	2.38	66.2	1,019	27,642	1,732,172	57,309,732	1,341.10	41,743.02
30–44	75.6	1.88	62.8	1,617	67,550	1,239,966	73,618,104	2,138.78	107,583.47
45–49	92.5	2.16	70.7	1,835	55,721	369,717	16,911,217	1,983.01	78,815.71
60+	136.7	4.47	96.4	934	13,724	59,163	1,304,226	683.40	14,241.64
Total Select	86.8	1.17	67.6	5,544	167,079	3,928,422	157,863,046	6,388.	24,706.
Policy Years 16 and Over from 16 Companies									
Ultimate Experience by Attained Age									
15–29	87.4	5.17	81.0	286	1,369	326,542	1,588,378	327.42	1,691.46
30–44	81.2	3.14	67.0	669	4,071	482,553	3,264,648	823.63	6,079.00
45–59	74.8	1.24	72.0	3,666	24,582	719,388	4,953,882	4,900.30	34,146.04
60–74	83.9	0.78	77.3	11,443	50,456	554,963	2,632,908	13,645.53	65,285.51
75+	91.3	0.85	88.6	11,536	35,492	152,028	479,723	12,639.29	40,041.36
Total Ultimate	85.4	0.51	78.8	27,600	115,970	2,235,474	12,919,538	32,336.	14,724.
Grand Total	85.6	0.47	71.8	33,144	283,049	6,163,896	170,782,585	38,724.	39,430.

*Shown in $1,000 units.

TABLE 2A

CANADIAN STANDARD ORDINARY EXPERIENCE BETWEEN POLICY ANNIVERSARIES IN 1987 AND 1988
MALES LIVES ONLY—EXPECTED CA 69–75 TABLES

	Ratio A/E		Actual Deaths		Exposures		Expected Deaths	
	Number	Amount	Number	Amount*	Number	Amount*	Number	Amount*
Policy Years 1 to 15 from 16 Companies								
Select Experience by Policy Year								
1	83.5	71.8	291	18,019	284,430	21,119,069	348.60	25,106.18
2	105.0	52.5	414	13,641	271,879	18,839,172	394.45	25,958.97
3	77.8	51.3	316	13,839	256,041	16,640,205	406.41	26,995.92
4	90.4	58.0	381	13,873	232,304	12,920,435	421.59	23,904.55
5	95.0	77.5	428	17,402	215,802	10,866,384	450.49	22,452.59
6–10	84.2	73.1	1,190	43,893	638,750	23,608,296	1,412.82	60,025.96
11–15	80.7	79.7	1,038	20,209	444,991	7,943,979	1,286.73	25,371.01
By Issue Age								
0–4	54.0	47.5	81	1,342	278,614	4,597,857	149.95	2,821.95
5–29	81.3	67.8	800	22,098	1,003,000	36,358,657	983.81	32,586.41
30–44	74.9	62.2	1,183	56,103	793,225	55,776,058	1,579.26	90,240.51
45–59	89.7	69.8	1,366	50,100	236,606	14,207,068	1,522.69	71,783.07
60+	129.4	90.7	628	11,233	32,752	997,899	485.40	12,383.25
Total Select	86.0	67.1	4,058	140,876	2,344,197	111,937,540	4,721.	209,815.
Policy Years 16 and Over from 16 Companies								
Ultimate Experience by Attained Age								
15–29	91.5	81.2	235	1,151	192,365	1,060,685	256.81	1,416.54
30–44	81.0	65.6	519	3,549	337,357	2,742,176	641.00	5,411.64
45–59	72.2	71.5	3,048	22,963	564,122	4,473,909	4,220.44	32,122.92
60–74	83.2	76.8	9,601	46,736	424,725	2,359,275	11,538.42	60,857.60
75+	92.7	88.0	9,377	31,245	113,845	413,788	10,011.54	35,504.25
Total Ultimate	85.1	78.1	22,780	105,643	1,632,414	11,049,832	26,768.	135,313.
Grand Total	85.2	71.4	26,838	246,519	3,976,611	122,987,372	31,489.	345,128.

*Shown in $1,000 units.

TABLE 2B

CANADIAN STANDARD ORDINARY EXPERIENCE BETWEEN POLICY ANNIVERSARIES IN 1987 AND 1988
FEMALE LIVES ONLY—EXPECTED CA 69–75 TABLES

	Ratio A/E		Actual Deaths		Exposures		Expected Deaths	
	Number	Amount	Number	Amount*	Number	Amount*	Number	Amount*
Policy Years 1 to 15 from 16 Companies								
Select Experience by Policy Year								
1	67.4	54.0	100	3,325	207,053	9,959,533	148.35	6,155.72
2	102.6	66.7	150	3,601	193,436	8,512,984	146.27	5,395.24
3	77.0	51.1	112	2,516	179,509	7,089,438	145.45	4,924.98
4	108.6	75.2	166	3,198	167,374	5,349,982	152.89	4,251.95
5	106.6	93.4	167	3,618	151,297	4,238,315	156.70	3,872.08
6–10	86.6	78.1	450	7,155	434,607	8,359,142	519.51	9,156.75
11–15	85.7	79.9	341	2,789	250,946	2,415,941	397.70	3,489.99
By Issue Age								
0–4	63.2	59.3	58	1,100	248,790	4,121,910	91.73	1,856.38
5–29	61.3	60.6	219	5,544	729,171	20,950,949	357.29	9,156.42
30–44	77.6	66.0	434	11,447	446,739	17,842,000	559.51	17,342.89
45–59	101.9	79.9	469	5,621	133,111	2,704,149	460.32	7,032.64
60+	154.5	134.0	306	2,490	26,411	306,327	198.00	1,858.39
Total Select	89.1	70.3	1,486	26,203	1,584,222	45,925,335	1,667.	37,247.
Policy Years 16 and Over from 16 Companies								
Ultimate Experience by Attained Age								
15–29	72.2	79.5	51	218	134,177	527,693	70.60	274.92
30–44	80.5	77.5	144	512	143,122	518,600	178.99	660.66
45–59	92.1	80.0	587	1,509	150,664	465,072	637.60	1,885.63
60–74	88.2	79.8	1,608	2,815	120,581	242,582	1,822.24	3,528.86
75+	85.0	86.9	1,772	2,922	33,618	53,664	2,084.73	3,361.58
Total Ultimate	86.8	82.1	4,162	7,976	582,162	1,807,613	4,794.	9,712.
Grand Total	87.4	72.8	5,648	34,178	2,166,384	47,732,948	6,461.	46,958.

*Shown in $1,000 units.

TABLE 2C

Canadian Standard Ordinary Experience between Policy Anniversaries in 1987 and 1988
Sex Not Known—Expected CA 69–75 Tables

	Ratio A/E		Actual Deaths		Exposures		Expected Deaths	
	Number	Amount	Number	Amount*	Number	Amount*	Number	Amount*
Policy Years 1 to 15 from 16 Companies								
Select Experience by Policy Year								
1	0.0	0.0	0	0	0	0	0.00	0.00
2	0.0	0.0	0	0	0	25	0.00	0.02
3	0.0	0.0	0	0	2	21	0.00	0.05
4	0.0	0.0	0	0	0	0	0.00	0.00
5	0.0	0.0	0	0	1	26	0.00	0.02
6–10	0.0	0.0	0	0	0	0	0.00	0.00
11–15	0.0	0.0	0	0	0	100	0.00	0.17
By Issue Age								
0–4	0.0	0.0	0	0	0	0	0.00	0.00
5–29	0.0	0.0	0	0	1	126	0.00	0.19
30–44	0.0	0.0	0	0	2	46	0.00	0.07
45–59	0.0	0.0	0	0	0	0	0.00	0.00
60+	0.0	0.0	0	0	0	0	0.00	0.00
Total Select	0.0	0.0	0	0	3	172	0.	0.
Policy Years 16 and Over from 16 Companies								
Ultimate Experience by Attained Age								
15–29	0.0	0.0	0	0	0	0	0.00	0.00
30–44	164.8	157.3	6	11	2,074	3,872	3.64	6.70
45–59	73.4	80.3	31	110	4,602	14,900	42.26	137.49
60–74	82.1	100.6	234	905	9,657	31,051	284.87	899.05
75+	87.4	112.8	387	1,326	4,565	12,270	443.02	1,175.52
Total Ultimate	85.0	106.0	658	2,352	20,898	62,093	774.	2,219.
Grand Total	85.0	106.0	658	2,352	20,901	62,265	774.	2,219.

*Shown in $1,000 units.

TABLE 3

CANADIAN STANDARD ORDINARY EXPERIENCE BETWEEN POLICY ANNIVERSARIES IN 1987 AND 1988
EXPECTED CA 69–75 TABLES
POLICY YEARS 1 TO 15 FROM 16 COMPANIES

Select Experience	Ratio A/E		Actual Deaths		Exposures		Expected Deaths	
	Number	Amount	Number	Amount*	Number	Amount*	Number	Amount*
Medical Males								
By Policy Year								
1	77.7	78.6	30	4,358	14,338	2,833,513	38.59	5,543.81
2	79.3	24.8	41	1,822	16,650	3,219,502	51.68	7,354.39
3	81.6	45.1	50	3,759	15,553	2,965,213	61.28	8,334.31
4	73.4	41.2	46	3,212	13,371	2,336,895	62.69	7,788.86
5	105.7	74.0	85	5,559	14,909	2,046,171	80.43	7,511.26
6–10	88.1	72.8	343	20,163	71,537	6,596,506	389.45	27,678.62
11–15	77.2	79.1	443	11,558	91,223	2,837,169	573.58	14,620.45
By Issue Age								
0–4	96.3	51.2	3	36	6,685	135,261	3.11	70.37
5–29	61.4	35.7	33	973	43,112	2,516,743	53.78	2,722.17
30–44	65.3	53.6	232	14,955	106,382	12,602,885	355.44	27,901.79
45–59	87.0	69.1	512	27,506	66,947	6,953,161	588.66	39,787.44
60+	100.5	83.4	258	6,961	14,455	626,920	256.71	8,349.94
Total	82.5	64.0	1,038	50,430	237,581	22,834,971	1,258.	78,832.
Medical Females								
By Policy Year								
1	148.2	59.4	20	327	6,713	466,930	13.50	551.13
2	129.9	61.2	20	369	6,340	458,951	15.40	602.06
3	135.6	34.3	18	173	5,104	348,538	13.27	505.25
4	144.6	50.8	18	220	4,136	237,974	12.45	433.61
5	166.4	101.9	28	467	4,981	223,319	16.83	458.70
6–10	128.0	88.5	124	1,538	23,701	717,052	96.86	1,737.97
11–15	83.3	77.3	94	823	22,745	330,734	112.78	1,064.33
By Issue Age								
0–4	0.0	0.0	0	0	4,264	78,534	1.28	28.76
5–29	113.6	89.9	11	289	15,152	615,636	9.68	321.87
30–44	80.3	49.1	33	891	20,547	1,282,161	41.10	1,816.17
45–59	104.2	75.3	126	1,574	22,330	649,059	120.95	2,088.02
60+	140.6	106.0	152	1,164	11,427	158,107	108.08	1,098.02
Total	114.6	73.2	322	3,918	73,720	2,783,497	281.	5,353.

*Shown in $1,000 units.

TABLE 3—*Continued*

Select Experience	Ratio A/E		Actual Deaths		Exposures		Expected Deaths	
	Number	Amount	Number	Amount*	Number	Amount*	Number	Amount*
Nonmedical Males								
By Policy Year								
1	88.3	86.2	210	11,408	235,934	14,187,045	237.80	13,229.18
2	121.0	70.4	319	8,949	224,608	12,510,201	263.55	12,715.18
3	79.0	58.1	203	7,706	214,033	11,329,210	256.89	13,257.24
4	98.1	75.9	260	8,471	196,922	8,751,683	265.04	11,157.39
5	96.6	81.1	250	7,757	176,811	6,992,026	258.73	9,560.42
6–10	89.5	84.1	583	14,946	480,258	12,296,363	651.06	17,778.70
11–15	84.8	76.1	468	5,591	321,155	4,203,937	551.94	7,346.52
By Issue Age								
0–4	53.8	48.1	78	1,306	269,858	4,418,586	145.09	2,712.30
5–29	82.6	72.4	737	20,062	923,534	31,551,785	892.44	27,705.23
30–44	82.7	74.1	772	30,589	565,988	31,341,498	933.32	41,275.11
45–59	114.2	91.5	464	10,660	82,041	2,813,031	406.26	11,650.06
60+	224.3	130.0	242	2,212	8,300	145,566	107.91	1,701.94
Total	92.3	76.2	2,293	64,829	1,849,721	70,270,465	2,485.	85,045.
Nonmedical Females								
By Policy Year								
1	55.6	52.6	64	2,463	185,636	8,589,011	115.10	4,685.33
2	98.5	63.5	110	2,569	174,548	7,410,238	111.62	4,043.84
3	71.3	56.0	79	2,100	163,514	6,263,409	110.74	3,749.65
4	102.3	75.0	120	2,427	154,769	4,780,036	117.31	3,233.89
5	96.9	73.8	110	2,042	137,314	3,680,700	113.48	2,766.18
6–10	71.4	60.7	229	3,320	380,282	6,749,576	320.91	5,465.97
11–15	85.8	75.0	213	1,498	219,672	1,944,121	248.17	1,997.19
By Issue Age								
0–4	63.8	60.2	57	1,085	242,743	4,006,754	89.32	1,803.48
5–29	59.8	57.0	204	4,885	700,380	19,783,122	340.89	8,574.95
30–44	77.3	61.1	361	7,907	394,267	14,506,385	467.26	12,937.39
45–59	108.9	90.8	219	2,146	71,986	1,070,052	201.14	2,363.19
60+	216.9	150.9	84	397	6,359	50,779	38.72	263.04
Total	81.3	63.3	925	16,419	1,415,735	39,417,092	1,137.	25,942.

*Shown in $1,000 units.

TABLE 3—*Continued*

Select Experience	Ratio A/E		Actual Deaths		Exposures		Expected Deaths	
	Number	Amount	Number	Amount*	Number	Amount*	Number	Amount*
Paramedical Males								
By Policy Year								
1	73.8	36.7	49	2,189	28,768	3,777,062	66.37	5,966.51
2	66.5	49.3	49	2,720	26,031	2,833,378	73.66	5,517.36
3	75.2	47.7	62	2,364	22,478	2,086,838	82.50	4,956.29
4	79.9	44.2	75	2,190	22,011	1,831,856	93.86	4,958.30
5	83.5	75.9	93	4,086	24,082	1,828,187	111.33	5,380.91
6–10	70.9	60.3	264	8,783	86,955	4,715,399	372.31	14,568.54
11–15	78.8	89.9	127	3,061	32,610	902,664	161.19	3,402.98
By Issue Age								
0–4	0.0	0.0	0	0	420	8,268	0.20	4.91
5–29	87.4	53.7	29	1,053	30,485	2,026,835	33.16	1,962.49
30–44	61.1	50.6	174	10,405	115,727	11,384,025	285.00	20,563.15
45–59	74.1	59.4	388	11,874	86,470	4,343,032	523.61	20,002.13
60+	107.3	92.9	128	2,060	9,833	213,224	119.24	2,218.20
Total	74.8	56.7	719	25,392	242,935	17,975,385	961.	44,751.
Paramedical Females								
By Policy Year								
1	75.4	57.1	13	473	10,861	760,549	17.24	828.16
2	98.9	88.6	17	600	9,324	530,518	17.20	677.62
3	76.7	40.7	15	242	8,213	379,125	19.54	594.65
4	121.0	94.3	28	551	8,469	331,971	23.13	584.45
5	109.9	171.3	29	1,109	9,002	334,296	26.39	647.20
6–10	95.3	117.6	97	2,296	30,624	892,514	101.74	1,952.80
11–15	92.5	109.2	34	468	8,529	141,087	36.75	428.47
By Issue Age								
0–4	0.0	0.0	0	0	316	5,860	0.10	2.23
5–29	58.0	172.5	3	360	9,107	407,712	5.17	208.65
30–44	79.7	104.9	39	2,599	28,901	1,898,769	48.95	2,479.00
45–59	89.0	73.8	122	1,876	38,170	963,253	137.05	2,539.94
60+	136.0	187.1	69	905	8,528	94,465	50.72	483.53
Total	96.3	100.5	233	5,740	85,022	3,370,060	242.	5,713.

*Shown in $1,000 units.

TABLE 4

Canadian Standard Ordinary Experience
Comparison of Ratios (A/E) by Amount—Expected CIA 69–75 Tables

Combined Data	Grouping	Policy Year							
		1980–81	1981–82	1982–83	1983–84	1984–85	1985–86	1986–87	1987–88
Male and Female	Select and Ultimate	80.1	82.4	79.6	74.9	82.4	80.3	76.5	71.8
Male	Select and Ultimate	79.4	82.0	78.7	74.3	83.2	80.5	77.0	71.4
Female	Select and Ultimate	80.4	83.3	84.8	74.4	72.9	75.4	72.4	72.8
Male and Female	Select	76.0	80.8	76.9	68.9	81.6	73.4	74.2	67.6
Male	Select	75.7	81.0	75.7	68.4	83.3	73.3	74.9	67.1
Female	Select	78.9	79.2	86.8	72.8	70.5	74.0	70.4	70.3
Male and Female	Ultimate	84.5	84.0	82.6	81.7	83.4	90.1	79.8	78.8
Male	Ultimate	83.7	83.0	82.1	81.0	83.2	90.0	79.9	78.1
Female	Ultimate	84.2	92.2	79.4	79.3	80.3	80.0	79.3	82.1
Medical Male	Select	71.7	85.9	74.1	65.9	95.9	70.2	76.8	64.0
Nonmedical Male	Select	83.0	75.0	80.9	65.1	73.5	75.0	78.3	76.2
Paramedical Male	Select	78.2	73.6	71.7	80.4	71.4	76.6	64.7	56.7
Medical Female	Select	89.5	73.0	129.3	79.3	60.1	86.8	90.5	73.2
Nonmedical Female	Select	75.9	81.2	74.1	70.2	72.6	70.9	63.8	63.3
Paramedical Female	Select	68.1	82.5	72.3	74.3	73.2	75.0	79.7	100.5

TABLE 5

1987–1988 EXPERIENCE RATIO BY DEPARTURE FROM INTERCOMPANY EXPERIENCE RATIO BY AMOUNT EXPECTED CA 69–75 TABLES

Percentage Departure	Number of Companies	Actual Claims*	Percentage of Claims
Within 5%	3	60,107	21.2%
5% to 10%	3	46,115	16.3
10% to 15%	2	73,355	25.9
15% to 20%	5	73,425	25.9
20% and Over	3	30,046	10.6
	16	283,049	100.0%

*Shown in $1,000 units.

TABLE 6

CANADIAN STANDARD ORDINARY EXPERIENCE BETWEEN POLICY ANNIVERSARIES IN 1987 AND 1988 EXPECTED CA 69–75 TABLE

	Ratio A/E		Exposure		Actual Deaths	
	Number	Amount	Number	Amount*	Number	Amount*
Medical Males						
Ages						
0–29	63.3	36.1	49,797	2,652,004	36	1,009
30–54	75.3	60.2	159,308	18,302,019	584	34,417
55+	98.2	79.5	28,476	1,880,947	418	15,005
Policy Years						
1–5	85.5	51.2	74,821	13,401,296	252	18,709
6–15	81.6	75.0	162,760	9,433,675	786	31,721
Total	82.5	64.0	237,581	22,834,971	1,038	50,430
Nonmedical Males						
Ages						
0–29	78.6	70.2	1,193,392	35,970,371	815	21,367
30–54	88.7	76.7	636,937	33,839,919	1,110	38,859
55+	187.3	116.2	19,392	460,175	368	4,603
Policy Years						
1–5	96.9	73.9	1,048,308	53,770,165	1,242	44,292
6–15	87.4	81.7	801,413	16,500,300	1,051	20,537
Total	92.3	76.2	1,849,721	70,270,465	2,293	64,829
Paramedical Males						
Ages						
0–29	86.9	53.5	30,905	2,035,103	29	1,053
30–54	66.2	52.7	183,339	15,091,569	431	18,989
55+	93.6	79.3	28,691	848,713	259	5,350
Policy Years						
1–5	76.7	50.6	123,370	12,357,322	328	13,548
6–15	73.3	65.9	119,565	5,618,063	391	11,844
Total	74.8	56.7	242,935	17,975,385	719	25,392

*Shown in $1,000 units.

TABLE 6—*Continued*

	Ratio A/E		Exposure		Actual Deaths	
	Number	Amount	Number	Amount*	Number	Amount*
Medical Females						
Ages						
0–29	100.3	82.7	19,416	694,170	11	289
30–54	85.4	59.4	36,717	1,803,996	103	2,000
55+	139.2	99.5	17,587	285,331	208	1,629
Policy Years						
1–5	145.6	61.0	27,274	1,735,712	104	1,557
6–15	104.0	84.3	46,446	1,047,786	218	2,361
Total	114.6	73.2	73,720	2,783,497	322	3,918
Nonmedical Females						
Ages						
0–29	60.7	57.5	943,123	23,789,875	261	5,970
30–54	82.2	64.3	455,416	15,476,540	518	9,649
55+	190.3	144.3	17,196	150,676	146	800
Policy Years						
1–5	85.0	62.8	815,781	30,723,395	483	11,601
6–15	77.7	64.6	599,954	8,693,697	442	4,818
Total	81.3	63.3	1,415,735	39,417,092	925	16,419
Paramedical Females						
Ages						
0–29	57.0	170.7	9,423	413,572	3	360
30–54	88.7	92.0	56,312	2,690,176	125	4,090
55+	109.6	122.0	19,287	266,312	105	1,289
Policy Years						
1–5	98.6	89.3	45,869	2,336,459	102	2,975
6–15	94.6	116.1	39,153	1,033,600	131	2,764
Total	96.3	100.5	85,022	3,370,060	233	5,740

*Shown in $1,000 units.

TABLE 6—*Continued*

	Ratio A/E		Exposure		Actual Deaths	
	Number	Amount	Number	Amount*	Number	Amount*
Males Combined (Ultimate)						
Ages						
15–44	84.0	68.8	529,722	3,802,860	754	4,699
45–69	77.7	73.5	891,406	6,389,295	8,913	54,026
70+	91.1	85.4	211,286	857,677	13,113	46,917
Total	85.1	78.1	1,632,414	11,049,832	22,780	105,643
Females Combined (Ultimate)						
Ages						
15–44	78.1	78.1	277,299	1,046,294	195	730
45–69	85.9	75.1	241,980	656,986	1,514	3,155
70+	88.2	89.5	62,883	104,333	2,453	4,090
Total	86.8	82.1	582,162	1,807,613	4,162	7,976
All Codes—Select						
Ages						
0–29	73.2	64.8	2,259,576	66,029,499	1,158	30,084
30–54	80.4	64.6	1,537,594	87,906,801	2,880	108,271
55+	123.0	86.9	131,252	3,926,746	1,506	28,724
Policy Years						
1–5	91.1	62.4	2,159,128	115,535,588	2,525	93,033
6–15	83.5	75.5	1,769,294	42,327,458	3,019	74,046
Total	86.8	67.6	3,928,422	157,863,046	5,544	167,079
All Codes—Ultimate						
Ages						
15–44	83.0	70.0	809,095	4,853,026	955	5,440
45–69	78.9	73.8	1,144,761	7,083,583	10,592	57,870
70+	90.4	86.2	281,618	982,930	16,053	52,660
Total	85.4	78.8	2,235,474	12,919,538	27,600	115,970

*Shown in $1,000 units.

TABLE 7A

STANDARD MEDICAL AND NONMEDICAL ISSUES FOR MALES AND FEMALES COMBINED
DISTRIBUTION BY CAUSE OF DEATH AND AMOUNT OF DEATH CLAIMS FOR POLICY YEAR 1987–1988
POLICY YEARS 1–5
(AMOUNTS SHOWN IN $1,000 UNITS)

Age at Issue	Amount	Percentage	Amount	Percentage	Amount	Percentage	Amount	Percentage	Amount	Percentage
							Nervous System and Mental Diseases			
	Infective and Parasitic Diseases (Tuberculosis, etc.) (01–17)*		Malignant Neoplasms (18–33)*		Diabetes Mellitus (37)*		Vascular Lesions (42)*		Other (41, 43–47)*	
0–9	20	1.1	177	10.1	0	0.0	13	0.7	10	0.6
10–19	87	3.0	92	3.2	0	0.0	0	0.0	10	0.3
20–29	30	0.3	1,251	10.6	40	0.3	414	3.5	50	0.4
30–39	251	1.1	5,080	22.0	110	0.5	485	2.1	450	2.0
40–49	513	2.2	7,699	33.3	0	0.0	1,782	7.7	96	0.4
50–59	143	0.6	10,057	39.6	20	0.1	778	3.1	315	1.2
Total	1,045	1.2	24,355	27.7	170	0.2	3,473	3.9	931	1.1
	Diseases of the Heart and Circulatory System						Diseases of the Digestive System			
	Arteriosclerotic and Degenerative Heart Disease (50,5A)*		Hypertensive and Rheumatic, etc. (49, 51–55)*		Respiratory Diseases Pneumonia and Influenza, etc. (56–63)*		Cirrhosis of the Liver (70)*		Other (64–69, 71–72)*	
0–9	22	1.3	20	1.1	0	0.0	0	0.0	68	3.9
10–19	95	3.3	10	0.3	60	2.1	0	0.0	0	0.0
20–29	276	2.3	167	1.4	200	1.7	50	0.4	65	0.6
30–39	1,364	5.9	1,307	5.7	613	2.7	25	0.1	98	0.4
40–49	3,390	14.7	2,680	11.6	153	0.7	111	0.5	138	0.6
50–59	4,966	19.5	1,650	6.5	433	1.7	105	0.4	113	0.4
Total	10,113	11.5	5,834	6.6	1,459	1.7	291	0.3	481	0.5

TABLE 7A—*Continued*

Age at Issue	Amount	Percentage	Amount	Percentage	Amount	Percentage	Amount	Percentage	Amount	Percentage
	Genito-Urinary Diseases (Nephritis, etc.) (73–77)*		Motor Vehicle Accidents (88)*		Other Accidents and Homicides (89–96, 98)*		All Other Diseases			
							Suicides (97)*		Unknown Causes (Other Codes†)*	
0–9	0	0.0	365	20.9	202	11.6	10	0.6	839	48.1
10–19	0	0.0	1,559	53.6	505	17.4	280	9.6	211	7.2
20–29	0	0.0	4,048	34.3	2,184	18.5	1,255	10.6	1,776	15.0
30–39	40	0.2	4,480	19.4	2,839	12.3	2,344	10.2	3,585	15.5
40–49	100	0.4	995	4.3	710	3.1	2,703	11.7	2,039	8.8
50–59	37	0.1	2,023	8.0	1,192	4.7	515	2.0	3,073	12.1
Total	177	0.2	13,471	15.3	7,632	8.7	7,106	8.1	11,522	13.1
	AIDS (02)*									
0–9	15	0.9								
10–19	0	0.0								
20–29	362	3.1								
30–39	470	2.0								
40–49	204	0.9								
50–59	40	0.2								
Total	1,091	1.2								

*1980, codes for cause of death.
†(34–36, 38–40, 48, 78–83, 85–87, 99).

TABLE 7B

STANDARD MEDICAL AND NONMEDICAL ISSUES FOR MALES AND FEMALES COMBINED
DISTRIBUTION BY CAUSE OF DEATH AND AMOUNT OF DEATH CLAIMS FOR POLICY YEAR 1987–1988
POLICY YEARS 6–15
(AMOUNTS SHOWN IN $1,000 UNITS)

Age at Issue	Amount	Percentage	Amount	Percentage	Amount	Percentage	Amount	Percentage	Amount	Percentage
							Nervous System and Mental Diseases			
	Infective and Parasitic Diseases (Tuberculosis, etc.) (01–17)*		Malignant Neoplasms (18–33)*		Diabetes Mellitus (37)*		Vascular Lesions (42)*		Other (41, 43–47)*	
0–9	0	0.0	143	12.6	0	0.0	0	0.0	98	8.6
10–19	5	0.3	361	20.1	3	0.1	35	2.0	17	0.9
20–29	135	1.7	1,760	21.7	38	0.5	203	2.5	38	0.5
30–39	214	1.1	6,394	32.6	28	0.1	560	2.9	74	0.4
40–49	196	1.0	9,307	48.4	200	1.0	496	2.6	194	1.0
50–59	61	0.3	6,337	33.3	57	0.3	292	1.5	192	1.0
Total	611	0.9	24,303	35.3	325	0.5	1,586	2.3	612	0.9
	Diseases of the Heart and Circulatory System						Diseases of the Digestive System			
	Arteriosclerotic and Degenerative Heart Disease (50,5A)*		Hypertensive and Rheumatic, etc. (49, 51–55)*		Respiratory Diseases Pneumonia and Influenza, etc. (56–63)*		Cirrhosis of the Liver (70)*		Other (64–69, 71–72)*	
0–9	17	1.5	45	3.9	54	4.7	0	0.0	10	0.9
10–19	15	0.8	25	1.4	0	0.0	0	0.0	35	2.0
20–29	485	6.0	239	2.9	159	2.0	0	0.0	80	1.0
30–39	2,774	14.2	871	4.4	458	2.3	318	1.6	258	1.3
40–49	3,081	16.0	1,338	7.0	703	3.7	2	0.0	172	0.9
50–59	3,309	17.4	2,734	14.4	1,297	6.8	520	2.7	107	0.6
Total	9,681	14.0	5,251	7.6	2,670	3.9	840	1.2	662	1.0

TABLE 7B—*Continued*

Age at Issue	Amount	Percentage	Amount	Percentage	Amount	Percentage	Amount	Percentage	Amount	Percentage
	Genito-Urinary Diseases (Nephritis, etc.) (73–77)*		Motor Vehicle Accidents (88)*		Other Accidents and Homicides (89–96, 98)*		All Other Diseases			
							Suicides (97)*		Unknown Causes (Other Codes†)*	
0–9	0	0.0	301	26.4	152	13.4	70	6.1	249	21.9
10–19	0	0.0	439	24.5	442	24.6	276	15.4	142	7.9
20–29	23	0.3	1,204	14.8	1,619	19.9	878	10.8	1,260	15.5
30–39	55	0.3	1,164	5.9	1,320	6.7	2,235	11.4	2,874	14.7
40–49	220	1.1	286	1.5	346	1.8	598	3.1	2,098	10.9
50–59	608	3.2	614	3.2	171	0.9	124	0.7	2,602	13.7
Total	905	1.3	4,007	5.8	4,050	5.9	4,180	6.1	9,227	13.4
	AIDS (02)*									
0–9	0	0.0								
10–19	59	3.3								
20–29	184	2.3								
30–39	729	3.7								
40–49	155	0.8								
50–59	298	1.6								
Total	1,424	2.1								

*1980, codes for cause of death.
†(34–36, 38–40, 48, 78–83, 85–87, 99).

TABLE 7C

Standard Medical and Nonmedical Issues for Males and Females Combined
Distribution by Cause of Death and Amount of Death Claims for Policy Year 1987–1988
Policy Years 16 and Over
(Amounts Shown in $1,000 Units)

Attained Age	Amount	Percentage	Amount	Percentage	Amount	Percentage	Amount	Percentage	Amount	Percentage
							Nervous System and Mental Diseases			
	Infective and Parasitic Diseases (Tuberculosis, etc.) (01–17)*		Malignant Neoplasms (18–33)*		Diabetes Mellitus (37)*		Vascular Lesions (42)*		Other (41, 43–47)*	
15–19	0	0.0	31	7.7	0	0.0	5	1.3	10	2.5
20–29	5	0.5	114	11.3	8	0.8	7	0.7	41	4.1
30–39	22	1.3	469	28.7	5	0.3	4	0.2	17	1.1
40–49	123	1.8	2,085	31.1	0	0.0	114	1.7	75	1.1
50–59	491	2.7	6,255	35.0	29	0.2	302	1.7	162	0.9
60–69	419	1.4	9,714	32.9	33	0.1	1,004	3.4	676	2.3
70–99	1,079	2.3	10,351	21.9	72	0.2	3,025	6.4	1,068	2.3
Total	2,139	2.0	29,018	27.8	148	0.1	4,462	4.3	2,050	2.0
	Diseases of the Heart and Circulatory System						Diseases of the Digestive System			
	Arteriosclerotic and Degenerative Heart Disease (50,5A)*		Hypertensive and Rheumatic, etc. (49, 51–55)*		Respiratory Diseases Pneumonia and Influenza, etc. (56–63)*		Cirrhosis of the Liver (70)*		Other (64–69, 71–72)*	
15–19	25	6.3	0	0.0	15	3.8	0	0.0	5	1.3
20–29	47	4.7	25	2.4	15	1.5	17	1.7	6	0.6
30–39	96	5.9	214	13.1	33	2.0	7	0.4	5	0.3
40–49	1,145	17.1	446	6.7	182	2.7	97	1.4	103	1.5
50–59	4,169	23.3	1,622	9.1	377	2.1	301	1.7	465	2.6
60–69	6,455	21.8	3,783	12.8	1,121	3.8	165	0.6	542	1.8
70–99	8,749	18.5	6,702	14.2	3,759	8.0	95	0.2	483	1.0
Total	20,687	19.8	12,792	12.3	5,503	5.3	682	0.7	1,609	1.5

TABLE 7C—*Continued*

Attained Age	Amount	Percentage	Amount	Percentage	Amount	Percentage	Amount	Percentage	Amount	Percentage
	Genito-Urinary Diseases Nephritis, etc.) (73–77)*		Motor Vehicle Accidents (88)*		Other Accidents and Homicides (89–96, 98)*		All Other Diseases: Suicides (97)*		All Other Diseases: Unknown Causes (Other Codes†)*	
15–19	0	0.0	200	50.4	38	9.6	38	9.7	30	7.5
20–29	2	0.2	214	21.2	204	20.2	140	13.9	164	16.3
30–39	8	0.5	82	5.0	182	11.1	179	11.0	310	19.0
40–49	70	1.0	331	4.9	392	5.8	327	4.9	1,209	18.0
50–59	41	0.2	267	1.5	365	2.0	582	3.3	2,463	13.8
60–69	473	1.6	288	1.0	377	1.3	255	0.9	4,257	14.4
70–99	680	1.4	121	0.3	297	0.6	18	0.0	10,670	22.6
Total	1,274	1.2	1,502	1.4	1,854	1.8	1,539	1.5	19,103	18.3
	AIDS (02)*									
15–19	0	0.0								
20–29	8	0.8								
30–39	55	3.4								
40–49	150	2.2								
50–59	277	1.5								
60–69	342	1.2								
70–99	362	0.8								
Total	1,194	1.1								

*1980, codes for cause of death.
†(34–36, 38–40, 48, 78–83, 85–87, 99).

TABLE 8

CANADIAN STANDARD ORDINARY EXPERIENCE BETWEEN POLICY ANNIVERSARIES IN 1987 AND 1988
EXPECTED CA 69–75 TABLES
POLICY YEARS 1 TO 15 FROM 14 COMPANIES

Select Experience	Ratio A/E		Actual Deaths		Exposures		Expected Deaths	
	Number	Amount	Number	Amount*	Number	Amount*	Number	Amount*
Male Smokers								
By Policy Year								
1	126.9	150.6	81	5,905	53,079	3,488,744	63.83	3,920.71
2	205.3	92.0	206	3,938	54,985	3,208,600	100.35	4,279.09
3	127.4	88.7	101	4,204	50,726	3,018,741	79.25	4,736.69
4	128.7	77.5	97	2,804	42,612	2,030,676	75.38	3,619.94
5	106.0	79.7	91	2,676	44,588	1,786,221	85.82	3,357.54
6–10	108.5	87.9	162	5,817	72,203	2,748,562	149.27	6,615.07
By Issue Age								
0–4	21.4	20.6	3	54	24,172	440,180	14.05	263.43
5–14	43.5	27.4	5	60	20,179	398,250	11.50	219.12
15–24	124.4	117.2	73	2,155	57,884	1,886,018	58.68	1,839.13
25–34	99.5	76.0	92	4,243	104,475	6,465,360	92.44	5,579.43
35–44	118.3	105.5	144	8,970	68,123	5,030,369	121.77	8,501.75
45–54	120.7	93.8	154	6,169	30,043	1,657,301	127.63	6,572.95
55–64	191.8	102.0	172	3,188	10,900	395,456	89.67	3,124.93
65+	240.4	95.4	95	506	2,816	35,900	39.51	530.05
Total	133.0	95.2	738	25,345	318,592	16,308,834	555.	26,631.
Male Nonsmokers								
By Policy Year								
1	73.3	50.8	92	5,636	92,907	8,421,256	125.49	11,092.61
2	63.3	41.7	86	4,876	88,551	7,585,773	135.82	11,706.68
3	51.4	39.6	81	5,131	90,902	7,150,756	157.52	12,944.03
4	60.9	55.7	94	6,534	78,864	5,705,372	154.43	11,734.98
5	62.1	62.0	93	6,357	65,623	4,396,808	149.72	10,248.46
6–10	68.7	63.6	141	9,155	78,254	5,027,167	205.19	14,388.23
By Issue Age								
0–4	30.8	26.8	4	73	20,619	408,792	13.00	272.61
5–14	36.3	19.2	3	30	14,478	285,569	8.27	156.50
15–24	69.6	63.9	62	2,586	88,269	4,144,397	89.04	4,044.97
25–34	68.3	60.7	98	7,145	166,302	13,749,684	143.44	11,766.69
35–44	55.4	50.9	118	10,891	122,993	12,682,824	213.19	21,384.65
45–54	56.1	43.4	134	9,119	58,586	5,400,466	238.91	21,014.18
55–64	70.0	53.2	126	6,362	21,820	1,558,123	180.07	11,955.77
65+	92.7	84.4	42	1,482	3,006	113,876	45.32	1,757.10
Total	63.0	52.1	587	37,688	496,073	38,343,731	931.	72,352.

*Shown in $1,000 units.

TABLE 8—*Continued*

Select Experience	Ratio A/E		Actual Deaths		Exposures		Expected Deaths	
	Number	Amount	Number	Amount*	Number	Amount*	Number	Amount*
Male Unclassified								
By Policy Year								
1	74.1	64.2	118	6,478	138,444	9,209,069	159.28	10,092.86
2	77.1	48.4	122	4,827	128,343	8,044,798	158.27	9,973.21
3	79.0	49.2	134	4,579	114,413	6,470,708	169.63	9,315.19
4	99.1	53.0	190	4,535	110,828	5,184,387	191.78	8,549.64
5	113.5	94.6	244	8,369	105,591	4,683,355	214.96	8,846.59
6–10	83.8	74.1	887	28,920	488,293	15,832,568	1,058.37	39,022.66
By Issue Age								
0–4	60.2	53.1	74	1,214	233,823	3,748,884	122.90	2,285.92
5–14	88.3	81.3	91	1,337	121,283	2,447,086	103.05	1,643.64
15–24	81.8	68.5	263	5,244	311,994	7,676,120	321.57	7,658.83
25–34	75.6	64.3	469	16,051	461,683	21,967,237	620.68	24,974.50
35–44	72.5	55.8	565	19,564	258,562	15,401,801	779.45	35,057.71
45–54	89.3	78.7	661	21,088	103,769	4,929,698	739.80	26,810.41
55–64	101.4	100.2	431	10,519	32,807	1,014,596	425.24	10,503.22
65+	146.8	152.8	179	2,900	5,611	99,550	121.93	1,897.70
Total	84.5	70.3	2,733	77,917	1,529,532	57,284,972	3,235.	110,832.
Female Smokers								
By Policy Year								
1	102.6	98.5	25	966	37,128	1,772,377	24.36	981.43
2	179.5	137.0	55	1,301	37,515	1,571,637	30.64	949.61
3	107.5	56.2	29	510	35,763	1,382,611	26.98	907.35
4	110.3	81.9	29	545	31,728	908,826	26.29	665.70
5	134.8	117.8	39	712	31,634	719,968	28.94	604.19
6–10	132.7	126.1	60	1,229	45,741	990,930	45.21	974.57
By Issue Age								
0–4	133.8	136.6	12	227	21,863	391,406	8.97	166.15
5–14	38.2	57.4	2	55	17,717	331,858	5.23	95.84
15–24	92.9	123.9	19	756	55,223	1,708,596	20.44	610.47
25–34	85.1	80.0	31	1,266	66,388	3,093,174	36.42	1,583.42
35–44	113.4	96.7	50	1,528	35,323	1,403,035	44.08	1,579.85
45–54	116.7	107.3	42	772	15,469	333,213	36.00	719.49
55–64	243.2	178.0	53	454	6,157	75,511	21.79	255.35
65+	293.4	262.9	28	204	1,415	11,616	9.54	77.52
Total	130.2	103.4	237	5,262	219,555	7,348,409	182.	5,088.

*Shown in $1,000 units.

TABLE 8—*Continued*

Select Experience	Ratio A/E		Actual Deaths		Exposures		Expected Deaths	
	Number	Amount	Number	Amount*	Number	Amount*	Number	Amount*
Female Nonsmokers								
By Policy Year								
1	48.7	35.9	25	960	67,601	4,119,915	51.38	2,678.33
2	66.1	48.6	32	1,173	60,612	3,511,729	48.42	2,411.76
3	66.7	52.7	35	1,231	61,727	3,110,100	52.51	2,337.03
4	76.6	62.0	40	1,252	53,931	2,328,106	52.22	2,019.64
5	75.2	95.0	38	1,554	44,572	1,584,585	50.53	1,634.72
6–10	50.5	48.3	32	898	49,179	1,531,086	63.42	1,860.58
By Issue Age								
0–4	102.0	109.0	9	205	19,501	383,769	8.82	188.02
5–14	50.8	49.3	2	35	13,180	246,976	3.94	71.05
15–24	45.5	36.8	12	386	72,349	2,953,255	26.40	1,050.38
25–34	54.7	41.7	34	1,534	115,084	7,136,706	62.17	3,677.90
35–44	47.8	52.0	41	2,333	72,146	4,074,468	85.79	4,483.51
45–54	56.6	58.8	38	1,297	30,168	1,062,723	67.17	2,205.08
55–64	86.6	59.8	39	564	12,604	283,718	45.06	944.43
65+	139.2	214.9	27	713	2,743	48,374	19.40	331.62
Total	63.3	54.6	202	7,067	337,775	16,189,989	319.	12,952.
Female Unclassified								
By Policy Year								
1	68.9	56.0	50	1,399	102,324	4,067,241	72.61	2,495.96
2	93.7	55.4	63	1,127	95,309	3,429,617	67.20	2,033.88
3	72.8	46.1	48	775	82,019	2,596,726	65.95	1,680.60
4	130.4	89.4	97	1,401	81,715	2,113,049	74.39	1,566.62
5	116.5	82.8	90	1,352	75,091	1,933,762	77.23	1,633.17
6–10	87.1	79.5	358	5,028	339,687	5,837,126	410.88	6,321.60
By Issue Age								
0–4	50.0	44.5	37	668	207,426	3,346,735	73.95	1,502.20
5–14	63.8	62.1	24	398	102,264	2,078,760	37.61	640.81
15–24	63.8	55.7	71	1,032	221,890	4,204,646	111.37	1,851.28
25–34	65.3	65.3	149	3,566	267,544	7,826,196	228.01	5,458.67
35–44	85.4	76.0	218	4,101	136,802	3,735,278	255.33	5,396.13
45–54	100.7	84.4	234	2,275	59,593	905,294	232.36	2,694.30
55–64	129.5	99.8	200	1,161	25,295	241,553	154.39	1,163.28
65+	157.0	134.1	114	671	6,078	48,473	72.62	499.96
Total	89.8	72.2	1,047	13,872	1,026,892	22,386,935	1,166.	19,207.

*Shown in $1,000 units.

TABLE 9

CANADIAN STANDARD ORDINARY EXPERIENCE BETWEEN POLICY ANNIVERSARIES IN 1987 AND 1988
EXPECTED CA 69–75 TABLES
POLICY YEARS 1 TO 15 FROM 16 COMPANIES

	Ratio A/E		Actual Deaths		Exposures		Expected Deaths	
	Number	Amount	Number	Amount*	Number	Amount*	Number	Amount*
Permanent								
By Issue Age								
0–29	74.6	68.0	1,090	23,614	2,106,597	50,428,571	1,462.03	34,717.30
30–54	82.9	70.1	2,321	55,570	1,168,221	40,569,255	2,800.15	79,229.38
55+	126.4	102.1	1,382	20,398	114,790	2,202,664	1,093.67	19,976.90
By Policy Year								
1–5	95.9	70.5	2,164	54,211	1,810,322	66,701,831	2,256.50	76,942.20
6–15	84.8	79.6	2,629	45,371	1,579,286	26,498,659	3,099.35	56,981.39
Total	89.5	74.4	4,793	99,582	3,389,608	93,200,490	5,356.	133,924.
Term								
By Issue Age								
0–29	59.0	49.5	66	3,768	137,650	9,940,061	111.80	7,609.58
30–54	71.8	60.7	528	44,087	343,789	37,507,738	735.07	72,606.79
55+	86.4	60.4	76	6,075	11,193	1,346,401	87.98	10,063.39
By Policy Year								
1–5	69.7	54.4	307	30,874	311,707	36,638,876	440.27	56,769.71
6–15	73.4	68.8	363	23,056	180,925	12,155,323	494.58	33,510.05
Total	71.7	59.7	670	53,930	492,632	48,794,199	935.	90,280.
Term Rider								
By Issue Age								
0–29	0.0	73.7	0	2,635	0	4,849,120	0.00	3,574.50
30–54	0.0	62.0	0	7,277	0	7,490,389	0.00	11,736.50
55+	0.0	56.3	0	453	0	118,775	0.00	804.13
By Policy Year								
1–5	0.0	60.6	0	5,894	0	9,144,939	0.00	9,729.88
6–15	0.0	70.0	0	4,471	0	3,313,345	0.00	6,385.24
Total	0.0	64.3	0	10,365	0	12,458,284	0.00	16,115.

*Shown in $1,000 units.

TABLE 9—*Continued*

	Ratio A/E		Actual Deaths		Exposures		Expected Deaths	
	Number	Amount	Number	Amount*	Number	Amount*	Number	Amount*
Permanent Term								
By Issue Age								
0–29	15.7	12.0	1	60	10,046	777,863	6.37	501.10
30–54	65.2	34.4	27	1,373	24,827	2,331,327	41.43	3,987.39
55+	112.6	81.9	48	1,798	5,256	258,785	42.64	2,194.54
By Policy Year								
1–5	72.9	38.2	54	2,130	36,069	3,043,377	74.05	5,574.06
6–15	134.3	99.4	22	1,102	4,060	324,597	16.39	1,108.96
Total	84.4	48.4	76	3,232	40,129	3,367,974	90.	6,683.
Other								
By Issue Age								
0–29	38.8	37.1	1	7	5,283	33,886	2.58	18.88
30–54	99.5	97.9	4	39	757	8,093	4.02	39.82
55+	0.0	0.0	0	0	13	121	0.23	1.98
By Policy Year								
1–5	0.0	0.0	0	0	1,030	6,566	0.38	2.44
6–15	77.5	77.8	5	45	5,023	35,534	6.45	58.23
Total	71.4	73.8	5	45	6,053	42,100	7.	61.
Unknown								
By Issue Age								
0–29	0.0	0.0	0	0	0	0	0.00	0.00
30–54	0.0	0.0	0	0	0	0	0.00	0.00
55+	0.0	0.0	0	0	0	0	0.00	0.00
By Policy Year								
1–5	0.0	0.0	0	0	0	0	0.00	0.00
6–15	0.0	0.0	0	0	0	0	0.00	0.00
Total	0.0	0.0	0	0	0	0	0.	0.

*Shown in $1,000 units.

TABLE 9—*Continued*

	Ratio A/E		Actual Deaths		Exposures		Expected Deaths	
	Number	Amount	Number	Amount*	Number	Amount*	Number	Amount*
				Permanent (Ultimate)				
By Attained Age								
15–44	83.6	72.3	950	5,227	801,225	4,586,785	1,136.09	7,230.08
45–69	79.0	74.3	10,424	54,913	1,117,192	6,493,572	13,190.32	73,930.14
70+	90.4	86.2	16,046	52,609	281,414	981,933	17,741.37	60,997.49
Total	85.5	79.3	27,420	112,749	2,199,831	12,062,290	32,068.	142,158.
				Term (Ultimate)				
By Attained Age								
15–44	49.2	41.4	6	84	5,920	92,246	12.20	202.92
45–69	66.0	79.6	142	2,389	24,793	364,931	215.13	2,999.31
70+	134.4	145.0	3	31	33	294	2.23	21.38
Total	65.7	77.7	151	2,504	30,746	457,471	230.	3,224.
				Term Rider (Ultimate)				
By Attained Age								
15–44	0.0	40.0	0	130	0	165,943	0.00	324.41
45–69	0.0	31.4	0	427	0	211,298	0.00	1,358.92
70+	0.0	55.8	0	12	0	339	0.00	21.52
Total	0.0	33.4	0	569	0	377,580	0	1,705

*Shown in $1,000 units.

TABLE 9—*Continued*

	Ratio A/E		Actual Deaths		Exposures		Expected Deaths	
	Number	Amount	Number	Amount*	Number	Amount*	Number	Amount*
Permanent Term (Ultimate)								
By Attained Age								
15–44	0.0	0.0	0	0	0	0	0.00	0.00
45–69	0.0	0.0	0	0	0	0	0.00	0.00
70+	0.0	0.0	0	0	0	0	0.00	0.00
Total	0.0	0.0	0	0	0	0	0.	0.
Other (Ultimate)								
By Attained Age								
15–44	0.0	0.0	0	0	1,950	8,053	2.76	13.04
45–69	98.8	113.4	26	140	2,776	13,782	26.30	123.61
70+	41.0	43.8	4	9	171	364	9.77	20.55
Total	76.9	94.9	30	149	4,897	22,199	39.	157.
Unknown (Ultimate)								
By Attained Age								
15–44	0.0	0.0	0	0	0	0	0.00	0.00
45–69	0.0	0.0	0	0	0	0	0.00	0.00
70+	0.0	0.0	0	0	0	0	0.00	0.00
Total	0.0	0.0	0	0	0	0	0.	0.

REPORT OF THE SUBCOMMITTEE ON ANNUITY MORTALITY COMMITTEE ON EXPECTED EXPERIENCE OF THE CANADIAN INSTITUTE OF ACTUARIES

INDIVIDUAL ANNUITANT MORTALITY STUDY POLICY YEARS 1980–1988

This report was prepared by the Subcommittee on Annuity Mortality of the Committee on Life Insurance Expected Experience of the Canadian Institute of Actuaries. The Canadian Institute of Actuaries has given the Society of Actuaries permission to reproduce this report as part of the Society's expansion of its experience studies. Discussions of this report as well as of any experience study are encouraged. The Canadian Institute and the Society intend to cooperate in experience studies to benefit actuaries in both Canada and the United States.

---

1. INTRODUCTION

Work on the Individual Annuitant Mortality Study began in 1983. The first data were submitted in 1984. It has been a lengthy process getting all the submissions clear of errors. Some inconsistencies remain. However, because we do not have any reason to believe that any errors remain which are large enough to invalidate the aggregate results, we are publishing our study at this time.

This study will become an annual publication. We expect it to be sent out about a year after the end of the policy year under study.

Not all contributing companies have finished with their systems for submitting data. We are still expecting some additional submissions for the years covered by this report. We may also receive some revisions to data submitted. Later reports will incorporate these changes to our data and may not agree entirely with this report.

2. DESCRIPTION OF THE STUDY

The study considers experience under Canadian individual annuities. Most of the policies studied are in the payout status, but in some cases experience is included during the deferred period provided the policy has no cash value or right to change the policy.

The study is done on a policy year basis; that is, the year of study runs between successive policy anniversaries. The *year of experience,* as the year under study is known, is referred to by the calendar year in which the policy year ends. The anniversary is with respect to the *determination date.* This is the day on which the income was determined and may not be changed; there is a final disposition of funds on that date. Usually the determination date will be the same as the issue date. In the case of an accumulation type of annuity, the determination date would most likely be the date when the policy changes from accumulation status to payout status.

The study uses a ten-year select period. Since there is no published annuitant mortality table with the ten-year select period, the expected for both the select and ultimate periods is calculated using an aggregate table: the 1983 Basic table, which appears in *TSA* XXXIII (1981): 695.

Data are segregated by single life policies, joint policies in which both annuitants are still alive at the beginning of the policy year and joint policies for which only one annuitant is alive at the beginning of the year. All companies had a very low mortality ratio (that is, ratio of actual to expected mortality) for female experience under joint policies with both alive. It is likely that the payee is usually a male, and when the female dies, no need is seen to report the death to the insurance company. Experience under male lives is closer to single life experience, but still too low to be believed. The overall mortality ratio for males in single life policies and in joint policies with both alive is 95 percent and 73 percent, respectively; 105 percent and 35 percent, respectively, for females. Because of the problems with joint data, only single life data are included in this report.

RRSP policies, RPP policies and nonregistered policies are studied separately.

Experience is studied separately by refund and nonrefund. A refund policy is one which provides for the possibility of some payment after the death of the annuitant. The most common refund provision is a continuation of payments for at least a specified number of years. There is very little exposure for nonrefund policies.

All reports are done on the basis of age nearest birthday. Most data were contributed on this basis. Age last birthday data were split half to the age indicated and half to the next age.

The following gives an overview of the data included in the study. Only single life data are included in the table.

Year of Experience	Number of Companies	Number Exposed	Number of Deaths	Ratio A/E by Income
1981	4	36,744	912	85.4%
1982	4	43,173	1,294	88.9
1983	6	56,875	1,440	85.2
1984	6	64,009	1,837	95.9
1985	7	99,451	2,787	96.5
1986	7	108,914	3,281	108.7
1987	5	106,537	3,210	100.6
1988	4	104,113	3,084	97.3

3. CAUTIONS

There are some known inconsistencies in the data. We do not know how serious the inconsistencies are, but we do not believe them to be consequential.

Only single life data are included in the report. Joint data were excluded because of the problems of underreporting of deaths.

The data are not homogenous. Only two companies contributed data for all years of experience. However, the largest four companies are the same for each of the last four years.

There are more deaths in the select period than in the ultimate and substantially more exposure. Therefore, the aggregate mortality ratios represent the effects of the growth in the annuity market and are not representative of the experience of a cohort.

4. OBSERVATIONS

There is no clear trend of mortality improvement. On the contrary, the least squares regression line of the mortality ratios is positively sloped (implying mortality increasing) for both males and females. This is quite surprising. However, only two companies have data spanning all years of experience, and both of these had one year of exceptionally light mortality in the early 1980s. It may be that a different trend would have been observed if all companies had contributed data for all years.

As an aside on the trend in mortality, it is interesting to note that most companies showed a high year for mortality in 1986, and for some 1987 was high as well. The nuclear reactor at Chernobyl exploded on 26 April 1986, and a radioactive plume reached us about two weeks later. The uptick in American mortality in the summer of 1986 is noted in *The Economist*, 30 January 1988, p. 67. (Deaths in the summer of 1986 would fall partly in the 1985–86 policy year and partly in 1986–87.)

Although the data are collected on a 10-select basis, there appears to be no effect of selection, except perhaps in the first policy year. This supports the present practice of using aggregate data for constructing annuitant mortality tables. It may be that our reports would be more useful if the detail were by attained age on aggregate data rather than using attained age only for ultimate data.

As expected, mortality ratios for RPP business are significantly higher than for RRSP and nonregistered business. We also might have expected that RRSP mortality ratios would be higher than nonregistered, but surprisingly, the opposite is true. It appears that we can state that RRSP mortality is lighter than nonregistered with a fairly high degree of confidence. RRSP and nonregistered mortality are closer together (RRSP still lower) in the ultimate period, but this probably reflects the fact that virtually all ultimate RRSP business would have been written when deregistration was the only alternative to a life annuity.

There appears to be a significant degree of antiselection by amount for males, but not for females.

Nonrefund business shows lower mortality ratios than on refund business, particularly at the early durations. Since there is very little nonrefund business, it is not clear that any valid inferences can be drawn. It must also be borne in mind that refund business is far from homogenous. Business is classified as refund if there is any certain period at all. Thus, a 5-year certain period is combined with certain to age 90.

The following table summarizes aggregate single life mortality ratios.

Year of Experience	Number of Policies		Annualized Income	
	Male	Female	Male	Female
1981	0.911	0.797	0.896	0.823
1982	1.072	1.087	0.909	0.914
1983	0.963	0.925	0.835	0.993
1984	1.074	0.966	0.986	0.820
1985	1.026	0.994	0.961	1.009
1986	1.057	1.138	1.010	1.236
1987	1.071	1.114	0.963	1.077
1988	1.026	1.064	0.938	1.080
All	1.035	1.035	0.953	1.049

5. CONCLUSIONS

In spite of the lack of homogeneity in the data, some qualitative inferences can be drawn.

1. The 1983 Basic table appears to be reasonably consistent with actual experience.
2. Registration type should be taken into account in forming a mortality assumption.

6. CONTRIBUTING COMPANIES

The following table of contributing companies shows the proportion of deaths, on single life policies, submitted for all years of study. The number of years submitted differs from company to company. At present, the distribution of data is not well balanced. The balance should improve when all companies contribute data each year.

Aetna Canada	0.3%
Canada Life	34.3
Confederation Life	7.0
Crown Life	6.5
Great-West Life	14.6
Industrielle-Alliance	0.1
Manufacturers Life	10.5
Mutual Life	26.1
Standard Life	0.5

7. INDEX TO TABLES

TABLE 1

CANADIAN INDIVIDUAL ANNUITANT EXPERIENCE BETWEEN POLICY ANNIVERSARIES IN 1980 AND 1988
ALL COMPANIES TO DATE
MALE AND FEMALE COMBINED; EXPECTED: 1983 BASIC MALE AND FEMALE (*TSA* XXXIII, 695)
SINGLE LIFE POLICIES ONLY; ALL TAX TYPES COMBINED, BOTH REFUND AND NONREFUND

	Exposures		Actual Deaths		Expected Deaths		Ratio A/E	
	Number	Income	Number	Income	Number	Income	Number	Income
				Select Experience — Policy Years 1 to 10				
By Policy Year								
1	75,788	239,119,685	919	2,665,649	1,061.74	3,410,098	86.6	78.2
2	71,356	217,842,928	1,105	3,312,894	1,110.61	3,394,576	99.5	97.6
3	65,838	195,455,616	1,135	3,465,548	1,124.97	3,317,374	100.9	104.5
4	60,543	174,315,413	1,130	2,875,865	1,130.04	3,166,027	100.0	90.8
5	54,094	146,946,576	1,186	2,972,531	1,107.54	2,923,342	107.1	101.7
6–10	177,172	362,982,159	4,773	8,715,763	4,601.97	9,049,932	103.7	96.3
By Issue Age								
0–59	58,980	254,183,334	514	1,612,141	406.07	1,476,583	126.6	109.2
60–64	121,412	311,926,055	1,751	3,961,282	1,565.92	3,909,908	111.8	101.3
65–69	207,612	445,408,516	4,109	8,263,097	4,139.10	8,788,040	99.3	94.0
70 and over	116,788	325,144,474	3,875	10,171,731	4,025.79	11,086,818	96.3	91.7
Total Select	504,791	1,336,662,377	10,248	24,008,250	10,136.88	25,261,349	101.1	95.0
				Ultimate Experience — Policy Years 11 and Over				
By Attained Age								
0–69	19,481	26,703,174	290	340,643	198.66	257,737	146.0	132.2
70–74	26,140	27,360,007	662	881,874	597.42	664,998	110.8	132.6
75–79	49,802	47,954,267	2,023	1,877,536	1,945.93	1,962,213	103.9	95.7
80–84	35,579	32,611,409	2,424	2,303,714	2,263.02	2,153,567	107.1	107.0
85–89	16,380	12,749,859	1,776	1,504,252	1,641.28	1,295,926	108.2	116.1
90 and over	9,487	6,581,206	1,662	1,168,092	1,649.10	1,136,438	100.8	102.8
Total Ultimate	156,868	153,959,920	8,836	8,076,110	8,295.42	7,470,879	106.5	108.1
Grand Total	661,659	1,490,622,297	19,084	32,084,360	18,432.30	32,732,228	103.5	98.0

TABLE 2

CANADIAN INDIVIDUAL ANNUITANT EXPERIENCE BETWEEN POLICY ANNIVERSARIES IN 1980 AND 1988
ALL COMPANIES TO DATE
MALE LIVES ONLY; EXPECTED: 1983 BASIC MALE (*TSA* XXXIII, 695)
SINGLE LIFE POLICIES ONLY; ALL TAX TYPES COMBINED, BOTH REFUND AND NONREFUND

	Exposures		Actual Deaths		Expected Deaths		Ratio A/E	
	Number	Income	Number	Income	Number	Income	Number	Income
Select Experience — Policy Years 1 to 10								
By Policy Year								
1	40,414	140,988,638	623	1,869,829	704.48	2,407,295	88.4	77.7
2	38,647	131,080,337	763	2,374,767	742.66	2,416,352	102.7	98.3
3	36,231	120,465,254	798	2,523,115	757.40	2,384,700	105.4	105.8
4	33,827	108,856,108	758	1,932,200	768.01	2,296,796	98.7	84.1
5	31,054	94,441,497	818	2,087,394	767.62	2,163,961	106.6	96.5
6–10	108,142	250,580,758	3,458	6,609,754	3,336.85	7,014,286	103.6	94.2
By Issue Age								
0–59	32,098	163,249,018	318	1,114,497	274.24	1,142,899	115.8	97.5
60–64	65,418	192,775,453	1,185	2,800,431	1,067.87	2,925,652	111.0	95.7
65–69	124,250	291,205,962	3,103	6,467,908	3,028.79	6,832,679	102.4	94.7
70 and over	66,549	199,182,160	2,613	7,014,224	2,706.12	7,782,159	96.6	90.1
Total Select	288,315	846,412,592	7,218	17,397,059	7,077.02	18,683,391	102.0	93.1
Ultimate Experience — Policy Years 11 and Over								
By Attained Age								
0–69	9,018	15,599,168	177	258,119	118.13	179,128	149.8	144.1
70–74	12,328	15,961,073	381	592,488	369.53	478,197	103.0	123.9
75–79	27,809	31,817,163	1,382	1,338,360	1,314.49	1,501,210	105.1	89.2
80–84	19,028	20,911,866	1,523	1,643,923	1,424.64	1,560,728	106.9	105.3
85–89	6,349	5,776,982	810	733,468	739.33	668,278	109.6	109.8
90 and over	2,975	2,355,997	537	464,555	571.51	452,143	93.9	102.7
Total Ultimate	77,505	92,422,247	4,808	5,030,912	4,537.63	4,839,685	106.0	104.0
Grand Total	365,820	938,834,839	12,026	22,427,971	11,614.65	23,523,075	103.5	95.3

TABLE 3

CANADIAN INDIVIDUAL ANNUITANT EXPERIENCE BETWEEN POLICY ANNIVERSARIES IN 1980 AND 1988
ALL COMPANIES TO DATE
FEMALE LIVES ONLY; EXPECTED: 1983 BASIC FEMALE (*TSA* XXXIII, 695);
SINGLE LIFE POLICIES ONLY; ALL TAX TYPES COMBINED, BOTH REFUND AND NONREFUND

	Exposures		Actual Deaths		Expected Deaths		Ratio A/E	
	Number	Income	Number	Income	Number	Income	Number	Income
Select Experience — Policy Years 1 to 10								
By Policy Year								
1	35,374	98,131,047	296	795,820	357.26	1,002,803	82.9	79.4
2	32,709	86,762,591	342	938,127	367.95	978,224	92.9	95.9
3	29,607	74,990,362	337	942,433	367.57	932,674	91.7	101.0
4	26,716	65,459,305	372	943,665	362.03	869,231	102.8	108.6
5	23,040	52,505,079	368	885,137	339.91	759,380	108.3	116.6
6–10	69,030	112,401,401	1,315	2,106,009	1,265.12	2,035,646	103.9	103.5
By Issue Age								
0–59	26,882	90,934,316	197	497,645	131.83	333,684	149.1	149.1
60–64	55,994	119,150,602	566	1,160,851	498.05	984,255	113.5	117.9
65–69	83,362	154,202,554	1,006	1,795,189	1,110.31	1,955,361	90.6	91.8
70 and over	50,239	125,962,314	1,262	3,157,507	1,319.67	3,304,659	95.6	95.5
Total Select	216,476	490,249,785	3,030	6,611,191	3,059.85	6,577,959	99.0	100.5
Ultimate Experience — Policy Years 11 and Over								
By Attained Age								
0–69	10,464	11,104,006	113	82,524	80.53	78,609	140.3	105.0
70–74	13,812	11,398,934	282	289,386	227.89	186,800	123.5	154.9
75–79	21,994	16,137,105	641	539,176	631.44	461,003	101.5	117.0
80–84	16,551	11,699,543	901	659,791	838.37	592,839	107.5	111.3
85–89	10,032	6,972,877	966	770,784	901.95	627,648	107.1	122.8
90 and over	6,512	4,225,210	1,126	703,538	1,077.60	684,295	104.4	102.8
Total Ultimate	79,363	61,537,673	4,028	3,045,198	3,757.79	2,631,194	107.2	115.7
Grand Total	295,839	551,787,458	7,058	9,656,389	6,817.64	9,209,153	103.5	104.9

TABLE 4

CANADIAN INDIVIDUAL ANNUITANT EXPERIENCE BETWEEN POLICY ANNIVERSARIES IN 1980 AND 1988
ALL COMPANIES TO DATE
MALE LIVES ONLY; EXPECTED: 1983 BASIC MALE (*TSA* XXXIII, 695)
SINGLE LIFE POLICIES ONLY; RRSP ONLY, BOTH REFUND AND NONREFUND

	Exposures		Actual Deaths		Expected Deaths		Ratio A/E	
	Number	Income	Number	Income	Number	Income	Number	Income
Select Experience — Policy Years 1 to 10								
By Policy Year								
1	27,966	93,347,950	431	1,348,598	495.92	1,664,245	86.9	81.0
2	28,065	92,635,210	530	1,712,845	550.17	1,799,410	96.3	95.2
3	26,334	85,353,234	571	1,789,816	564.08	1,789,835	101.2	100.0
4	24,180	73,999,401	548	1,512,125	566.86	1,691,226	96.7	89.4
5	21,819	62,551,129	563	1,447,313	557.61	1,555,705	101.0	93.0
6–10	71,285	158,676,616	2,318	4,226,428	2,272.60	4,717,187	102.0	89.6
By Issue Age								
0–59	13,068	59,337,044	124	282,222	122.69	461,252	100.7	61.2
60–64	43,555	131,050,768	779	1,918,183	703.02	1,967,954	110.7	97.5
65–69	89,433	216,616,771	2,209	4,865,687	2,189.61	5,073,416	100.9	95.9
70 and over	53,594	159,558,958	1,850	4,971,034	1,991.91	5,714,986	92.9	87.0
Total Select	199,649	566,563,540	4,961	12,037,125	5,007.23	13,217,608	99.1	91.1
Ultimate Experience — Policy Years 11 and Over								
By Attained Age								
0–69	3,477	7,530,643	67	136,581	45.24	83,801	148.1	163.0
70–74	5,324	8,463,113	152	321,810	160.57	255,458	94.7	126.0
75–79	12,509	16,572,545	594	652,877	588.53	779,452	100.8	83.8
80–84	8,896	11,290,253	660	877,225	661.34	837,278	99.7	104.8
85–89	1,541	1,771,539	197	208,955	173.95	198,074	113.0	105.5
90 and over	198	140,091	32	19,440	34.28	23,769	91.9	81.8
Total Ultimate	31,944	45,768,183	1,700	2,216,886	1,663.91	2,177,832	102.2	101.8
Grand Total	231,593	612,331,723	6,661	14,254,011	6,671.13	15,395,440	99.8	92.6

TABLE 5

CANADIAN INDIVIDUAL ANNUITANT EXPERIENCE BETWEEN POLICY ANNIVERSARIES IN 1980 AND 1988
ALL COMPANIES TO DATE
MALE LIVES ONLY; EXPECTED: 1983 BASIC MALE (*TSA* XXXIII, 695)
SINGLE LIFE POLICIES ONLY; RPP ONLY, BOTH REFUND AND NONREFUND

	Exposures		Actual Deaths		Expected Deaths		Ratio A/E	
	Number	Income	Number	Income	Number	Income	Number	Income
Select Experience — Policy Years 1 to 10								
By Policy Year								
1	1,546	7,073,869	25	60,890	21.73	91,018	115.0	66.9
2	1,473	6,425,508	25	44,237	22.46	91,590	111.3	48.3
3	1,415	5,995,311	28	71,137	24.21	95,306	115.7	74.6
4	1,344	5,390,812	43	74,734	25.01	94,391	171.9	79.2
5	1,242	4,596,486	31	75,818	25.06	90,064	123.7	84.2
6–10	5,660	13,606,524	190	522,973	145.05	348,650	131.0	150.0
By Issue Age								
0–59	2,350	9,346,782	29	106,130	21.56	79,725	134.5	133.1
60–64	3,178	12,636,959	70	255,285	53.72	195,720	130.3	115.1
65–69	6,241	17,238,827	204	462,302	149.03	380,305	136.6	121.6
70 and over	912	3,865,943	40	56,073	39.21	155,269	100.7	36.1
Total Select	12,680	43,088,510	342	849,789	263.51	811,019	129.8	104.8
Ultimate Experience — Policy Years 11 and Over								
By Attained Age								
0–69	1,814	1,939,818	35	25,731	24.25	26,947	144.3	95.5
70–74	1,276	1,522,518	45	96,235	37.81	45,022	119.0	213.7
75–79	3,317	4,045,886	191	203,979	157.76	190,399	121.1	107.1
80–84	2,332	2,346,158	198	191,761	174.92	175,553	113.2	109.2
85–89	880	761,169	119	110,405	103.06	88,804	115.5	124.3
90 and over	449	325,281	95	83,580	80.54	55,722	118.0	149.9
Total Ultimate	10,065	10,940,829	683	711,690	578.33	582,498	118.1	122.2
Grand Total	22,745	54,029,339	1,025	1,561,479	841.85	1,393,517	121.8	112.1

TABLE 6

CANADIAN INDIVIDUAL ANNUITANT EXPERIENCE BETWEEN POLICY ANNIVERSARIES IN 1980 AND 1988
ALL COMPANIES TO DATE
MALE LIVES ONLY; EXPECTED: 1983 BASIC MALE (*TSA* XXXIII, 695)
SINGLE LIFE POLICIES ONLY; NONREGISTERED ONLY, BOTH REFUND AND NONREFUND

	Exposures		Actual Deaths		Expected Deaths		Ratio A/E	
	Number	Income	Number	Income	Number	Income	Number	Income
Select Experience — Policy Years 1 to 10								
By Policy Year								
1	10,902	40,566,819	167	460,341	186.83	652,033	89.4	70.6
2	9,109	32,019,619	208	617,685	170.03	525,352	122.3	117.6
3	8,482	29,116,709	199	662,162	169.12	499,559	117.7	132.5
4	8,303	29,465,895	167	345,341	176.14	511,179	94.8	67.6
5	7,993	27,293,882	224	564,263	184.96	518,192	121.1	108.9
6–10	31,197	78,297,618	950	1,860,353	919.20	1,948,449	103.4	95.5
By Issue Age								
0–59	16,681	94,565,192	165	726,145	129.99	601,922	126.9	120.6
60–64	18,685	49,087,726	337	656,964	311.14	761,978	108.2	86.2
65–69	28,577	57,350,365	690	1,139,920	690.15	1,378,958	100.0	82.7
70 and over	12,043	35,757,260	724	1,987,117	675.00	1,911,904	107.2	103.9
Total Select	75,986	236,760,542	1,915	4,510,145	1,806.28	4,654,763	106.0	96.9
Ultimate Experience — Policy Years 11 and Over								
By Attained Age								
0–69	3,728	6,128,707	75	95,807	48.64	68,380	154.2	140.1
70–74	5,729	5,975,443	184	174,444	171.15	177,716	107.2	98.2
75–79	11,983	11,198,732	597	481,505	568.20	531,359	105.1	90.6
80–84	7,801	7,275,455	665	574,938	588.38	547,896	113.0	104.9
85–89	3,928	3,244,274	495	414,109	462.32	381,400	107.0	108.6
90 and over	2,329	1,890,625	410	361,535	456.69	372,602	89.8	97.0
Total Ultimate	35,496	35,713,235	2,425	2,102,336	2,295.39	2,079,354	105.6	101.1
Grand Total	111,482	272,473,777	4,340	6,612,481	4,101.67	6,734,118	105.8	98.2

TABLE 7

CANADIAN INDIVIDUAL ANNUITANT EXPERIENCE BETWEEN POLICY ANNIVERSARIES IN 1980 AND 1988
ALL COMPANIES TO DATE
FEMALE LIVES ONLY; EXPECTED: 1983 BASIC FEMALE (*TSA* XXXIII, 695)
SINGLE LIFE POLICIES ONLY; RRSP ONLY, BOTH REFUND AND NONREFUND

	Exposures		Actual Deaths		Expected Deaths		Ratio A/E	
	Number	Income	Number	Income	Number	Income	Number	Income
Select Experience — Policy Years 1 to 10								
By Policy Year								
1	25,817	63,271,476	200	503,161	250.44	617,413	79.9	81.5
2	24,651	59,268,514	231	561,808	263.82	631,242	87.6	89.0
3	22,083	51,538,547	222	534,112	259.51	603,362	85.5	88.5
4	19,413	42,946,454	240	521,180	250.29	551,817	95.9	94.4
5	16,168	33,028,918	213	454,053	226.69	463,438	94.0	98.0
6–10	40,610	59,035,235	649	954,819	679.20	962,985	95.6	99.2
By Issue Age								
0–59	10,694	27,963,644	103	230,651	58.62	128,252	175.7	179.8
60–64	38,907	80,520,465	356	746,369	340.38	656,917	104.6	113.6
65–69	63,510	115,301,109	706	1,246,961	831.32	1,438,359	84.9	86.7
70 and over	35,633	85,303,927	590	1,305,153	699.62	1,606,727	84.3	81.2
Total Select	148,742	309,089,144	1,755	3,529,133	1,929.94	3,830,256	90.9	92.1
Ultimate Experience — Policy Years 11 and Over								
By Attained Age								
0–69	2,102	2,256,529	33	22,859	17.70	18,806	183.6	121.5
70–74	3,414	2,967,456	74	86,467	56.30	48,423	131.4	178.6
75–79	5,475	4,032,885	165	124,371	154.28	112,544	106.9	110.5
80–84	2,624	2,003,203	129	102,321	127.61	98,250	100.7	104.1
85–89	441	361,542	39	36,103	37.15	29,728	103.6	121.4
90 and over	38	19,014	9	5,862	5.43	2,622	156.5	223.5
Total Ultimate	14,092	11,640,627	447	377,982	398.48	310,374	112.2	121.8
Grand Total	162,834	320,729,771	2,202	3,907,115	2,328.42	4,140,629	94.6	94.4

TABLE 8

CANADIAN INDIVIDUAL ANNUITANT EXPERIENCE BETWEEN POLICY ANNIVERSARIES IN 1980 AND 1988
ALL COMPANIES TO DATE
FEMALE LIVES ONLY; EXPECTED: 1983 BASIC FEMALE (*TSA* XXXIII, 695)
SINGLE LIFE POLICIES ONLY; RPP ONLY, BOTH REFUND AND NONREFUND

	Exposures		Actual Deaths		Expected Deaths		Ratio A/E	
	Number	Income	Number	Income	Number	Income	Number	Income
Select Experience — Policy Years 1 to 10								
By Policy Year								
1	783	2,433,900	10	25,035	5.74	17,191	174.1	145.6
2	758	2,213,764	9	24,262	6.24	17,678	144.3	137.2
3	670	1,922,092	7	17,160	6.16	17,138	113.7	100.1
4	591	1,620,738	9	15,188	6.18	16,231	145.5	93.6
5	528	1,262,958	8	30,411	5.77	13,622	138.7	223.2
6–10	1,721	2,704,975	34	56,547	21.39	31,921	158.9	177.1
By Issue Age								
0–59	1,306	3,140,949	13	34,304	5.97	13,384	217.6	256.3
60–64	1,503	4,023,634	24	66,633	13.18	32,743	178.3	203.5
65–69	1,883	4,088,422	28	53,552	23.75	48,267	117.9	110.9
70 and over	360	905,422	13	14,115	8.57	19,387	145.8	72.8
Total Select	5,051	12,158,427	77	168,603	51.48	113,781	149.6	148.2
Ultimate Experience — Policy Years 11 and Over								
By Attained Age								
0–69	683	543,329	11	7,031	5.04	4,473	208.3	157.2
70–74	533	443,487	10	7,009	8.77	7,298	114.0	96.0
75–79	1,109	859,671	23	18,312	31.97	24,741	71.9	74.0
80–84	768	449,662	52	26,227	38.85	22,734	133.9	115.4
85–89	354	264,162	32	19,362	30.86	23,340	103.7	83.0
90 and over	95	55,910	25	11,108	14.45	8,737	169.6	127.1
Total Ultimate	3,541	2,616,220	152	89,047	129.93	91,323	117.0	97.5
Grand Total	8,592	14,774,647	229	257,650	181.41	205,104	126.2	125.6

TABLE 9

Canadian Individual Annuitant Experience between Policy Anniversaries in 1980 and 1988
All Companies To Date
Female Lives Only; Expected: 1983 Basic Female (*TSA* XXXIII, 695)
Single Life Policies Only; Nonregistered Only, Both Refund and Nonrefund

	Exposures		Actual Deaths		Expected Deaths		Ratio A/E	
	Number	Income	Number	Income	Number	Income	Number	Income
Select Experience — Policy Years 1 to 10								
By Policy Year								
1	8,774	32,425,671	86	267,624	101.08	368,199	85.1	72.7
2	7,300	25,280,313	102	352,057	97.90	329,304	104.2	106.9
3	6,854	21,529,723	108	391,161	101.90	312,174	106.0	125.3
4	6,712	20,892,113	123	407,297	105.56	301,183	116.5	135.2
5	6,344	18,213,203	147	400,673	107.46	282,320	136.8	141.9
6–10	26,699	50,661,191	632	1,094,643	564.53	1,040,741	112.0	105.2
By Issue Age								
0–59	14,883	59,829,723	81	232,690	67.23	192,047	119.7	121.2
60–64	15,584	34,606,503	186	347,849	144.48	294,596	128.7	118.1
65–69	17,970	34,813,023	272	494,677	255.24	468,735	106.6	105.5
70 and over	14,247	39,752,965	660	1,838,240	611.48	1,678,545	107.9	109.5
Total Select	62,683	169,002,214	1,198	2,913,455	1,078.43	2,633,922	111.1	110.6
Ultimate Experience — Policy Years 11 and Over								
By Attained Age								
0–69	7,679	8,304,149	70	52,635	57.78	55,329	121.1	95.1
70–74	9,866	7,987,991	198	195,910	162.83	131,079	121.3	149.5
75–79	15,410	11,244,550	453	396,494	445.19	323,718	101.8	122.5
80–84	13,159	9,246,678	721	531,243	671.91	471,855	107.2	112.6
85–89	9,237	6,347,174	896	715,320	833.95	574,579	107.4	124.5
90 and over	6,380	4,150,286	1,093	686,568	1,057.72	672,936	103.3	102.0
Total Ultimate	61,730	47,280,826	3,429	2,578,169	3,229.38	2,229,498	106.2	115.6
Grand Total	124,413	216,283,040	4,627	5,491,624	4,307.81	4,863,419	107.4	112.9

TABLE 10

CANADIAN INDIVIDUAL ANNUITANT EXPERIENCE BETWEEN POLICY ANNIVERSARIES IN 1980 AND 1981
ALL COMPANIES TO DATE
MALE LIVES ONLY; EXPECTED: 1983 BASIC MALE (*TSA* XXXIII, 695)
SINGLE LIFE POLICIES ONLY; ALL TAX TYPES COMBINED, BOTH REFUND AND NONREFUND

	Exposures		Actual Deaths		Expected Deaths		Ratio A/E	
	Number	Income	Number	Income	Number	Income	Number	Income
Select Experience — Policy Years 1 to 10								
By Policy Year								
1	3,579	10,574,511	53	139,194	59.13	161,674	89.6	86.1
2	2,461	5,253,622	41	120,282	45.72	94,973	89.7	126.6
3	1,878	3,271,151	31	54,502	38.22	64,834	81.1	84.1
4	1,614	2,247,245	34	42,038	36.24	49,513	93.8	84.9
5	1,828	2,946,780	51	62,279	44.45	70,433	114.7	88.4
6–10	5,059	5,658,168	149	129,550	155.07	179,575	96.1	72.1
By Issue Age								
0–59	2,204	6,475,123	21	21,121	18.25	43,749	112.3	48.3
60–64	3,458	5,868,293	62	66,330	54.01	83,464	113.9	79.5
65–69	7,376	11,099,096	161	212,076	166.58	236,000	96.4	89.9
70 and over	3,382	6,508,966	117	248,319	140.00	257,789	83.2	96.3
Total Select	16,419	29,951,477	359	547,845	378.84	621,002	94.8	88.2
Ultimate Experience — Policy Years 11 and Over								
By Attained Age								
0–69	448	562,059	10	20,274	6.62	8,612	151.1	235.4
70–74	573	692,289	24	34,530	17.11	20,427	140.3	169.0
75–79	1,317	1,186,039	59	52,475	62.76	55,805	93.2	94.0
80–84	915	797,219	53	50,670	69.63	60,190	75.4	84.2
85–89	427	318,100	42	25,948	50.22	38,019	82.6	68.2
90 and over	231	173,562	26	18,121	41.35	32,647	61.7	55.5
Total Ultimate	3,908	3,729,267	212	202,016	247.68	215,701	85.6	93.7
Grand Total	20,327	33,680,744	571	749,861	626.52	836,703	91.1	89.6

TABLE 11

CANADIAN INDIVIDUAL ANNUITANT EXPERIENCE BETWEEN POLICY ANNIVERSARIES IN 1980 AND 1981
ALL COMPANIES TO DATE
FEMALE LIVES ONLY; EXPECTED: 1983 BASIC FEMALE (*TSA* XXXIII, 695)
SINGLE LIFE POLICIES ONLY; ALL TAX TYPES COMBINED, BOTH REFUND AND NONREFUND

	Exposures		Actual Deaths		Expected Deaths		Ratio A/E	
	Number	Income	Number	Income	Number	Income	Number	Income
Select Experience — Policy Years 1 to 10								
By Policy Year								
1	2,520	4,801,318	18	29,617	24.36	46,666	73.9	63.5
2	1,576	2,548,387	12	17,751	16.42	25,369	73.1	70.0
3	1,182	1,474,401	10	18,008	14.38	18,676	69.5	96.4
4	1,051	1,174,357	6	7,303	13.26	14,903	45.3	49.0
5	1,112	1,285,099	13	24,899	16.73	22,626	77.7	110.0
6–10	3,394	3,011,525	52	52,936	65.86	68,764	79.0	77.0
By Issue Age								
0–59	2,139	3,725,105	5	4,668	9.99	13,731	50.0	34.0
60–64	2,938	3,356,215	14	10,665	25.31	26,715	53.3	39.9
65–69	3,893	4,238,002	39	49,691	49.15	50,841	78.3	97.7
70 and over	1,866	2,975,767	54	85,491	66.56	105,717	81.1	80.9
Total Select	10,835	14,295,087	111	150,514	151.01	197,003	73.5	76.4
Ultimate Experience — Policy Years 11 and Over								
By Attained Age								
0–69	799	593,461	11	7,343	6.11	4,461	171.7	164.6
70–74	990	645,994	10	12,043	16.38	10,754	58.0	112.0
75–79	1,333	741,293	29	26,183	38.19	21,359	75.9	122.6
80–84	1,126	627,113	47	25,698	57.95	32,415	80.2	79.3
85–89	842	456,679	59	26,906	76.07	41,027	77.6	65.6
90 and over	493	239,077	76	36,712	81.92	39,558	92.2	92.8
Total Ultimate	5,582	3,303,616	230	134,883	276.63	149,573	83.1	90.2
Grand Total	16,417	17,598,703	341	285,397	427.64	346,576	79.7	82.3

TABLE 12

CANADIAN INDIVIDUAL ANNUITANT EXPERIENCE BETWEEN POLICY ANNIVERSARIES IN 1981 AND 1982
ALL COMPANIES TO DATE
MALE LIVES ONLY; EXPECTED: 1983 BASIC MALE (*TSA* XXXIII, 695)
SINGLE LIFE POLICIES ONLY; ALL TAX TYPES COMBINED, BOTH REFUND AND NONREFUND

	Exposures		Actual Deaths		Expected Deaths		Ratio A/E	
	Number	Income	Number	Income	Number	Income	Number	Income
Select Experience — Policy Years 1 to 10								
By Policy Year								
1	4,150	17,510,091	57	128,335	70.49	264,845	80.9	48.5
2	3,535	10,435,092	53	136,745	64.41	175,125	82.3	78.1
3	2,419	5,112,124	57	124,122	49.07	99,048	116.2	125.3
4	1,848	3,215,533	43	43,367	41.38	69,869	103.9	62.1
5	1,579	2,204,137	40	56,738	38.88	52,598	102.9	107.9
6–10	6,029	7,811,261	213	279,965	185.92	242,655	114.6	115.4
By Issue Age								
0–59	2,564	10,838,278	25	63,992	20.81	69,651	120.1	91.9
60–64	4,165	9,696,485	66	87,644	64.19	130,556	102.8	67.1
65–69	8,658	16,012,101	198	287,519	196.25	335,872	100.9	85.6
70 and over	4,175	9,741,375	174	330,118	168.89	368,062	103.0	89.7
Total Select	19,560	46,288,238	463	769,272	450.14	904,141	102.9	85.1
Ultimate Experience — Policy Years 11 and Over								
By Attained Age								
0–69	498	569,005	13	5,366	6.94	8,109	187.3	66.2
70–74	655	770,087	19	13,354	19.37	22,684	95.5	58.9
75–79	1,435	1,312,049	73	66,198	68.36	61,931	106.0	106.9
80–84	1,029	928,288	93	73,222	77.11	69,620	120.6	105.2
85–89	502	347,165	68	33,099	58.86	40,300	115.5	82.1
90 and over	252	225,765	51	84,390	46.15	42,123	110.5	200.3
Total Ultimate	4,369	4,152,358	316	275,628	276.79	244,767	114.2	112.6
Grand Total	23,929	50,440,596	779	1,044,900	726.93	1,148,908	107.2	90.9

TABLE 13

CANADIAN INDIVIDUAL ANNUITANT EXPERIENCE BETWEEN POLICY ANNIVERSARIES IN 1981 AND 1982
ALL COMPANIES TO DATE
FEMALE LIVES ONLY; EXPECTED: 1983 BASIC FEMALE (*TSA* XXXIII, 695)
SINGLE LIFE POLICIES ONLY; ALL TAX TYPES COMBINED, BOTH REFUND AND NONREFUND

	Exposures		Actual Deaths		Expected Deaths		Ratio A/E	
	Number	Income	Number	Income	Number	Income	Number	Income
Select Experience — Policy Years 1 to 10								
By Policy Year								
1	3,140	8,434,126	28	52,422	29.90	79,408	93.7	66.0
2	2,506	4,766,850	31	37,740	26.75	51,290	115.9	73.6
3	1,566	2,528,358	21	46,623	17.98	27,768	116.8	167.9
4	1,172	1,455,791	14	14,147	15.40	19,681	90.9	71.9
5	1,045	1,167,078	17	17,772	14.57	16,370	116.7	108.6
6–10	3,887	3,806,310	61	64,495	73.48	84,930	83.0	75.9
By Issue Age								
0–59	2,322	5,419,961	12	10,730	10.87	19,326	110.4	55.5
60–64	3,562	5,031,266	34	42,421	30.20	38,643	110.9	109.8
64–69	4,994	6,774,988	55	68,082	62.38	78,646	87.4	86.6
70 and over	2,439	4,932,299	72	111,968	74.62	142,832	96.5	78.4
Total Select	13,316	22,158,513	172	233,199	178.07	279,447	96.6	83.5
Ultimate Experience — Policy Years 11 and Over								
By Attained Age								
0–69	852	687,322	11	5,779	6.20	4,818	169.4	119.9
70–74	1,023	654,135	23	12,649	16.89	10,810	133.2	117.0
75–79	1,454	846,309	54	30,250	41.62	23,987	128.5	126.1
80–84	1,165	663,497	48	20,460	59.60	33,920	80.5	60.3
85–89	884	501,471	90	47,376	79.98	44,959	112.5	105.4
90 and over	551	279,199	119	55,858	91.31	45,921	129.8	121.6
Total Ultimate	5,928	3,631,932	343	172,372	295.61	164,415	116.0	104.8
Grand Total	19,244	25,790,445	515	405,571	473.69	443,862	108.7	91.4

TABLE 14

CANADIAN INDIVIDUAL ANNUITANT EXPERIENCE BETWEEN POLICY ANNIVERSARIES IN 1982 AND 1983
ALL COMPANIES TO DATE
MALE LIVES ONLY; EXPECTED: 1983 BASIC MALE (*TSA* XXXIII, 695)
SINGLE LIFE POLICIES ONLY; ALL TAX TYPES COMBINED, BOTH REFUND AND NONREFUND

	Exposures		Actual Deaths		Expected Deaths		Ratio A/E	
	Number	Income	Number	Income	Number	Income	Number	Income
Select Experience — Policy Years 1 to 10								
By Policy Year								
1	5,124	18,969,309	79	257,302	90.34	325,813	87.4	79.0
2	5,397	24,981,600	77	266,676	98.37	398,564	78.3	66.9
3	4,458	14,680,652	76	190,676	86.66	256,597	87.7	74.3
4	3,144	7,119,302	56	81,747	67.63	146,966	82.8	55.6
5	2,623	5,281,896	74	106,465	62.79	121,192	117.9	87.8
6–10	9,299	17,558,704	294	479,502	279.20	483,405	105.3	99.2
By Issue Age								
0–59	4,121	21,359,036	19	50,726	32.40	136,931	57.1	37.0
60–64	6,782	19,386,744	85	159,976	105.27	273,245	80.3	58.5
65–69	12,645	28,994,314	299	553,233	292.31	628,872	102.1	88.0
70 and over	6,499	18,851,370	255	618,435	255.03	693,488	99.8	89.2
Total Select	30,045	88,591,463	656	1,382,368	685.00	1,732,536	95.8	79.8
Ultimate Experience — Policy Years 11 and Over								
By Attained Age								
0–69	747	842,701	10	9,715	9.94	11,076	100.6	87.7
70–74	1,059	1,249,782	39	39,067	31.60	37,376	123.4	104.5
75–79	2,135	2,019,303	118	96,569	101.82	95,192	115.9	101.4
80–84	1,546	1,436,045	95	98,807	115.27	108,099	82.0	91.4
85–89	662	493,984	93	92,736	76.97	57,072	120.8	162.5
90 and over	326	221,047	30	20,341	59.78	41,632	49.3	48.9
Total Ultimate	6,473	6,262,861	384	357,233	395.38	350,447	97.1	101.9
Grand Total	36,518	94,854,324	1,040	1,739,601	1,080.38	2,082,983	96.3	83.5

TABLE 15

CANADIAN INDIVIDUAL ANNUITANT EXPERIENCE BETWEEN POLICY ANNIVERSARIES IN 1982 AND 1983
ALL COMPANIES TO DATE
FEMALE LIVES ONLY; EXPECTED: 1983 BASIC FEMALE (*TSA* XXXIII, 695)
SINGLE LIFE POLICIES ONLY; ALL TAX TYPES COMBINED, BOTH REFUND AND NONREFUND

	Exposures		Actual Deaths		Expected Deaths		Ratio A/E	
	Number	Income	Number	Income	Number	Income	Number	Income
Select Experience — Policy Years 1 to 10								
By Policy Year								
1	4,290	12,032,953	31	54,297	42.82	119,402	72.4	45.5
2	3,786	11,781,793	39	133,415	39.95	116,898	97.6	114.1
3	2,886	5,787,865	33	75,758	33.30	66,934	99.1	113.2
4	1,863	3,059,851	30	40,263	22.74	35,622	131.9	113.0
5	1,379	1,872,372	22	27,167	19.36	28,319	113.6	95.9
6–10	5,361	6,417,581	105	122,188	94.65	122,201	110.9	100.0
By Issue Age								
0–59	3,082	9,140,286	20	34,073	14.68	32,912	132.8	103.5
60–64	5,318	9,993,854	55	81,761	45.27	77,350	120.4	105.7
65–69	7,232	12,291,978	94	157,668	90.70	143,548	103.6	109.8
70 and over	3,934	9,526,298	92	179,586	102.17	235,565	90.0	76.2
Total Select	19,565	40,952,415	260	453,088	252.82	489,375	102.8	92.6
Ultimate Experience — Policy Years 11 and Over								
By Attained Age								
0–69	1,108	1,055,236	9	15,304	8.02	6,904	112.2	221.7
70–74	1,365	883,288	11	9,429	22.35	14,493	49.2	65.1
75–79	2,053	1,241,078	47	54,085	58.62	35,039	80.2	154.4
80–84	1,647	1,004,380	90	66,465	84.14	51,059	106.4	130.2
85–89	1,094	620,701	84	52,132	97.40	55,035	86.2	94.7
90 and over	736	381,136	96	58,899	121.09	62,358	78.9	94.5
Total Ultimate	8,002	5,185,818	336	256,312	391.62	224,887	85.8	114.0
Grand Total	27,567	46,138,233	596	709,400	644.44	714,262	92.5	99.3

TABLE 16

CANADIAN INDIVIDUAL ANNUITANT EXPERIENCE BETWEEN POLICY ANNIVERSARIES IN 1983 AND 1984
ALL COMPANIES TO DATE
MALE LIVES ONLY; EXPECTED: 1983 BASIC MALE (*TSA* XXXIII, 695)
SINGLE LIFE POLICIES ONLY; ALL TAX TYPES COMBINED, BOTH REFUND AND NONREFUND

	Exposures		Actual Deaths		Expected Deaths		Ratio A/E	
	Number	Income	Number	Income	Number	Income	Number	Income
Select Experience — Policy Years 1 to 10								
By Policy Year								
1	4,234	12,149,589	73	193,395	73.88	222,120	98.8	87.1
2	5,162	18,870,821	115	397,069	99.51	355,069	115.6	111.8
3	5,339	24,749,108	118	462,530	106.86	431,363	110.4	107.2
4	4,400	14,484,881	82	217,427	94.30	279,665	87.0	77.7
5	3,117	7,141,428	71	131,719	73.82	163,289	96.2	80.7
6–10	10,670	21,061,258	321	592,582	320.45	586,848	100.2	101.0
By Issue Age								
0–59	4,215	21,524,669	46	193,226	34.89	147,524	130.4	131.0
60–64	7,582	22,078,417	135	362,076	120.06	325,066	112.0	111.4
65–69	13,865	32,780,478	339	733,042	327.77	737,216	103.4	99.4
70 and over	7,261	22,073,522	261	706,379	286.09	828,548	91.2	85.3
Total Select	32,922	98,457,085	780	1,994,722	768.81	2,038,354	101.5	97.9
Ultimate Experience — Policy Years 11 and Over								
By Attained Age								
0–69	808	1,039,117	23	18,283	10.57	12,538	212.8	145.8
70–74	1,204	1,365,686	38	26,923	35.63	40,333	106.6	66.8
75–79	2,546	2,753,159	97	104,846	120.73	129,583	80.3	80.9
80–84	1,905	1,764,986	193	175,040	142.62	133,328	135.3	131.3
85–89	729	594,822	83	53,076	84.44	68,846	98.3	77.1
90 and over	398	278,894	116	68,661	74.06	53,178	156.0	129.1
Total Ultimate	7,589	7,796,663	549	446,828	468.06	437,806	117.3	102.1
Grand Total	40,511	106,253,748	1,329	2,441,550	1,236.87	2,476,160	107.4	98.6

TABLE 17

CANADIAN INDIVIDUAL ANNUITANT EXPERIENCE BETWEEN POLICY ANNIVERSARIES IN 1983 AND 1984
ALL COMPANIES TO DATE
FEMALE LIVES ONLY; EXPECTED: 1983 BASIC FEMALE (*TSA* XXXIII, 695)
SINGLE LIFE POLICIES ONLY; ALL TAX TYPES COMBINED, BOTH REFUND AND NONREFUND

	Exposures		Actual Deaths		Expected Deaths		Ratio A/E	
	Number	Income	Number	Income	Number	Income	Number	Income
Select Experience — Policy Years 1 to 10								
By Policy Year								
1	3,759	9,219,448	23	42,125	38.58	95,808	59.6	44.0
2	4,331	12,117,874	30	94,559	47.43	132,125	63.2	71.6
3	3,771	11,685,141	32	84,712	43.86	127,039	73.0	66.7
4	2,863	5,721,885	29	35,273	36.43	73,094	79.6	48.3
5	1,862	3,044,821	27	53,960	25.21	39,300	107.1	137.3
6–10	5,897	7,387,933	98	106,475	103.92	144,459	94.3	73.7
By Issue Age								
0–59	3,152	9,906,841	19	49,203	15.46	37,229	122.9	132.2
60–64	6,037	12,029,454	50	83,830	52.20	95,665	95.8	87.6
65–69	8,471	15,012,104	76	91,515	107.87	179,722	70.0	50.9
70 and over	4,824	12,228,704	95	192,558	119.89	299,209	78.8	64.4
Total Select	22,483	49,177,102	239	417,104	295.42	611,825	80.9	68.2
Ultimate Experience — Policy Years 11 and Over								
By Attained Age								
0–69	1,180	1,217,310	14	5,099	8.71	7,948	160.7	64.2
70–74	1,452	1,061,460	23	14,864	23.80	17,284	96.7	86.0
75–79	2,321	1,521,230	52	36,702	66.80	43,248	77.1	84.9
80–84	1,762	1,057,492	122	80,641	89.92	53,732	135.1	150.1
85–89	1,196	714,471	110	69,520	106.76	63,852	102.6	108.9
90 and over	822	432,602	146	89,564	137.43	72,593	105.9	123.4
Total Ultimate	8,732	6,004,564	465	296,389	433.41	258,657	107.3	114.6
Grand Total	31,215	55,181,666	704	713,493	728.84	870,482	96.6	82.0

TABLE 18

CANADIAN INDIVIDUAL ANNUITANT EXPERIENCE BETWEEN POLICY ANNIVERSARIES IN 1984 AND 1985
ALL COMPANIES TO DATE
MALE LIVES ONLY; EXPECTED: 1983 BASIC MALE (*TSA* XXXIII, 695)
SINGLE LIFE POLICIES ONLY; ALL TAX TYPES COMBINED, BOTH REFUND AND NONREFUND

	Exposures		Actual Deaths		Expected Deaths		Ratio A/E	
	Number	Income	Number	Income	Number	Income	Number	Income
Select Experience — Policy Years 1 to 10								
By Policy Year								
1	6,754	24,510,789	121	393,607	117.80	423,318	102.7	93.0
2	5,947	16,320,745	133	354,208	117.69	332,198	113.0	106.6
3	6,549	23,380,082	148	477,964	139.73	481,542	105.9	99.3
4	6,671	29,833,008	158	428,569	146.72	557,473	107.7	76.9
5	5,371	16,426,922	127	374,209	129.16	357,205	98.3	104.8
6–10	17,759	34,181,228	547	862,732	561.10	1,014,557	97.5	85.0
By Issue Age								
0–59	5,152	27,241,229	51	162,355	43.87	183,830	115.1	88.3
60–64	10,913	32,293,873	197	453,014	175.98	478,747	111.7	94.6
65–69	21,440	50,402,820	548	1,074,779	526.82	1,174,625	103.9	91.5
70 and over	11,547	34,714,853	440	1,201,142	465.54	1,329,092	94.4	90.4
Total Select	49,051	144,652,774	1,234	2,891,289	1,212.20	3,166,293	101.8	91.3
Ultimate Experience — Policy Years 11 and Over								
By Attained Age								
0–69	1,356	2,087,051	29	37,339	16.66	24,704	171.0	151.1
70–74	1,862	2,513,420	59	197,311	55.47	74,962	105.5	263.2
75–79	4,210	4,892,728	203	196,642	198.36	229,628	102.3	85.6
80–84	2,972	3,153,263	236	263,604	222.09	234,409	106.0	112.5
85–89	1,013	916,171	126	110,874	118.30	105,741	106.1	104.9
90 and over	468	375,966	80	57,772	92.42	73,244	86.6	78.9
Total Ultimate	11,880	13,938,598	731	863,540	703.30	742,690	103.9	116.3
Grand Total	60,931	158,591,372	1,965	3,754,829	1,915.51	3,908,983	102.6	96.1

TABLE 19

CANADIAN INDIVIDUAL ANNUITANT EXPERIENCE BETWEEN POLICY ANNIVERSARIES IN 1984 AND 1985
ALL COMPANIES TO DATE
FEMALE LIVES ONLY; EXPECTED: 1983 BASIC FEMALE (*TSA* XXXIII, 695)
SINGLE LIFE POLICIES ONLY; ALL TAX TYPES COMBINED, BOTH REFUND AND NONREFUND

	Exposures		Actual Deaths		Expected Deaths		Ratio A/E	
	Number	Income	Number	Income	Number	Income	Number	Income
Select Experience — Policy Years 1 to 10								
By Policy Year								
1	5,918	17,172,734	41	127,372	61.17	176,464	67.0	72.2
2	5,186	12,293,219	52	140,407	61.94	154,816	83.9	90.7
3	5,461	14,891,866	52	175,758	67.67	182,864	76.8	96.1
4	4,738	14,716,842	57	151,957	62.29	175,513	91.5	86.6
5	3,535	6,727,486	65	100,907	50.89	99,576	127.7	101.3
6–10	10,049	12,878,433	195	259,237	194.64	264,450	100.2	98.0
By Issue Age								
0–59	3,913	13,737,422	31	65,557	19.14	48,653	161.9	134.7
60–64	8,931	19,205,603	79	148,994	77.95	153,323	101.4	97.2
65–69	13,669	24,886,796	143	255,124	181.59	309,236	78.8	82.5
70 and over	8,375	20,850,760	209	485,964	219.93	542,471	95.0	89.6
Total Select	34,887	78,680,580	462	955,638	498.61	1,053,683	92.7	90.7
Ultimate Experience — Policy Years 11 and Over								
By Attained Age								
0–69	1,537	1,702,271	17	13,596	11.52	11,744	147.6	115.8
70–74	2,084	1,835,661	46	33,564	34.22	29,816	133.0	112.6
75–79	3,408	2,591,231	117	97,513	98.13	74,217	119.2	131.4
80–84	2,511	1,820,212	122	82,675	128.03	93,034	95.3	88.9
85–89	1,626	1,261,272	162	205,310	146.52	114,244	110.2	179.7
90 and over	1,026	634,347	157	106,058	171.69	104,027	91.4	102.0
Total Ultimate	12,191	9,844,993	620	538,714	590.11	427,082	105.1	126.1
Grand Total	47,078	88,525,573	1,082	1,494,352	1,088.72	1,480,765	99.4	100.9

TABLE 20

CANADIAN INDIVIDUAL ANNUITANT EXPERIENCE BETWEEN POLICY ANNIVERSARIES IN 1985 AND 1986
ALL COMPANIES TO DATE
MALE LIVES ONLY; EXPECTED: 1983 BASIC MALE (*TSA* XXXIII, 695)
SINGLE LIFE POLICIES ONLY; ALL TAX TYPES COMBINED, BOTH REFUND AND NONREFUND

	Exposures		Actual Deaths		Expected Deaths		Ratio A/E	
	Number	Income	Number	Income	Number	Income	Number	Income
Select Experience — Policy Years 1 to 10								
By Policy Year								
1	5,710	18,853,742	89	367,534	103.13	337,132	86.3	109.0
2	6,799	24,891,808	151	423,320	130.92	471,789	115.3	89.7
3	5,906	16,391,581	131	430,479	129.53	367,721	101.1	117.1
4	6,537	23,715,852	172	563,170	154.68	538,149	111.2	104.6
5	6,629	30,020,452	177	598,741	157.63	608,320	112.3	98.4
6–10	19,884	45,633,064	657	1,278,765	613.99	1,286,677	107.0	99.4
By Issue Age								
0–59	5,296	28,388,550	58	271,288	47.10	209,287	122.1	129.6
60–64	11,737	36,614,944	209	507,439	195.19	563,154	107.1	90.1
65–69	22,100	55,509,584	597	1,349,818	548.42	1,324,059	108.8	101.9
70 and over	12,333	38,993,421	514	1,533,465	499.16	1,513,286	103.0	101.3
Total Select	51,465	159,506,499	1,377	3,662,009	1,289.88	3,609,787	106.8	101.4
Ultimate Experience — Policy Years 11 and Over								
By Attained Age								
0–69	1,800	3,507,085	27	51,551	22.77	35,532	118.6	145.1
70–74	2,303	3,055,933	62	91,463	69.23	92,388	89.6	99.0
75–79	5,114	6,173,163	263	257,666	240.13	290,394	109.5	88.7
80–84	3,399	3,949,026	256	289,083	253.33	291,397	101.1	99.2
85–89	1,060	1,004,723	131	130,292	123.89	116,215	105.3	112.1
90 and over	437	361,524	88	68,397	85.76	71,097	102.0	96.2
Total Ultimate	14,111	18,051,452	826	888,450	795.11	897,024	103.9	99.0
Grand Total	65,576	177,557,951	2,203	4,550,459	2,084.99	4,506,811	105.7	101.0

TABLE 21

CANADIAN INDIVIDUAL ANNUITANT EXPERIENCE BETWEEN POLICY ANNIVERSARIES IN 1985 AND 1986
ALL COMPANIES TO DATE
FEMALE LIVES ONLY; EXPECTED: 1983 BASIC FEMALE (*TSA* XXXIII, 695)
SINGLE LIFE POLICIES ONLY; ALL TAX TYPES COMBINED, BOTH REFUND AND NONREFUND

	Exposures		Actual Deaths		Expected Deaths		Ratio A/E	
	Number	Income	Number	Income	Number	Income	Number	Income
Select Experience — Policy Years 1 to 10								
By Policy Year								
1	5,629	15,972,830	69	187,957	59.26	174,729	116.4	107.6
2	6,027	17,498,152	76	218,506	68.99	199,016	110.2	109.8
3	5,219	12,459,550	86	273,733	69.27	173,440	124.2	157.8
4	5,522	15,182,893	89	296,185	76.53	203,712	116.3	145.4
5	4,772	15,057,305	81	281,613	67.02	191,162	120.9	147.3
6–10	11,951	18,111,709	270	382,060	220.07	339,230	122.7	112.6
By Issue Age								
0–59	4,319	15,775,529	31	107,040	21.81	58,953	142.1	181.6
60–64	9,869	22,863,363	134	265,232	88.13	188,231	152.1	140.9
65–69	15,190	30,025,909	243	486,966	203.24	379,569	119.6	128.3
70 and over	9,743	25,617,639	263	780,816	247.95	654,537	106.1	119.3
Total Select	39,120	94,282,439	671	1,640,054	561.12	1,281,290	119.6	128.0
Ultimate Experience — Policy Years 11 and Over								
By Attained Age								
0–69	1,766	2,012,222	16	11,166	13.82	14,316	112.2	78.0
70–74	2,412	2,181,716	54	63,926	39.83	35,609	134.3	179.5
75–79	3,741	3,002,179	91	85,611	107.17	85,937	84.4	99.6
80–84	2,699	2,061,510	152	113,894	134.93	103,482	112.3	110.1
85–89	1,618	1,205,473	155	116,349	145.27	108,799	106.7	106.9
90 and over	1,008	683,680	190	118,475	164.00	109,025	115.9	108.7
Total Ultimate	13,243	11,146,777	656	509,420	605.02	457,169	108.4	111.4
Grand Total	52,363	105,429,216	1,327	2,149,474	1,166.15	1,738,458	113.8	123.6

TABLE 22

CANADIAN INDIVIDUAL ANNUITANT EXPERIENCE BETWEEN POLICY ANNIVERSARIES IN 1986 AND 1987
ALL COMPANIES TO DATE
MALE LIVES ONLY; EXPECTED: 1983 BASIC MALE (*TSA* XXXIII, 695)
SINGLE LIFE POLICIES ONLY; ALL TAX TYPES COMBINED, BOTH REFUND AND NONREFUND

	Exposures		Actual Deaths		Expected Deaths		Ratio A/E	
	Number	Income	Number	Income	Number	Income	Number	Income
Select Experience — Policy Years 1 to 10								
By Policy Year								
1	5,563	18,920,294	70	191,320	99.51	335,488	70.3	57.0
2	4,799	15,126,684	111	347,852	96.03	298,352	115.6	116.6
3	5,945	21,582,596	134	488,638	125.07	444,178	107.1	110.0
4	5,096	13,311,626	114	276,093	122.78	328,206	92.9	84.1
5	5,777	20,313,812	159	481,542	150.56	515,621	105.6	93.4
6–10	20,920	62,502,533	707	1,537,023	635.87	1,636,669	111.2	93.9
By Issue Age								
0–59	4,664	25,770,955	53	147,214	42.38	191,171	123.9	77.0
60–64	11,286	35,771,487	250	654,720	191.58	571,541	130.2	114.6
65–69	20,588	52,579,058	516	1,226,906	519.74	1,292,142	99.2	95.0
70 and over	11,563	37,636,046	478	1,293,629	476.12	1,503,661	100.3	86.0
Total Select	48,100	151,757,545	1,295	3,322,468	1,229.82	3,558,515	105.3	93.4
Ultimate Experience — Policy Years 11 and Over								
By Attained Age								
0–69	1,913	4,499,079	38	72,245	24.29	46,703	154.4	154.7
70–74	2,514	3,609,867	69	120,945	75.56	109,037	91.3	110.9
75–79	5,741	7,404,754	283	306,537	270.61	349,971	104.4	87.6
80–84	3,674	4,597,307	322	388,921	276.07	342,853	116.6	113.4
85–89	1,014	1,053,823	148	144,645	118.67	122,953	124.3	117.6
90 and over	452	363,630	79	75,116	89.57	69,822	87.6	107.6
Total Ultimate	15,306	21,528,459	937	1,108,407	854.78	1,041,339	109.6	106.4
Grand Total	63,406	173,286,004	2,232	4,430,875	2,084.60	4,599,854	107.1	96.3

TABLE 23

CANADIAN INDIVIDUAL ANNUITANT EXPERIENCE BETWEEN POLICY ANNIVERSARIES IN 1986 AND 1987
ALL COMPANIES TO DATE
FEMALE LIVES ONLY; EXPECTED: 1983 BASIC FEMALE (*TSA* XXXIII, 695)
SINGLE LIFE POLICIES ONLY; ALL TAX TYPES COMBINED, BOTH REFUND AND NONREFUND

	Exposures		Actual Deaths		Expected Deaths		Ratio A/E	
	Number	Income	Number	Income	Number	Income	Number	Income
Select Experience — Policy Years 1 to 10								
By Policy Year								
1	5,220	14,692,401	38	123,671	53.38	150,753	71.2	82.0
2	4,659	12,489,191	48	153,530	53.90	149,924	89.1	102.4
3	5,411	15,392,484	47	106,161	68.41	191,896	68.7	55.3
4	4,835	11,164,947	69	177,391	70.33	168,213	98.1	105.5
5	5,024	13,498,113	78	204,259	76.46	198,082	102.0	103.1
6–10	13,780	28,605,191	285	605,301	244.91	468,690	116.4	129.1
By Issue Age								
0–59	4,042	16,550,175	36	67,513	20.63	61,306	172.1	110.1
60–64	9,883	23,325,275	101	267,217	90.75	201,064	111.3	132.9
65–69	15,262	30,742,815	184	300,092	208.72	402,847	87.9	74.5
70 and over	9,743	25,224,063	245	735,491	247.30	662,341	99.1	111.0
Total Select	38,929	95,842,327	565	1,370,313	567.40	1,327,558	99.6	103.2
Ultimate Experience — Policy Years 11 and Over								
By Attained Age								
0–69	1,744	2,125,769	19	13,057	13.98	15,571	136.0	83.9
70–74	2,433	2,301,288	63	65,756	40.30	37,922	156.3	173.4
75–79	3,995	3,243,086	131	102,656	114.68	92,480	114.2	111.0
80–84	2,842	2,247,607	166	150,166	143.25	113,286	115.5	132.6
85–89	1,524	1,208,431	182	134,205	138.01	110,251	131.9	121.7
90 and over	997	756,793	191	121,617	164.19	120,690	116.0	100.8
Total Ultimate	13,535	11,882,973	751	587,456	614.41	490,200	122.2	119.8
Grand Total	52,464	107,725,300	1,316	1,957,769	1,181.81	1,817,758	111.4	107.7

TABLE 24

CANADIAN INDIVIDUAL ANNUITANT EXPERIENCE BETWEEN POLICY ANNIVERSARIES IN 1987 AND 1988
ALL COMPANIES TO DATE
MALE LIVES ONLY; EXPECTED: 1983 BASIC MALE (*TSA* XXXIII, 695)
SINGLE LIFE POLICIES ONLY; ALL TAX TYPES COMBINED, BOTH REFUND AND NONREFUND

	Exposures		Actual Deaths		Expected Deaths		Ratio A/E	
	Number	Income	Number	Income	Number	Income	Number	Income
Select Experience — Policy Years 1 to 10								
By Policy Year								
1	5,300	19,500,313	81	199,142	90.20	336,905	89.8	59.1
2	4,547	15,199,965	82	328,615	90.00	290,282	91.1	113.2
3	3,737	11,297,960	103	294,204	82.26	239,416	125.2	122.9
4	4,517	14,928,661	99	279,789	104.28	326,955	94.9	85.6
5	4,130	10,106,070	119	275,701	110.34	275,303	107.8	100.1
6–10	18,522	56,174,542	570	1,449,635	585.24	1,583,899	97.4	91.5
By Issue Age								
0–59	3,885	21,651,179	48	204,576	34.53	160,756	137.6	127.3
60–64	9,497	31,065,211	184	509,234	161.59	499,879	113.6	101.9
65–69	17,580	43,828,514	447	1,030,537	450.91	1,103,893	99.1	93.4
70 and over	9,791	30,662,609	376	1,082,740	415.30	1,288,232	90.5	84.0
Total Select	40,753	127,207,511	1,054	2,827,086	1,062.33	3,052,761	99.2	92.6
Ultimate Experience — Policy Years 11 and Over								
By Attained Age								
0–69	1,451	2,493,073	29	43,348	20.34	31,853	140.2	136.1
70–74	2,160	2,704,010	72	68,898	65.56	80,988	109.1	85.1
75–79	5,313	6,075,968	287	257,430	251.70	288,706	114.0	89.2
80–84	3,590	4,285,734	276	304,577	268.53	320,831	102.8	94.9
85–89	944	1,048,196	121	142,800	107.99	119,134	112.0	119.9
90 and over	413	355,609	69	71,759	82.42	68,400	83.7	104.9
Total Ultimate	13,869	16,962,589	853	888,810	796.53	909,912	107.1	97.7
Grand Total	54,622	144,170,100	1,907	3,715,896	1,858.86	3,962,673	102.6	93.8

TABLE 25

CANADIAN INDIVIDUAL ANNUITANT EXPERIENCE BETWEEN POLICY ANNIVERSARIES IN 1987 AND 1988
ALL COMPANIES TO DATE
FEMALE LIVES ONLY; EXPECTED: 1983 BASIC FEMALE (*TSA* XXXIII, 695)
SINGLE LIFE POLICIES ONLY; ALL TAX TYPES COMBINED, BOTH REFUND AND NONREFUND

	Exposures		Actual Deaths		Expected Deaths		Ratio A/E	
	Number	Income	Number	Income	Number	Income	Number	Income
Select Experience — Policy Years 1 to 10								
By Policy Year								
1	4,898	15,805,237	48	178,359	47.79	159,573	100.4	111.8
2	4,638	13,267,125	54	142,219	52.56	148,786	102.7	95.6
3	4,111	10,770,697	56	161,680	52.71	144,057	106.2	112.2
4	4,672	12,982,739	78	221,146	65.06	178,493	119.9	123.9
5	4,311	9,852,805	65	174,560	69.68	163,945	93.3	106.5
6–10	14,711	32,182,719	249	513,317	267.61	542,923	93.0	94.5
By Issue Age								
0–59	3,915	16,678,999	44	158,862	19.24	61,574	226.1	258.0
60–64	9,459	23,345,575	100	260,732	88.25	203,265	113.3	128.3
65–69	14,652	30,229,963	174	386,053	206.66	410,951	84.2	93.9
70 and over	9,316	24,606,786	233	585,635	241.26	661,988	96.4	88.5
Total Select	37,341	94,861,322	550	1,391,281	555.40	1,337,777	99.0	104.0
Ultimate Experience — Policy Years 11 and Over								
By Attained Age								
0–69	1,478	1,710,416	18	11,181	12.17	12,848	143.8	87.0
70–74	2,054	1,835,393	54	77,156	34.12	30,113	156.8	256.2
75–79	3,690	2,950,700	122	106,177	106.23	84,736	114.4	125.3
80–84	2,801	2,217,735	157	119,794	140.55	111,911	111.3	107.0
85–89	1,248	1,004,380	125	118,988	111.93	89,480	111.7	133.0
90 and over	881	818,378	153	116,357	145.96	130,123	104.8	89.4
Total Ultimate	12,150	10,537,000	627	549,652	550.96	459,211	113.8	119.7
Grand Total	49,491	105,398,322	1,177	1,940,933	1,106.37	1,796,988	106.4	108.0

REPORT OF THE SUBCOMMITTEE ON ANNUITY MORTALITY
COMMITTEE ON EXPECTED EXPERIENCE
OF THE CANADIAN INSTITUTE OF ACTUARIES

IMPROVEMENT IN ANNUITANT MORTALITY—CANADA

This report was prepared by the Subcommittee on Annuity Mortality of the Committee on Life Insurance Expected Experience of the Canadian Institute of Actuaries. The Canadian Institute of Actuaries has given the Society of Actuaries permission to reproduce this report as part of the Society's expansion of its experience studies. Discussions of this report as well as of any experience study are encouraged. The Canadian Institute and the Society intend to cooperate in experience studies to benefit actuaries in both Canada and the United States.

INTRODUCTION

An analysis of mortality over the last century or more clearly indicates that rates of death have declined dramatically. These improvements have not occurred uniformly during the twentieth century, as can be seen from the table below, which is derived from U.S. population data.[1]

Period	Annual Mortality Reduction	
	Males	Females
1900–1936	0.8%	0.9%
1936–1954	1.6	2.5
1954–1968	−0.2	0.8
1968–1982	1.8	2.1
1982–	small	small

Because of these variations, it is difficult to predict the future change in mortality, especially for a particular period of time. Future improvements in mortality will depend upon such factors as medical advances, the presence of environmental pollutants, exercise and nutrition, the misuse of drugs, the incidence of violence, and the prevalence of cigarette smoking. For example, it has been estimated[2] that the decline in smoking prevalence alone has

[1]Social Security Administration: *Actuarial Study No. 105.*
[2]Thomas W. Reese, FSA, "U.S. Smoking Trends," *Product Development News*, Sept. 1989.

accounted for an average mortality improvement from 1965 to 1987 of about 0.6 percent per annum for males and about 0.2 percent annually for females.

The impact of unexpected events such as AIDS is difficult to predict. AIDS is expected to influence mortality primarily for males in the age range 25 to 45. Based on U.S. population data, it has been estimated[3] that the impact of AIDS on average annual mortality improvement over the period 1983–88 has been as follows:

REDUCTION IN AVERAGE ANNUAL MORTALITY IMPROVEMENT DUE TO AIDS—1983 TO 1988

Ages	Male	Female
15–24	0.5%	0.2%
25–34	2.5	0.8
35–44	2.1	0.6
45–54	0.6	0.0
55–	0.0	0.0

Nevertheless, it is most likely that mortality will continue to improve for the foreseeable future especially for annuitants where the impact of AIDS is expected to be small. The level of improvement is not clear and is open to all kinds of speculation. Assembled below are a variety of sources of information on mortality improvement to assist the actuary in making decisions in this area.

HISTORICAL SCALES

Table 1 shows various scales that have been proposed over the last 40 years. The variety is due, in part, to the fact that they were published at different times and thus reflect the then-current knowledge about longevity. Nevertheless, the more recent scales, Scales G and H, were both recommended in 1983 by two Society of Actuaries committees on annuities. Their difference may be due to subjective thinking rather than to underlying differences between individual and group annuitants. Scales I and J were presented in a recent (1989) paper entitled "The Effects of Mortality on Individual Annuities" by Naftali Teitelbaum (*TSA* XL, Part II, p. 653). These scales assumed mortality improvement greater than previous scales.

Despite the fact there are major differences in the rates of mortality improvement in the various projection scales, the more recent ones all differentiate by sex as well as attained age.

[3]Tillinghast Update, "Population Mortality—1988 Results."

TABLE 1

ANNUITY PROJECTION SCALES

Age	A 1949	B 1949	C 1952	D 1971	E	G 1983	H 1983	I 1989	J 1989	P76 1979
					Male					
20	2.80	1.25	1.25	0.65	0.65	0.14	0.14	0.29	0.44	0.50
30	2.40	1.25	1.25	0.65	0.65	0.49	0.49	0.68	0.83	0.50
40	2.00	1.25	1.25	0.65	0.65	2.00	2.00	2.30	2.60	0.50
50	1.60	1.25	1.25	0.65	0.65	1.75	1.75	2.00	2.24	0.50
55	1.40	1.23	1.25	0.65		1.60	1.60	1.88	2.20	0.50
60	1.20	1.20	1.20	0.65	0.65	1.50	1.50	1.77	2.02	0.50
63				0.65	0.65	1.50	1.50			0.50
65	1.00	1.10	1.25	0.63		1.50	1.50	1.69	1.81	0.50
68				0.60	0.45	1.45	1.45			0.50
70	0.80	0.95	1.25			1.35	1.35	1.50	1.60	0.50
73				0.50	0.45	1.25	1.25			0.50
75	0.60	0.75	1.00	0.46		1.25	1.25	1.40	1.50	0.50
78				0.40	0.45	1.25	1.25			0.50
80	0.40	0.50	0.67			1.25	1.25	1.40	1.50	0.50
83				0.30	0.45	1.25	1.15			0.50
85	0.20	0.25	0.33	0.26		1.25	0.95	1.40	1.50	0.50
88				0.20	0.45	1.20	0.70			
90	0.00	0.00	0.00			1.10	0.60	1.34	1.50	0.30
92					0.45	1.00	0.50			
95				0.06		1.00	0.26	1.21	1.38	0.10
97				0.02		1.00	0.10			
98				0.00		0.75	0.07			
99						0.50	0.03			
100						0.25	0.00			0.00
					Female					
20	2.80	1.25	1.25	1.30		0.50	0.50	0.70	0.80	1.30
30	2.40	1.25	1.25	1.30		1.05	1.05	1.39	1.67	1.30
40	2.00	1.25	1.25	1.30		2.25	2.25	2.59	3.12	1.30
50	1.60	1.25	1.25	1.30		2.00	2.00	2.22	2.35	1.30
55	1.40	1.23	1.25	1.30		1.85	1.85	2.05	2.16	1.30
60	1.20	1.20	1.20	1.30		1.75	1.75	1.92	1.92	1.40
63				1.30		1.75	1.75			
65	1.00	1.10	1.25	1.28		1.75	1.75	1.90	1.86	1.50
68				1.25		1.75	1.75			
70	0.80	0.95	1.25			1.75	1.75	1.96	2.11	1.60
73				1.15		1.70	1.70			
75	0.60	0.75	1.00	1.09		1.60	1.60	1.85	2.25	1.75
78				1.00		1.50	1.50			
80	0.40	0.50	0.67			1.50	1.50	1.75	2.25	1.90
83				0.80		1.50	1.40			
85	0.20	0.25	0.33	0.68		1.50	1.20	1.75	2.19	1.60
88				0.50		1.45	0.90			
90	0.00	0.00	0.00			1.35	0.70	1.57	1.91	1.20
92						1.25	0.50			
95				0.08		1.25	0.35	1.45	1.69	0.80
97				0.00		1.25	0.25			
98						1.00	0.17			
99						0.75	0.08			
100						0.50	0.00			0.40

POPULATION DATA

While population data do not reflect specifically the mortality of annuitants, the data have the advantage of being on large homogenous exposures with mortality results being available at regular intervals on a timely basis. The use of population data for mortality projections of annuitant mortality is examined in greater detail in a 1979 CIA paper by Donald M. Keith entitled "Mortality Projections Based on Population Data." The subcommittee believes that population data are the most reliable source for tracking the historical improvement in rates of mortality, especially in Canada where the amount of data on annuitants is relatively small and not sufficient for mortality trend studies. The following table is derived from Canada Life Tables published by Statistics Canada. Using mortality rates from quinquennial reports, annual rates of mortality improvement can be computed for various periods of time.

AVERAGE ANNUAL RATES OF IMPROVEMENT
OF CANADIAN POPULATION MORTALITY

Ages	1921–31	1931–41	1941–51	1951–61	1961–71	1971–76	1976–81	1981–86
				Males				
55–60	0.01%	−0.25%	−0.08%	0.44%	0.51%	0.47%	2.51%	2.19%
60–65	−0.41	−0.48	−0.10	0.25	0.30	0.92	2.15	1.80
65–70	−0.33	−0.28	0.50	0.03	−0.04	0.99	1.53	1.37
70–75	0.24	−0.22	0.69	0.01	0.14	0.63	1.48	0.97
75–80	−0.07	−0.17	0.68	0.45	0.29	0.41	1.08	0.60
80–85	−0.25	−0.17	0.54	0.54	0.38	0.26	1.03	0.38
85–90	−0.02	−0.11	0.19	0.72	0.45	−0.11	0.96	0.02
				Females				
55–60	0.04%	1.02%	2.03%	1.98%	1.04%	1.35%	1.64%	1.62%
60–65	−0.16	1.03	1.34	1.92	1.46	1.29	1.55	1.17
65–70	0.49	0.54	1.68	1.52	1.69	1.29	1.58	1.20
70–75	0.54	0.57	1.15	1.67	1.59	1.46	1.82	1.05
75–80	−0.03	0.42	1.05	1.46	1.73	1.66	1.83	0.58
80–85	−0.33	0.34	0.65	1.03	1.63	1.30	1.84	0.74
85–90	0.07	−0.03	0.51	0.59	1.33	0.91	1.66	0.30

A more comprehensive set of statistics (derived from Statistics Canada Life Tables) is provided in Tables 2A (male) and 2B (female). From the mid-1970s to the mid-1980s, mortality improvement was much greater than in previous periods. However, current opinion suggests that these rates of improvement are expected to decrease somewhat in future years (see next section).

TABLE 2A

ANNUAL RATE OF MORTALITY IMPROVEMENT
CANADIAN POPULATION—MALE

Age	5-Year Periods Ending												
	1926	1931	1936	1941	1946	1951	1956	1961	1966	1971	1976	1981	1986
1–5	1.13%	1.08%	1.93%	5.98%	7.63%	7.20%	4.85%	5.24%	2.73%	2.55%	3.45%	5.47%	4.00%
5–10	5.75	0.63	2.34	4.35	3.67	5.56	5.61	2.91	1.08	1.73	3.07	5.99	5.84
10–15	2.00	3.50	1.43	2.91	3.77	4.84	4.92	2.27	0.88	0.95	3.62	2.13	4.56
15–20	3.22	0.19	3.53	1.40	3.05	3.94	1.49	1.47	−1.40	−2.80	−0.72	3.25	3.81
20–25	2.73	−0.41	4.61	0.17	4.65	1.93	1.42	0.74	−2.19	−0.07	−0.14	3.34	2.54
25–30	2.98	−0.23	3.10	2.51	4.11	3.14	1.40	1.92	−0.79	0.97	−0.14	1.42	1.74
30–35	2.23	−1.05	1.39	3.46	4.14	1.92	2.05	2.68	−0.36	−0.35	1.15	2.93	−0.44
35–40	1.98	−0.97	1.44	2.41	3.10	3.40	2.29	0.06	0.74	0.15	0.36	3.65	2.20
40–45	1.52	−0.90	1.25	0.71	2.30	1.87	2.48	0.90	−1.08	−0.20	1.51	3.72	2.47
45–50	1.74	−1.44	0.05	0.46	0.69	1.07	1.68	0.28	0.23	0.28	0.46	3.44	3.39
50–55	1.24	−2.72	0.72	−0.74	1.13	−0.60	1.14	0.61	−0.41	0.67	0.86	2.90	2.82
55–60	1.46	−1.46	0.20	−0.70	0.73	−0.90	0.69	0.19	0.09	0.92	0.47	2.51	2.19
60–65	0.60	−1.43	−1.71	0.74	0.23	−0.44	0.06	0.44	−0.11	0.70	0.92	2.15	1.80
65–70	0.16	−0.82	0.08	−0.63	0.11	0.89	−0.37	0.43	−0.38	0.30	0.99	1.53	1.37
70–75	1.07	−0.59	−0.27	−0.17	1.04	0.33	0.29	−0.27	0.38	−0.10	0.63	1.48	0.97
75–80	0.37	−0.52	0.21	−0.55	1.07	0.28	0.36	0.54	0.06	0.51	0.41	1.08	0.60
80–85	0.47	−0.99	−0.74	0.39	1.23	−0.15	0.26	0.83	0.31	0.46	0.26	1.03	0.38
85–90	0.01	−0.05	−0.06	−0.16	0.61	−0.22	0.99	0.45	0.03	0.87	−0.11	0.96	0.02

Age	10-Year Periods Ending												
	1926	1931	1936	1941	1946	1951	1956	1961	1966	1971	1976	1981	1986
1–5		1.11%	1.51%	3.98%	6.81%	7.41%	6.03%	5.05%	3.99%	2.64%	3.00%	4.47%	4.74%
5–10		3.22	1.49	3.35	4.01	4.62	5.58	4.27	2.00	1.40	2.40	4.54	5.91
10–15		2.75	2.47	2.18	3.34	4.31	4.88	3.60	1.58	0.92	2.29	2.88	3.55
15–20		1.72	1.87	2.47	2.23	3.50	2.72	1.48	0.05	−2.10	−1.75	1.28	3.53
20–25		1.17	2.13	2.42	2.43	3.30	1.67	1.08	−0.71	−1.12	−0.10	1.62	2.95
25–30		1.39	1.45	2.80	3.31	3.63	2.27	1.66	0.58	0.09	0.42	0.64	1.58
30–35		0.61	0.18	2.43	3.80	3.04	1.98	2.36	1.17	−0.36	0.40	2.04	1.26
35–40		0.52	0.24	1.93	2.76	3.25	2.85	1.18	0.40	0.45	0.26	2.02	2.93
40–45		0.32	0.18	0.98	1.51	2.09	2.18	1.69	−0.08	−0.64	0.66	2.62	3.10
45–50		0.16	−0.69	0.25	0.57	0.88	1.37	0.98	0.25	0.25	0.37	1.96	3.41
50–55		−0.72	−0.98	−0.01	0.20	0.27	0.27	0.87	0.10	0.14	0.77	1.89	2.86
55–60		0.01	−0.62	−0.25	0.02	−0.08	−0.10	0.44	0.14	0.51	0.70	1.49	2.35
60–65		−0.41	−1.57	−0.48	0.49	−0.10	−0.19	0.25	0.17	0.30	0.81	1.53	1.97
65–70		−0.33	−0.37	−0.28	−0.26	0.50	0.27	0.03	0.02	−0.04	0.65	1.26	1.45
70–75		0.24	−0.43	−0.22	0.44	0.69	0.31	0.01	0.06	0.14	0.26	1.06	1.23
75–80		−0.07	−0.16	−0.17	0.26	0.68	0.32	0.45	0.30	0.29	0.46	0.75	0.84
80–85		−0.25	−0.86	−0.17	0.81	0.54	0.05	0.54	0.57	0.38	0.36	0.64	0.70
85–90		−0.02	−0.05	−0.11	0.22	0.19	0.39	0.72	0.24	0.45	0.38	0.43	0.49

TABLE 2A—*Continued*

Age	15-Year Periods Ending												
	1926	1931	1936	1941	1946	1951	1956	1961	1966	1971	1976	1981	1986
1–5			1.38%	3.02%	5.21%	6.94%	6.57%	5.77%	4.28%	3.52%	2.91%	3.83%	4.31%
5–10			2.93	2.45	3.46	4.53	4.95	4.70	3.22	1.91	1.96	3.61	4.97
10–15			2.31	2.62	2.71	3.84	4.51	4.02	2.70	1.37	1.82	2.24	3.44
15–20			2.33	1.72	2.66	2.80	2.83	2.30	0.53	−0.89	−1.64	−0.06	2.13
20–25			2.33	1.48	3.17	2.27	2.67	1.36	0.00	−0.50	−0.79	1.06	1.93
25–30			1.96	1.80	3.24	3.26	2.89	2.16	0.85	0.71	0.02	0.75	1.01
30–35			0.87	1.29	3.00	3.18	2.71	2.22	1.46	0.66	0.15	1.25	1.22
35–40			0.83	0.97	2.32	2.97	2.93	1.93	1.03	0.32	0.42	1.40	2.08
40–45			0.63	0.36	1.42	1.63	2.22	1.75	0.78	−0.12	0.08	1.69	2.57
45–50			0.12	−0.31	0.40	0.74	1.15	1.01	0.73	0.26	0.32	1.40	2.44
50–55			−0.24	−0.90	0.37	−0.07	0.56	0.38	0.45	0.29	0.38	1.49	2.20
55–60			0.08	−0.65	0.08	−0.29	0.18	0.00	0.32	0.40	0.50	1.30	1.73
60–65			−0.84	−0.80	−0.24	0.18	−0.05	0.02	0.13	0.34	0.50	1.26	1.62
65–70			−0.19	−0.46	−0.15	0.13	0.21	0.32	−0.11	0.12	0.30	0.94	1.30
70–75			0.07	−0.34	0.20	0.40	0.55	0.12	0.14	0.01	0.30	0.67	1.03
75–80			0.02	−0.29	0.24	0.27	0.57	0.39	0.32	0.37	0.33	0.67	0.70
80–85			−0.41	−0.44	0.30	0.49	0.45	0.31	0.47	0.53	0.34	0.58	0.56
85–90			−0.03	−0.09	0.13	0.08	0.46	0.41	0.49	0.45	0.27	0.58	0.29

Age	20-Year Periods Ending												
	1926	1931	1936	1941	1946	1951	1956	1961	1966	1971	1976	1981	1986
1–5				2.55%	4.19%	5.71%	6.42%	6.24%	5.02%	3.85%	3.50%	3.56%	3.88%
5–10				3.29	2.76	3.99	4.80	4.44	3.81	2.85	2.20	2.98	4.17
10–15				2.46	2.91	3.25	4.11	3.96	3.24	2.27	1.94	1.90	2.82
15–20				2.09	2.05	2.98	2.47	2.49	1.39	−0.29	−0.85	−0.39	0.92
20–25				1.80	2.28	2.86	2.05	2.19	0.49	−0.02	−0.41	0.26	1.43
25–30				2.10	2.39	3.22	2.79	2.65	1.43	0.88	0.50	0.37	1.00
30–35				1.52	2.01	2.73	2.90	2.70	1.58	1.01	0.79	0.85	0.83
35–40				1.23	1.51	2.59	2.80	2.22	1.63	0.81	0.33	1.24	1.60
40–45				0.65	0.85	1.53	1.84	1.89	1.05	0.53	0.29	1.00	1.89
45–50				0.21	−0.06	0.56	0.97	0.93	0.82	0.62	0.31	1.11	1.90
50–55				−0.36	−0.39	0.13	0.24	0.57	0.19	0.50	0.44	1.02	1.82
55–60				−0.12	−0.30	−0.16	−0.04	0.18	0.02	0.47	0.42	1.00	1.53
60–65				−0.44	−0.54	−0.29	0.15	0.08	−0.01	0.27	0.49	0.92	1.39
65–70				−0.30	−0.32	0.11	0.00	0.27	0.14	−0.01	0.33	0.61	1.05
70–75				0.01	0.00	0.24	0.37	0.35	0.19	0.08	0.16	0.60	0.75
75–80				−0.12	0.05	0.25	0.29	0.56	0.31	0.37	0.38	0.52	0.65
80–85				−0.21	−0.02	0.19	0.44	0.54	0.31	0.46	0.46	0.51	0.53
85–90				−0.06	0.08	0.04	0.30	0.46	0.31	0.58	0.31	0.44	0.44

TABLE 2A—*Continued*

Age	1926	1931	1936	1941	1946	1951	1956	1961	1966	1971	1976	1981	1986
	25-Year Periods Ending												
1–5					3.59%	4.80%	5.54%	6.19%	5.55%	4.53%	3.77%	3.90%	3.65%
5–10					3.36	3.32	4.31	4.42	3.78	3.40	2.89	2.97	3.56
10–15					2.73	3.30	3.58	3.75	3.35	2.79	2.54	1.97	2.44
15–20					2.29	2.43	2.69	2.27	1.73	0.57	−0.38	−0.02	0.46
20–25					2.37	2.21	2.57	1.79	1.33	0.38	−0.04	0.35	0.72
25–30					2.50	2.54	2.86	2.62	1.97	1.34	0.68	0.68	0.64
30–35					2.05	1.99	2.60	2.85	2.10	1.19	1.04	1.22	0.59
35–40					1.60	1.89	2.53	2.26	1.93	1.34	0.72	1.00	1.43
40–45					0.98	1.05	1.72	1.65	1.30	0.80	0.73	0.98	1.30
45–50					0.30	0.17	0.79	0.84	0.79	0.71	0.59	0.95	1.57
50–55					−0.06	−0.43	0.33	0.31	0.38	0.28	0.58	0.93	1.38
55–60					0.05	−0.42	0.01	0.00	0.16	0.20	0.47	0.84	1.24
60–65					−0.31	−0.52	−0.22	0.21	0.04	0.13	0.40	0.82	1.10
65–70					−0.22	−0.07	0.02	0.09	0.14	0.18	0.19	0.58	0.76
70–75					0.22	0.07	0.25	0.25	0.36	0.13	0.19	0.43	0.67
75–80					0.12	0.10	0.27	0.34	0.46	0.35	0.37	0.52	0.53
80–85					0.08	−0.05	0.20	0.51	0.50	0.34	0.42	0.58	0.49
85–90					0.07	0.02	0.23	0.33	0.37	0.42	0.45	0.44	0.36

Age	1926	1931	1936	1941	1946	1951	1956	1961	1966	1971	1976	1981	1986
	30-Year Periods Ending												
1–5						4.20%	4.81%	5.49%	5.62%	5.05%	4.35%	4.06%	3.92%
5–10						3.73	3.71	4.08	3.87	3.44	3.34	3.41	3.45
10–15						3.08	3.57	3.37	3.28	2.95	2.93	2.47	2.41
15–20						2.56	2.27	2.48	1.67	0.99	0.35	0.23	0.63
20–25						2.30	2.08	2.27	1.14	1.10	0.29	0.53	0.72
25–30						2.61	2.35	2.70	2.06	1.80	1.09	0.80	0.86
30–35						2.03	2.00	2.61	2.32	1.69	1.19	1.36	0.94
35–40						1.91	1.96	2.12	2.01	1.63	1.18	1.22	1.20
40–45						1.13	1.29	1.59	1.20	1.05	0.92	1.23	1.23
45–50						0.43	0.42	0.70	0.73	0.71	0.67	1.07	1.36
50–55						−0.15	−0.17	0.38	0.19	0.43	0.38	0.97	1.25
55–60						−0.10	−0.24	0.04	0.02	0.29	0.25	0.82	1.07
60–65						−0.33	−0.42	−0.11	0.16	0.15	0.26	0.70	0.99
65–70						−0.03	−0.12	0.09	0.01	0.16	0.31	0.42	0.71
70–75						0.24	0.11	0.16	0.27	0.28	0.21	0.41	0.52
75–80						0.14	0.14	0.32	0.29	0.47	0.36	0.49	0.53
80–85						0.04	0.00	0.31	0.48	0.49	0.33	0.52	0.54
85–90						0.02	0.19	0.27	0.28	0.45	0.34	0.53	0.37

TABLE 2A—*Continued*

Age	35-Year Periods Ending						
	1956	1961	1966	1971	1976	1981	1986
1–5	4.29%	4.87%	5.10%	5.19%	4.83%	4.51%	4.05%
5–10	4.00	3.59	3.66	3.57	3.39	3.72	3.76
10–15	3.35	3.39	3.02	2.95	3.05	2.81	2.77
15–20	2.41	2.16	1.94	1.04	0.74	0.77	0.75
20–25	2.17	1.89	1.64	0.97	0.92	0.73	0.82
25–30	2.44	2.29	2.21	1.90	1.53	1.14	0.94
30–35	2.03	2.10	2.19	1.95	1.61	1.44	1.10
35–40	1.96	1.69	1.93	1.74	1.45	1.53	1.36
40–45	1.32	1.24	1.21	1.00	1.12	1.33	1.41
45–50	0.61	0.40	0.64	0.67	0.67	1.07	1.40
50–55	0.03	−0.06	0.27	0.26	0.49	0.75	1.23
55–60	0.01	−0.17	0.05	0.15	0.31	0.57	1.01
60–65	−0.27	−0.30	−0.11	0.23	0.26	0.54	0.85
65–70	−0.08	−0.04	0.02	0.05	0.28	0.49	0.55
70–75	0.25	0.05	0.19	0.22	0.33	0.39	0.49
75–80	0.18	0.20	0.28	0.32	0.46	0.46	0.51
80–85	0.07	0.12	0.31	0.48	0.46	0.43	0.50
85–90	0.16	0.22	0.23	0.37	0.37	0.42	0.46

Age	50-Year Periods Ending			
	1971	1976	1981	1986
1–5	4.06%	4.29%	4.72%	4.93%
5–10	3.38	3.11	3.64	3.99
10–15	2.76	2.92	2.78	3.10
15–20	1.43	1.04	1.34	1.37
20–25	1.38	1.09	1.47	1.26
25–30	1.92	1.61	1.77	1.64
30–35	1.62	1.52	1.91	1.73
35–40	1.47	1.31	1.77	1.85
40–45	0.89	0.89	1.35	1.48
45–50	0.51	0.38	0.87	1.20
50–55	0.11	0.07	0.63	0.85
55–60	0.13	0.03	0.42	0.62
60–65	−0.09	−0.06	0.30	0.65
65–70	−0.02	0.06	0.30	0.43
70–75	0.17	0.13	0.34	0.46
75–80	0.23	0.24	0.40	0.44
80–85	0.21	0.19	0.39	0.50
85–90	0.25	0.24	0.34	0.34

Age	40-Year Periods Ending						
	1956	1961	1966	1971	1976	1981	1986
1–5		4.41%	4.61%	4.79%	4.97%	4.91%	4.45%
5–10		3.87	3.28	3.42	3.51	3.72	3.99
10–15		3.21	3.08	2.76	3.03	2.93	3.03
15–20		2.29	1.72	1.36	0.83	1.06	1.16
20–25		1.99	1.39	1.43	0.83	1.23	0.96
25–30		2.37	1.91	2.05	1.65	1.52	1.21
30–35		2.11	1.79	1.88	1.85	1.78	1.20
35–40		1.72	1.57	1.71	1.57	1.73	1.62
40–45		1.27	0.95	1.03	1.07	1.45	1.47
45–50		0.57	0.38	0.59	0.64	1.02	1.36
50–55		0.11	−0.10	0.32	0.34	0.79	1.01
55–60		0.03	−0.14	0.16	0.19	0.59	0.78
60–65		−0.18	−0.27	−0.01	0.32	0.50	0.69
65–70		−0.02	−0.09	0.05	0.17	0.44	0.60
70–75		0.18	0.09	0.16	0.27	0.48	0.47
75–80		0.22	0.18	0.31	0.34	0.54	0.48
80–85		0.17	0.15	0.33	0.45	0.53	0.42
85–90		0.20	0.20	0.31	0.31	0.45	0.37

Age	60-Year Periods Ending			
	1971	1976	1981	1986
1–5			4.13%	4.36%
5–10			3.57	3.58
10–15			2.78	2.99
15–20			1.41	1.46
20–25			1.42	1.40
25–30			1.71	1.61
30–35			1.69	1.47
35–40			1.56	1.58
40–45			1.18	1.26
45–50			0.75	0.89
50–55			0.41	0.54
55–60			0.36	0.42
60–65			0.18	0.29
65–70			0.19	0.29
70–75			0.32	0.31
75–80			0.32	0.34
80–85			0.28	0.27
85–90			0.28	0.28

TABLE 2B

ANNUAL RATE OF MORTALITY IMPROVEMENT
CANADIAN POPULATION—FEMALE

Age	5-Year Periods Ending												
	1926	1931	1936	1941	1946	1951	1956	1961	1966	1971	1976	1981	1986
1–5	0.72%	1.64%	2.17%	6.32%	7.79%	7.74%	4.85%	5.48%	3.69%	1.74%	3.87%	5.99%	2.68%
5–10	6.25	1.91	0.61	5.96	4.77	6.96	7.09	3.16	−0.37	2.37	2.93	5.27	5.03
10–15	2.98	1.60	3.60	4.90	4.84	7.00	5.53	5.68	−0.87	−0.01	3.12	3.28	3.83
15–20	1.44	1.13	4.25	5.03	2.86	9.36	6.96	1.77	−0.38	−2.29	1.38	2.95	1.57
20–25	1.44	1.11	3.62	5.83	3.70	10.26	7.96	2.08	0.67	−0.22	0.87	3.02	2.66
25–30	2.73	−1.25	3.69	4.85	6.17	9.12	5.52	3.75	1.49	−0.08	2.91	0.67	3.95
30–35	3.00	−0.97	2.01	5.76	4.77	7.69	6.31	3.16	−0.10	−0.22	3.06	3.70	1.62
35–40	2.63	0.20	1.39	4.86	4.75	5.25	6.26	1.55	1.05	−0.28	2.32	3.11	4.05
40–45	2.28	−0.56	2.00	2.85	3.73	3.03	4.85	2.33	0.30	−0.14	2.38	2.52	2.44
45–50	2.19	−0.71	1.19	2.10	2.20	2.43	3.63	2.26	0.60	1.19	0.20	3.51	1.68
50–55	3.28	−1.70	0.55	1.85	1.88	2.60	2.72	1.52	0.61	0.92	1.96	1.46	1.46
55–60	2.49	−2.46	1.32	0.71	2.21	1.84	1.93	2.03	0.98	1.10	1.35	1.64	1.62
60–65	1.16	−1.50	−0.09	2.13	1.18	1.51	1.76	2.09	1.33	1.60	1.29	1.55	1.17
65–70	1.47	−0.50	0.56	0.53	1.65	1.71	1.73	1.30	1.78	1.59	1.29	1.58	1.20
70–75	2.18	−1.12	−0.13	1.27	0.92	1.37	2.06	1.29	1.85	1.34	1.46	1.82	1.05
75–80	0.70	−0.76	0.76	0.09	1.52	0.58	1.09	1.83	1.58	1.88	1.66	1.83	0.58
80–85	0.06	−0.73	−0.31	0.97	0.83	0.47	0.91	1.16	1.25	2.01	1.30	1.84	0.74
85–90	−0.55	0.69	0.05	−0.11	0.42	0.59	0.80	0.38	0.98	1.67	0.91	1.66	0.30

Age	10-Year Periods Ending												
	1926	1931	1936	1941	1946	1951	1956	1961	1966	1971	1976	1981	1986
1–5		1.18%	1.90%	4.26%	7.06%	7.77%	6.31%	5.16%	4.59%	2.72%	2.81%	4.93%	4.35%
5–10		4.11	1.26	3.32	5.37	5.87	7.02	5.14	1.41	1.01	2.65	4.11	5.15
10–15		2.29	2.61	4.26	4.87	5.92	6.27	5.60	2.46	−0.44	1.57	3.20	3.56
15–20		1.29	2.70	4.64	3.95	6.17	8.17	4.40	0.70	−1.33	−0.44	2.17	2.26
20–25		1.28	2.37	4.73	4.77	7.04	9.12	5.06	1.38	0.23	0.33	1.95	2.84
25–30		0.76	1.25	4.27	5.51	7.66	7.34	4.64	2.63	0.71	1.43	1.79	2.32
30–35		1.03	0.53	3.91	5.27	6.24	7.00	4.75	1.54	−0.16	1.43	3.38	2.67
35–40		1.43	0.80	3.14	4.80	5.00	5.75	3.93	1.30	0.39	1.03	2.71	3.58
40–45		0.87	0.73	2.43	3.29	3.38	3.95	3.60	1.32	0.08	1.13	2.45	2.48
45–50		0.75	0.24	1.65	2.15	2.32	3.03	2.94	1.43	0.89	0.69	1.87	2.60
50–55		0.82	−0.57	1.21	1.87	2.24	2.66	2.12	1.06	0.76	1.44	1.71	1.46
55–60		0.04	−0.55	1.02	1.46	2.03	1.88	1.98	1.51	1.04	1.23	1.49	1.63
60–65		−0.16	−0.79	1.03	1.66	1.34	1.64	1.92	1.71	1.46	1.45	1.42	1.36
65–70		0.49	0.03	0.54	1.09	1.68	1.72	1.52	1.54	1.69	1.44	1.43	1.39
70–75		0.54	−0.63	0.57	1.09	1.15	1.72	1.67	1.57	1.59	1.40	1.64	1.44
75–80		−0.03	0.00	0.42	0.81	1.05	0.84	1.46	1.70	1.73	1.77	1.75	1.21
80–85		−0.33	−0.52	0.34	0.90	0.65	0.69	1.03	1.20	1.63	1.66	1.57	1.29
85–90		0.07	0.37	−0.03	0.16	0.51	0.70	0.59	0.68	1.33	1.29	1.28	0.98

TABLE 2B—*Continued*

Age	15-Year Periods Ending												
	1926	1931	1936	1941	1946	1951	1956	1961	1966	1971	1976	1981	1986
1–5			1.51%	3.40%	5.45%	7.29%	6.80%	6.03%	4.67%	3.65%	3.10%	3.88%	4.19%
5–10			2.95	2.85	3.81	5.90	6.28	5.75	3.34	1.73	1.66	3.53	4.42
10–15			2.73	3.38	4.45	5.59	5.79	6.07	3.49	1.64	0.76	2.14	3.41
15–20			2.28	3.48	4.05	5.79	6.43	6.09	2.83	−0.29	−0.42	0.70	1.97
20–25			2.06	3.54	4.39	6.64	7.35	6.83	3.62	0.85	0.44	1.23	2.19
25–30			1.74	2.46	4.91	6.73	6.95	6.16	3.60	1.74	1.45	1.18	2.52
30–35			1.36	2.31	4.20	6.08	6.26	5.74	3.16	0.96	0.92	2.20	2.80
35–40			1.41	2.17	3.68	4.95	5.42	4.37	2.98	0.78	1.04	1.72	3.16
40–45			1.25	1.44	2.86	3.21	3.87	3.41	2.51	0.84	0.86	1.59	2.45
45–50			0.90	0.87	1.83	2.25	2.76	2.77	2.17	1.35	0.66	1.64	1.80
50–55			0.73	0.25	1.43	2.11	2.40	2.28	1.62	1.02	1.16	1.45	1.62
55–60			0.47	−0.13	1.42	1.59	1.99	1.93	1.65	1.37	1.15	1.36	1.53
60–65			−0.14	0.19	1.08	1.61	1.48	1.79	1.73	1.67	1.41	1.48	1.34
65–70			0.52	0.20	0.91	1.30	1.70	1.58	1.61	1.56	1.55	1.49	1.35
70–75			0.32	0.01	0.69	1.19	1.45	1.57	1.73	1.49	1.55	1.54	1.44
75–80			0.24	0.03	0.79	0.73	1.07	1.17	1.50	1.76	1.71	1.79	1.36
80–85			−0.32	−0.02	0.50	0.76	0.73	0.85	1.11	1.48	1.52	1.72	1.29
85–90			0.06	0.21	0.12	0.30	0.61	0.59	0.72	1.01	1.19	1.41	0.96

Age	20-Year Periods Ending												
	1926	1931	1936	1941	1946	1951	1956	1961	1966	1971	1976	1981	1986
1–5				2.74%	4.51%	6.03%	6.68%	6.47%	5.45%	3.95%	3.70%	3.83%	3.58%
5–10				3.71	3.34	4.61	6.20	5.51	4.26	3.10	2.03	2.57	3.91
10–15				3.28	3.75	5.09	5.57	5.76	4.38	2.63	2.01	1.40	2.57
15–20				2.98	3.33	5.41	6.09	5.29	4.51	1.58	0.13	0.43	0.92
20–25				3.02	3.58	5.89	6.97	6.06	5.32	2.67	0.85	1.09	1.59
25–30				2.53	3.40	5.98	6.43	6.16	5.01	2.70	2.03	1.25	1.88
30–35				2.48	2.93	5.08	6.14	5.50	4.31	2.32	1.49	1.63	2.05
35–40				2.29	2.82	4.07	5.28	4.47	3.55	2.18	1.16	1.56	2.31
40–45				1.65	2.02	2.91	3.62	3.49	2.64	1.86	1.23	1.27	1.81
45–50				1.20	1.20	1.98	2.59	2.63	2.23	1.93	1.06	1.38	1.65
50–55				1.01	0.66	1.72	2.26	2.18	1.87	1.45	1.25	1.24	1.45
55–60				0.53	0.46	1.52	1.67	2.00	1.70	1.51	1.37	1.27	1.43
60–65				0.43	0.44	1.19	1.65	1.64	1.67	1.69	1.58	1.44	1.40
65–70				0.52	0.56	1.12	1.41	1.60	1.63	1.60	1.49	1.56	1.41
70–75				0.56	0.24	0.86	1.41	1.41	1.64	1.63	1.48	1.62	1.42
75–80				0.20	0.41	0.74	0.82	1.26	1.27	1.60	1.74	1.74	1.49
80–85				0.00	0.19	0.49	0.79	0.84	0.95	1.33	1.43	1.60	1.48
85–90				0.02	0.26	0.24	0.43	0.55	0.69	0.96	0.99	1.31	1.14

TABLE 2B—*Continued*

Age	25-Year Periods Ending												
	1926	1931	1936	1941	1946	1951	1956	1961	1966	1971	1976	1981	1986
1–5					3.77%	5.17%	5.80%	6.44%	5.92%	4.72%	3.93%	4.16%	3.60%
5–10					3.93	4.07	5.11	5.60	4.36	3.88	3.07	2.69	3.07
10–15					3.59	4.41	5.18	5.59	4.47	3.52	2.73	2.27	1.89
15–20					2.96	4.57	5.72	5.24	4.18	3.19	1.54	0.70	0.66
20–25					3.15	4.95	6.31	6.01	5.00	4.24	2.32	1.29	1.41
25–30					3.27	4.58	5.89	5.90	5.24	4.02	2.74	1.76	1.80
30–35					2.94	3.90	5.33	5.55	4.40	3.42	2.47	1.94	1.62
35–40					2.78	3.31	4.52	4.55	3.79	2.80	2.20	1.56	2.06
40–45					2.07	2.22	3.30	3.36	2.86	2.09	1.96	1.49	1.51
45–50					1.40	1.45	2.31	2.53	2.23	2.03	1.58	1.56	1.44
50–55					1.19	1.05	1.92	2.12	1.87	1.68	1.55	1.29	1.28
55–60					0.87	0.74	1.60	1.75	1.80	1.58	1.48	1.42	1.34
60–65					0.58	0.65	1.30	1.73	1.57	1.66	1.61	1.57	1.39
65–70					0.75	0.80	1.24	1.39	1.64	1.62	1.54	1.51	1.49
70–75					0.63	0.47	1.10	1.38	1.50	1.58	1.60	1.55	1.50
75–80					0.47	0.44	0.81	1.03	1.32	1.39	1.61	1.76	1.51
80–85					0.17	0.25	0.58	0.87	0.92	1.16	1.33	1.51	1.43
85–90					0.10	0.33	0.35	0.42	0.64	0.89	0.95	1.12	1.11

Age	30-Year Periods Ending												
	1926	1931	1936	1941	1946	1951	1956	1961	1966	1971	1976	1981	1986
1–5						4.44%	5.12%	5.74%	5.99%	5.24%	4.58%	4.28%	3.92%
5–10						4.44	4.58	4.78	4.63	4.03	3.73	3.44	3.08
10–15						4.17	4.59	5.26	4.54	3.74	3.45	2.82	2.53
15–20						4.05	4.97	5.07	4.32	3.13	2.89	1.78	0.85
20–25						4.38	5.46	5.62	5.14	4.15	3.69	2.43	1.52
25–30						4.27	4.73	5.53	5.18	4.38	3.83	2.40	2.13
30–35						3.75	4.31	4.97	4.63	3.65	3.36	2.68	1.88
35–40						3.20	3.81	4.03	3.97	3.13	2.72	2.36	1.98
40–45						2.23	2.67	3.14	2.86	2.37	2.14	2.05	1.64
45–50						1.57	1.82	2.30	2.21	2.06	1.72	1.91	1.58
50–55						1.42	1.33	1.86	1.87	1.71	1.72	1.53	1.32
55–60						1.03	0.94	1.68	1.62	1.68	1.54	1.51	1.45
60–65						0.74	0.84	1.43	1.67	1.58	1.60	1.60	1.51
65–70						0.91	0.95	1.25	1.45	1.63	1.57	1.55	1.46
70–75						0.75	0.73	1.13	1.46	1.47	1.56	1.63	1.47
75–80						0.49	0.55	0.98	1.12	1.42	1.44	1.65	1.56
80–85						0.22	0.36	0.67	0.93	1.11	1.18	1.41	1.39
85–90						0.18	0.41	0.36	0.51	0.81	0.89	1.07	0.99

TABLE 2B—*Continued*

Age	35-Year Periods Ending						
	1956	1961	1966	1971	1976	1981	1986
1–5	4.50%	5.17%	5.45%	5.39%	5.04%	4.78%	4.05%
5–10	4.82	4.38	4.07	4.31	3.88	3.95	3.67
10–15	4.36	4.75	4.41	3.91	3.65	3.43	2.96
15–20	4.47	4.52	4.31	3.41	2.88	2.90	1.75
20–25	4.90	4.99	4.92	4.39	3.69	3.59	2.47
25–30	4.45	4.59	4.97	4.45	4.17	3.39	2.62
30–35	4.12	4.14	4.26	3.95	3.56	3.41	2.53
35–40	3.64	3.49	3.61	3.38	3.01	2.77	2.60
40–45	2.61	2.62	2.74	2.44	2.37	2.19	2.11
45–50	1.87	1.88	2.06	2.06	1.79	1.98	1.87
50–55	1.61	1.36	1.68	1.73	1.75	1.69	1.52
55–60	1.16	1.10	1.58	1.55	1.64	1.55	1.52
60–65	0.88	1.02	1.42	1.66	1.54	1.59	1.54
65–70	1.03	1.00	1.33	1.47	1.58	1.57	1.50
70–75	0.94	0.81	1.23	1.44	1.47	1.60	1.55
75–80	0.57	0.73	1.07	1.23	1.45	1.50	1.49
80–85	0.32	0.47	0.76	1.09	1.13	1.28	1.32
85–90	0.27	0.41	0.45	0.68	0.82	1.00	0.96

Age	50-Year Periods Ending			
	1971	1976	1981	1986
1–5	4.25%	4.55%	4.98%	5.03%
5–10	3.91	3.57	3.91	4.34
10–15	3.56	3.57	3.74	3.76
15–20	3.07	3.06	3.24	2.98
20–25	3.70	3.64	3.83	3.74
25–30	3.64	3.66	3.84	3.87
30–35	3.18	3.19	3.65	3.61
35–40	2.79	2.76	3.05	3.31
40–45	2.08	2.09	2.40	2.44
45–50	1.71	1.52	1.94	1.99
50–55	1.43	1.30	1.61	1.70
55–60	1.23	1.11	1.51	1.54
60–65	1.12	1.14	1.44	1.56
65–70	1.19	1.17	1.37	1.44
70–75	1.11	1.03	1.32	1.44
75–80	0.93	1.03	1.28	1.27
80–85	0.67	0.79	1.05	1.15
85–90	0.50	0.64	0.74	0.76

Age	40-Year Periods Ending						
	1956	1961	1966	1971	1976	1981	1986
1–5		4.62%	4.98%	5.00%	5.20%	5.16%	4.52%
5–10		4.62	3.80	3.86	4.14	4.05	4.08
10–15		4.53	4.06	3.87	3.81	3.61	3.48
15–20		4.14	3.92	3.51	3.16	2.89	2.73
20–25		4.55	4.46	4.30	3.96	3.61	3.48
25–30		4.36	4.21	4.35	4.25	3.74	3.46
30–35		4.00	3.62	3.71	3.84	3.58	3.19
35–40		3.38	3.19	3.13	3.24	3.02	2.93
40–45		2.58	2.33	2.38	2.43	2.39	2.23
45–50		1.92	1.72	1.95	1.83	2.01	1.94
50–55		1.60	1.26	1.59	1.76	1.71	1.66
55–60		1.27	1.08	1.52	1.52	1.64	1.56
60–65		1.04	1.06	1.44	1.61	1.54	1.54
65–70		1.06	1.10	1.36	1.45	1.58	1.52
70–75		0.98	0.94	1.25	1.44	1.51	1.53
75–80		0.73	0.84	1.17	1.28	1.50	1.38
80–85		0.42	0.57	0.91	1.11	1.22	1.21
85–90		0.29	0.48	0.60	0.71	0.93	0.91

Age	60-Year Periods Ending			
	1971	1976	1981	1986
1–5			4.36%	4.52%
5–10			3.94	3.84
10–15			3.50	3.57
15–20			2.92	2.93
20–25			3.41	3.51
25–30			3.34	3.44
30–35			3.22	3.10
35–40			2.78	2.90
40–45			2.14	2.16
45–50			1.74	1.70
50–55			1.48	1.33
55–60			1.27	1.20
60–65			1.17	1.17
65–70			1.23	1.20
70–75			1.19	1.10
75–80			1.07	1.06
80–85			0.82	0.87
85–90			0.63	0.70

Don Keith, in his paper on mortality improvement, concluded that, if the actuary decided to adjust population data when applied to annuitant mortality, the adjustments could be positive or negative, but in no event should they be very large for an indefinite period.

FUTURE PROJECTIONS—SOCIAL SECURITY RESEARCH

The projected costs of social insurance plans in Canada and the United States are affected to a great extent by the future outlook for mortality. Information on mortality improvement is contained in:

(1) Social Security Administration (United States)
Population Projections: 1989 Actuarial Study No. 105

Past reduction in mortality has varied greatly by cause of death. Because it is expected that future reduction in mortality rates will also vary greatly by cause of death, the SSA analyzed death rates for the years 1968 through 1986 by age group and sex for ten groups of causes of death. Table 3 shows the average annual percentage reductions in central death rates during 1968–86 (Table 7 in SSA *Actuarial Study No. 105*). Using this guide, the Social Security Administration postulates annual percentage improvements in central death rates by sex and the ten leading causes of death. Three alternatives in ultimate annual percentage reductions in death rates were postulated with Alternative II considered the most likely; see Table 4. Using central death rates by age group, sex and calendar year as published in SSA *Actuarial Study No. 105*, annual percentage reductions in mortality can be computed. Table 5 shows projected mortality according to Alternative II for the period 1990 to 2030 in ten-year steps, and for the period 2030 to 2080.

(2) Canada Pension Plan
10th and 11th Statutory Reports

Table 6 shows future assumed mortality rates used in the last two CPP statutory reports. From these data, the annual compound rates of mortality improvement were computed.

The methodology used to project mortality rates is described in the Eleventh Actuarial Report and is summarized as follows:

1. Mortality rates in the 1985–87 Canada Life Tables are assumed to be applicable for 1986.

TABLE 3

AVERAGE ANNUAL PERCENTAGE REDUCTIONS IN CENTRAL DEATH RATES DURING 1968–86 BY AGE GROUP, SEX, AND CAUSE OF DEATH

Age Group	Cause of Death										
	Total*	Heart Disease	Cancer	Vascular Disease	Violence	Respiratory Disease	Infancy	Digestive Disease	Diabetes Mellitus	Cirrhosis (Liver)	Other†
					Male						
0	4.55	−3.97	2.65	1.28	5.72	11.75	5.30	6.76	7.70	3.77	−2.99
1–4	3.04	−2.22	3.82	6.65	2.51	8.65	2.10	1.68	7.14	5.42	2.55
5–9	3.65	−0.38	3.87	7.40	3.39	6.99	4.42	4.38	6.23	8.32	3.30
10–14	2.69	0.56	2.76	8.23	2.45	4.96	3.08	5.41	5.63	2.46	2.40
15–19	1.94	0.32	2.83	7.18	1.55	5.94	2.90	6.26	6.03	7.63	3.48
20–24	1.77	0.73	2.84	7.18	1.38	6.11	2.76	6.71	4.58	5.07	3.48
25–29	1.12	1.19	2.09	6.08	0.88	4.77	3.83	5.98	4.17	2.76	1.09
30–34	1.22	2.43	1.60	6.01	1.03	3.72	2.88	4.44	3.28	2.26	0.39
35–39	2.15	3.45	1.71	5.84	1.72	4.66	2.95	3.90	2.54	3.26	1.31
40–44	2.56	3.44	1.16	5.59	2.11	4.76	2.75	3.87	1.97	3.67	1.68
45–49	2.62	3.47	0.65	5.12	2.39	4.47	3.54	3.86	1.84	3.51	1.67
50–54	2.27	3.09	0.01	5.03	2.52	3.65	4.09	3.11	2.08	2.95	1.23
55–59	2.21	3.05	−0.14	5.24	2.94	2.96	3.06	3.15	2.04	2.75	1.08
60–64	2.09	2.90	−0.22	5.22	3.25	2.30	1.70	2.91	2.20	2.51	0.71
65–69	1.59	2.36	−0.71	4.90	2.85	1.03	0.84	2.47	2.22	1.32	−0.04
70–74	1.32	2.06	−0.96	4.66	2.26	0.10	−0.31	1.95	2.17	0.14	−0.93
75–79	1.12	1.82	−1.13	4.43	1.79	−0.75	−0.19	1.41	1.96	−0.13	−1.80
80–84	1.10	1.69	−1.25	4.43	2.03	−1.47	−1.83	0.79	1.90	−0.28	−2.27
85–89	1.12	1.64	−1.43	4.50	2.14	−2.01	−0.10	−0.04	1.88	0.30	−2.43
90–94	1.12	1.49	−1.72	4.48	2.55	−1.77	−2.06	−1.00	0.58	1.02	−2.52
Total	1.60	2.16	−0.64	4.68	1.95	0.32	4.97	1.89	2.04	2.21	−0.66

TABLE 3—*Continued*

Age Group	Cause of Death										
	Total*	Heart Disease	Cancer	Vascular Disease	Violence	Respiratory Disease	Infancy	Digestive Disease	Diabetes Mellitus	Cirrhosis (Liver)	Other†
	Female										
0	4.32	−3.42	3.28	1.70	5.46	12.14	4.84	6.81	8.69	4.89	−2.62
1–4	3.30	−2.60	3.98	6.48	2.77	8.45	2.87	0.28	4.44	6.69	3.01
5–9	3.52	−0.34	3.89	5.96	3.12	6.65	4.74	3.62	6.45	9.38	2.96
10–14	2.62	0.36	2.88	6.14	1.79	5.61	2.43	5.92	6.72	9.23	2.79
15–19	1.81	1.21	2.51	7.33	0.77	5.66	3.53	5.77	5.70	11.03	3.22
20–24	1.99	0.98	2.27	7.30	0.73	5.98	3.11	7.57	5.38	6.48	3.34
25–29	2.25	1.77	1.94	6.95	1.01	5.54	3.33	6.40	4.12	3.82	2.97
30–34	2.89	3.39	1.80	7.73	1.76	5.24	3.60	6.27	3.97	4.16	3.03
35–39	3.42	4.12	1.79	7.30	2.57	5.62	2.55	5.44	3.03	5.93	3.77
40–44	3.11	3.41	1.52	6.18	2.79	5.02	3.11	4.72	2.84	5.77	3.39
45–49	2.62	2.90	1.21	5.54	2.89	3.56	4.20	4.03	3.16	5.18	2.45
50–54	1.89	2.50	0.38	5.00	2.98	1.82	2.82	3.02	2.58	3.75	1.79
55–59	1.58	2.56	−0.12	5.00	3.05	0.31	2.78	2.71	2.96	2.90	1.04
60–64	1.16	2.36	−0.89	4.83	3.03	−1.30	1.85	1.93	2.71	1.36	0.08
65–69	0.90	2.11	−1.45	4.67	2.61	−2.75	1.16	1.18	2.91	−0.55	−1.04
70–74	1.35	2.37	−1.20	4.85	2.58	−2.73	−0.75	1.02	3.32	−1.34	−1.57
75–79	1.77	2.43	−0.60	4.92	3.25	−1.87	−1.55	0.73	3.42	−1.54	−2.30
80–84	1.93	2.30	−0.38	4.78	3.91	−0.91	−1.39	0.15	2.91	−1.32	−2.84
85–89	1.78	1.96	−0.32	4.41	4.53	−0.66	−2.08	−0.66	1.83	−0.33	−3.22
90–94	1.43	1.41	−0.80	3.98	5.03	−0.40	−3.14	−1.64	0.12	−0.07	−3.34
Total	1.74	2.17	−0.41	4.70	2.54	−0.17	4.56	1.12	2.85	2.32	−0.84

*Includes AIDS.
†Excludes AIDS.
Note: The average annual percentage reduction is the complement of the exponential of the least-squares line through the logarithms of the central death rates.
Source: SSA *Actuarial Study No. 105.*

TABLE 4

ASSUMED ULTIMATE ANNUAL PERCENTAGE REDUCTIONS IN DEATH RATES BY ALTERNATIVE, SEX, AGE GROUP, AND CAUSES

Sex and Age Group	Cause of Death									
	I	II	III	IV	V	VI	VII	VIII	IX	X
					Alternative I					
Male										
<15	0.3	0.2	0.7	0.3	0.3	0.8	0.6	0.5	0.3	0.0
15–64	0.6	0.1	0.9	0.2	0.2	0.6	0.4	0.4	0.2	0.0
65+	0.5	0.0	0.8	0.3	0.0	0.4	0.2	0.3	0.1	0.0
Female										
<15	0.3	0.2	0.7	0.3	0.3	0.8	0.6	0.5	0.3	0.0
15–64	0.6	0.1	0.9	0.2	0.2	0.6	0.4	0.4	0.2	0.0
65+	0.5	0.0	0.8	0.3	0.0	0.4	0.2	0.3	0.1	0.0
					Alternative II					
Male										
<15	0.6	0.5	1.2	0.6	0.5	1.5	0.8	0.8	0.5	0.2
15–64	1.0	0.3	1.4	0.3	0.3	1.3	0.6	0.7	0.3	0.2
65+	0.8	0.2	1.3	0.4	0.2	1.1	0.4	0.6	0.2	0.2
Female										
<15	0.6	0.5	1.2	0.6	0.5	1.5	0.8	0.8	0.5	0.2
15–64	1.0	0.3	1.4	0.4	0.3	1.3	0.6	0.8	0.4	0.2
65+	0.9	0.2	1.3	0.5	0.2	1.1	0.4	0.6	0.2	0.2
					Alternative III					
Male										
<15	0.9	1.3	1.4	0.9	0.6	2.0	1.0	1.0	0.8	0.4
15–64	1.3	1.2	1.8	0.6	0.5	1.8	0.9	0.9	0.6	0.4
65+	1.1	1.1	1.7	0.8	0.4	1.6	0.8	0.9	0.6	0.4
Female										
<15	0.9	1.3	1.4	0.9	0.6	2.0	1.0	1.0	0.8	0.4
15–64	1.3	1.3	1.8	0.8	0.5	1.8	0.9	1.0	0.7	0.4
65+	1.2	1.2	1.7	0.9	0.4	1.6	0.8	0.9	0.6	0.4

Source: SSA *Actuarial Study No. 105.*

TABLE 5

ANNUAL IMPROVEMENT IN MORTALITY RATES—ALTERNATIVE II
SOCIAL SECURITY ADMINISTRATION *ACTUARIAL STUDY NO.* 105.

Age Group	Annual Improvement in Mortality from 1990 to 2000	2000 to 2010	2010 to 2020	2020 to 2030	1990 to 2030	2030 to 2080
Male						
1–4	1.96%	1.37%	0.60%	0.58%	1.13%	0.53%
5–9	2.69	1.51	0.50	0.53	1.31	0.52
10–14	2.29	1.26	0.56	0.50	1.16	0.53
15–19	1.63	0.86	0.33	0.32	0.79	0.31
20–24	0.88	1.22	0.32	0.30	0.68	0.28
25–29	−1.05	2.04	0.29	0.24	0.39	0.23
30–34	−1.88	2.55	0.31	0.20	0.31	0.20
35–39	−1.89	2.73	0.38	0.21	0.37	0.20
40–44	−0.41	2.22	0.45	0.34	0.65	0.29
45–49	0.56	1.78	0.48	0.41	0.81	0.36
50–54	1.18	1.17	0.52	0.47	0.84	0.44
55–59	1.46	0.93	0.54	0.50	0.86	0.47
60–64	1.46	0.85	0.54	0.52	0.84	0.49
65–69	1.08	0.60	0.44	0.42	0.63	0.39
70–74	0.83	0.50	0.44	0.43	0.55	0.40
75–79	0.63	0.44	0.45	0.44	0.49	0.41
80–84	0.54	0.43	0.47	0.46	0.47	0.42
85–89	0.47	0.41	0.48	0.47	0.46	0.43
90–94	0.46	0.43	0.50	0.49	0.47	0.45
Female						
1–4	1.98%	1.46%	0.59%	0.55%	1.15%	0.53%
5–9	2.41	1.43	0.62	0.56	1.26	0.48
10–14	2.17	1.07	0.54	0.57	1.09	0.52
15–19	1.26	0.76	0.41	0.42	0.71	0.39
20–24	1.33	0.84	0.43	0.40	0.75	0.40
25–29	0.31	1.67	0.38	0.36	0.68	0.33
30–34	−0.58	2.20	0.35	0.29	0.57	0.26
35–39	1.49	1.56	0.44	0.36	0.96	0.34
40–44	2.07	1.27	0.46	0.41	1.06	0.39
45–49	2.05	1.05	0.48	0.45	1.01	0.42
50–54	1.45	0.82	0.48	0.46	0.80	0.43
55–59	1.09	0.61	0.47	0.46	0.66	0.43
60–64	0.64	0.46	0.49	0.47	0.51	0.45
65–69	0.30	0.30	0.41	0.40	0.35	0.37
70–74	0.60	0.39	0.44	0.43	0.47	0.40
75–79	0.97	0.54	0.49	0.48	0.62	0.44
80–84	1.15	0.64	0.55	0.53	0.72	0.49
85–89	1.05	0.66	0.59	0.57	0.72	0.53
90–94	0.79	0.63	0.62	0.61	0.66	0.56

TABLE 6

CANADA PENSION PLAN—ASSUMED RATES OF MORTALITY IMPROVEMENT

Age	Mortality Rates Canada Life Tables		Rates Assumed for 1986 in Report 10	Mortality Rates Assumed for Year 2100		Annual Rates of Mortality Improvement from 1986 to 2100	
	1980–82	1985–87		Report 10	Report 11	Report 10	Report 11
Male							
1	0.81	0.67	0.78	0.53	0.27	0.34%	0.79%
5	0.39	0.30	0.38	0.25	0.12	0.37	0.80
10	0.22	0.18	0.21	0.12	0.08	0.49	0.71
20	1.53	1.30	1.50	1.17	0.64	0.22	0.62
30	1.32	1.30	1.30	1.05	0.83	0.19	0.39
40	2.23	1.97	2.15	1.38	0.95	0.39	0.64
50	6.28	5.32	6.09	4.17	2.50	0.33	0.66
60	16.28	14.68	15.77	10.57	7.75	0.35	0.56
70	39.07	36.73	38.13	27.96	21.21	0.27	0.48
80	89.41	86.65	87.31	64.61	52.59	0.26	0.44
90	187.75	191.97	185.77	136.21	114.49	0.27	0.45
Female							
1	0.66	0.62	0.63	0.40	0.24	0.40%	0.83%
5	0.27	0.22	0.26	0.16	0.07	0.42	1.00
10	0.18	0.14	0.18	0.10	0.05	0.51	0.90
20	0.47	0.42	0.46	0.38	0.20	0.17	0.65
30	0.57	0.51	0.56	0.37	0.26	0.36	0.59
40	1.32	1.12	1.27	0.76	0.53	0.45	0.65
50	3.38	3.12	3.28	2.21	1.68	0.35	0.54
60	8.04	7.51	7.84	5.71	4.23	0.28	0.50
70	19.83	18.67	19.35	14.08	10.23	0.28	0.53
80	54.01	51.73	52.04	33.30	27.19	0.39	0.56
90	143.51	144.15	142.87	92.33	72.61	0.38	0.60

Source: CPP Statutory Reports 10 and 11.

2. To reflect anticipated sustained improvements in life expectancy, these rates were projected to the year 2100 using the following annual rates of decrease:
   (a) For 1987 to 2010, the annual rates of decrease (varying by age, sex and calendar year) were determined by interpolation between (i) the average reduction in rates experienced in Canada between 1976 and 1986, and (ii) the constant rates of decrease, described in (b) below, in respect of the period 2011 to 2100.
   (b) For 2011 and later years, the annual rates of decrease (varying by age and sex only, not by calendar year) are those identified as "Alternative II (medium)" in *Actuarial Study No. 102* (Social Security Area Population Projection) prepared by the Office of the Actuary of the U.S. Social Security Administration.
3. To account for AIDS, which was ignored in the above steps, male mortality was increased for the years 1989 to 2018 by the increments estimated by the Canadian Institute of Actuaries' Task Force on AIDS in its November 1988 Report of the Subcommittee on Modeling. A constant level of new infections is assumed to hold from 1984 to 1988 and to decrease gradually from that level to zero in 1999. On the basis of the cumulative number of deaths attributable to AIDS (as reported by the Federal Centre for AIDS), female mortality was also increased but by only 10% of the above increments for males.
4. The following table shows the impact on the expectation of life of using the mortality improvement described.

EXPECTATION OF LIFE (YEARS)

	1986		2100	
	Male	Female	Male	Female
At Birth	73.0	79.7	80.3	86.9
At Age 65	14.9	19.1	19.3	24.5

IMPACT OF MORTALITY IMPROVEMENT ON ANNUITY VALUES

Table 7 shows the impact on an immediate annuity of $1,000 per month of using mortality according to the 1983 Basic Table along with improvement according to Scales G and H. Two projection approaches are employed: (1) a generation approach, whereby the mortality rate depends on sex, attained age and the calendar year in which that age is reached, and (2) a static approach using 17 years of mortality improvement from 1983 for all ages.

TABLE 7

IMPACT ON ANNUITY VALUES OF VARIOUS PROJECTION SCALES AND METHODS OF PROJECTION: RATIO OF ANNUITY VALUES TO BASE
(1983 BASIC TABLE WITH NO PROJECTION AT 10.0% INTEREST FOR 20 YEARS AND 5.0% THEREAFTER)

	Immediate Life Annuity				Immediate Life Annuity with 10 Years Certain			
	Projection				Projection			
Age at Birthday in 1990	Scale G Generation #1	Scale G Static #2	Scale H Generation #3	Scale H Static #4	Scale G Generation #1	Scale G Static #2	Scale H Generation #3	Scale H Static #4
				Male				
60	104.1%	103.7%	103.6%	103.5%	103.5%	102.8%	103.0%	102.6%
65	104.5	104.5	103.9	104.2	103.5	103.0	102.9	102.8
70	104.9	105.6	104.2	105.1	103.3	103.2	102.7	102.8
75	105.5	107.1	104.5	106.2	102.9	103.1	102.0	102.4
				Female				
60	103.9%	103.1%	103.3%	102.8%	103.6%	102.6%	102.9%	102.3%
65	104.4	103.9	103.6	103.5	103.7	103.0	103.0	102.6
70	104.8	105.0	103.9	104.4	103.7	103.3	102.9	102.8
75	105.4	106.4	104.2	105.4	103.5	103.5	102.4	102.6

1. Scale G with projection from 1983 using a generation approach.
2. Scale G with projection from 1983 to 2000 (static approach).
3. Scale H with projection from 1983 using a generation approach.
4. Scale H with projection from 1983 to 2000 (static approach).

VIEW OF THE ANNUITY MORTALITY SUBCOMMITTEE

The Annuity Mortality Subcommittee of the CIA Expected Experience Committee makes the following observations and suggestions regarding mortality improvement on individual annuitants:

1. While there is no general agreement as to the level of change, annuitant mortality is expected to continue to improve in the future.
2. The subcommittee feels there are insufficient data from the Canadian Annuitant Mortality study to be able to recommend a particular scale for Canadian annuitants. However, a review of all the evidence available with an emphasis on research based on population data suggests that Scale G rates of mortality improvement are probably conservative at ages over 65 in forecasting mortality improvement over the foreseeable future.
3. The scale of mortality improvement rates chosen by the actuary should vary by sex and attained age. Table 8 compares the rates of mortality improvement from several sources. For example, based on this information, an assumption for mortality improvement over the next 20 years

for males might be 1.25 percent at age 65 decreasing to 0.50 percent at age 90 and over. For female annuitants, a reasonable assumption might be 1.50 percent at age 65 decreasing to 0.75 percent at age 90 and over.

TABLE 8

RATES OF MORTALITY IMPROVEMENT—COMPARISONS

Age	G	H	P76	Canada Life Tables Improvement to 1986 from			SSA *Study No. 105* Improvement from		CPP 11th Report Improvement from 1986 to 2100
				1976	1966	1956	1990 to 2000	1990 to 2030	
Male									
55	1.60	1.60	0.50	2.35	1.53	1.07	1.46	0.86	
60	1.50	1.50	0.50	1.97	1.39	0.99	1.46	0.84	0.56
65	1.50	1.50	0.50	1.45	1.05	0.71	1.08	0.63	
70	1.35	1.35	0.50	1.23	0.75	0.52	0.83	0.55	0.48
75	1.25	1.25	0.50	0.84	0.65	0.53	0.63	0.49	
80	1.25	1.25	0.50	0.70	0.53	0.54	0.54	0.47	0.44
85	1.25	0.95	0.50	0.49	0.44	0.37	0.47	0.46	
90	1.10	0.60	0.30				0.46	0.47	0.45
95	1.00	0.26	0.10						
100	0.25	0.00	0.00						
Female									
55	1.85	1.85	1.30	1.63	1.43	1.45	1.09	0.66	
60	1.75	1.75	1.40	1.36	1.40	1.51	0.64	0.51	0.50
65	1.75	1.75	1.50	1.39	1.41	1.46	0.30	0.35	
70	1.75	1.75	1.60	1.44	1.42	1.47	0.60	0.47	0.53
75	1.60	1.60	1.75	1.21	1.49	1.56	0.97	0.62	
80	1.50	1.50	1.90	1.29	1.48	1.39	1.15	0.72	0.56
85	1.50	1.20	1.60	0.98	1.14	0.99	1.05	0.72	
90	1.35	0.70	1.20				0.79	0.66	0.60
95	1.25	0.35	0.80						
100	0.50	0.00	0.40						

4. The generation approach is preferred for determining mortality rates which include improvement. The use of a static table may be used as an approximation, but such a table should be tested for its continued appropriateness from year to year, and updated where necessary. This is because, compared to a generation table, a static table will tend to release margins more quickly.

BIBLIOGRAPHY

Title/Subject	Scale (S)	Source
"A New Mortality Basis for Annuities" by Wilmer A. Jenkins and Edward A. Lew	A and B	*TSA* I (1949), p. 369
"Group Annuity Mortality" by Ray M. Peterson	C	*TSA* IV (1952), p. 246
1971 Annuity Mortality Tables	D and E	*TSA* XXIII, Part I (1971)
Report of the Committee to Recommend a New Mortality Basis for Individual Annuity Valuation (Derivation of the 1983 Table *a*)	G	*TSA* XXXIII (1981), p. 675
Development of the 1983 Group Annuity Mortality Table, Committee on Annuities	H	*TSA* XXXV (1983), p. 859
Population Mortality—Canada		Canada Life Tables (quinquennial to 1985–87)
Social Insurance—Canada		10th and 11th Statutory Reports on the Canada Pension Plan
Social Insurance—United States		*Actuarial Study No. 105* "Population Projections: 1989"
"The Effects of Mortality on Individual Annuities" by Naftali Teitelbaum	I and J	*TSA* XL, Part II (1988), p. 653
"Mortality Projections Based on Population Data" by Donald M. Keith	P76	CIA paper (December 1979) Discussed at March 1980 CIA general membership meeting
Mortality Trends		Panel Discussion #3 CIA *Proceedings* 1985–86 Volume XVII, No. 1, p. 55

REPORT OF THE LIFE INSURANCE MARKETING AND RESEARCH ASSOCIATION, INC.

I. 1987–88 LONG-TERM ORDINARY LAPSE SURVEY IN THE UNITED STATES*

PREFACE

This report was prepared in the Financial Research Department of the Life Insurance Marketing and Research Association, Inc. LIMRA has given the Society of Actuaries permission to reproduce this study as part of the Society's expansion of its experience studies. Discussions of this report as well as of any experience study are encouraged. LIMRA and the Society intend to work together to expand this report and seek additional data contributors. The Canadian version of this study appears as Part II.

INTRODUCTION

Annual Survey

This annual long-term lapse study examines the lapsation of ordinary insurance in the U.S. between 1987 and 1988 policy anniversaries. It is designed to assist companies with developing new products and in monitoring marketing and product performance.

In past reports, lapse rates were percentages of face amounts in force at the beginning of 1987 policy anniversaries that lapse on or before 1988 policy anniversaries. (See Appendix A for the definitions used in this study.) This year, the report also examines the percent of policies in force at the beginning of 1987 policy anniversaries that lapse on or before 1988 policy anniversaries.

Lapse rates by face amount and number of policies are measured for seven types of ordinary insurance plans:

- Traditional whole life
- Interest-sensitive whole life
- Individual pension trust
- Graded-premium whole life—Type 1 (traditional type premium)
- Graded-premium whole life—Type 2 (yearly renewable term, YRT, type premium)

- YRT
- Level face amount term (excluding YRT).

Universal life persistency is examined in a separate report.

Lapse rates are measured for policy years 1, 2, 3–5, 6–10, and 11 and over. These policy years correspond to issue years 1987, 1986, 1985–1983, 1982–1978, and 1977 and earlier.

The report touches on each of the seven products, highlighting certain details. The report examines trends in whole life and YRT lapse rates for a constant group of companies that participated in both this year's and last year's studies. Average face amount persisting and lapsing throughout the year are analyzed for whole life and YRT, as are variations of lapse rates by company for these two products. At the end of the report, quartiles and averages are given for the products. Appendix A supplies definitions of in-force business, lapses, and products.

In-Depth Survey

The report also presents an in-depth look at lapse rates for YRT on these bases:

- Number of policies
- Face amount
- Annualized premium.

For each of these measures, the in-depth section shows lapse rates for specific issue ages by policy year. Issue ages include 20–29, 30–39, 40–49, 50–59, and all issue ages combined. Policy years include individual years 1–10 and combined policy years 11 and over.

A look at a constant group of companies that participated in the 1983–1984 study and the 1987–1988 study is included.

ABOUT THE SAMPLE

Twenty-five companies participated in this year's study. Twenty-four of these companies provided both face amount lapsing and the number of policies lapsing; one company was able to provide only face amount lapsing. Table A shows the total face amount in force at the beginning of the 1987–1988 policy year; Table B shows the total number of policies in force at the beginning of the 1987–1988 policy year.

TABLE A

FACE AMOUNT IN FORCE (BILLIONS) ON 1987 ANNIVERSARIES
(25 COMPANIES)

Issue Year	Traditional Whole Life	Interest-Sensitive Whole Life	Individual Pension Trust	Graded-Premium Type 1	Graded-Premium Type 2	Level Term	
						YRT	Other
1987*	$ 47.0	$ 8.5	$ 1.9	$ 2.0	$ 1.7	$ 67.2	$ 7.2
Before 1987	268.5	42.5	9.6	8.7	18.3	172.4	20.0
Total In Force	$315.5	$51.0	$11.5	$10.7	$20.0	$239.6	$27.2

*For issue year 1987, amounts in force on 1987 anniversaries correspond to amounts sold during that year.

TABLE B

NUMBER OF POLICIES IN FORCE (THOUSANDS) ON 1987 ANNIVERSARIES
(24 COMPANIES)

Issue Year	Traditional Whole Life	Interest-Sensitive Whole Life	Individual Pension Trust	Graded-Premium Type 1	Graded-Premium Type 2	Level Term	
						YRT	Other
1987*	1,090	133	37	20	6	412	105
Before 1987	18,320	650	324	180	89	1,227	570
Total In Force	19,410	783	361	200	95	1,639	675

*For issue year 1987, amounts in force on 1987 anniversaries correspond to amounts sold during that year.

LAPSE RATES BY PRODUCT TYPE

As a quick overview, Table C summarizes median face amount lapse rates by policy year, and Table D summarizes median policy count lapse rates by policy year.

TABLE C

PERCENTAGE OF FACE AMOUNT LAPSING BY PRODUCT TYPE
(25 COMPANIES)

Policy Year	Traditional Whole Life	Interest-Sensitive Whole Life	Individual Pension Trust	Graded-Premium Type 1	Graded-Premium Type 2	Level Term	
						YRT	Other
1	16.7%	16.4%	16.6%	—	—	17.8%	14.6%
2	11.5	14.2	12.0	—	—	18.7	15.2
3–5	10.5	9.7	15.6	13.1%	20.3%	17.2	15.4
6–10	11.3	—	14.2	11.8	18.0	13.9	12.5
11 and Over	8.2	—	10.0	8.2	—	9.4	8.9

—Insufficient data.

TABLE D

PERCENTAGE OF POLICIES LAPSING BY PRODUCT TYPE
(24 COMPANIES)

Policy Year	Traditional Whole Life	Interest-Sensitive Whole Life	Individual Pension Trust	Graded-Premium Type 1	Graded-Premium Type 2	Level Term	
						YRT	Other
1	17.1%	14.0%	16.7%	—	—	19.2%	14.4%
2	10.7	13.5	20.6	—	—	18.5	19.3
3–5	8.6	7.5	16.5	10.8%	22.1%	17.0	17.1
6–10	9.5	—	15.8	10.6	17.5	13.6	12.2
11 and Over	6.0	—	9.6	6.9	—	10.9	9.3

—Insufficient data.

LAPSE RATES BY COMPANY SIZE

Figure 1 shows median face amount lapse rates for *traditional whole life*. These lapse rates for all companies range from 16.7 percent in policy year 1, to 8.2 percent in policy years 11 and over. Lapse rates fluctuate between 10.5 percent and 11.5 percent in the middle durations. Large writers of whole life ($10 billion or more) have lower lapse rates than small writers in all durations. For large writers, the first-year lapse rate is 15.1 percent, which is about twice as large as the lapse rates in their remaining durations. For small writers, the first-year lapse rate is 17.7 percent, which decreases to 8.9 percent by policy years 11 and over.

Figure 1 — Median Face Amount Lapse Rates for Traditional Whole Life

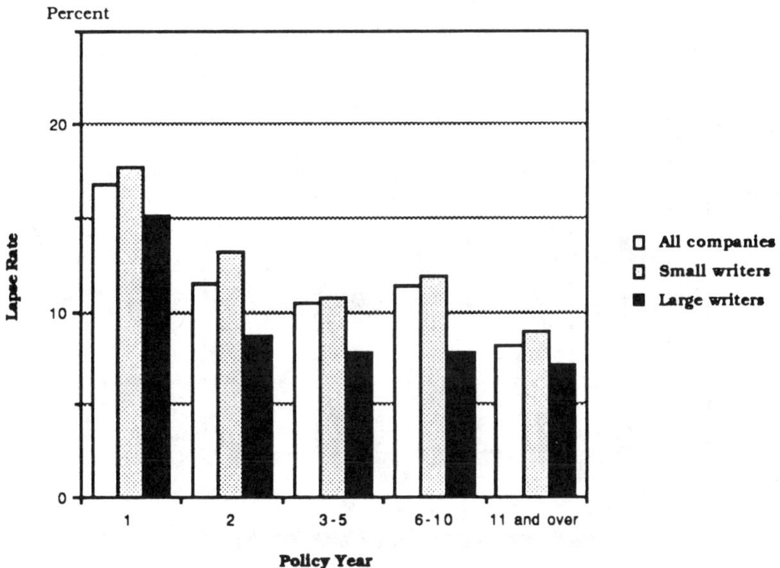

Figure 2 shows median face amount lapse rates for *yearly renewable term* insurance. For all companies, lapse rates peak in duration 2 at 18.7 percent and then decrease to 9.4 percent by policy years 11 and over. Companies that write a large amount of yearly renewable term insurance ($5 billion or more) exhibit lower lapse rates than small writers, especially in policy year 2, policy years 3–5, and policy years 6–10. For large writers, the lapse rates range from 17.5 percent in policy year 1, to 8.9 percent in policy years 11 and over. For small writers, the first-year lapse rate is 18.1 pecent; the lapse rate is 11.3 percent in policy years 11 and over.

Figure 2 — Median Face Amount Lapse Rates for Yearly Renewable Term

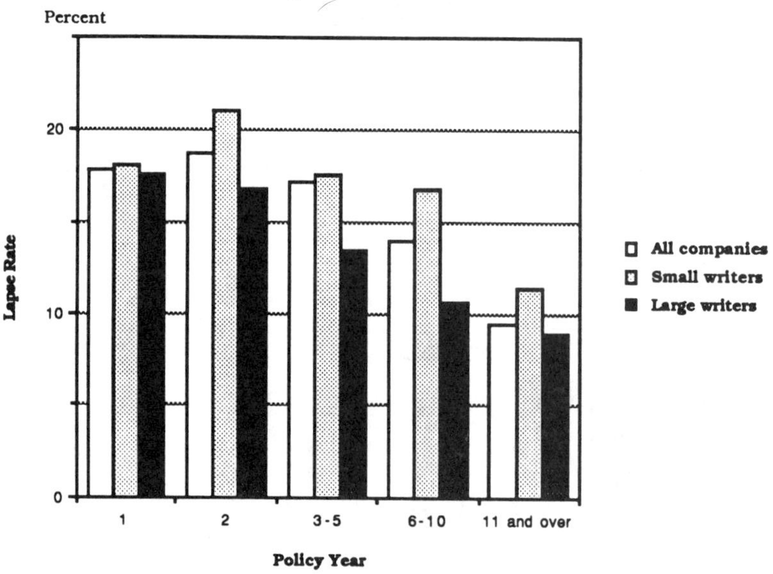

LAPSE RATES BY FACE AMOUNT AND NUMBER OF POLICIES

Figure 3 shows median lapse rates by face amount and number of policies for *traditional whole life*. Lapse rates by number of policies are lower than lapse rates by face amount in all but policy year 1. Lapse rates by face amount range from 16.7 percent in policy year 1, to 8.2 percent in policy years 11 and over; lapse rates by number of policies range from 17.1 percent in policy year 1, to 6 percent in policy years 11 and over.

Figure 3 — Median Lapse Rates for Traditional Whole Life

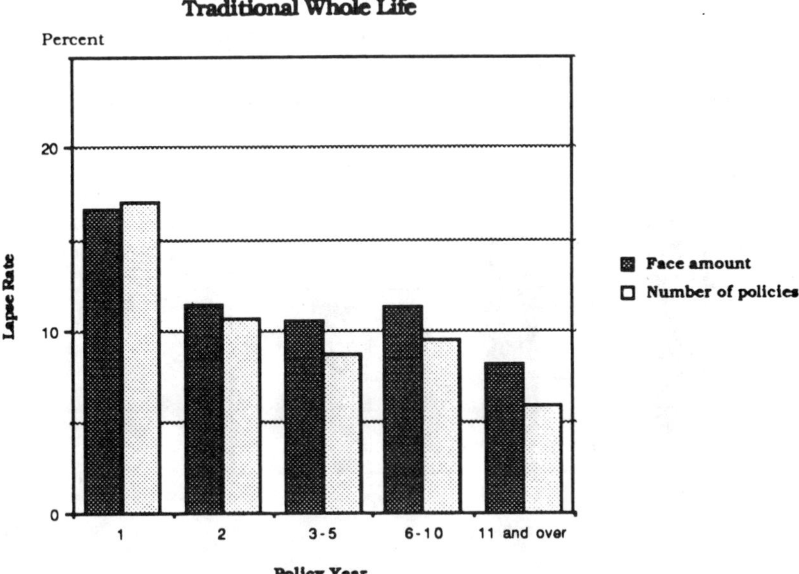

Figure 4 shows median lapse rates by face amount and number of policies for *interest-sensitive whole life*. Data are shown only for the first three durations because of limited data in the older policy years. Lapse rates decrease in both measures through the first five policy years. Lapse rates by face amount range from 16.4 percent to 9.7 percent, and lapse rates by number of policies range from 14 percent to 7.5 percent.

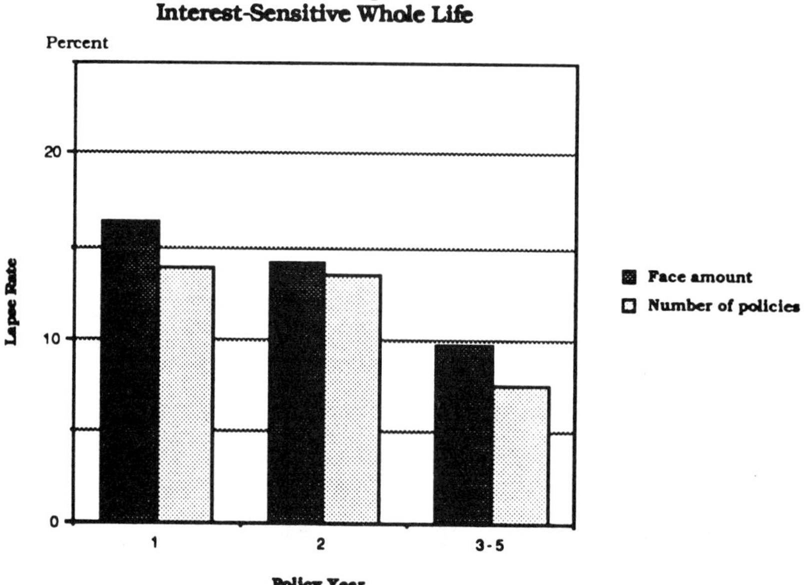

Figure 4 — Median Lapse Rates for Interest-Sensitive Whole Life

Figure 5 shows median lapse rates by face amount and number of policies for *individual pension trust*. For both measures lapse rates are close in all durations except for policy year 2. The lapse rate for this duration by face amount is 12 percent while by number of policies it is 20.6 percent.

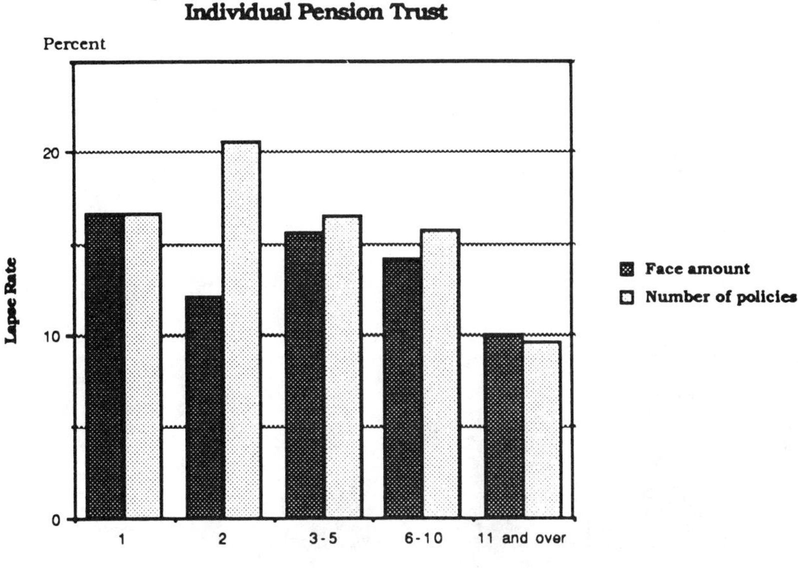

Figure 6 shows median lapse rates by face amount and number of policies for *graded-premium whole life—Type 1*. Because of insufficient data for the first two policy years, data are shown only for policy years 3 and over. Lapse rates by number of policies are lower than face amount lapse rates in all three durations. Lapse rates by face amount begin with 13.1 percent in policy years 3–5 and end with 8.2 percent in policy years 11 and over; lapse rates by number of policies range from 10.8 percent to 6.9 percent in these durations.

Figure 6 — Median Lapse Rates for Graded-Premium Whole Life — Type 1

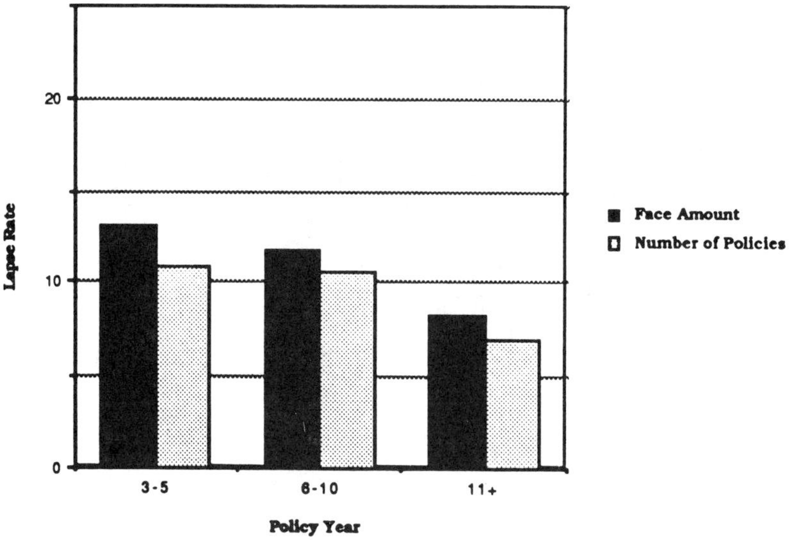

Figure 7 shows median lapse rates by face amount and number of policies for *graded-premium whole life—Type 2*. The limited amount of data in recent policy years points to the effect of the Tax Reform Act of 1984 on the sale of this product. Graded-premium whole life—Type 2 has the highest lapse rates among all products.

Figure 7 — Median Lapse Rates for Graded-Premium Whole Life — Type 2

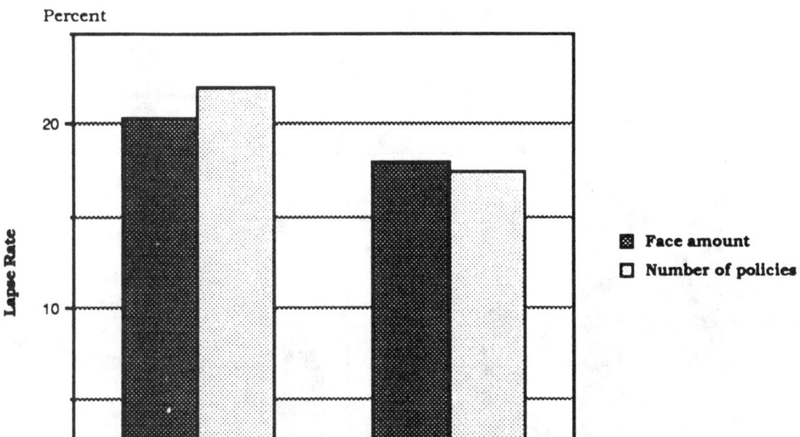

Figure 8 shows median lapse rates by face amount and number of policies for *yearly renewable term*. Face amount lapse rates peak in policy year 2 at 18.7 percent. Lapse rates decrease through the next durations ending at 9.4 percent in policy years 11 and over. Lapse rates by number of policies decrease through the durations beginning at 19.2 percent in policy year 1 and ending at 10.9 percent in policy years 11 and over.

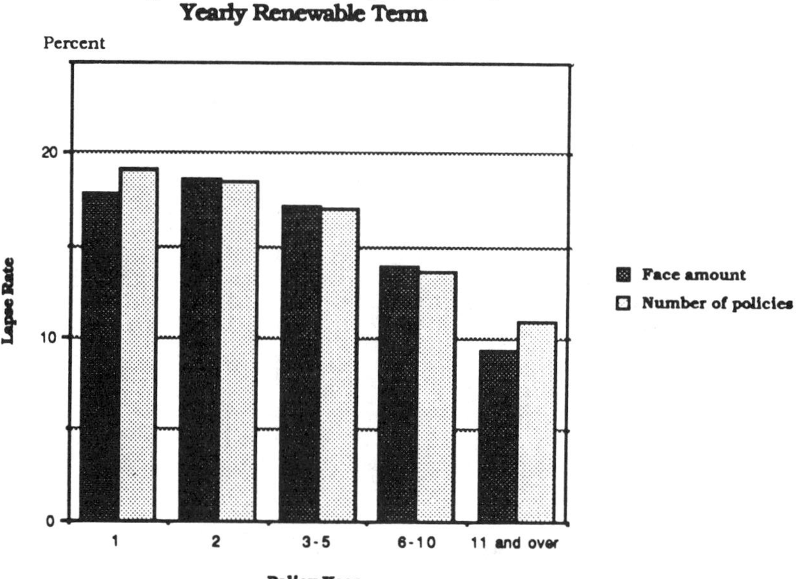

Figure 9 shows median lapse rates by face amount and number of policies for *level term (excluding YRT)* which includes products such as five-year renewable term and ten-year renewable term. Lapse rates for both measures are very close in early and later durations. For the middle years, policy year 2 and policy years 3–5, lapse rates by number of policies are higher.

Figure 9 — Median Lapse Rates for Level Term (excluding YRT)

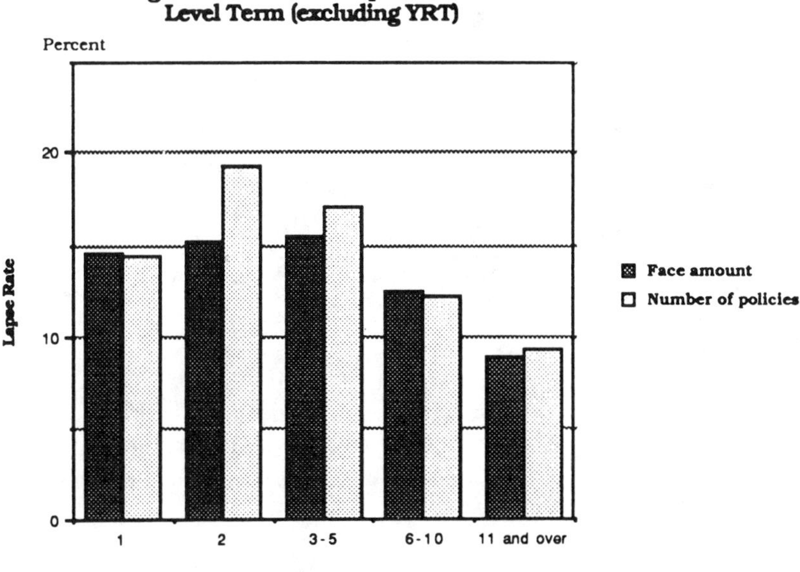

AVERAGE FACE AMOUNT PERSISTING AND LAPSING

Medians and averages are shown in Table E for average face amount persisting and lapsing for traditional whole life. Overall, the average face amount persisting is slightly less than the average face amount lapsing. Medians of average face amount persisting and lapsing are close to 50 percent less than the corresponding averages in the first five policy years.

TABLE E

AVERAGE FACE AMOUNT PERSISTING AND LAPSING FOR TRADITIONAL WHOLE LIFE (24 COMPANIES)

	Average Face Amount Persisting		Average Face Amount Lapsing	
Policy Year	Median	Average*	Median	Average*
1	$26,561	$56,120	$26,608	$56,401
2	24,616	50,417	27,199	57,954
3–5	22,307	49,009	26,249	47,094
6–10	17,821	28,411	21,771	31,585
11 and Over	7,315	8,683	9,987	12,912

*All companies receive equal weight; company size does not affect the results.

Table F shows average face amount persisting and lapsing for yearly renewable term; medians and averages are provided for both measures. In policy year 1, policy year 2, and policy years 11 and over, the medians and averages for average face amount persisting are greater than the average face amount lapsing medians and averages.

TABLE F

AVERAGE FACE AMOUNT PERSISTING AND LAPSING FOR YEARLY RENEWABLE TERM (23 COMPANIES)

	Average Face Amount Persisting		Average Face Amount Lapsing	
Policy Year	Median	Average*	Median	Average*
1	$161,075	$166,619	$133,832	$159,146
2	158,180	174,873	159,713	171,538
3–5	128,948	146,847	132,015	144,592
6–10	101,821	107,317	109,953	113,480
11 and over	81,896	89,192	66,438	81,543

*All companies receive equal weight: company size does not affect the results.

TRENDS IN WHOLE LIFE LAPSE RATES

Figure 10 shows 1987 and 1988 face amount lapse rates for a constant group of companies. The average lapse rates for these companies have decreased in all durations. However, the decrease in policy year 2 and policy years 11 and over is slight.

Figure 10 — Whole Life Lapse Rates for Constant Group

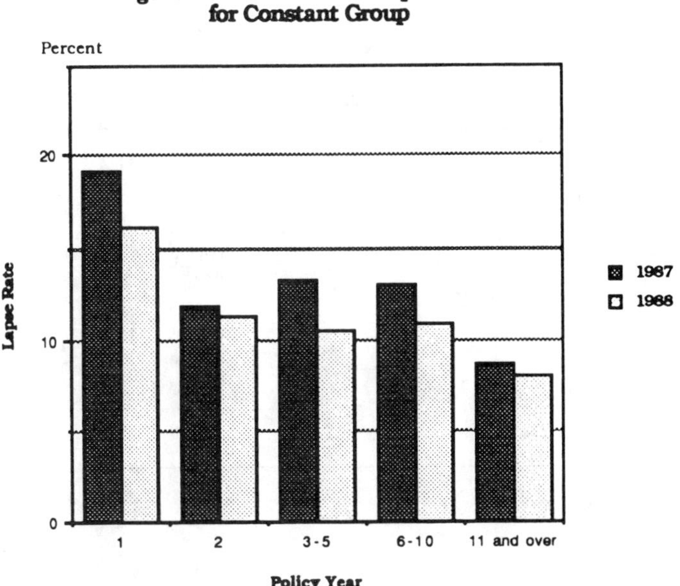

Table G summarizes the number of companies with decreases in face amount lapse rates and the number of companies with increases in face amount lapse rates.

TABLE G

INCREASES AND DECREASES IN WHOLE LIFE LAPSE RATES

	Number of Companies	Average Lapse Rate	
		1987	1988
Policy Year 1			
Increase	9	12.8	15.1
Decrease	11	24.3	18.5
All	20	19.1	17.0
Policy Year 2			
Increase	4	9.4	10.5
Decrease	16	13.1	11.1
All	20	12.0	11.4
Policy Years 3–5			
Increase	1	10.0	10.5
Decrease	19	13.0	10.2
All	20	12.8	10.2
Policy Years 6–10			
Increase	1	15.3	16.8
Decrease	19	12.6	10.4
All	20	12.8	10.7
Policy Years 11 and Over			
Increase	4	8.7	9.2
Decrease	15	9.0	8.0
All	19	8.9	8.3

TRENDS IN YEARLY RENEWABLE TERM LAPSE RATES

Figure 11 shows 1987 and 1988 face amount lapse rates for a constant group of companies. Yearly renewable term lapse rates have increased in policy year 1, policy year 2, and policy years 3–5 and have decreased in the two later durations.

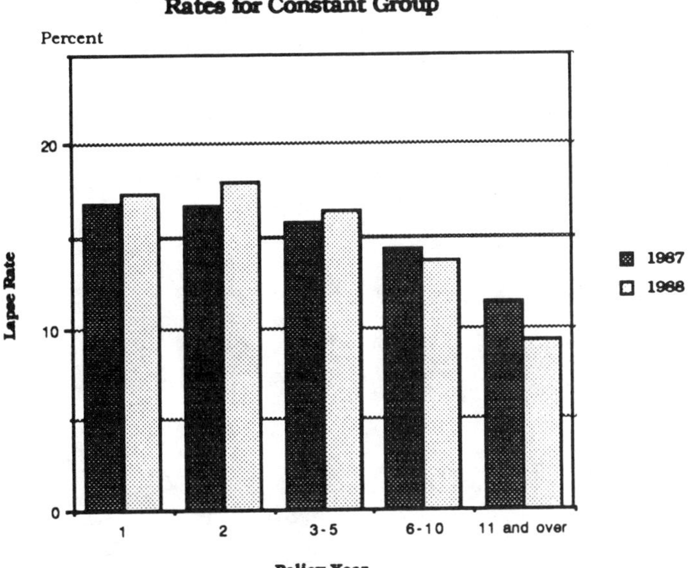

Table H summarizes the number of companies with decreases in face amount lapse rates and the number of companies with increases in lapse rates.

TABLE H

INCREASES AND DECREASES IN YEARLY RENEWABLE TERM LAPSE RATES

	Number of Companies	Average Lapse Rate	
		1987	1988
Policy Year 1			
Increase	10	14.2	21.1
Decrease	9	17.9	15.0
All	19	16.0	18.2
Policy Year 2			
Increase	12	17.1	19.8
Decrease	8	21.9	17.0
All	20	19.0	18.7
Policy Years 3–5			
Increase	5	16.4	22.2
Decrease	14	16.2	14.0
All	19	16.3	16.1
Policy Years 6–10			
Increase	6	15.6	20.7
Decrease	13	14.5	12.1
All	19	14.8	14.8
Policy Years 11 and Over			
Increase	4	9.2	12.8
Decrease	9	11.9	9.8
All	13	11.1	10.7

VARIATION OF LAPSES AMONG COMPANIES

Table I shows the variations of façe amount lapse rates by companies for traditional whole life insurance. Fifty-eight percent of the companies have lapse rates greater than 15 percent in policy year 1. In policy years 3–5, all but two companies have lapse rates less than 15 percent. All of the companies have lapse rates less than 15 percent in policy years 11 and over; 78 percent are below 10 percent.

TABLE I

VARIATIONS OF WHOLE LIFE LAPSE RATES

	Policy Year		
Lapse Rates	1	3–5	11 and Over
20% and Over	9	0	0
15–19.99%	5	2	0
10–14.99	4	11	5
Under 10.00	6	12	18
Total Number of Companies	24	25	23

Table J shows the variations of face amount lapse rates for yearly renewable term insurance. In policy year 1, 65 percent of the companies have lapse rates greater than 15 percent. In policy years 3–5, 61 percent of the companies have lapse rates above 15 percent. Lapse rates in policy years 11 and over improve; only one company has a lapse rate greater than 15 percent. Fifty-six percent of the companies in this duration have lapse rates less than 10 percent.

TABLE J

VARIATIONS OF YEARLY RENEWABLE TERM LAPSE RATES

	Policy Year		
Lapse Rates	1	3–5	11 and Over
20% and Over	6	3	0
15–19.99%	9	11	1
10–14.99	6	5	6
Under 10.00	2	4	9
Total Number of Companies	23	23	16

LAPSE RATES BY FACE AMOUNT

TABLE 1

TRADITIONAL WHOLE LIFE
(25 COMPANIES)

Policy Year	First Quartile	Median	Third Quartile	Average*
1	9.1%	16.7%	24.4%	17.2%
2	7.3	11.5	16.6	11.6
3–5	7.0	10.5	12.7	9.9
6–10	7.8	11.3	12.6	10.7
11 and Over	7.1	8.2	9.8	8.5

*All companies receive equal weight; company size does not affect the results.

TABLE 2

INTEREST-SENSITIVE WHOLE LIFE
(9 COMPANIES)

Policy Year	Median	Average*
1	16.4%	17.5%
2	14.2	15.5
3–5	9.7	8.1

*All companies receive equal weight; company size does not affect the results.

TABLE 3

INDIVIDUAL PENSION TRUST
(15 COMPANIES)

Policy Year	First Quartile	Median	Third Quartile	Average*
1	9.6%	16.6%	25.6%	16.3%
2	7.0	12.0	20.4	16.7
3–5	8.5	15.6	21.6	16.6
6–10	8.1	14.2	22.1	15.0
11 and Over	6.3	10.0	12.6	10.4

*All companies receive equal weight; company size does not affect the results.

TABLE 4

GRADED-PREMIUM WHOLE LIFE—TYPE 1
(8 COMPANIES)

Policy Year	Median	Average*
3–5	13.1%	14.9%
6–10	11.8	11.8
11 and Over	8.2	8.6

*All companies receive equal weight; company size does not affect the results.

TABLE 5

GRADED-PREMIUM WHOLE LIFE—TYPE 2
(7 COMPANIES)

Policy Year	Median	Average*
3–5	20.3%	20.3%
6–10	18.0	16.5

*All companies receive equal weight; company size does not affect the results.

TABLE 6

YEARLY RENEWABLE TERM
(24 COMPANIES)

Policy Year	First Quartile	Median	Third Quartile	Average*
1	14.4%	17.8%	21.6%	18.9%
2	14.8	18.7	24.5	19.0
3–5	13.2	17.2	18.7	16.4
6–10	10.0	13.9	17.9	14.7
11 and Over	7.2	9.4	13.4	10.1

*All companies receive equal weight; company size does not affect the results.

TABLE 7

OTHER LEVEL TERM
(17 COMPANIES)

Policy Year	First Quartile	Median	Third Quartile	Average*
1	12.5%	14.6%	22.1%	17.2%
2	12.3	15.2	19.9	16.5
3–5	12.2	15.4	21.7	17.6
6–10	10.4	12.5	17.8	16.1
11 and Over	6.7	8.9	12.2	9.6

*All companies receive equal weight; company size does not affect the results.

LAPSE RATES BY NUMBER OF POLICIES

TABLE 8

TRADITIONAL WHOLE LIFE
(24 COMPANIES)

Policy Year	First Quartile	Median	Third Quartile	Average*
1	10.1%	17.1%	21.7%	17.3%
2	8.1	10.7	13.6	10.8
3–5	6.1	8.6	11.1	8.8
6–10	6.8	9.5	11.4	9.3
11 and Over	5.2	6.0	7.2	6.3

*All companies receive equal weight; company size does not affect the results.

TABLE 9

INTEREST-SENSITIVE WHOLE LIFE
(7 COMPANIES)

Policy Year	Median	Average*
1	14.0%	15.5%
2	13.5	13.3
3–5	7.5	7.2

*All companies receive equal weight; company size does not affect the results.

TABLE 10

INDIVIDUAL PENSION TRUST
(13 COMPANIES)

Policy Year	First Quartile	Median	Third Quartile	Average*
1	12.5%	16.7%	23.0%	17.5%
2	12.1	20.6	23.6	18.8
3–5	13.1	16.5	28.5	20.3
6–10	11.2	15.8	26.9	17.3
11 and Over	7.8	9.6	14.7	12.3

*All companies receive equal weight; company size does not affect the results.

TABLE 11

GRADED-PREMIUM WHOLE LIFE—TYPE 1
(6 COMPANIES)

Policy Year	Median	Average*
3–5	10.8%	12.2%
6–10	10.6	11.3
11 and Over	6.9	7.9

*All companies receive equal weight; company size does not affect the results.

TABLE 12

GRADED-PREMIUM WHOLE LIFE—TYPE 2
(5 COMPANIES)

Policy Year	Median	Average*
3–5	22.1%	21.1%
6–10	17.5	18.8

*All companies receive equal weight; company size does not affect the results.

TABLE 13

YEARLY RENEWABLE TERM
(23 COMPANIES)

Policy Year	First Quartile	Median	Third Quartile	Average*
1	15.7%	19.2%	22.1%	19.2%
2	13.6	18.5	24.5	19.0
3–5	12.7	17.0	18.6	16.2
6–10	11.1	13.6	16.0	13.8
11 and Over	7.8	10.9	12.9	10.7

*All companies receive equal weight; company size does not affect results.

TABLE 14

OTHER LEVEL TERM
(15 COMPANIES)

Policy Year	First Quartile	Median	Third Quartile	Average*
1	13.0%	14.4%	26.1%	17.7%
2	13.0	19.3	20.5	17.6
3–5	13.1	17.1	21.5	17.2
6–10	9.0	12.2	15.6	13.2
11 and Over	6.1	9.3	11.8	9.8

*All companies receive equal weight; company size does not affect the results.

Lapse Rates by Policy Year

TABLE 15

PERCENTAGE OF POLICIES LAPSING
(17 COMPANIES)

Policy Year	First Quartile	Median	Third Quartile	Average*
1	14.0%	19.3%	22.7%	18.4%
2	14.2	17.8	24.6	19.1
3	12.9	17.3	23.0	17.2
4	12.3	14.2	17.0	14.6
5	11.5	14.5	15.9	13.8
6	11.3	13.4	15.2	13.4
7	10.5	13.3	15.8	13.4
8	10.1	12.0	14.2	12.5
9	9.5	10.9	16.2	12.1
10	9.0	11.6	17.8	12.8
11 and Over	8.0	10.1	12.9	10.5

*All companies receive equal weight; company size does not affect the results.

TABLE 16

PERCENTAGE OF FACE AMOUNT LAPSING
(18 COMPANIES)

Policy Year	First Quartile	Median	Third Quartile	Average*
1	12.2%	17.2%	21.7%	17.0%
2	14.2	18.6	24.6	19.3
3	12.9	16.6	21.0	16.9
4	11.2	15.2	19.5	17.2
5	10.9	13.9	17.1	14.3
6	10.1	13.3	17.8	13.8
7	10.7	12.8	15.8	13.1
8	9.7	13.2	15.2	13.2
9	9.5	12.8	16.1	13.2
10	9.6	11.5	16.9	13.8
11 and Over	7.9	9.1	13.3	10.2

*All companies receive equal weight; company size does not affect the results.

TABLE 17

PERCENTAGE OF ANNUALIZED PREMIUM LAPSING
(15 COMPANIES)

Policy Year	First Quartile	Median	Third Quartile	Average*
1	13.5%	16.7%	20.9%	16.8%
2	13.5	16.7	21.7	17.6
3	13.7	16.5	21.3	18.2
4	11.6	13.6	19.5	16.3
5	11.4	12.9	17.4	14.2
6	9.9	12.6	16.3	14.3
7	9.4	11.7	15.0	12.1
8	8.9	12.0	13.8	12.1
9	10.2	13.7	18.4	15.0
10	8.0	11.5	15.3	13.6
11 and Over	7.6	9.5	13.1	10.1

*All companies receive equal weight; company size does not affect the results.

Median Lapse Rates by Issue Age

TABLE 18

PERCENTAGE OF POLICIES LAPSING

	Issue Ages			
Policy Year	20–29	30–39	40–49	50–59
1	24.4%	18.6%	16.9%	15.8%
2	22.6	16.5	16.9	14.9
3	20.3	16.0	13.4	16.3
4	18.1	13.9	13.3	13.8
5	16.3	13.0	14.7	15.0
6	14.9	12.2	11.7	11.2
7	12.0	13.0	11.8	14.7
8	13.1	10.8	13.5	—
9	10.2	11.2	10.3	—
10	9.2	10.8	11.4	—
11 and Over	8.0	8.3	11.3	—

—Insufficient data.

TABLE 19

PERCENTAGE OF FACE AMOUNT LAPSING

Policy Year	Issue Ages			
	20–29	30–39	40–49	50–59
1	23.0%	18.1%	14.7%	14.1%
2	22.3	17.4	18.3	18.7
3	18.4	15.1	15.8	16.8
4	16.0	12.0	12.9	14.2
5	15.1	11.7	12.2	16.7
6	13.2	12.4	11.4	11.1
7	11.3	12.1	12.5	13.7
8	13.2	11.5	13.8	10.7
9	12.7	11.5	14.6	—
10	8.2	10.5	11.5	—
11 and Over	10.6	8.8	13.0	—

—Insufficient data.

TABLE 20

PERCENTAGE OF ANNUALIZED PREMIUM LAPSING

Policy Year	Issue Ages			
	20–29	30–39	40–49	50–59
1	26.0%	18.5%	15.6%	13.8%
2	21.5	16.9	15.4	17.1
3	19.1	16.6	15.5	18.0
4	17.6	13.2	13.8	15.5
5	16.0	12.0	12.2	15.5
6	14.3	12.0	11.2	12.2
7	13.5	10.7	12.3	11.8
8	14.4	11.6	14.0	11.9
9	12.7	12.6	16.9	—
10	—	11.7	—	—
11 and Over	—	8.7	12.4	—

—Insufficient data.

Three Measures of Lapsation — Companies Reporting All Three Measures

TABLE 21

COMPARISON OF MEDIAN LAPSE RATES BY UNIT OF MEASURE
(15 COMPANIES)

Policy Year	Lapse Rates By: Number of Policies	Face Amount	Annualized Premium
1	19.3%	17.1%	16.7%
2	16.6	17.5	16.7
3	16.9	16.2	15.7
4	14.7	13.6	13.4
5	13.8	13.3	12.4
6	13.4	12.7	12.6
7	12.8	12.5	11.7
8	11.9	12.9	12.1
9	10.5	12.8	12.8
10	11.6	11.5	12.6
11 and Over	9.3	9.0	9.5

Average Size Lapsing and Persisting

TABLE 22

AVERAGE FACE AMOUNT PERSISTING AND LAPSING
(17 COMPANIES)

	Median		Average	
Policy Year	Lapsing	Persisting	Lapsing	Persisting
1	$137,000	$165,000	$143,000	$165,000
2	161,000	163,000	157,000	160,000
3	142,000	146,000	143,000	145,000
4	128,000	132,000	136,000	142,000
5	135,000	129,000	129,000	130,000
6	106,000	104,000	112,000	114,000
7	105,000	96,000	104,000	102,000
8	97,000	90,000	99,000	93,000
9	93,000	85,000	100,000	91,000
10	94,000	87,000	106,000	93,000
11 and Over	66,000	95,000	82,000	87,000

TABLE 23

ANNUALIZED PREMIUMS PER POLICY
(15 COMPANIES)

Policy Year	Median		Average	
	Lapsing	Persisting	Lapsing	Persisting
1	$320	$380	$350	$380
2	420	390	380	400
3	390	370	390	390
4	390	410	420	410
5	440	420	460	440
6	460	440	550	480
7	470	490	490	500
8	510	520	480	480
9	640	520	610	500
10	550	570	570	550
11 and Over	540	530	490	540

Distribution of In Force and Lapses

TABLE 24

DISTRIBUTION OF IN FORCE BY NUMBER OF POLICIES,
FACE AMOUNT, AND ANNUALIZED PREMIUM

Policy Year	Number of Policies	Face Amount	Annualized Premium
1	25.2%	29.1%	20.7%
2	19.0	21.4	17.1
3	14.2	14.3	13.0
4	10.7	10.4	10.8
5	14.0	12.8	16.5
6	7.7	6.4	9.9
7	3.2	2.4	4.6
8	2.0	1.4	2.9
9	1.0	0.7	1.4
10	0.6	0.3	0.8
11 and Over	2.3	0.7	2.2
	100.0%	100.0%	100.0%

TABLE 25

DISTRIBUTION OF LAPSES BY NUMBER OF POLICIES, FACE AMOUNT, AND ANNUALIZED PREMIUM

Policy Year	Number of Policies	Face Amount	Annualized Premium
1	29.0%	30.1%	23.0%
2	21.7	23.5	17.2
3	14.1	14.1	13.1
4	9.5	9.4	12.0
5	13.0	12.9	16.5
6	6.5	5.8	8.3
7	2.3	1.8	3.9
8	1.4	1.1	2.3
9	0.7	0.5	1.3
10	0.4	0.2	0.7
11 and Over	1.3	0.5	1.8
	100.0%	100.0%	100.0%

Early 1980s vs. Late 1980s (Constant Group of Companies)

TABLE 26

PERCENTAGE OF POLICIES LAPSING (12 COMPANIES)

	Median		Average*	
Policy Year	1984	1988	1984	1988
1	20.5%	21.5%	19.5%	21.4%
2	21.4	18.8	22.3	18.7
3	41.0	16.9	20.9	16.6
4	18.4	13.9	20.3	14.6
5	18.5	14.7	20.2	13.7

*All companies receive equal weight; company size does not affect the results.

TABLE 27

PERCENTAGE OF FACE AMOUNT LAPSING (12 COMPANIES)

	Median		Average*	
Policy Year	1984	1988	1984	1988
1	18.5%	17.9%	18.6%	19.7%
2	22.6	20.0	23.9	19.9
3	21.9	16.7	22.2	16.8
4	19.9	16.8	21.9	17.2
5	18.0	15.1	20.7	15.0

*All companies receive equal weight; company size does not affect the results.

TABLE 28

PERCENTAGE OF ANNUALIZED PREMIUM LAPSING
(8 COMPANIES)

Policy Year	Median		Average*	
	1984	1988	1984	1988
1	18.5%	19.9%	16.7%	19.7%
2	19.5	16.8	24.0	17.4
3	22.1	15.2	23.0	16.3
4	21.6	15.5	23.0	16.1
5	19.7	13.8	22.3	14.3

*All companies receive equal weight; company size does not affect the results.

TABLE 29

MEDIAN FACE AMOUNTS PER POLICY
(11 COMPANIES)

Policy Year	1984 Medians		1988 Medians	
	Lapsing	Persisting	Lapsing	Persisting
1	$ 90,000	$106,000	$135,000	$167,000
2	109,000	101,000	165,000	159,000
3	116,000	110,000	149,000	145,000
4	114,000	98,000	140,000	137,000
5	103,000	97,000	141,000	131,000

TABLE 30

AVERAGE FACE AMOUNTS PER POLICY
(11 COMPANIES)

Policy Year	1984 Averages*		1988 Averages*	
	Lapsing	Persisting	Lapsing	Persisting
1	$ 97,000	$108,000	$151,000	$178,000
2	111,000	102,000	169,000	167,000
3	115,000	106,000	158,000	155,000
4	110,000	101,000	153,000	149,000
5	107,000	99,000	146,000	142,000

*All companies receive equal weight; company size does not affect the results.

TABLE 31

MEDIAN ANNUALIZED PREMIUMS PER POLICY
(8 COMPANIES)

Policy Year	1984 Medians		1988 Medians	
	Lapsing	Persisting	Lapsing	Persisting
1	$300	$390	$430	$450
2	400	410	460	460
3	500	420	450	470
4	540	460	540	450
5	580	550	570	530

TABLE 32

AVERAGE ANNUALIZED PREMIUMS PER POLICY
(8 COMPANIES)

Policy Year	1984 Averages*		1988 Averages*	
	Lapsing	Persisting	Lapsing	Persisting
1	$320	$420	$440	$480
2	440	440	480	470
3	520	500	470	440
4	550	550	540	460
5	650	580	560	510

*All companies receive equal weight; company size does not affect the results.

APPENDIX A
DEFINITIONS OF IN-FORCE POLICIES AND LAPSES

In Force

A policy is considered in force if the first premium for the new policy year starting in 1987 is paid.

In-force business includes:

- Policies issued in 1987.
- Policies issued before 1987 where the premium due on the 1987 policy anniversary date is paid before the end of the grace period.

In-force business excludes:

- Policies that lapse before their 1987 anniversaries and that are on extended term or reduced paid-up status.
- Limited premium payment policies that are paid up.
- Single premium policies.

Examples of policies in force are:

- A policy issued in 1987 and the first premium is paid.
- A policy issued in 1986 and the premium due in the 13th policy month is paid.
- A policy issued in 1985 and the premium due in the 25th policy month is paid.

Lapse

A policy is considered a lapse if the first premium for the new policy year starting in 1987 is paid, but not all of the premium that comes due after the 1987 anniversary and before or on the 1988 anniversary date is paid.

Lapsed business includes:

- Policies surrendered after their 1987 anniversaries and before or on their 1988 anniversaries.
- Policies where a premium due after the 1987 anniversary and before or on the 1988 anniversary date is not paid by the end of the grace period.
- Term policies with renewal provisions that do not renew.
- Policies that go on extended term or reduced paid-up status.

Lapsed business excludes:

- Death claims.
- Automatic premium loaned policies.
- Expiries and maturities.
- Conversions.
- Policies that lapse during the 1987–1988 policy year but are reinstated before or on their 1988 anniversaries.
- Policies not taken.
- Policies where the waiver of premium provision applies.

Examples of policies that lapse are:

- A policy issued in 1987 and the policyowner has paid the first premium. If any premium for policy months 2 through 13 is not paid by the end of the grace period, the policy is a lapse.
- A policy issued in 1986 and the policyowner has paid the 13th policy month premium. If any premium for policy months 14 through 25 is not paid by the end of the grace period, the policy is a lapse.
- A policy issued in 1985 and the policyowner has paid the 25th policy month premium. If any premium for policy months 26 through 37 is not paid by the end of the grace period, the policy is a lapse.

An example of a policy that does not lapse is:

- A policy issued in 1986 is not considered a lapse if the 13th policy month premium and all premiums for policy months 14 through 25 are paid.

PRODUCT DEFINITIONS

Traditional Whole Life

Includes:
- Whole life policies with level premiums or indeterminate premiums with *fixed* cash values including continuous-pay and limited-pay plans.

Excludes:
- Universal life
- Variable life with flexible premiums
- Variable life with fixed premiums
- Interest-sensitive whole life
- Endowments
- Policies that are combinations of whole life and term plans
- Individual pension trust plans.

Yearly Renewable Term

Includes:
- Term policies with level face amounts.

Excudes:
- Graded premium whole life—Types 1 and 2
- Term riders.

Level Term (Other Than YRT)

Excludes:
- Nonlevel term
- Term riders.

Individual Pension Trust

Includes:
- All policies sold on a pension trust basis.

Interest-Sensitive Whole Life

Includes:
- Whole life plans that credit cash values with current interest rates. Premiums may be level, may vanish, or may be adjusted periodically.

Excludes:
- Universal life
- Individual pension trust.

Graded-Premium Whole Life—Type 1

Includes:
- Traditional graded-premium whole life: The premium may increase annually for 5 to 10 years and then level off at a premium comparable to a whole life continuous-pay plan.

Excludes:
- Graded-premium whole life—Type 2
- Individual pension trust.

Graded-Premium Whole Life—Type 2

Includes:
- Nontraditional graded-premium whole life: The initial premium is competitive with yearly renewable term policies. The premium increases annually for 10 to 20 years and then becomes level. Usually, the policy has no cash value for the first 10 years. Some of the products developed before 1984 were designed to take advantage of Section 818 C of the tax code. With the Tax Reform Act of 1984, the advantages were substantially reduced.

II. 1987–88 LONG-TERM ORDINARY LAPSE SURVEY IN CANADA*

PREFACE

This report was prepared in the Financial Research Department of the Life Insurance Marketing and Research Association, Inc. LIMRA has given the Society of Actuaries permission to reproduce this study as part of the Society's expansion of its experience studies. Discussions of this report as well as of any experience study are encouraged. LIMRA and the Society intend to work together to expand this report and seek additional data contributors. The United States version of this study appears as Part I.

INTRODUCTION

Annual Survey

This annual long-term lapse study examines the lapsation of ordinary insurance in Canada between 1987 and 1988 policy anniversaries. It is designed to assist companies with developing new products and in monitoring marketing and product performance.

In past reports, lapse rates were percentages of face amounts in force at the beginning of 1987 policy anniversaries that lapse on or before 1988 policy anniversaries. (See Appendix A for the definitions used in this study.) This year, the report also examines the percent of policies in force at the beginning of 1987 policy anniversaries that lapse on or before 1988 policy anniversaries.

Face amount lapse rates are measured for five types of ordinary insurance plans:

- Traditional whole life
- Interest-sensitive whole life
- Permanent term (sometimes referred to as term to 100)
- Five-year renewable term (5-YRT)
- Level face amount term (excluding 5-YRT).

Lapse rates are measured for policy years 1, 2, 3–5, 6–10, and 11 and over. These policy years correspond to issue years 1987, 1986, 1985–1983, 1982–1978, and 1977 and earlier.

This report touches on each of the five products, highlighting certain details. The report also examines trends in whole life and 5-YRT lapse rates for a constant group of companies that participated in both this year's and last year's studies, as well as variations of lapse rates by company for whole life and 5-YRT. The end of the report has detailed tables showing various statistics for each product. Appendix A supplies definitions of in-force business, lapses, and products.

In-Depth Survey

The report also presents an in-depth look at lapse rates for five-year renewable term on three bases:

- Number of policies
- Face amount
- Annualized premium.

Lapse rates and average size policies are analyzed for individual policy years 1–10 and combined policy years 11 and over.

ABOUT THE SAMPLE

Eleven companies participated in the study; 10 of these companies provided both face amount lapsing and number of policies lapsing; one company was only able to provide face amount lapsing. Table A shows the total face amount in force at the beginning of the 1987–1988 policy year, while Table B shows the total number of policies in force at the beginning of the 1987–1988 policy year.

TABLE A

FACE AMOUNT IN FORCE (BILLIONS) ON 1987 ANNIVERSARIES
(11 COMPANIES)

Issue Year	Traditional Whole Life	Interest-Sensitive Whole Life	Permanent Term	Level Term	
				5-YRT	Other
1987*	$ 5.0	$ 4.4	$0.9	$ 3.0	$ 2.9
Before 1987	27.8	13.6	2.1	13.1	8.4
Total In Force	$32.8	$18.0	$3.0	$16.1	$11.3

*For issue year 1987, amounts in force on 1987 anniversaries correspond to amounts sold during that year.

TABLE B

NUMBER OF POLICIES IN FORCE (THOUSANDS) ON 1987 ANNIVERSARIES (10 COMPANIES)

Issue Year	Traditional Whole Life	Interest-Sensitive Whole Life	Permanent Term	Level Term	
				5-YRT	Other
1987*	112	82	9	23	17
Before 1987	1,799	306	21	123	71
Total In Force	1,911	388	30	146	88

*For issue year 1987, amounts in force on 1987 anniversaries correspond to amounts sold during that year.

LAPSE RATES BY PRODUCT TYPE

As a quick overview, Table C summarizes the products by showing the individual median lapse rates by policy year and face amount. Table D summarizes the products by policy year and number of policies.

TABLE C

SUMMARY OF MEDIAN LAPSE RATES BY FACE AMOUNT (11 COMPANIES)

Policy Year	Traditional Whole Life	Interest-Sensitive Whole Life	Permanent Term	Level Term	
				5-YRT	Other
1	11.8%	14.2%	7.4%	13.0%	10.9%
2	10.5	10.8	11.1	14.4	12.2
3–5	8.0	10.9	9.8	16.8	13.7
6–10	8.3	—	—	15.0	12.6
11 and Over	6.1	—	—	12.1	10.0

—Insufficient data.

TABLE D

SUMMARY OF MEDIAN LAPSE RATES BY NUMBER OF POLICIES (10 COMPANIES)

Policy Year	Traditional Whole Life	Interest-Sensitive Whole Life	Permanent Term	Level Term	
				5-YRT	Other
1	12.2%	14.9%	11.6%	14.1%	13.1%
2	9.8	11.3	12.3	14.9	14.9
3–5	7.9	10.4	10.6	16.7	14.3
6–10	8.7	—	—	13.0	12.5
11 and Over	5.7	—	—	11.2	7.3

—Insufficient data.

LAPSE RATES BY FACE AMOUNT AND NUMBER OF POLICIES

Figure 1 shows median lapse rates by face amount and number of policies for *traditional whole life*. Lapse rates in both measures decrease in the first three durations, increase slightly in the fourth duration, and then decrease in the last duration.

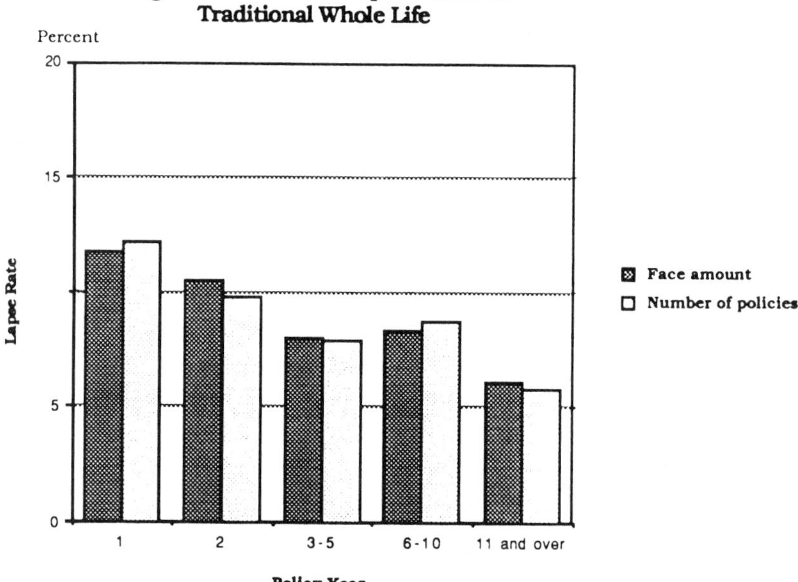

Figure 2 shows median lapse rates by face amount and number of policies for *interest-sensitive whole life*. Because of insufficient data in the later durations, lapse rates are only shown for the first three durations. Lapse rates by face amount range from 14.2 percent to 10.9 percent; lapse rates by number of policies range from 14.9 percent to 10.4 percent.

Figure 2 — Median Lapse Rates for Interest-Sensitive Whole Life

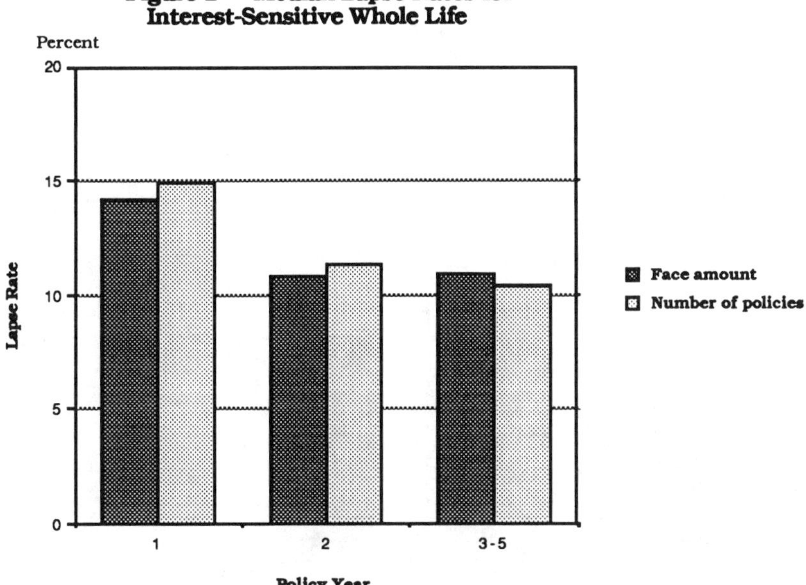

Figure 3 shows selected median lapse rates by face amount and number of policies for *permanent term* insurance (sometimes referred to as term to 100). In the first three durations, lapse rates by face amount are lower than rates by number of policies. The biggest difference occurs in policy year 1. The lapse rate by face amount is 7.4 percent, while the lapse rate by number of policies is 11.6 percent.

Figure 3 — Median Lapse Rates for Permanent Term

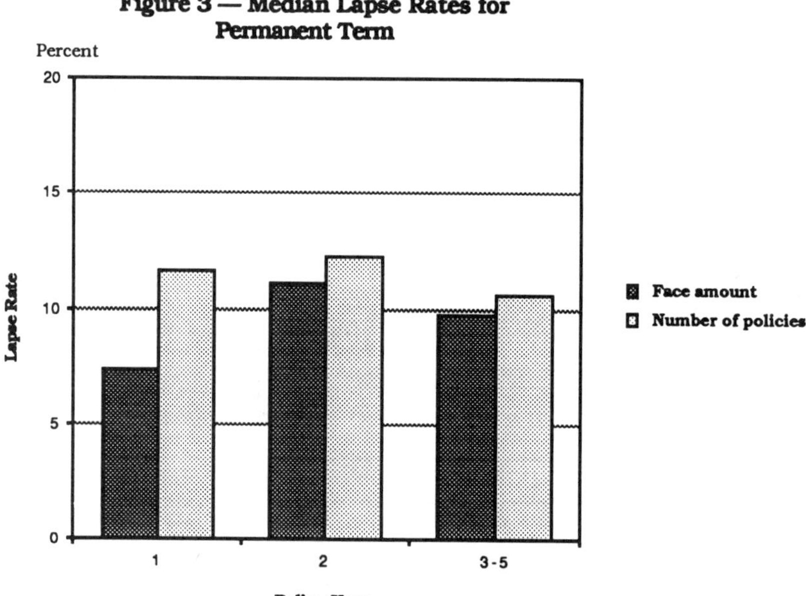

Figure 4 shows median lapse rates by face amount and number of policies for *five-year renewable term* insurance. Lapse rates peak in policy years 3–5. Note that a policy not renewing in the first month of the premium increase (61st month) is considered a fifth-policy-year lapse, not a sixth-policy-year lapse (see Appendix A for definitions of lapses).

Figure 4 — Median Lapse Rates for Five-Year Renewable Term

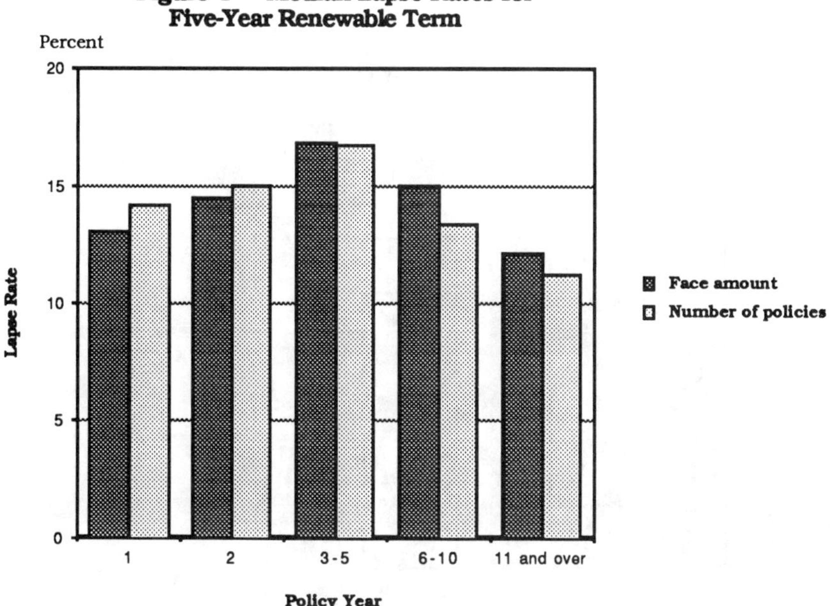

Figure 5 shows median lapse rates by face amount and number of policies for *level term (excluding 5-YRT)*. Lapse rates measured by face amount are lower than lapse rates by number of policies in all but the last two durations. Face amount lapse rates range from 10.9 percent in policy year 1 to 13.7 percent in policy years 3–5. Lapse rates measured by number of policies range from 13.1 percent in policy year 1 to 7.3 percent in policy years 11 and over.

Figure 5 — Median Lapse Rates for Level Term (excluding 5-YRT)

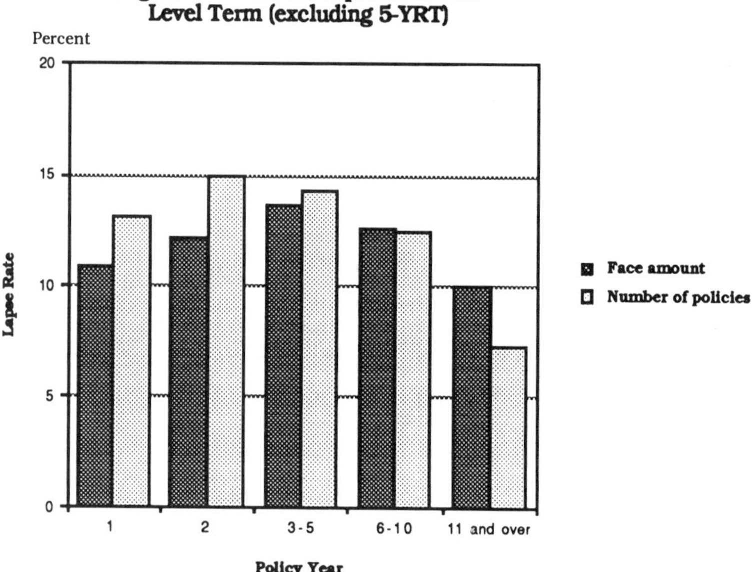

AVERAGE FACE AMOUNT PERSISTING AND LAPSING

Table E provides medians for average face amount persisting and lapsing for traditional whole life. Average face amount persisting is greater than average face amount lapsing only in policy year 1 and policy year 2.

TABLE E

AVERAGE FACE AMOUNT PERSISTING AND LAPSING FOR TRADITIONAL WHOLE LIFE (10 COMPANIES)

Policy Year	Average Face Amount	
	Persisting	Lapsing
1	$40,207	$34,977
2	40,642	36,398
3–5	25,555	27,346
6–10	20,798	21,374
11 and Over	7,903	8,298

Table F shows medians for average face amount lapsing and persisting for five-year renewable term. Average face amount persisting is greater than average face amount lapsing in policy year 1, policy year 2, and policy years 3–5.

TABLE F

AVERAGE FACE AMOUNT PERSISTING AND LAPSING FOR FIVE-YEAR RENEWABLE TERM (7 COMPANIES)

Policy Year	Average Face Amount	
	Persisting	Lapsing
1	$144,924	$118,218
2	159,411	153,060
3–5	135,917	133,698
6–10	95,587	104,597
11 and Over	49,118	54,662

TRENDS IN WHOLE LIFE FACE AMOUNT LAPSE RATES

Figure 6 shows 1987 and 1988 whole life lapse rates for a constant group of companies. The lapse rates for this group of companies have decreased from 1987 in all durations with the exception of policy years 1 and 2. Policy years 3–5 experienced the largest decrease.

Figure 6 — Whole Life Lapse Rates for Constant Group

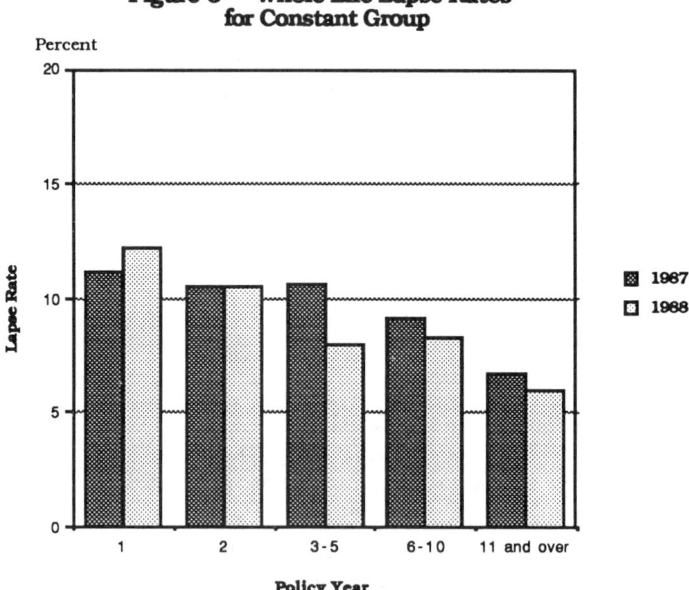

TRENDS IN FIVE-YEAR RENEWABLE TERM LAPSE RATES

Figure 7 shows 1987 and 1988 five-year renewable term lapse rates for a constant group of companies. Lapse rates have increased in policy year 2 and policy years 11 and over. The most substantial decrease occurs in policy years 6–10.

Figure 7 — Five-Year Renewable Term Lapse Rates for Constant Group

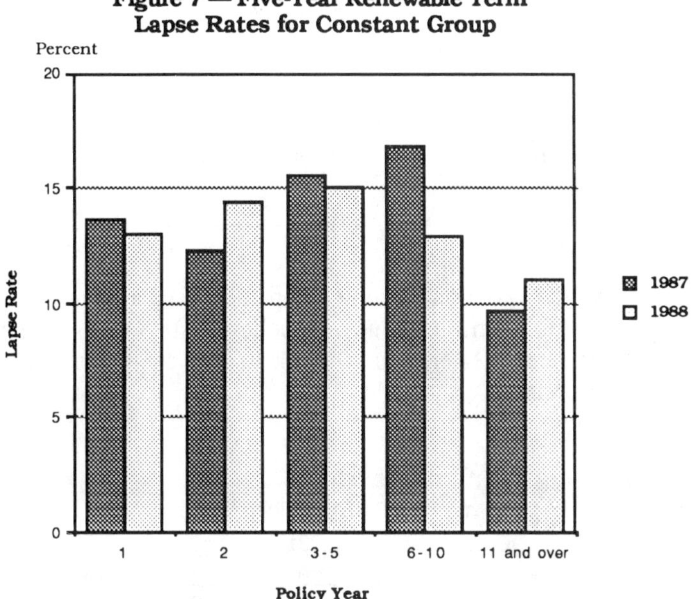

VARIATIONS AMONG COMPANIES' LAPSE RATES

Table G shows the face amount lapse rate variations across companies for whole life insurance. All companies in the three durations have lapse rates less than 20 percent. In policy year 1, nine companies have lapse rates less than 15 percent. In policy years 3–5 and policy years 11 and over, eight companies have lapse rates below 10 percent.

TABLE G

VARIATIONS OF WHOLE LIFE LAPSE RATES

Lapse Rate	Policy Year 1	3–5	11 and Over
20% and Over	0	0	0
15–19.99%	2	2	0
10–14.99	6	1	1
Under 10.00	3	8	8
Total Number of Companies	11	11	11

Table H shows the variations among companies' face amount lapse rates for five-year renewable term insurance. In policy years 3 to 5, all the companies have lapse rates greater than 10 percent; two companies have lapse rates above 20 percent.

TABLE H

VARIATIONS OF FIVE-YEAR RENEWABLE TERM LAPSE RATES

Lapse Rate	Policy Year 1	3–5	11 and Over
20% and Over	0	2	0
15–19.99%	2	3	1
10–14.99%	3	3	3
Under 10.00%	1	0	2
Total Number of Companies	6	8	6

LAPSE RATES BY FACE AMOUNT

TABLE 1

TRADITIONAL WHOLE LIFE
(11 COMPANIES)

Policy Year	Low	Median	High	Average*
1	3.5%	11.8%	16.9%	11.5%
2	6.0	10.5	18.3	10.3
3–5	5.6	8.0	16.3	9.3
6–10	4.6	8.3	20.7	9.0
11 and Over	4.0	6.1	14.3	7.2

*All companies receive equal weight; company size does not affect the results.

TABLE 2

INTEREST-SENSITIVE WHOLE LIFE
(6 COMPANIES)

Policy Year	Low	Median	High	Average*
1	3.4%	14.2%	15.7%	12.3%
2	5.1	10.8	16.4	10.5
3–5	5.5	10.9	21.7	13.3

*All companies receive equal weight; company size does not affect the results.

TABLE 3

PERMANENT TERM
(6 COMPANIES)

Policy Year	Low	Median	High	Average*
1	1.3%	7.4%	14.5%	7.8%
2	4.9	11.1	15.8	10.5
3–5	1.5	9.8	14.0	8.5

*All companies receive equal weight; company size does not affect the results.

TABLE 4

FIVE-YEAR RENEWABLE TERM
(9 COMPANIES)

Policy Year	Low	Median	High	Average*
1	8.3%	13.0%	17.2%	13.1%
2	11.3	14.4	19.1	14.5
3–5	11.6	16.8	24.6	16.9
6–10	10.0	15.0	21.8	15.5
11 and Over	7.5	12.1	15.6	11.7

*All companies receive equal weight; company size does not affect the results.

TABLE 5

LEVEL TERM (EXCLUDING 5-YRT)†
(10 COMPANIES)

Policy Year	Low	Median	High	Average*
1	2.4%	10.9%	23.7%	11.0%
2	9.9	12.2	21.6	13.2
3–5	7.2	13.7	24.1	14.8
6–10	8.7	12.6	24.6	13.5
11 and Over	5.5	10.0	18.9	10.6

*All companies receive equal weight; company size does not affect the results.

†One company's data were excluded because of atypical experience.

LAPSE RATES BY NUMBER OF POLICIES

TABLE 6

TRADITIONAL WHOLE LIFE
(10 COMPANIES)

Policy Year	Low	Median	High	Average*
1	9.8%	12.2%	18.1%	12.9%
2	6.8	9.8	14.2	10.2
3–5	6.3	7.9	16.7	9.2
6–10	5.3	8.7	19.8	10.1
11 and Over	3.5	5.7	9.9	6.2

*All companies receive equal weight; company size does not affect the results.

TABLE 7

INTEREST-SENSITIVE WHOLE LIFE
(6 COMPANIES)

Policy Year	Low	Median	High	Average*
1	4.0%	14.9%	17.4%	13.3%
2	6.1	11.3	17.0	11.2
3–5	4.7	10.4	23.4	13.1

*All companies receive equal weight; company size does not affect the results.

TABLE 8

PERMANENT TERM
(5 COMPANIES)

Policy Year	Low	Median	High	Average*
1	1.8%	11.6%	14.0%	9.6%
2	4.9	12.3	19.1	12.0
3–5	3.9	10.6	18.8	10.9

*All companies receive equal weight; company size does not affect the results.

TABLE 9

FIVE-YEAR RENEWABLE TERM
(8 COMPANIES)

Policy Year	Low	Median	High	Average*
1	7.7%	14.1%	21.7%	14.3%
2	12.9	14.9	20.5	15.6
3–5	12.0	16.7	19.6	15.6
6–10	9.3	13.3	17.1	13.3
11 and Over	7.0	11.2	14.1	10.7

*All companies receive equal weight; company size does not affect the results.

TABLE 10

LEVEL TERM (EXCLUDING 5-YRT)†
(8 COMPANIES)

Policy Year	Low	Median	High	Average*
1	3.0%	13.1%	29.2%	13.3%
2	9.4	14.9	24.9	15.9
3–5	9.7	14.3	26.0	16.1
6–10	7.4	12.5	21.7	12.4
11 and Over	4.3	7.3	13.9	8.3

*All companies receive equal weight; company size does not affect the results.

†One company's data were excluded because of atypical experience.

IN-DEPTH SURVEY—FIVE-YEAR RENEWABLE TERM

Lapse Rates by Policy Year

TABLE 11

PERCENTAGE OF POLICIES LAPSING
(6 COMPANIES)

Policy Year	Median	Average*
1	14.4%	15.4%
2	14.9	15.0
3	15.2	15.8
4	13.7	13.8
5	17.0	18.6
6	18.6	18.3
7	12.9	12.3
8	11.5	11.5
9	9.6	10.0
10	14.2	14.2
11 and Over	11.2	10.8

*All companies receive equal weight; company size does not affect the results.

TABLE 12

PERCENTAGE OF FACE AMOUNT LAPSING
(6 COMPANIES)

Policy Year	Median	Average*
1	16.2%	13.8%
2	14.4	13.9
3	14.1	15.3
4	11.1	12.3
5	16.0	20.8
6	22.0	20.9
7	13.4	13.4
8	13.9	13.7
9	9.7	9.2
10	13.8	16.7
11 and Over	13.2	12.2

*All companies receive equal weight; company size does not affect the results.

TABLE 13

PERCENTAGE OF ANNUALIZED PREMIUM LAPSING
(6 COMPANIES)

Policy Year	Median	Average*
1	13.3%	15.6%
2	15.4	15.6
3	11.6	12.4
4	10.4	10.3
5	15.3	27.2
6	15.3	16.6
7	14.5	14.6
8	11.5	10.3
9	8.5	8.2
10	13.9	20.5
11 and Over	10.6	10.4

*All companies receive equal weight; company size does not affect the results.

Average Size Policy Lapsing and Persisting

TABLE 14

FACE AMOUNTS PERSISTING AND LAPSING

Policy Year	Median		Average*	
	Lapsing	Persisting	Lapsing	Persisting
1	$118,000	$145,000	$107,000	$133,000
2	153,000	159,000	129,000	144,000
3	118,000	162,000	134,000	140,000
4	128,000	158,000	118,000	137,000
5	112,000	115,000	121,000	109,000
6	124,000	102,000	112,000	94,000
7	111,000	106,000	110,000	100,000
8	112,000	96,000	117,000	90,000
9	70,000	78,000	76,000	82,000
10	69,000	71,000	78,000	67,000
11 and Over	55,000	50,000	56,000	51,000

*All companies receive equal weight; company size does not affect the results.

Distribution of In Force and Lapses

TABLE 15

DISTRIBUTION OF IN FORCE

Policy Year	Number of Policies	Face Amount	Annualized Premium
1	13.5%	15.9%	11.0%
2	14.4	17.3	11.6
3	12.4	13.9	11.0
4	12.7	14.2	14.8
5	12.6	12.4	14.2
6	9.2	8.4	10.7
7	7.4	6.9	8.3
8	4.6	3.9	4.8
9	3.2	2.4	3.2
10	2.4	1.5	2.5
11 and Over	7.6	3.2	8.0
	100.0%	100.0%	100.0%

TABLE 16

DISTRIBUTION OF LAPSES

Policy Year	Number of Policies	Face Amount	Annualized Premium
1	14.4%	14.5%	9.1%
2	15.6	17.2	12.2
3	12.6	14.5	9.8
4	11.7	12.0	11.2
5	15.9	15.9	21.3
6	10.1	10.7	14.1
7	6.0	5.7	6.9
8	3.5	3.5	3.8
9	2.1	1.6	1.6
10	2.4	1.7	2.8
11 and Over	5.6	2.7	7.2
	100.0%	100.0%	100.0%

APPENDIX A

DEFINITIONS OF IN-FORCE POLICIES AND LAPSES

In Force

A policy is considered in force if the first premium for the new policy year starting in 1987 is paid.

In-force business includes:

- Policies issued in 1987.
- Policies issued before 1987 where the premium due on the 1987 policy anniversary date is paid before the end of the grace period.

In-force business excludes:

- Policies that lapse before their 1987 anniversaries and are on extended term or reduced paid-up status.
- Limited premium payment policies that are paid up.
- Single premium policies.

Examples of policies in force are:

- A policy issued in 1987 and the first premium is paid.
- A policy issued in 1986 and the premium due in the 13th policy month is paid.
- A policy issued in 1985 and the premium due in the 25th policy month is paid.

Lapse

A policy is considered a lapse if the first premium for the new policy year starting in 1987 is paid, but not all of the premium that comes due after the 1987 anniversary and before or on the 1988 anniversary date is paid.

Lapsed business includes:

- Policies surrendered after their 1987 anniversaries and before or on their 1988 anniversaries.
- Policies where a premium due after the 1987 anniversary and before or on the 1988 anniversary date is not paid by the end of the grace period.
- Term policies with renewal provisions that do not renew.
- Policies that are on extended-term or reduced paid-up status.

Lapsed business excludes:

- Death claims.
- Automatic premium loaned policies.
- Expiries and maturities.
- Conversions.
- Policies that lapse during the 1987–1988 policy year but are reinstated before or on their 1988 anniversaries.
- Policies not taken.
- Policies where the waiver-of-premium provision applies.

Examples of policies that lapse are:

- A policy issued in 1987 and the policyowner has paid the first premium. If any premium for policy months 2 through 13 is not paid by the end of the grace period, the policy is a lapse.
- A policy issued in 1986 and the policyowner has paid the 13th policy month premium. If any premium for policy months 14 through 25 is not paid by the end of the grace period, the policy is a lapse.
- A policy issued in 1985 and the policyowner has paid the 25th policy month premium. If any premium for policy months 26 through 37 is not paid by the end of the grace period, the policy is a lapse.

Example of a policy that does not lapse is:

- A policy issued in 1986 is not considered a lapse if the 13th policy month premium and all premiums for policy months 14 through 25 are paid.

PRODUCT DEFINITIONS

Traditional Whole Life

Includes:
- Whole life policies with level premiums or indeterminate premiums with *fixed* cash values including continuous pay and limited pay plans.

Excludes:
- Universal life
- Graded-premium whole life
- Interest-sensitive whole life
- Endowments
- Policies that are combinations of whole life and term plans
- Whole life plans used to fund a registered pension plan.

Five-Year Renewable Term

Includes:
- Level five-year term.

Excludes:
- Nonlevel term
- Permanent-term insurance
- Term riders.

Level Term (Excluding 5-YRT)

Includes:
- Term policies with level face amounts.

Excludes:
- Nonlevel term
- Permanent term insurance
- Term riders.

Interest-Sensitive Whole Life

Includes:
- Whole life plans that credit cash values with current interest rates. Premiums may be level, may vanish, or may be adjusted periodically.

Excludes:
- Universal life.

Permanent Term

Includes:

- Plans that provide coverage to age 100 and feature initial level death benefits and level premiums. Death benefits or premiums for these plans may be adjusted periodically (for example, every five years) to reflect changes in interest rates, mortality, and expenses. Typically the plans build no (or little) cash value and their only nonforfeiture value may be reduced paid-up coverage.

II. 1983–86 WHOLE LIFE LAPSATION IN THE UNITED STATES*†

PREFACE

This report was prepared in the Financial Research Department of the Life Insurance Marketing and Research Association, Inc. LIMRA has given the Society of Actuaries permission to reproduce this study as part of the Society's expansion of its experience studies. Discussions of this report as well as of any experience study are encouraged. LIMRA and the Society intend to work together to expand this report and seek additional data contributors. A report on lapse rates on ordinary life insurance policies in the U.S. for 1986–87 appears as Part I. The Canadian versions of these studies appear as Parts III and IV.

INTRODUCTION

As part of the annual Long-Term Lapse Survey, LIMRA has analyzed lapse rates on whole life insurance policies each year for the past three years. The analyses looked at the lapse experience between policy anniversaries from 1983 to 1984, from 1984 to 1985, and from 1985 to 1986. Compared with prior long-term lapse studies, these periods have unusually high lapses for policies in their renewal years.

This report examines the lapse experience over the combined three-year period. Only nonpension whole life policies having fixed or indeterminate premiums, both continuous-pay and limited-pay, are included. Single-premium, graded-premium, and flexible-premium products are excluded. Interest-sensitive whole life policies where the cash values are credited with current interest are also excluded.

The study measures lapses on three bases: face amount, annualized premium, and number of policies. All companies were able to provide face amount data and more than three-fourths of the companies provided premium and policy count data (31 companies are included in this study).

The study looks at how lapse rates vary by policyowners' issue age groups and by policy year. Issue age groups include 20–29, 30–39, 40–49, and 50–59 as well as all issue ages combined (including those under age 20 and

†This report replaces the one that appears in the *1985-86-87 Reports of Mortality, Morbidity and Other Experience*; that report contains incorrect bar graphs and should not be used.

over age 59). Policy-year durations consist of eight categories. Policy years 1–5 are examined separately; years 6–9 are grouped together; year 10 is looked at separately; and policies older than 10 years make up the last category.

OVERVIEW OF RESULTS

Percent of Policies Lapsing

Looking at average lapse rates, there is only a three percentage point difference between policy year 1 and policy year 2 (20 percent and 17 percent, respectively). For prior long-term lapse studies, the differences between first- and second-year lapse rates were much greater. For the next seven policy years (durations 3–9), average lapse rates are nearly level, ranging from 14 percent to 15 percent. Lapse rates then decline to only 12 percent for policy year 10 and 8 percent for policy years 11 and over.

Face Amount and Annualized Premium Lapsing

Policy year 1 shows average lapse rates of 19 percent of face amount and 17 percent of annualized premium. Lapse rates are virtually level for the next four policy years (durations 2–5) at 17 percent of face amount and 16 percent of annualized premium. For policy years 6 through 9, these lapse rates pick up slightly, then ultimately decrease to 10 percent for policy years 11 and over.

Variation by Company

About one-third of the companies that have relatively low first-year lapse rates also have low tenth-year lapse rates; for another third, a high first-year lapse rate is accompanied by a high tenth-year lapse rate. The remaining third of the companies experienced either low first-year and high tenth-year lapse rates, or high first-year and low tenth-year lapse rates.

Regardless of policy year, there is considerable variation in lapse experience across companies. For policy years 1–10, one quarter of the lapse rates are below 10 percent. Another quarter of the lapse rates generally exceed 20 percent.

For policies in force for more than 10 years, companies still lost an average of 8 percent of their policies and 10 percent of their face amount and premium. Large companies lost about 8.4 percent of face amount as compared with 11.6 percent for small companies—the average 1972 lapse experience for all participating companies was less than 3 percent.

THE DETAILS

The following section shows how the average (mean) percentage of policies and the percentage of face amount lapsing vary by policy year. For the remainder of this report, lapse rates are based on face amount, unless stated otherwise.

In calculating summary statistics, such as the mean percentage of policies lapsing, each company receives equal weight as long as the company has a minimum number of policies in force. The Appendix includes detailed tables and definitions used to determine lapses.

Mean Lapse Rates by Policy Year

Figure 1 shows average percentages of policies lapsing for 29 companies, while Figure 2 shows average percentages of face amount lapsing for 31 companies. These average lapse rates decline during the first four policy years, then increase slightly during the fifth policy year, and ultimately level off at 8 percent of policies and 10 percent of face amount for policies more than 10 years old. See Table 1 for details. Table A in the Appendix shows median lapse rates.

Figure 1 — Policy Count Lapse Rates

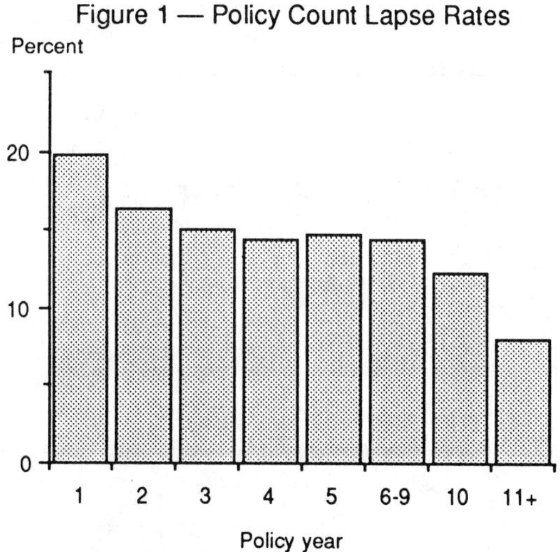

Figure 2 — Face Amount Lapse Rates

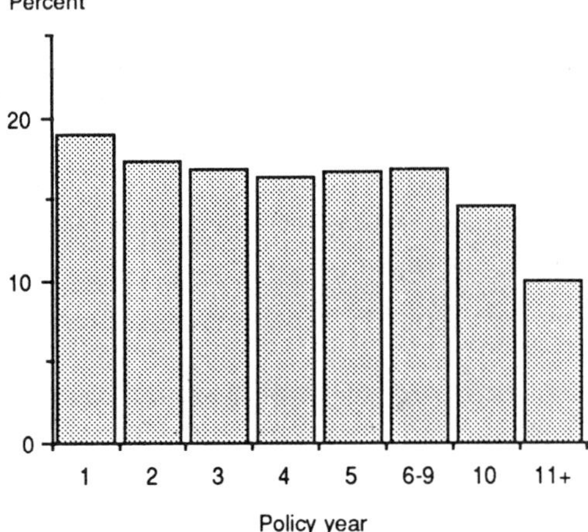

TABLE 1

LIMRA 1983–1986 Lapse Rates by Policy Year

Policy Year	Mean Lapse Rates: Number of Policies	Mean Lapse Rates: Face Amount
1	19.8%	19.0%
2	16.4	17.0
3	15.0	16.8
4	14.4	16.5
5	14.7	16.7
6–9	14.4	17.0
10	12.3	14.8
11 and over	8.0	10.0

Variation in Lapse Rates

Figure 3 shows (for selected years) mean lapse rates by policy year for two groups of companies, "size 1" and "size 2." Size 1 companies are those with at least $5 billion of whole life insurance in force (13 companies); size 2 companies are those with less than $5 billion of whole life insurance in force (18 companies). In the first 10 policy years, lapse rates for the size 1 companies in this study tend to be five to six percentage points lower than those for the size 2 companies. For policies more than 10 years old, the difference diminishes to approximately three percentage points (see Table B).

Figure 3 — Variation by Company Size

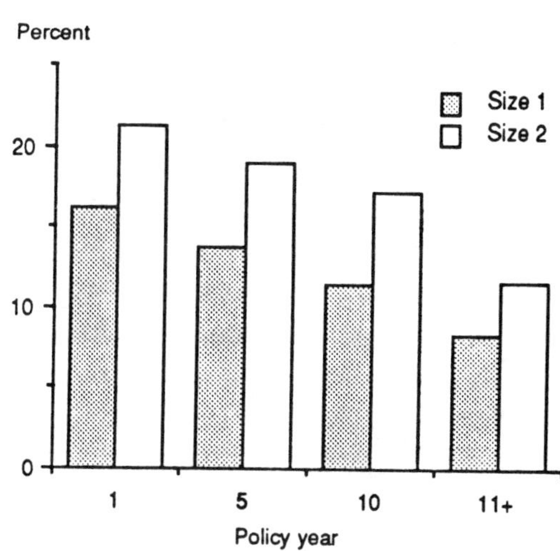

Figure 4 illustrates the variation of lapse rates across all 31 companies. Half of the companies have first-year lapse rates ranging from 10 percent to 25 percent. After the tenth policy year, half of the companies have lapse rates ranging from 7 percent to 11 percent (see Table C).

Figure 4 — Variation Across Companies

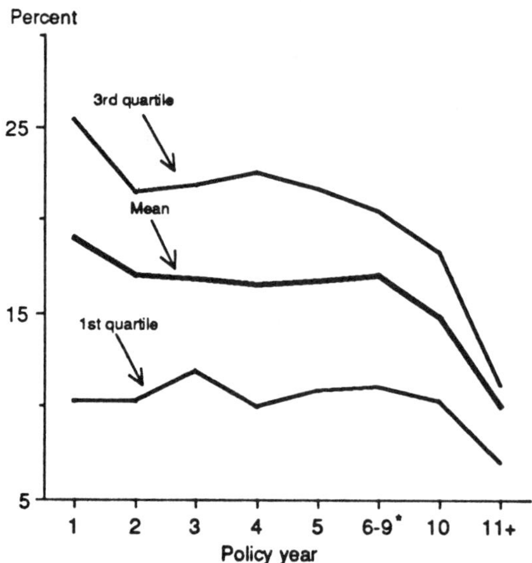

* Data for policy years 6 through 9 were collected in aggregate form.

Lapse Rates by Issue Age and Lapse Measure

Figure 5 shows first-year and tenth-year lapse rates by issue age. As in the past, relatively younger insureds tend to produce higher lapse rates. The first-year lapse rates decrease from 26.2 percent for issue ages 20–29 to 12.6 percent for issue ages 50–59. This trend toward higher lapse rates among younger insureds continues into later policy years but becomes less pronounced. By the tenth policy year, lapse rates decline to 16.4 percent and 11.2 percent for issue ages 20–29 and 50–59, respectively (see Table E).

Figure 5 — Mean Lapse Rates by Issue Age

Percent

30
20
10
0

20-29
30-39
40-49
50-59

1
10

Policy year

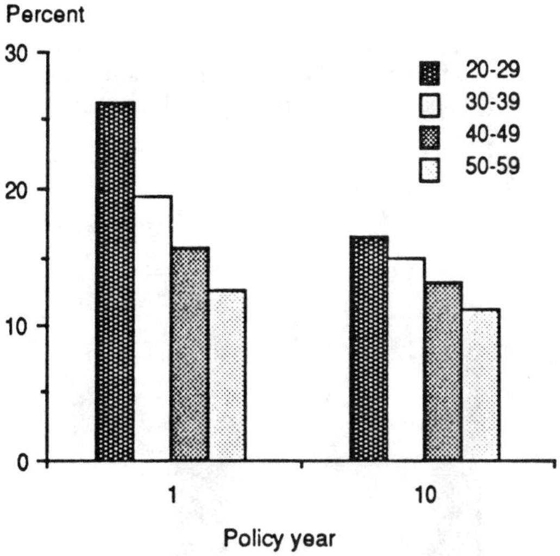

Figure 6 compares the percentage of policies lapsing with the percentage of face amount and annualized premium lapsing for both new issues and policies in their tenth year. In spite of many changes, such as higher lapses for policies in their renewal years, the pattern of these results matches patterns of previous LIMRA long-term lapse studies: In the first policy year, the average policy-count lapse rate is higher than the face-amount rate and the face-amount rate is higher than the premium lapse rate. This implies that relatively high face-amount, high premium policies have lower first-year lapse rates than lower face-amount policies with lower premiums. In renewal years, the policy-count lapse rates tend to be lower than premium lapse rates and premium lapse rates tend to be slightly lower than face-amount lapse rates (see Figures 7 and 8 and Table G).

Figure 6 — Mean Lapse Rates by Measure
(companies reporting all three measures)

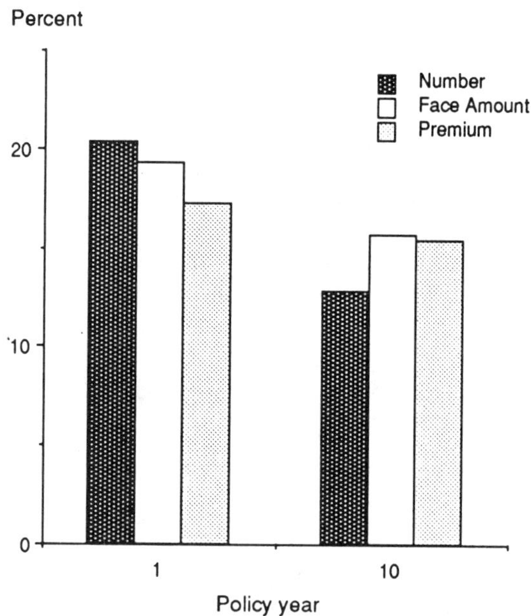

Average Policy Size

For policy years 3 and over, both the average face amount and the average size premium on lapsing policies are larger than the averages on policies remaining in force. This anomaly may be partly a result of unusual replacement activity during this time period. Figures 7 and 8 illustrate the pattern for selected policy years.

Figure 7 shows the average face amount per policy for policies that did not lapse and for policies that did lapse. In policy year 1, the average face amount persisting is slightly greater than the average size policy lapsing (see Table H).

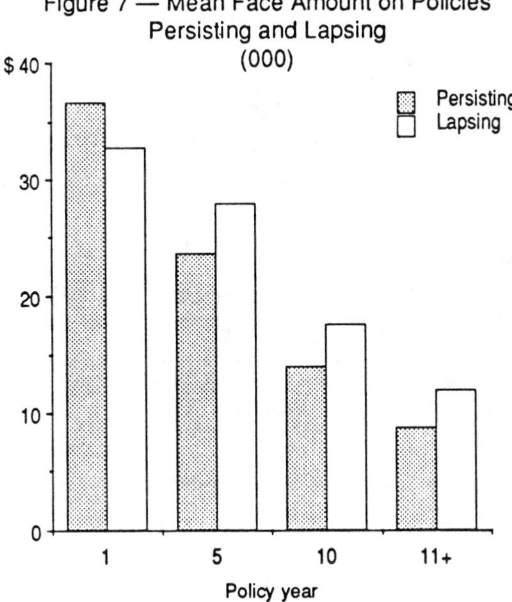

Figure 8 shows the same pattern for annualized premiums: Average annualized premium on *lapsing* policies in renewal years tends to be higher than annualized premium on policies remaining in force. For new issues, annualized premium on *persisting* policies tends to be higher than premium on lapsing policies (see Table I).

Figure 8 — Mean Annualized Premium on Policies Persisting and Lapsing

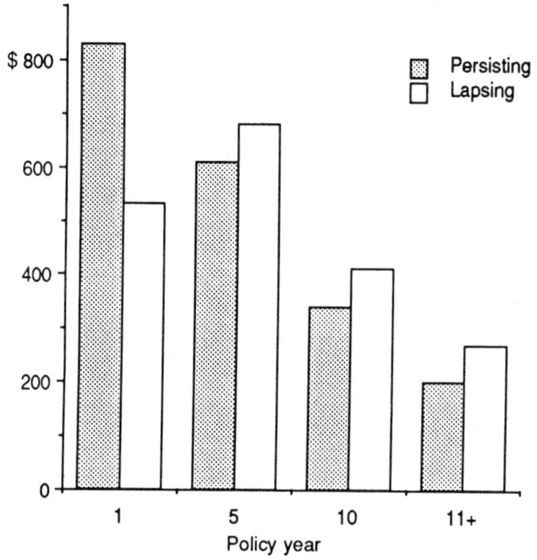

A Period of High Lapsation

Table 2 compares excerpts from LIMRA 1983–1986 lapse rates in this study with excerpts from some popular historical tables. Compared with prior LIMRA long-term lapse studies, the period from 1983 to 1986 has unusually high lapsation in the renewal years. The first-year lapse rate is not unusual; however, the renewal lapse rates are generally two to four times higher than the renewal lapse rates in these historical studies.

TABLE 2

COMPARISON OF VARIOUS LAPSE TABLES
(PERCENTAGE OF POLICIES LAPSING)

Policy Year	Linton Tables			Moorhead Tables			LIMRA Tables		
	A	B	C	R	S	T	'71–'72	'77–'78	'83–'86
1......	10.4%	20.4%	30.4%	7.0%	12.5%	20.0%	20.0%	16.4%	19.8%
5......	4.7	8.7	12.7	2.8	3.0	4.0	4.9	5.5	14.7
10......	3.6	6.1	8.6	1.7	2.4	3.0	2.8	3.6	12.3

The Linton tables were published by M.A. Linton in 1924 in the *Record of the American Institute of Actuaries*.* The Moorhead tables were published by E.J. Moorhead in 1960 in the *Transactions of the Society of Actuaries*.†

WHAT HIGH LAPSATION MEANS DOWN THE ROAD

To see how lapsation affects a company's in-force business, consider two hypothetical companies using some of the LIMRA lapse rates as summarized in Table 2. In 1988 each company has 100,000 policies in force; 15,000 are new issues and 85,000 are renewing policies. From 1989 through 1998, sales increase 10 percent each year, so in 1998 each company is writing 38,906 new policies. Let's assume Company A experiences LIMRA '71–'72 lapse rates, while Company B experiences LIMRA '83–'86 lapse rates over the next 10 years.

*Linton, M.A. "Returns under Agency Contracts," *RAIA* XII (1924): 283–319.
†Moorhead, E.J. "The Construction of Persistency Tables," *TSA* XII (1960): 545–63.

Figure 9 — Effect of Lapses on Policies in Force

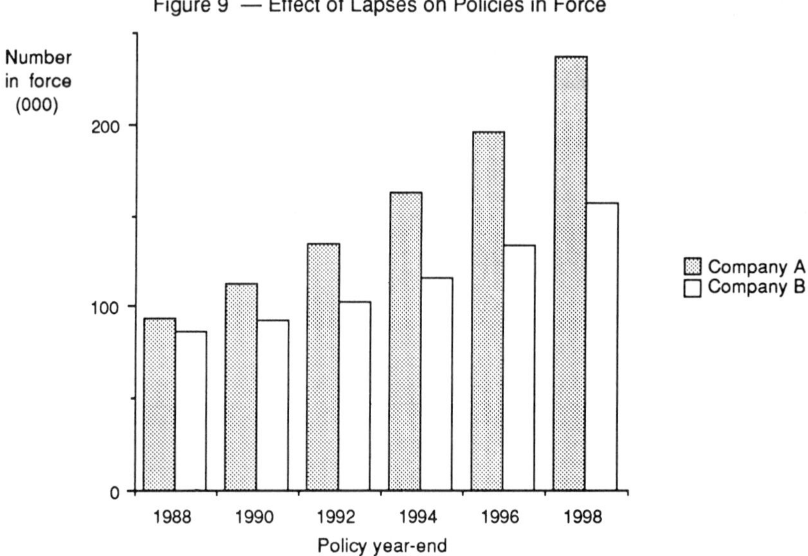

By the end of 1998, Company A has nearly 237,000 policies in force, while Company B has fewer than 157,000 policies in force. Each company writes over 275,000 new policies from 1988 through 1998, but the low-renewal-lapse Company A has a net gain of nearly 152,000 policies in force, compared with fewer than 72,000 policies for the high-renewal-lapse Company B.

The upshot: The high lapse company would have to sell nearly 175,000 more policies over the 1988-1998 period to achieve the same number of policies remaining in force as the low lapse company. This is equivalent to sustaining an annual sales growth rate of 17.4 percent—selling 420,000 policies instead of 275,000 policies from 1988 through 1998—to end up with 237,000 policies in force. Furthermore, this comparison does not address the much higher acquisition costs for new issues versus the costs involved for renewing business.

APPENDIX

TABLES

Table A presents LIMRA 1983–1986 median lapse rates. The remaining tables present lapse rates illustrated in Figures 3–8 of this report, in more detail.

TABLE A

MEDIAN LAPSE RATES BY POLICY YEAR

Policy Year	Median Lapse Rates	
	Number	Face Amount
1	20.0%	19.3%
2	15.4	16.7
3	15.2	15.3
4	13.5	15.0
5	13.5	14.4
6–9	12.4	16.3
10	10.9	12.9
11 and over	6.7	9.1

TABLE B

VARIATION IN LAPSE RATES BY COMPANY SIZE
(PERCENTAGE OF FACE AMOUNT LAPSING)

Policy Year	Median Lapse Rates	
	Size 1	Size 2
1............	16.2%	21.3%
2............	13.3	19.9
3............	13.5	19.2
4............	13.7	18.5
5............	13.7	18.9
6–9..........	12.8	20.0
10............	11.5	17.1
11 and over	8.4	11.6

TABLE C

VARIATION IN LAPSE RATES ACROSS COMPANIES
(PERCENTAGE OF FACE AMOUNT LAPSING)

Policy Year	Mean	Median	Range of Middle 50 Percent	
			Low	High
1.........	19.0%	19.3%	10.2%	25.3%
2.........	17.0	16.7	10.2	21.4
3.........	16.8	15.3	11.8	21.8
4.........	16.5	15.0	9.9	22.5
5.........	16.7	14.4	10.8	21.6
6–9.......	17.0	16.3	11.0	20.4
10.........	14.8	12.9	10.2	18.2
11 and over .	10.0	9.1	7.0	11.2

TABLE D

MEAN PERCENTAGE OF POLICIES LAPSING BY ISSUE AGE

Policy Year	Issue Age			
	20–29	30–39	40–49	50–59
1.........	26.4%	21.2%	17.2%	13.5%
2.........	22.5	19.4	14.5	10.5
3.........	20.3	17.7	12.9	9.9
4.........	18.8	17.3	13.0	10.0
5.........	18.7	17.4	13.2	10.3
6–9.......	18.5	16.7	12.0	8.7
10.........	15.5	13.1	9.8	7.3
11 and over .	9.7	7.8	5.9	4.4

TABLE E

MEAN PERCENTAGE OF FACE AMOUNT LAPSING BY ISSUE AGE

Policy Year	Issue Age			
	20–29	30–39	40–49	50–59
1.........	26.2%	19.5%	15.6%	12.6%
2.........	22.2	18.4	15.2	12.7
3.........	21.1	18.7	15.8	13.3
4.........	20.0	18.3	15.7	14.1
5.........	19.5	18.4	15.3	14.6
6–9.......	19.8	18.3	15.1	13.3
10.........	16.4	15.0	13.2	11.2
11 and over .	11.3	9.5	8.2	6.9

TABLE F

MEAN PERCENTAGE OF ANNUALIZED PREMIUM LAPSING BY ISSUE AGE

Policy Year	Issue Age 20–29	30–39	40–49	50–59
1.........	27.0%	21.4%	16.6%	12.8%
2.........	23.1	19.6	16.0	12.9
3.........	22.3	19.7	16.2	13.4
4.........	21.3	19.5	16.4	14.7
5.........	20.9	19.6	16.4	15.6
6–9.......	21.4	19.9	16.2	13.9
10.........	17.4	15.0	13.5	12.5
11 and over .	11.9	10.0	8.8	7.3

TABLE G

COMPARISON OF MEAN LAPSE RATES BY MEASURE (COMPANIES REPORTING ALL THREE MEASURES)

Policy Year	Number of Policies	Face Amount	Annualized Premium
1	20.3%	19.3%	17.2%
2	16.8	17.1	16.1
3	15.3	17.0	16.5
4	14.8	17.0	16.0
5	15.1	17.4	16.6
6–9	15.0	18.2	17.4
10	12.8	15.7	15.4
11 and over...	8.2	10.5	10.0

TABLE H

MEAN FACE AMOUNT PERSISTING AND LAPSING

Policy Year	Persisting	Lapsing
1............	$36,500	$32,600
2............	36,000	34,900
3............	29,800	35,500
4............	27,200	32,200
5............	23,600	27,800
6–9..........	17,600	21,700
10............	13,900	17,500
11 and over	8,700	11,900

TABLE I

MEAN ANNUALIZED PREMIUM PERSISTING AND LAPSING

Policy Year	Persisting	Lapsing
1	$830	$530
2............	820	680
3............	650	710
4............	640	700
5............	610	680
6–9..........	450	540
10............	340	410
11 and over	200	270

DEFINITIONS

Lapse Rate

Lapse rates are calculated by dividing the amounts lapsing by the corresponding amount in force. In calculating summary statistics for this report, each company's results receive equal weight, provided a minimum exposure criterion is met.

Policies lapsing because of nonpayment of premium are considered to lapse in the duration for which they were last in force, even if the grace period extends into the next policy year.

In Force

A policy is considered in force if the first premium at the beginning of the anniversary year is paid.

In-force business includes:

- New issues.
- Policies issued before the anniversary year under study where the premium due at the beginning of the anniversary year is paid before the end of the grace period.

In-force business excludes:

- Policies that lapsed before the beginning of the anniversary year under study even if the policies are on extended-term or reduced-paid-up status.
- Limited premium payment policies that are paid up.
- Single premium policies.

Lapse

A policy is considered a lapse if the policy is in force at the beginning of the anniversary year under study but not all of the premium that comes due during the anniversary year is paid, including the premium due on the policy's next anniversary.

Lapsed business includes:

- Policies surrendered during the anniversary year under study, including surrenders made at the end of the anniversary year, i.e., on next policy anniversaries.
- Policies where a premium comes due during the anniversary year under study, including the premium that comes due on the next policy anniversaries, but is not paid by the end of the grace period.
- Policies that go on reduced-paid-up or extended-term status.

Lapsed business excludes:

- Death claims.
- Automatic premium loaned policies.
- Lapses during the policy year that are reinstated before or on the next policy anniversary.
- Policies not taken.

CONTRIBUTING COMPANIES

Aetna Life & Casualty
Alfa Life*
American United Life
Baltimore Life
Business Men's Assurance
Canada Life (U.S.)
Connecticut Mutual Life
Equitable Life of the United States
Fidelity Union Life
Guardian Life of America
Horace Mann Life
IDS Life (Minnesota)
Jefferson-Pilot Life†
John Hancock Mutual Life
Liberty Life (South Carolina)
Lutheran Brotherhood

*Federated Guaranty at the time of the study.
†Jefferson Standard and Pilot Life made individual contributions.

Massachusetts Mutual Life
Metropolitan Life
Monumental Life
MONY
Northwestern Mutual Life
Principal Mutual Life
Prudential of America
Security-Connecticut Life
Security Life of Denver
Sun Life of Canada (U.S.)
Transamerica Occidental Life (California)
The Travelers
United of Omaha Life
USAA Life

IV. 1983–86 WHOLE LIFE LAPSATION IN CANADA*†

PREFACE

This report was prepared in the Financial Research Department of the Life Insurance Marketing and Research Association, Inc. LIMRA has given the Society of Actuaries permission to reproduce this study as part of the Society's expansion of its experience studies. Discussions of this report as well as of any experience study are encouraged. LIMRA and the Society intend to work together to expand this report and seek additional data contributors. A report on lapse rates on ordinary life insurance policies in Canada for 1986–87 appears as Part III. The United States versions of these studies appear as Parts I and II.

INTRODUCTION

As part of the annual Long-Term Lapse Survey, LIMRA has analyzed lapse rates on whole life insurance policies each year for the past three years. The analyses looked at lapse experience between policy anniversaries from 1983 to 1984, from 1984 to 1985, and from 1985 to 1986. Compared with prior long-term lapse studies, these periods have unusually high lapses for policies in their renewal years.

This report examines the lapse experience over the combined three-year period. Only nonpension whole life policies having fixed or indeterminate premiums, both continuous-pay and limited-pay, are included. Single premium, graded premium, and flexible-premium policies are excluded. Interest-sensitive whole life policies where the cash values are credited with current interest are also excluded.

The study measures lapses on three bases: number of policies, face amount, and annualized premium. Nearly all companies were able to provide policy count data and face amount data and more than three-fourths of the companies provided premium data (13 companies are included in this study).

The study looks at how lapse rates vary by policyowners' issue age groups and by policy year. Issue age groups include 20–29, 30–39, 40–49, and 50–59 as well as all issue ages combined (including those under age 20 and

†This report replaces the one that appears in the *1985-86-87 Reports of Mortality, Morbidity and Other Experience*; that report contains incorrect bar graphs and should not be used.

over age 59). Policy year durations consist of eight categories. Policy years 1–5 are examined separately; years 6–9 are grouped together; year 10 is looked at separately; and policies older than 10 years make up the last category.

OVERVIEW OF RESULTS

Percentage of Policies Lapsing

For average lapse rates, there is only a three percentage point difference between policy years 1 and 2 (16 percent and 13 percent, respectively). For the next eight policy years (durations 3–10), average lapse rates are nearly level, ranging from 10 percent to 11 percent. The average lapse rate ultimately declines to 6 percent for policy years 11 and over.

Face Amount and Annualized Premium Lapsing

Policy year 1 shows average lapse rates of 17 percent of face amount and 15 percent of annualized premium. Face amount and premium lapse rates decrease to approximately 10 percent for policy years 4 and 5. For policy years 6–9, lapses on relatively large size policies increase—the average percent of face amount lapsing increases two percentage points. For policy years 11 and over, the face amount and premium lapse rates average around 7 percent to 8 percent.

Variation by Company

There is considerable variation in lapse experience by company. For example, one quarter of the companies experienced first-year lapse rates below 14 percent, while another quarter experienced lapse rates above 19 percent. The average first-year lapse rate for large companies was approximately 15 percent, while the average first-year lapse rate for small companies was 20 percent.

More than half of the companies having relatively low first-year lapse rates also have relatively low tenth-year lapse rates. Four companies experienced the opposite of what might be expected—two experienced low first-year lapse rates and high tenth-year lapse rates, and two experienced high first-year and low tenth-year lapse rates.

For policies in force for more than 10 years, companies still lost an average of 7.8 percent of their in-force business. Larger companies lost about 7.6

percent of face amount as compared with 8.0 percent for smaller companies—the average 1977 lapse rate for all participating companies was less than 3 percent.

THE DETAILS

The next section shows how the average (mean) percentage of policies and the percentage of face amount lapsing vary by policy year. For the remainder of this report, average lapse rates are based on face amount, unless stated otherwise.

In calculating summary statistics, such as the mean percentage of policies lapsing, each company receives equal weight as long as the company has a minimum number of policies in force. The Appendix includes detailed tables and definitions used to determine lapses.

Mean Lapse Rates by Policy Year

Figures 1 and 2 show average lapse rates by age of policies as measured by the percentage of policies lapsing and the percentage of face amount lapsing (respectively) for all 13 companies. These average lapse rates decline during the first four policy years, then increase for policy years 5 and 6–9. For policy years 11 and over, these rates decline to 6 percent of policies and 8 percent of face amount. See Table 1 for details. Table A in the Appendix shows median lapse rates.

Figure 1 — Policy Count Lapse Rates

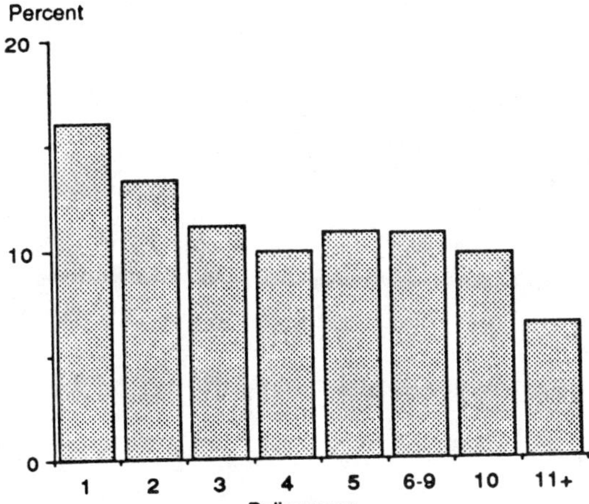

Figure 2 — Face Amount Lapse Rates

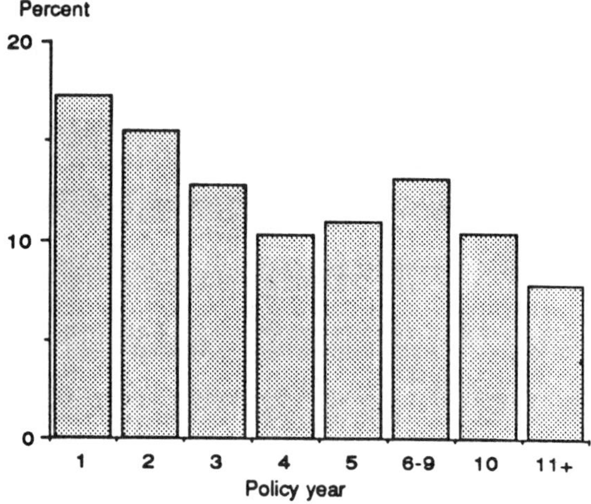

TABLE 1

LIMRA 1983–1986 LAPSE RATES BY POLICY YEAR

Policy Year	Mean Lapse Rates: Number of Policies	Mean Lapse Rates: Face Amount
1	16.1%	17.3%
2	13.3	15.5
3	11.1	12.8
4	9.9	10.3
5	10.8	10.9
6–9	10.7	13.1
10	9.7	10.4
11 and over...	6.4	7.8

Variation in Lapse Rates

Figure 3 shows (for selected years) mean lapse rates for two groups of companies. "Size 1" companies are those with more than $1 billion of whole life insurance in force (six companies); "size 2" companies are those with less than $1 billion of whole life insurance in force (seven companies). The first-year lapse rate for size 1 companies is more than five percentage points lower than that for size 2 companies. The difference in lapse rates is less than two percentage points for policy years 3 and over (see Table B).

Figure 3 — Variation by Company Size

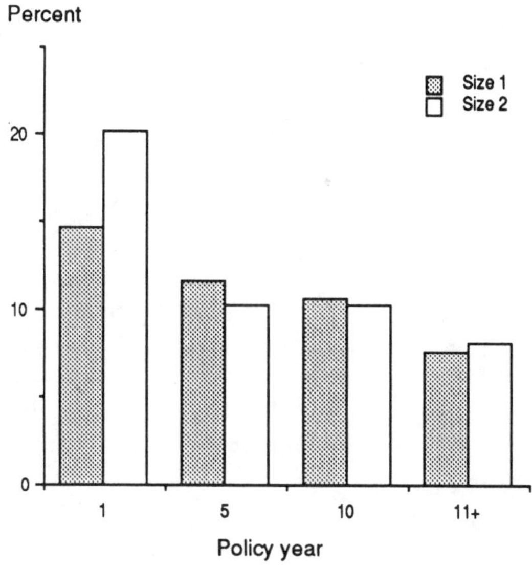

Figure 4 illustrates the variation of lapse rates across all 13 companies. Half the companies have first-year lapse rates ranging from 14 percent to 19 percent. After the tenth policy year, the spread narrows; for policy years 11 and over, half the companies have lapse rates ranging from 6.6 percent to 9 percent (see Table C).

Figure 4 — Variation Across Companies

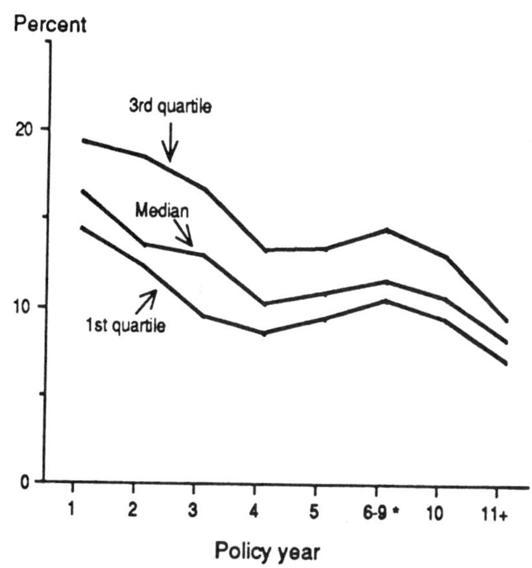

*Data for policy years 6 through 9 were collected in aggregate form.

Lapse Rates by Issue Age and Lapse Measure

Figure 5 shows average lapse rates by issue age for policy year 1 and policy years 11 and over. As in the past, relatively younger insureds tend to produce higher lapse rates. The first-year lapse rate ranges from 21 percent for issue ages 20–29, to 16 percent for issue ages 40–49, then decreases to 6.4 percent for issue ages 50–59. This trend toward higher lapse rates among younger insureds continues into later policy years but becomes less pronounced. In policy years 11 and over, lapse rates level off at approximately 8 percent and 6 percent for issue ages 20–29 and 40–49, respectively, and 5.6 percent for issue ages 50–59 (see Table E).

Figure 5 — Mean Lapse Rates by Issue Age

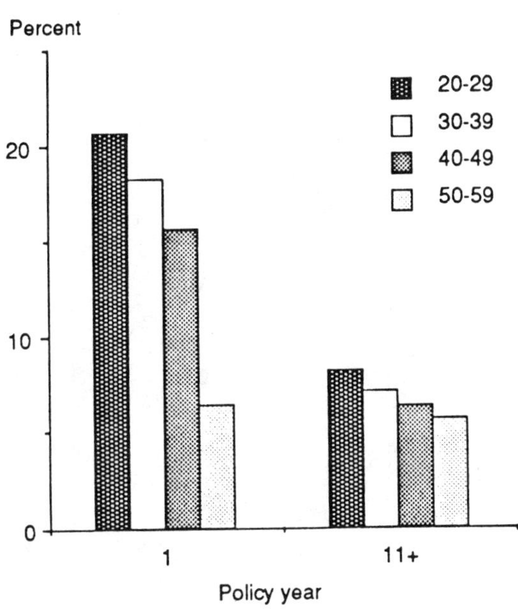

Figure 6 compares the percentage of face amount lapsing with the percentage of policies and annualized premium lapsing for policy years 1 and 10. The average first-year face-amount rate is slightly higher than the policy-count lapse rate, and the policy-count lapse rate is slightly higher than the annualized premium lapse rate. This implies that relatively high-face-amount, low-premium policies have higher first-year lapse rates than lower-face-amount policies with higher premiums. For policies in their tenth year, there is less variation; average lapse rates range between 9 percent and 10 percent (see Table G).

Figure 6 — Mean Lapse Rates by Measure
(companies reporting all three measures)

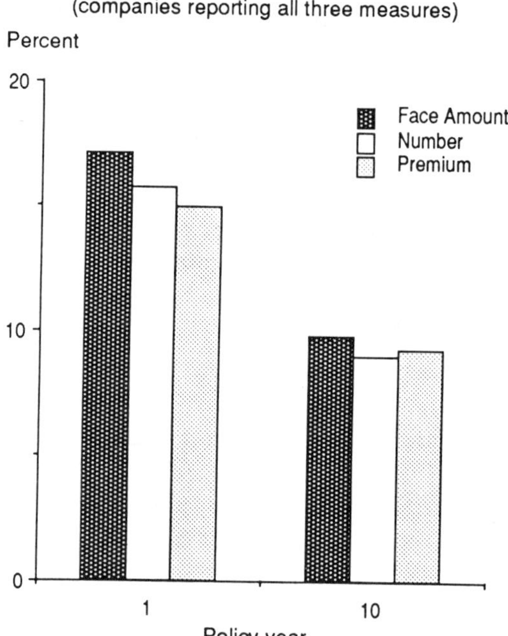

Average Policy Size

For policy years 11 and over, both the average face amount and average premium on lapsing policies are larger than average sizes on policies remaining in force. This result may be partly due to replacement activity during this time period. Figures 7 and 8 illustrate the pattern for selected policy years.

Figure 7 shows the average face amount per policy for policies that did not lapse and for policies that did lapse. In the first policy year there is little difference between the average size policy persisting and the average size policy lapsing. In policy years 11 and over, the average size policy lapsing is about 25 percent larger than the average size policy persisting (see Table H).

Figure 7 — Mean Face Amount
Persisting and Lapsing
(000)

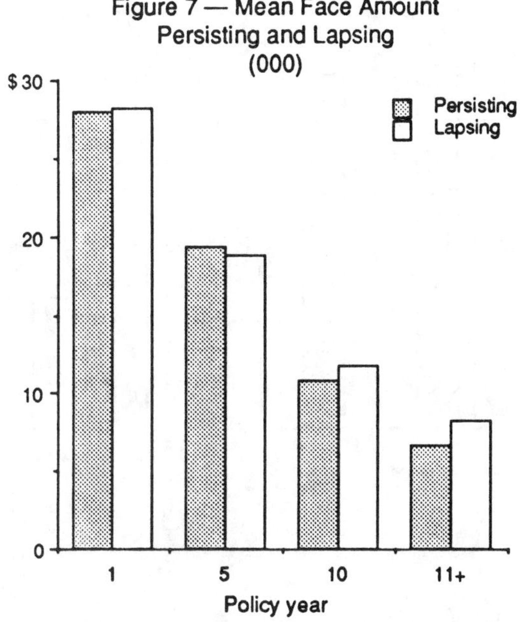

Figure 8 shows the pattern for annualized premiums. The greatest difference occurs in the fifth policy year where the average size premium on persisting policies is about 30 percent larger than the average size premium on lapsing policies. One company had an unusually large average size premium for persisting policies in policy year 5. Without this company, the average size premium for persisting policies is only about 6 percent larger than that for lapsing policies. The difference diminishes for policies more than 5 years old (see Table I).

Figure 8 — Mean Annualized Premium
Persisting and Lapsing

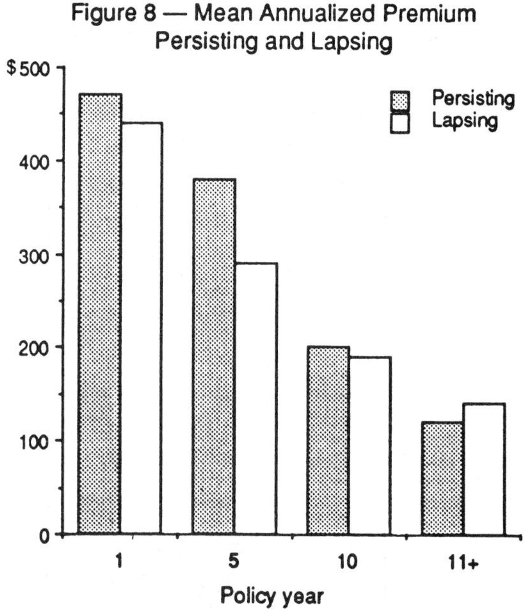

A Period of High Lapsation

Table 2 compares excerpts from LIMRA 1983–1986 lapse rates in this study with excerpts from some popular historical tables. Compared with prior LIMRA long-term lapse studies, the period from 1983 to 1986 has unusually high lapsation in the renewal years. The first-year lapse rate is not unusual; however, the renewal lapse rates are generally two to four times higher than the renewal lapse rates in these historical studies.

TABLE 2

COMPARISON OF VARIOUS LAPSE TABLES
(PERCENTAGE OF POLICIES LAPSING)

	Linton Tables			Moorhead Tables			LIMRA Tables	
Policy Year	A	B	C	R	S	T	1976–1977	1983–1986
1	10.4%	20.4%	30.4%	7.0%	12.5%	20.0%	12.7%	16.1%
5	4.7	8.7	12.7	2.8	3.0	4.0	4.2	10.8
10	3.6	6.1	8.6	1.7	2.4	3.0	3.1	9.7

The Linton tables were published by M.A. Linton in 1924 in the *Record of the American Institute of Actuaries*.* The Moorhead tables were published in 1960 in the *Transactions of the Society of Actuaries*.†

WHAT HIGH LAPSATION MEANS DOWN THE ROAD

To see how lapsation affects a company's in-force business, consider two hypothetical companies using some of the LIMRA lapse rates as summarized in Table 2. In 1988 each company has 50,000 policies in force; 10,000 are new issues and 40,000 are renewing policies. From 1989 through 1998, sales increase 10 percent each year, so in 1998 each company is writing 25,937 new policies. Let's assume Company A experiences LIMRA 1976–1977 lapse rates, while Company B experiences LIMRA 1983–1986 lapse rates over the next 10 years.

*Linton, M.A. "Returns under Agency Contracts," *RAIA* XIII (1924): 283–319.
†Moorhead, E.J. "The Construction of Persistency Tables," *TSA* XII (1960): 545–63.

Figure 9 — Effect of Lapses on Policies in Force

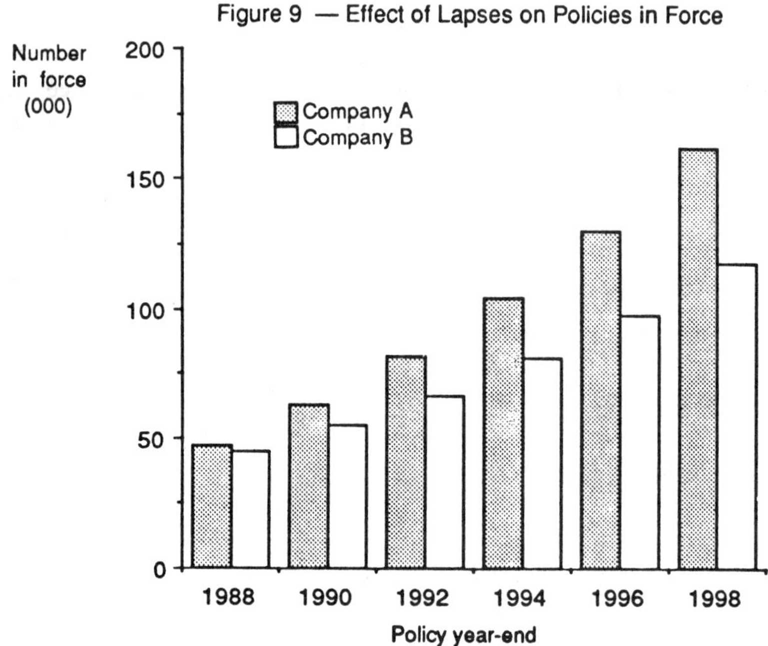

By the end of 1998, Company A has 162,000 policies in force, while Company B has fewer than 120,000 policies in force. Each company writes over 185,000 new policies from 1988 through 1998, but the low-renewal-lapse Company A has a net gain of nearly 122,000 policies in force, compared with fewer than 80,000 policies for the high-renewal-lapse Company B.

The upshot: The high-lapse company would have to sell nearly 80,000 more policies over the 1988–1998 period to achieve the same number of policies remaining in force as the low-lapse company. This is equivalent to sustaining an annual sales growth rate of 15.7 percent—selling 253,000 policies instead of 185,000 policies from 1988 through 1998—to end up with 162,000 policies in force. Furthermore, this comparison does not address the much higher acquisition costs for new issues versus the costs for renewing business.

APPENDIX

TABLES

Table A presents LIMRA 1983–1986 median lapse rates. The remaining tables present lapse rates illustrated in Figures 3–8 of this report in more detail.

TABLE A

MEDIAN LAPSE RATES BY POLICY YEAR
(PERCENTAGE OF FACE AMOUNT LAPSING)

Policy Year	Median Lapse Rates	
	Number	Face Amount
1	15.9%	15.9%
2	12.7	13.0
3	11.9	12.4
4	9.7	9.7
5	10.6	10.3
6–9	10.4	11.0
10	9.2	10.1
11 and over	6.4	7.8

TABLE B

VARIATION IN LAPSE RATES BY COMPANY SIZE
(PERCENTAGE OF FACE AMOUNT LAPSING)

Policy Year	Mean Lapse Rates	
	Size 1	Size 2
1	14.6%	20.1%
2	14.5	16.6
3	11.9	13.7
4	10.4	10.3
5	11.6	10.3
6–9	12.3	13.7
10	10.6	10.3
11 and over	7.6	8.0

TABLE C

VARIATION IN LAPSE RATES ACROSS COMPANIES
(PERCENTAGE OF FACE AMOUNT LAPSING)

Policy Year	Mean	Median	Range of Middle 50 Percent	
			Low	High
1.........	17.3%	15.9%	13.8%	18.8%
2.........	15.5	13.0	11.8	18.0
3.........	12.8	12.4	9.0	16.2
4.........	10.3	9.7	8.0	12.7
5.........	10.9	10.3	8.8	12.9
6–9.......	13.1	11.0	10.0	13.9
10.........	10.4	10.1	8.8	12.5
11 and over .	7.8	7.8	6.6	9.0

TABLE D

MEAN PERCENTAGE OF POLICIES LAPSING BY ISSUE AGE

Policy Year	Issue Age			
	20–29	30–39	40–49	50–59
1.........	18.5%	15.0%	11.8%	6.7%
2.........	16.0	13.6	9.7	4.9
3.........	14.4	11.8	7.6	4.3
4.........	11.8	10.0	7.3	4.5
5.........	12.8	11.3	7.8	5.4
6–9.......	13.1	10.8	8.0	5.8
10.........	11.8	10.2	7.2	—
11 and over .	6.9	5.8	5.0	4.0

—Insufficient exposure.

TABLE E

MEAN PERCENTAGE OF FACE AMOUNT LAPSING BY ISSUE AGE

Policy Year	Issue Age			
	20–29	30–39	40–49	50–59
1.........	20.6%	18.2%	15.6%	6.4%
2.........	18.0	16.7	14.8	5.4
3.........	16.0	13.7	9.8	8.1
4.........	13.3	11.8	10.1	6.8
5.........	13.4	11.7	8.4	8.8
6–9.......	13.7	12.3	10.2	8.1
10.........	12.3	11.5	8.0	—
11 and over .	8.1	7.1	6.3	5.6

—Insufficient exposure.

TABLE F

MEAN PERCENTAGE OF ANNUALIZED PREMIUM LAPSING BY ISSUE AGE

Policy Year	Issue Age			
	20–29	30–39	40–49	50–59
1	19.9%	16.3%	13.9%	5.2%
2	16.8	15.7	13.2	5.4
3	14.6	13.4	9.1	10.1
4	12.4	11.6	10.5	7.7
5	13.0	11.6	9.2	9.2
6–9	12.3	10.9	9.1	7.8
10	11.3	9.9	—	—
11 and over	7.6	6.6	5.7	5.3

—Insufficient exposure.

TABLE G

COMPARISON OF MEAN LAPSE RATES BY MEASURE (COMPANIES REPORTING ALL THREE MEASURES)

Policy Year	Face Amount	Number of Policies	Annualized Premium
1	17.1%	15.7%	14.9%
2	15.7	13.0	13.9
3	12.9	11.1	11.9
4	10.2	10.0	10.1
5	10.6	10.5	9.5
6–9	12.6	10.0	10.8
10	9.8	9.0	9.3
11 and over	7.1	5.9	7.2

TABLE H

MEAN FACE AMOUNT PERSISTING AND LAPSING

Policy Year	Persisting	Lapsing
1	$28,000	$28,200
2	22,800	25,100
3	20,800	22,900
4	20,700	19,800
5	19,300	18,800
6–9	13,300	17,100
10	10,800	11,700
11 and over	6,600	8,200

TABLE I

MEAN ANNUALIZED PREMIUM PERSISTING AND LAPSING

Policy Year	Persisting	Lapsing
1	$470	$440
2	360	380
3	350	370
4	330	320
5	380	290
6–9	240	240
10	200	190
11 and over	120	140

DEFINITIONS

Lapse Rate

Lapse rates are calculated by dividing the amounts lapsing by the corresponding amount in force. In calculating summary statistics in this report, each company's results receive equal weight, provided a minimum exposure criterion is met.

Policies lapsing because of nonpayment of premium are considered to lapse in the duration for which they were last in force, even if the grace period extends into the next policy year.

In Force

A policy is considered in force if the first premium at the beginning of the anniversary year is paid.

In-force business includes:

- New issues.
- Policies issued before the anniversary year under study where the premium due at the beginning of the anniversary year is paid before the end of the grace period.

In-force business excludes:

- Policies that lapsed before the beginning of the anniversary year under study even if the policies are on extended-term or reduced-paid-up status.
- Limited-premium-payment policies that are paid up.
- Single-premium policies.

Lapse

A policy is considered a lapse if the policy is in force at the beginning of the anniversary year under study but not all of the premium that comes due during the anniversary year is paid, including the premium due on the policy's next anniversary.

Lapsed business includes:

- Policies surrendered during the anniversary year under study, including surrenders made at the end of the anniversary year, i.e., on next policy anniversaries.
- Policies where a premium comes due during the anniversary year under study, including the premium that comes due on the next policy anniversaries, but is not paid by the end of the grace period.
- Policies that go on reduced-paid-up or extended-term status.

Lapsed business excludes:

- Death claims.
- Automatic premium loaned policies.
- Lapses during the policy year that are reinstated before or on the next policy anniversary.
- Policies not taken.

CONTRIBUTING COMPANIES

Canada Life
COLONIA Life
Commercial Union Life of Canada
Co-operators Life
Halifax Life
Industrial-Alliance Life*
Imperial Life of Canada
Metropolitan Life (Canada)
National Life of Canada
New York Life (Canada)
Standard Life (Canada)
Sun Life of Canada

*Alliance Mutual contributed to the 1983–1984 and 1984–1985 studies.